Learning Puppet 4

A Guide to Configuration Management and Automation

Jo Rhett

Beijing · Boston · Farnham · Sebastopol · Tokyo

Learning Puppet 4

by Jo Rhett

Printed in the United States of America.

Published by O'Reilly Media, Inc., 1005 Gravenstein Highway North, Sebastopol, CA 95472.

O'Reilly books may be purchased for educational, business, or sales promotional use. Online editions are also available for most titles (*http://safaribooksonline.com*). For more information, contact our corporate/institutional sales department: 800-998-9938 or *corporate@oreilly.com*.

Editor: Brian Anderson	**Indexer:** Judy McConville
Production Editor: Kristen Brown	**Interior Designer:** David Futato
Copyeditor: Rachel Monaghan	**Cover Designer:** Karen Montgomery
Proofreader: Jasmine Kwityn	**Illustrator:** Rebecca Demarest

April 2016:   First Edition

Revision History for the First Edition

2016-03-22:   First Release

See *http://oreilly.com/catalog/errata.csp?isbn=9781491907665* for release details.

978-1-491-90766-5

[LSI]

Table of Contents

Part II.   Creating Puppet Modules

Part III.   Using a Puppet Server

Part IV. Integrating Puppet

Foreword

I first met Jo Rhett online in the early 2000s. We were both active on the CFengine mailing lists, trying to administer production systems with methodologies that would come to be known as *infrastructure as code*. At the time, the concept of repeatable, convergent automation tools was fairly edgy, and the community that arose around the space also had its sharp edges. I seem to recall standing up at a LISA config management birds-of-a-feather session circa 2003, pointing at Mark Burgess, CFengine's author, and shouting, "You ruined my life! But you *saved* my life!"

Luke Kanies was also a CFengine user at the time, and was consistently exhorting the community to introspect its shortcomings and evolve to the next level. His edginess led to some pretty epic—though *mostly* collegial—debates, borne out in papers such as Steve Traugott's "Turing Equivalence in Systems Administration" and Luke's "ISConf: Theory, Practice, and Beyond."

Around 2005, Luke began writing a new tool in Ruby that was intended to address the problems with usability and flexibility he was running into with the rest of the ecosystem. Originally called Blink, the thing we know today as Puppet began its infancy as a CFengine "module" (actually a plugin, thus perpetuating an unfortunate relationship with English names that Puppet continues to this day), and Jo and I, along with the rest of the nascent configuration management community, followed its development with interest.

Fast-forward several years through a few iterations of Moore's law, and witness the resultant explosion in processing power, distributed systems complexity, and their attendant burden on operations folk. Puppet had matured to become the dominant *lingua franca* of infrastructure; the "tool wars" of the mid-2000s had achieved détente and our focus turned to culture, process, and the wider problems of tying infrastructure operations to business value: in a word, DevOps.

I'd done tens of thousands of infrastructure buildouts on Puppet and eventually came to work at Puppet Labs, the company Luke formed around supporting and productizing Puppet. Jo was consulting at large companies around Silicon Valley, pushing

Puppet to its limits and feeding bug fixes and feature requests into the community. As Puppet's new product manager, this relationship was a little different (and frankly, sometimes far less comfortable, on my end!) than working as peers on the same project, but over the past several years it's turned out to be hugely positive.

The thing I appreciate most about Jo, which I think shines through in the book you're about to read, is his sincere desire to help others. This is a core principle of the DevOps movement, usually stated as "sharing" or "empathy," and Jo's embodied it since the early days of CFengine. He consistently advocates for the "tough right thing" for the users, and while he will describe a range of possibilities with deep technical acumen and clear-eyed candor, in the end he'll steer us, the readers, in the direction that's going to work out the best in the long term.

Puppet's an amazing tool, but as the saying goes: "With great power comes great responsibility." Jo's depth of experience and empathy for other operations engineers make him the right person to show us how to use Puppet's power responsibly. This book is the result, and I'm deeply grateful to him for writing it.

— Eric Sorenson
Technical Product Manager
Puppet Platform
Portland, Oregon, September 24, 2015

Preface

Twenty years ago, it was common for a single server to provide services for hundreds of users. A system administrator was often responsible for as few as 10 servers. Most people used only one computer.

In 2015, it is common for a normal, everyday person to own and utilize more than five highly advanced and capable computers. Think about the devices you use on a daily basis: every one of them—the phone on your desk, the cell phone on your hip, the tablet you read from, your laptop, and even the car you drive—is thousands of times more powerful and capable than the large, room-sized servers used a few generations ago.

We live today in the midst of an information revolution. Systems capable of powerful computation that once required server rooms to contain are now able to be held in your hands. Explosive growth in the adoption and capabilities of modern technology has created a world full of computers. More and more devices every day contain powerful small computers that participate in the Internet of Things.

When I started my career, it was difficult to convince managers that every worker needed his or her own computer. Today, the workers are outnumbered by computers almost 20:1, and in certain industries by as much as 100:1. Advanced computing capability combined with cheap memory have revolutionized what businesses can accomplish with data. Even small teams of people utilize and depend upon thousands of computers. Every one of these devices needs to be managed. It's simply not possible to do it all by hand.

For this, we use Puppet.

Who This Book Is For

This book is primarily aimed at system administrators and operations or DevOps engineers. If you are responsible for development or production nodes, this book will provide you with immediately useful tools to make your job easier than ever before. If you run a high-uptime production environment, you're going to learn how Puppet can enforce standards throughout the implementation. Soon you'll wonder how you ever got along without it.

No matter what you call yourself, if you feel that you spend too much time managing computers, then this book is for you. You'd like to get it done faster so you can focus on something else. You'd like to do it more consistently, so that you don't have to chase down one-off problems in your reports. Or you've got some new demands that you're looking for a way to solve. If any of these statements fit, Puppet will be one of the best tools in your toolbox.

What to Expect from Me

This book will not be a heavy tome filled with reference material irrelevant to the day-to-day system administrator—exactly the opposite. Throughout this book we will never stray from one simple goal: using Puppet to manage real-life administration concerns.

This book will never tell you to run a script and not tell you what it does, or why. I hate trying to determine what an installation script did, and I won't do this to you. In this book you will build up the entire installation by hand. Every step you take will be useful to you in a production deployment. You'll know where every configuration file lives. You'll learn every essential configuration parameter and what it means.

By the time you have finished this book, you'll know how Puppet works inside and out. You will have the tools and knowledge to deploy Puppet seamlessly throughout your environment.

What You Will Need

You may use any modern Linux, Mac, or Windows system and successfully follow the hands-on tutorials in this book.

While there are some web dashboards for Puppet, the process of configuring and running Puppet will be performed through the command line. We will help you install all necessary software.

A beginner to system administration can follow every tutorial in this book. Any experience with scripts, coding, or configuration management will enhance what you can get out of this book, but is not necessary. It is entirely possible to deploy Puppet to manage complex environments without writing a single line of code.

Part II documents how to build custom modules for Puppet. You will create modules using the Puppet configuration language that will be taught in this book. When you've become an expert in building Puppet modules, you may want to add new extensions to the Puppet configuration language. Some extensions are currently only supported in the Ruby language:

Faces
Add-on subcommands for puppet

Providers
Implementation methods for resource types

Syntax checkers
A tool for validating input

Types
New resources not built into Puppet

Reference materials such as Michael Fitzgerald's *Learning Ruby* (*http://bit.ly/learning-ruby*) can be helpful when creating extensions for a custom Puppet module.

What You'll Find in This Book

The Introduction provides an overview of what Puppet does, how it works, and why you want to use it.

Part I will get you up and running with a working Puppet installation. You will learn how to write declarative Puppet policies to produce consistency in your systems. This part will also cover the changes to the language in Puppet 4.

Part II will introduce you to Puppet modules, the building blocks used for Puppet policies. You will learn how to find and evaluate Puppet modules. You'll learn how to distinguish *Puppet Supported* and *Puppet Approved* modules. You'll learn tips for managing configuration data in Hiera. Finally, you'll learn how to build, test, and publish your own Puppet modules.

Part III will help you install the new Puppet Server and the deprecated but stable Puppet master. You'll learn how to centralize the certificate authority, or use a third-party provider. You will configure an *external node classifier* (*ENC*). You'll find advice and gain experience on how to scale Puppet servers for high availability and performance.

Part IV will review dashboards and orchestration tools that supplement and complement Puppet. The web dashboards provide a way to view the node status and history of changes made by Puppet. The orchestration tools enable you to interact instantly with Puppet nodes for massively parallel orchestration events.

Every step of the way you'll perform hands-on installation and configuration of every component. There are no magic scripts, no do-it-all installers. You'll see how easy it is to deploy Puppet from scratch, and experience firsthand the power of the tools it provides. You'll finish this book with everything you need to build out a production service.

Throughout this book you'll find commentary and practical advice that is based on years of experience deploying, scaling, and tuning Puppet environments. You will find advice about managing small shops, large commercial enterprises, and globally distributed teams. You'll also learn several ways to scale Puppet to thousands of nodes.

How to Use This Book

This book provides explicit instructions for configuring and using Puppet from the command line without the use of external tools beyond your favorite text editor.

The book will help you create Puppet *manifests* and Puppet *modules* that utilize every feature of Puppet. You will create configuration policies to handle your specific needs from the examples in this book.

Everything you learn in this book can be done entirely from your laptop or workstation without any impact on production environments. However, it will teach you everything necessary to deploy Puppet in real environments, and will include numerous tips and recommendations for production use.

IPv6 Ready

Every example with IP addresses will include both IPv4 and IPv6 statements. If you're only using one of these protocols, you can ignore the other. Puppet will happily use any combination of them. Specific advice for managing Puppet in dual-stack IPv6 environments can be found in multiple parts of the book.

SSL is now TLS

You are likely familiar with the term *SSL* when referring to transport layer security and encryption. You're also likely aware that SSL v3 was renamed TLS 1.0 when it became an IETF standard. At this time, all versions of SSL and up to TLS 1.1 are subject to known exploits. Rather than constantly refer to both terms (SSL/TLS) throughout this book, I will refer to it only by the new name (TLS). This is technically more accurate, as Puppet 4 requires TLS 1.2 and will not accept SSL connections.

Conventions Used in This Book

The following typographical conventions are used in this book:

Italic
> Indicates new terms, URLs, email addresses, filenames, and file extensions.

`Constant width`
> Used for program listings, as well as within paragraphs to refer to program elements such as variable or function names, databases, data types, environment variables, statements, and keywords.

`Constant width bold`
> Shows commands or other text that should be typed literally by the user.

`Constant width italic`
> Shows text that should be replaced with user-supplied values or by values determined by context.

 This element signifies a tip or suggestion.

 This element signifies a general note.

 This element indicates a warning or caution.

Safari® Books Online

 *Safari Books Online* is an on-demand digital library that delivers expert content in both book and video form from the world's leading authors in technology and business.

Technology professionals, software developers, web designers, and business and creative professionals use Safari Books Online as their primary resource for research, problem solving, learning, and certification training.

Safari Books Online offers a range of plans and pricing for enterprise, government, education, and individuals.

Members have access to thousands of books, training videos, and prepublication manuscripts in one fully searchable database from publishers like O'Reilly Media, Prentice Hall Professional, Addison-Wesley Professional, Microsoft Press, Sams, Que, Peachpit Press, Focal Press, Cisco Press, John Wiley & Sons, Syngress, Morgan Kaufmann, IBM Redbooks, Packt, Adobe Press, FT Press, Apress, Manning, New Riders, McGraw-Hill, Jones & Bartlett, Course Technology, and hundreds more. For more information about Safari Books Online, please visit us online.

How to Contact Us

Please address comments and questions concerning this book to the publisher:

> O'Reilly Media, Inc.
> 1005 Gravenstein Highway North
> Sebastopol, CA 95472
> 800-998-9938 (in the United States or Canada)
> 707-829-0515 (international or local)
> 707-829-0104 (fax)

We have a web page for this book, where we list errata, examples, and any additional information. You can access this page at *http://bit.ly/learningPuppet4*.

To comment or ask technical questions about this book, send email to *bookquestions@oreilly.com*.

For more information about our books, courses, conferences, and news, see our website at http://www.oreilly.com.

Find us on Facebook: *http://facebook.com/oreilly*

Follow us on Twitter: *http://twitter.com/oreillymedia*

Watch us on YouTube: *http://www.youtube.com/oreillymedia*

Acknowledgments

I owe a deep debt of gratitude to Nova, Kevin, Andy, Lance, and far too many other friends whom I have neglected while adding "just one more essential thing" (more than a hundred times) to this book. I lack the words to express how thankful I am that you are in my life, and have apparently forgiven me for being a ghost over the last year.

Growing and improving happens only by surrounding yourself with smart people. The following individuals have provided incalculable feedback and insight that has influenced my learning process, and deserve both accolades for their technical efforts and my sincere appreciation for their advice:

- Corey Quinn
- R.I. Pienaar
- Chris Barbour
- William Jiminez
- Rob Nelson

There are far too many Puppet Labs employees to list who have accepted, rejected, and negotiated my suggestions, feedback, and patches to Puppet and related tools. Thank you for your assistance over the years. We all appreciate your efforts far more than we remember to share with you.

I owe a drink and many thanks to many people who provided input and feedback on the book during the writing process, including but definitely not limited to the technical reviewers:

- Eric Sorenson, Puppet Labs
- Anna Kennedy, Redpill-Linpro
- Nick Fagerlund, Puppet Labs

If you find that the examples in this book work well for you, it's likely due to the helpful feedback provided by numerous readers who posted errata on the book page or comments on the Safari book that helped me address concerns I would have missed. Their insights have been invaluable and deeply appreciated.

And finally, I'd like to thank my O'Reilly editor, Brian Anderson, who gave me excellent guidance on the book and was a pleasure to work with. I'm likewise deeply indebted to my patient and helpful production and copy editors, Kristen and Rachel, without whom my jumbled pile of letters wouldn't make any sense at all.

All of us who use Puppet today owe significant gratitude to Luke Kaines, who conceived of Puppet and continues to direct its growth in Puppet Labs. His vision and foresight made all of this possible.

Introduction

This book will teach you how to install and use Puppet for managing computer systems. It will introduce you to how Puppet works, and how it provides value. To better understand Puppet and learn the basics, you'll set up a testing environment, which will evolve as your Puppet knowledge grows. You'll learn how to declare and evaluate configuration policy for hundreds of nodes.

This book covers modern best practices for Puppet. You'll find tips throughout the book labeled Best Practice.

You'll learn how to update Puppet 2 or Puppet 3 puppet code for the increased features and improved parser of Puppet 4. You'll learn how to deploy the new Puppet Server. You'll have a clear strategy for upgrading older servers to Puppet 4 standards. You'll learn how to run Puppet services over IPv6 protocol.

Most important of all, this book will cover how to scale your Puppet installation to handle thousands of nodes. You'll learn multiple strategies for handling diverse and heterogenous environments, and reasons why each of these approaches may or may not be appropriate for your needs.

What Is Puppet?

Puppet manages configuration data, including users, packages, processes, and services—in other words, any resource of the node you can define. Puppet can manage complex and distributed components to ensure service consistency and availability. In short, Puppet brings computer systems into compliance with a configuration policy.

Puppet can ensure configuration consistency across servers, clients, your router, and that computer on your hip. Puppet utilizes a flexible hierarchy of data sources combined with node-specific data to tune the policy appropriately for each node. Puppet can help you accomplish a variety of tasks. For example, you can use it to do any of the following:

- Deploy new systems with consistent configuration and data installed.
- Upgrade security and software packages across the enterprise.
- Roll out new features and capabilities to existing systems painlessly.
- Adjust system configurations to make new data sources available.
- Decrease the cost and effort involved in minor changes on hundreds of systems.
- Simplify the effort and personnel involved in software deployments.
- Automate buildup and teardown of replica systems to test proposed changes.
- Repurpose existing computer resources for a new use within minutes.
- Gather a rich data set of information about the infrastructure and computing resources.
- Provide a clear and reviewable change control mechanism.

Twenty years ago, people were impressed that I was responsible for 100 servers. At a job site last year, I was responsible for over 17,000 servers. At my current job I'd have to go check somewhere to find out, as we scale up and down dynamically based on load. These days, my Puppet code spins up more servers while I'm passed out asleep than I did in the first 10 years of my career. You can achieve this only by fully embracing what Puppet provides.

I was recently reminded of something I quipped to a CEO almost six years ago:

> You can use Puppet to do more faster if you have ten nodes.
> You must use Puppet if you have ten hundred nodes.

Puppet enables you to make a lot of changes both quickly and consistently. You don't have to write out every step, you only have to define how it should be. You are not required to write out the process for evaluating and adjusting each platform. Instead, you utilize the Puppet configuration language to declare the final state of the computing resources. Thus, we describe Puppet as *declarative*.

Why Declarative

When analyzing hand-built automation systems, you'll invariably find commands such as the following:

```
$ echo "param: newvalue" >> configuration-file
```

This command appends a new parameter and value to a configuration file. This works properly the first time you run it. However, if the same operation is run again, the file has the value twice. This isn't a desirable effect in configuration management. To avoid this, you'd have to write code that checks the file for the configuration parameter and its current value, and then makes any necessary changes.

Language that describes the actions to perform is called *imperative*. It defines what to do, and how to do it. It must define every change that should be followed to achieve the desired configuration. It must also deal with any differences in each platform or operating system.

When managing computer systems, you want the operations applied to be *idempotent*, where the operation achieves the same results every time it executes. This allows you to apply and reapply (or converge) the configuration policy and always achieve the desired state.

To achieve a configuration state no matter the existing conditions, the specification must avoid describing the actions required to reach the desired state. Instead, the specification should describe the desired state itself, and leave the evaluation and resolution up to the interpreter.

Language that declares the final state is called *declarative*. Declarative language is much easier to read, and less prone to breakage due to environment differences. Puppet was designed to achieve consistent and repeatable results. Every time Puppet evaluates the state of the node, it will bring the node to a state consistent with the specification.

How Puppet Works

Any node you control contains an application named `puppet agent`. The agent evaluates and applies *Puppet manifests*, or files containing Puppet configuration language that declares the desired state of the node. The agent evaluates the state of each component described in a manifest, and determines whether or not any change is necessary. If the component needs to be changed, the agent makes the requested changes and logs the event.

If Puppet is configured to utilize a centralized Puppet server, Puppet will send the node's data to the server, and receive back a *catalog* containing only the node's specific policy to enforce.

Now you might be thinking to yourself, "What if I only want the command executed on a subset of nodes?" Puppet provides many different ways to classify and categorize nodes to limit which resources should be applied to which nodes. You can use node facts such as hostname, operating system, node type, Puppet version, and many others. Best of all, new criteria custom to your environment can be easily created.

The Puppet agent evaluates the state of only one node. In this model, you can have agents on tens, hundreds, or thousands of nodes evaluating their catalogs and applying changes on their nodes at exactly the same time. The localized state machine ensures a scalable and fast parallel execution environment.

Why Use Puppet

As we have discussed, Puppet provides a well-designed infrastructure for managing the state of many nodes simultaneously. Here are a few reasons to use it:

- Puppet utilizes a node's local data to customize the policy for each specific node: hundreds of values specific to the node—including hostname, operating system, memory, networking configuration, and many node-specific details—are used to tune the policy appropriately.
- Puppet agents can handle OS-specific differences, allowing you to write a single manifest that will be applied by OS-specific *providers* on each node.
- Puppet agents can be invoked with specific tags, allowing a filtered run that only performs operations that match those tags during a given invocation.
- Puppet uses a decentralized approach where each node evaluates and converges its own Puppet catalog separately. No node is waiting for another node to complete.
- Puppet agents report back success, failure, and convergence results for each resource, and the entire run.
- Orchestration systems such as the Marionette Collective (MCollective) can invoke and control the Puppet agent for instantaneous large-scale changes.

In Part I, you will learn how to write simple declarative language that will make changes only when necessary.

In Part II, you will create a module that uses Puppet to install and configure the Puppet agent. This kind of recursion is not only possible but common.

In Part III, you will learn how to use Puppet masters and Puppet Server to offload and centralize catalog building, report processing, and backup of changed files.

In Part IV, you will use MCollective to orchestrate immediate changes with widespread Puppet agents.

Puppet provides a flexible framework for policy enforcement that can be customized for any environment. After reading this book and using Puppet for a while, you'll be able to tune your environment to exactly your needs. Puppet's declarative language not only allows but encourages creativity.

Is Puppet DevOps?

While Puppet is a tool used by many DevOps teams, using Puppet will not by itself give you all the benefits of adopting DevOps practices within your team.

In practice, Puppet is used by many classic operations teams who handle all change through traditional planning and approval processes. It provides them with many benefits, most especially a readable, somewhat self-documenting description of what is deployed on any system. This provides tremendous value to operations where change management control and auditing are primary factors.

On the other hand, the ability to manage rapid change across many systems that Puppet provides has also cracked open the door to DevOps for many operations teams. Classic operations teams were often inflexible because they were responsible for the previously difficult task of tracking and managing change. Puppet makes it possible to not only track and manage change, but to implement locally customized change quickly and seamlessly across thousands of nodes. This makes it possible for operations teams to embrace practices that are flexible for changing business needs.

You don't have to be working with developers to utilize DevOps practices. This is a common misconception of DevOps. The developer in DevOps is not a different person or team, it is you! There are many teams which utilize DevOps practices that don't support developers; rather, they manage systems that support a completely different industry. You are participating in DevOps when you utilize Agile development processes to develop code that implements operations and infrastructure designs.

What Is DevOps?

I feel that it is essential to refer to the Agile Manifesto, because it is the base on which DevOps practices emerged. It may help you to mentally replace *software* with *services* when reading the manifesto:

> We are uncovering better ways of developing
> software by doing it and helping others do it.
> Through this work we have come to value:

> **Individuals and interactions** over processes and tools
> **Working software** over comprehensive documentation
> **Customer collaboration** over contract negotiation
> **Responding to change** over following a plan

> That is, while there is value in the items on the right,
> we value the items on the left more.

The DevOps term was first used to refer to the application of Agile software development practices to systems administration. The original DevOps discussion group was named "Agile System Administration." This led to a conference in Belgium named "DevOpsDays," which was the first appearance of the name. After the conference, the hashtag *#devops* was used to continue the discussion on Twitter.

While DevOps teams customize their Agile practices for needs specific to operations processes, embracing DevOps practices provides many advantages to Agile development teams. Agile Scrum-based *continuous integration* (*CI*) can also include *continuous delivery* (*CD*) when the operations teams utilize DevOps practices.

Perhaps the biggest source of confusion comes when people try to compare using Puppet (a tool) to implement DevOps practices, and the idea of "valuing individuals and interactions over processes and tools." It is easiest to explain this by first outlining the reasons that operations teams were historically perceived as inflexible. The tools available for managing software within the enterprise used to be shockingly limited. Many times a very small change, or a customization for one group, would require throwing away the software management tool and embracing another. That's a tremendous amount of work for an operations team.

When using Puppet, if an individual can make a case for the value of a change (interaction), then rolling out a local customization usually involves only a small refactoring of the code. Applying changes becomes easy, and thus avoids a conflict between valuable requests and the limitations of the tools available. Discussion of the merits of the change has higher value than processes used to protect operations teams from unmanageable change.

No tool or set of tools, product, or job title will give an operations team all the benefits of utilizing DevOps practices. I have seen far too many teams with all of the keywords, all of the titles, and none of the philosophy. It's not a product, it's an evolving practice. You don't get the benefits without changing how you think.

I highly recommend making the effort to fully understand both Agile processes and DevOps practices and methodologies. Don't skimp. Someone on your team who is good at promoting and guiding others should be fully trained on Agile processes. Get the people responsible for creating change out to conferences where they can learn from others' experiences, such as DevOps Days (*http://www.devopsdays.org/*), PuppetConf (*http://puppetconf.com/*), and O'Reilly's Velocity (*http://velocityconf.com/*) conference.

That's not an obligatory push of the publisher's conference. Many people consider John Allspaw's "10+ Deploys Per Day: Dev and Ops Cooperation," which was presented at Velocity 2009, to be a founding cornerstone of the DevOps movement. Velocity was the first large conference to add DevOps items to its agenda, and DevOps practices are a major focus of the conference today.

Puppet is a great tool, and you'll find that it's even more valuable when used with DevOps practices. While this is not a book about DevOps, it will present many useful tools and strategies for practicing DevOps in your organization.

Time to Get Started

As we proceed, this book will show you how Puppet can help you do more, and do it faster and more consistently than ever before. You'll learn how to extend Puppet to meet your specific needs:

- You'll install Puppet and get it working seamlessly to control files, packages, services, and the Puppet daemon.
- You'll discover an active community of Puppet developers who develop modules and other Puppet plugins on the Puppet Forge and GitHub.
- You'll build your own custom fact. You'll use this fact within your Puppet manifest to handle something unique to your environment.
- You'll build your own custom Puppet module. You'll learn how to test the module safely prior to deploying in your production environment.
- You'll learn how to package your module and upload it to a Puppet Forge.
- You'll learn how to configure Puppet Server, allowing you to centralize Puppet services within a campus or around the globe.
- You'll tour the ecosystem of components that utilize, extend, and enhance Puppet within your environment.

By the time you finish this book, you will understand not just how powerful Puppet is, but also exactly how it works. You'll have the knowledge and understanding to debug problems within any part of the infrastructure. You'll know what to tune as your deployment grows. You'll have a resource to use for further testing as your knowledge and experience expands.

It's time to get declarative.

## PART I

Controlling with Puppet Apply

In this part, you'll learn about the Puppet configuration language and how to think in a declarative manner. You'll set up a testing environment that you can use to learn Puppet while reading this book. You'll be able to continue to use this setup to develop and test your Puppet code long after you have finished this book.

To start, you will install Puppet and create your first Puppet manifests. You'll learn how to utilize resources, how to associate them, and how to order and limit the changes upon them.

When you finish this part of the book, you'll have a solid understanding of the Puppet configuration language. As you make your way through the chapters in this part, you will write and test your own Puppet manifests. This part establishes a foundation of modern best practices from which you can explore Puppet's features and capabilities.

## CHAPTER 1

Thinking Declarative

If you have experience writing shell, Ruby, Python, or Perl scripts that make changes to a system, you've very likely been performing *imperative programming*. Imperative programming issues commands that change a target's state, much as the imperative grammatical mood in natural language expresses commands for people to act on.

You may be using *procedural programming* standards, where state changes are handled within procedures or subroutines to avoid duplication. This is a step toward declarative programming, but the main program still tends to define each operation, each procedure to be executed, and the order in which to execute them in an imperative manner.

While it can be useful to have a background in procedural programming, a common mistake is to attempt to use Puppet to make changes in an imperative fashion. The very best thing you can do is forget everything you know about imperative or procedural programming.

If you are new to programming, don't feel intimidated. People without a background in imperative or procedural programming can often learn good Puppet practices faster.

Writing good Puppet manifests requires declarative programming. When it comes to maintaining configuration on systems, you'll find declarative programming to be easier to create, easier to read, and easier to maintain. Let's show you why.

Handling Change

The reason that you need to cast aside imperative programming is to handle change better.

When you write code that performs a sequence of operations, that sequence will make the desired change the first time it is run. If you run the same code the second time in a row, the same operations will either fail or create a different state than desired. Here's an example:

```
$ sudo useradd -u 1001 -g 1001 -c "Joe User" -m joe
$ sudo useradd -u 1001 -g 1000 -c "Joe User" -m joe
useradd: user 'joe' already exists
```

So then you need to change the code to handle that situation:

```
# bash excerpt
getent passwd $USERNAME > /dev/null 2> /dev/null
if [ $? -ne 0 ]; then
    useradd -u $UID -g $GID -c "$COMMENT" -s $SHELL -m $USERNAME
else
    usermod -u $UID -g $GID -c "$COMMENT" -s $SHELL -m $USERNAME
fi
```

OK, that's six lines of code and all we've done is ensure that the username isn't already in use. What if we need to check to ensure the UID is unique, the GID is valid, and that the password expiration is set? You can see that this will be a very long script even before we adjust it to ensure it works properly on multiple operating systems.

This is why we say that imperative programming doesn't handle change very well. It takes a lot of code to cover every situation you need to test.

Using Idempotence

When managing computer systems, you want the operations applied to be *idempotent*, where the operation achieves the same results every time it executes. Idempotence allows you to apply and reapply (or converge) a configuration manifest and always achieve the desired state.

In order for imperative code to be idempotent, it needs to have instructions for how to compare, evaluate, and apply not just every resource, but also each attribute of the resource. As you saw in the previous section, even the simplest of operations will quickly become ponderous and difficult to maintain.

What is an Idempotent Operation?

In mathematics and computer science, idempotent operations are those that can be applied multiple times without changing the result beyond the initial application. The word literally means "[the quality of] having the same power," from the Latin roots *idem* + *potent* "same" + "power."[1] Here are some examples of idempotent and non-idempotent math and code:

`any number^1`	**Idempotent**	A number to the power of 1 is the same
`value = value * 2`	**Non-idempotent**	Will double every time
`value = value * 2 / 2`	**Idempotent**	Remains the same value
`echo "Good!" >> /some/file`	**Non-idempotent**	File will keep growing
`echo "Good!" > /some/file`	**Idempotent**	File will always have the same content

The simplistic final example avoids having to compare the state of the item by simply overwriting it every time. This only works in a limited set of situations. Most changes require evaluation to determine what changes are necessary.

Declaring Final State

As we mentioned in Introduction, for a configuration state to be achieved no matter the conditions, the configuration language must avoid describing the actions required to reach the desired state. Instead, the configuration language should describe the desired state itself, and leave the actions up to the interpreter. Language that declares the final state is called *declarative*.

Rather than writing extensive imperative code to handle every situation, it is much simpler to declare what you want the final state to be. In other words, instead of including dozens of lines of comparison, the code reflects only the desired final state of the resource (a user account, in this example). Here we will introduce you to your first bit of Puppet configuration language, a resource declaration for the same user we created earlier:

---

1 First seen in George Boole's book *The Mathematical Analysis of Logic*, originally published in 1847.

```
user { 'joe':
  ensure     => present,
  uid        => '1001',
  gid        => '1000',
  comment    => 'Joe User',
  managehome => true,
}
```

As you can see, the code is not much more than a simple text explanation of the desired state. A user named *Joe User* should be *present*, a home directory for the user should be created, and so on. It is very clear, very easy to read. Exactly how the user should be created is not within the code, nor are instructions for handling different operating systems.

Declarative language is much easier to read, and less prone to breakage due to environment differences. Puppet was designed to achieve consistent and repeatable results. You describe what the final state of the resource should be, and Puppet will evaluate the resource and apply any necessary changes to reach that state.

Reviewing Declarative Programming

Conventional programming languages create change by listing exact operations that should be performed. Code that defines each state change and the order of changes is known as *imperative programming*.

Good Puppet manifests are written with declarative programming. Instead of defining exactly how to make changes, in which you must write code to test and compare the system state before making that change, you instead declare how it should be. It is up to the Puppet agent to evaluate the current state and apply the necessary changes.

As this chapter has demonstrated, declarative programming is easier to create, easier to read, and easier to maintain.

## CHAPTER 2

Creating a Learning Environment

In this chapter, we will create a virtualized environment suitable for learning and testing Puppet. We will utilize Vagrant and VirtualBox to set up this environment on your desktop or laptop. You can keep using this environment long after you have finished this book, or rebuild it quickly any time you'd like to test something new.

If you are an experienced developer or operations engineer, you are welcome to use a testing environment of your own choice. Anything that can host multiple Linux nodes will work. Puppet's needs are minimal. Any of the following would be suitable for use as a Puppet test lab:

- A spare system that you can install Linux on
- An Amazon Web Services (AWS) Free Tier instance (*http://amzn.to/1Rro5qL*)
- An OpenStack DevStack development instance (*http://bit.ly/1UHnoig*)
- A VMware Free vSphere ESXi solo instance (*http://vmw.re/1TUxTjq*)
- A Vagrant development environment (*http://www.vagrantup.com/*) on your personal computer

You can build your own test lab using one of the preceding solutions, or you can use an existing test lab you maintain. In all cases, I recommend using an OS compatible with RedHat Enterprise Linux 7 for learning purposes. The CentOS platform is freely available, and fully supported by both Red Hat and Puppet Labs. This will allow you to breeze through the learning exercises without distractions.

We recommend and are going to use Vagrant for the remainder of this book, for the following reasons:

- It is easier for you to set up and get started quickly.
- You can more easily carry it with you, and restart it at any time.
- The Vagrant setup includes the Puppet manifests shown in this book.
- You can always build one of the other environments later for a comparison point.

If you plan to use your own testing environment, skip ahead to "Initializing Non-Vagrant Systems" on page 22.

Installing Vagrant

If you are going to follow the recommendation to use Vagrant, let's get started installing it. You'll need to download two packages.

Go to VirtualBox Downloads (*https://www.virtualbox.org/wiki/Downloads*) and download the appropriate platform package for your system.

Next, go to Vagrant Downloads (*https://www.vagrantup.com/downloads.html*) and download the appropriate platform package for your system.

Install these packages according to the instructions for your operating system. I've included detailed instructions for Windows and Mac users in the following subsections. If you're running Vagrant on Linux or another platform, I'm going to assume you are expert enough to handle this installation yourself.

Installing Vagrant on Mac

First, you should run the VirtualBox installer. Open the VirtualBox DMG image file you downloaded and click on the *Virtualbox.pkg* installer, as shown in Figure 2-1.

Accept the license and the installer will complete the installation.

Next, you should run the Vagrant installer. Open the Vagrant DMG image file you downloaded and click on the *Vagrant.pkg* installer, as shown in Figure 2-2.

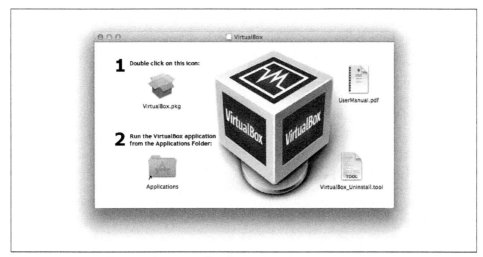

Figure 2-1. VirtualBox package installer for Mac

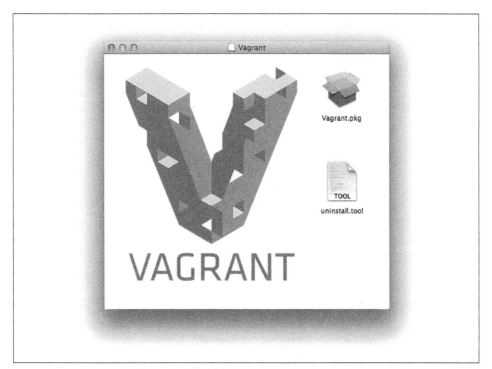

Figure 2-2. Vagrant package installer for Mac

Likewise, accept the license agreement and the installer will complete the installation.

Finally, if you don't already have it, you will need to install Xcode on your machine. Perform the following steps:

1. Pull down on the Apple logo at the top left of your screen.
2. Select "App Store…"
3. In the App Store, type xcode into the search bar on the right.
4. The top-left application should be Xcode Developer Tools.
5. Click GET and then click INSTALL APP beneath its name.

Installing Git Tools on Windows

On Windows platforms, you must install Git and its tools in order to use Vagrant successfully.

Open your browser to Git Source Code Management (*http://git-scm.com/*) and click the Downloads for Windows link (*http://git-scm.com/download/win*) on the lower right of the page. Run the installer when the download completes.

Accept the default components.

On the "Adjusting your PATH environment" screen, select "Use Git from the Windows Command Prompt," as shown in Figure 2-3.

Figure 2-3. Select "Use Git from the Windows Prompt"

On the "Configuring the line ending conversions" screen (as shown in Figure 2-4), any option will work successfully for this book. Select the default option if you are unsure. You can change this later.

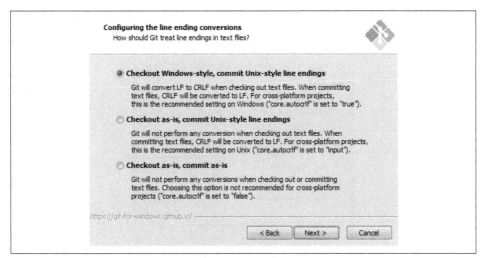

Figure 2-4. Choose which line endings you prefer

Select the MinTTY terminal emulator on the following screen (Figure 2-5).

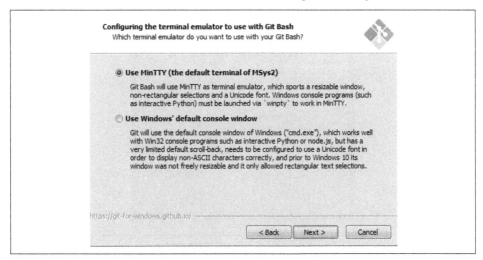

Figure 2-5. Choose the MinTTY terminal for the Bash shell

Accept the final prompts to complete the installation.

Installing VirtualBox on Windows

Vagrant will use the VirtualBox virtualization engine to run the test systems. Installing VirtualBox is very straightforward. Run the VirtualBox installer package that you downloaded on the previous page.

Click Next to start the installation, and then click Next again to install all features (Figure 2-6).

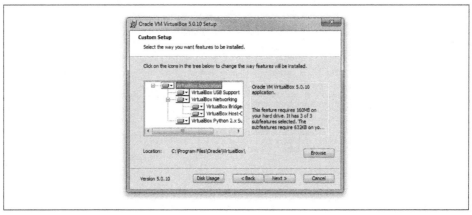

Figure 2-6. Install all features (the default choice)

You can disable the options to create shortcuts (Figure 2-7), as these won't be necessary for the learning environment.

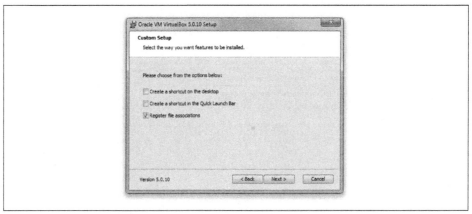

Figure 2-7. Select only the "Register file associations" checkbox

Accept the warning about a short interruption to networking (Figure 2-8). In most situations, you won't notice any effect.

Figure 2-8. VirtualBox network interruption notice

To install VirtualBox, click Install, as shown in Figure 2-9.

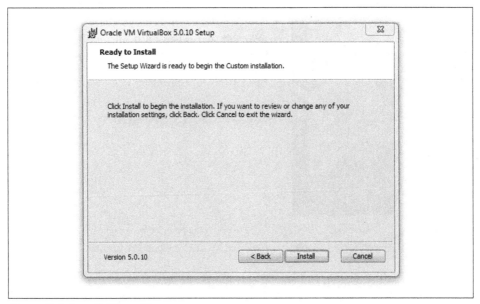

Figure 2-9. Install VirtualBox

At this point, you'll be prompted to install several virtualization drivers (Figure 2-10). You can either choose to always trust software from Oracle, or click Install for each one.

Figure 2-10. Oracle drivers

Disable the checkbox to start VirtualBox after installation (Figure 2-11). Vagrant will start it automatically.

Figure 2-11. Disable autostart

Installing Vagrant on Windows

Now we should install Vagrant. Run the Vagrant installer package that you downloaded (Figure 2-12).

Figure 2-12. Vagrant installer for Windows

You'll need to accept the license agreement, as shown in Figure 2-13.

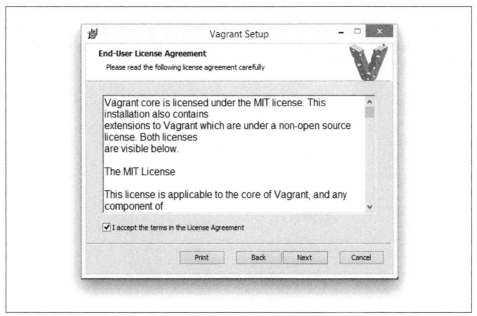

Figure 2-13. License agreement

Select where you want to install Vagrant. As Figure 2-14 shows, I prefer to install Vagrant in the normal system location for 64-bit programs. It doesn't matter which path you choose here.

Figure 2-14. Select an installation path for Vagrant

Once you get to the confirmation screen acknowledging completion of the installation, you can exit the Setup Wizard by clicking Finish (Figure 2-15).

Figure 2-15. Click Finish to complete the installation

Windows systems will need to reboot, as shown in Figure 2-16.

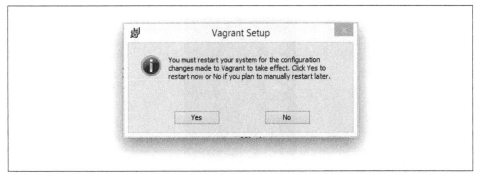

Figure 2-16. Restart after installation

Starting a Bash Shell

At this point, you'll need to start a Bash prompt. We'll be using Bash for the remainder of this book, so now is a good time to become comfortable using it.

On a Macintosh, follow these steps:

1. Open Finder.
2. In the sidebar on the left, click on Applications.
3. Open the Utilities folder.
4. Start the Terminal application.

On Windows 7 and before, follow these steps:

1. From the taskbar, click on the Windows Start button.
2. Select All Programs.
3. Select Git.
4. Click on Git Bash.

On Windows 8, follow these steps:

1. From the Metro desktop, click the down-arrow icon at the bottom left.
2. Scroll to the right and locate the Git section.
3. Click on Git Bash.

On Windows 10 (see Figure 2-17), follow these steps:

1. From the taskbar, click the Windows Start button.
2. Select the first item, All Apps.
3. Scroll to G.
4. Expand the arrow next to Git.
5. Click on Git Bash.

Figure 2-17. Windows 10: Git Bash

On Linux or any other platform, use the terminal prompt of your choice.

You may use any third-party terminal or command prompt that you prefer. Two popular choices are ConEmu (*https://conemu.github.io/en/*) for Windows and iTerm2 (*https://www.iterm2.com/*) for Mac. Tabbed session support will be helpful, as you'll log in to multiple instances at the same time in some exercises.

No matter which operating system you are using, the instructions assume you will start at a command prompt in your home directory.

Downloading a Box

To save some time later, you can download the virtual box image used as the base system for our learning environment (as mentioned before, we'll use CentOS 7, as it is well supported by all Puppet Labs programs and modules):

```
$ vagrant box add --provider virtualbox puppetlabs/centos-7.2-64-nocm
==> box: Loading metadata for box 'puppetlabs/centos-7.2-64-nocm'
    box: URL: https://atlas.hashicorp.com/puppetlabs/centos-7.2-64-nocm
==> box: Adding box 'puppetlabs/centos-7.2-64-nocm' (v1.0.2)
        for provider: virtualbox
    box: Downloading: https://atlas.hashicorp.com/puppetlabs/boxes/
        centos-7.2-64-nocm/versions/1.0.2/providers/virtualbox.box
==> box: Successfully added box 'puppetlabs/centos-7.2-64-nocm' (v1.0.2)
```

You may note that there are boxes at this site that already have Puppet installed. I want you to go through the installation of Puppet on a stock system so that you have that experience.

Cloning the Learning Repository

Now we'll download a repository that contains virtual machine configurations and learning materials. Starting in your home directory, use `git` to clone the following repository:

```
$ git clone https://github.com/jorhett/learning-puppet4
Cloning into 'learning-puppet4'...
remote: Counting objects: 64, done.
remote: Total 64 (delta 0), reused 0 (delta 0)
Unpacking objects: 100% (64/64), done.
Checking connectivity... done.
$ cd learning-puppet4
```

As shown, change into the *learning-puppet4* directory. All further instructions will assume you are in this directory.

Install the Vagrant vbguest Plugin

Now you should install the `vagrant-vbguest` plugin. This plugin ensures that the VirtualBox extensions on the virtual machine are kept up to date.

```
$ vagrant plugin install vagrant-vbguest
Installing the 'vagrant-vbguest' plugin. This can take a few minutes...
Installed the plugin 'vagrant-vbguest (0.11.0)'!
```

In particular, this plugin helps avoid problems that happen when a new kernel is installed, such as the */vagrant* shared mount not being available.

Initializing the Vagrant Setup

The learning repository contains a *Vagrantfile* that lists the systems we'll use in this book. If you are familiar with Vagrant, you'll know that we can easily start these systems with `vagrant up`. We'll do that now to initialize a client system for learning Puppet:

```
$ vagrant up client
Bringing machine 'client' up with 'virtualbox' provider...
==> client: Importing base box 'centos65'...
==> client: Matching MAC address for NAT networking...
==> client: Setting the name of the VM: learning-puppet4_client_14150820_51797
==> client: Clearing any previously set network interfaces...
==> client: Preparing network interfaces based on configuration...
    client: Adapter 1: nat
    client: Adapter 2: hostonly
```

```
==> client: Forwarding ports...
    client: 22 => 2222 (adapter 1)
==> client: Booting VM...
==> client: Waiting for machine to boot. This may take a few minutes...
    client: SSH address: 127.0.0.1:2222
    client: SSH username: vagrant
    client: SSH auth method: private key
    client: Warning: Connection timeout. Retrying...
==> client: Machine booted and ready!
==> client: Checking for guest additions in VM...
==> client: Setting hostname...
==> client: Configuring and enabling network interfaces...
==> client: Mounting shared folders...
    client: /vagrant => /Users/jorhett/puppet-intro
```

Debugging Vagrant Problems

If the machine fails to boot, check for warnings or errors in the *VBox.log* file for this machine. VirtualBox creates a *VirtualBox VMs* directory in your home directory, with a subdirectory for each virtual machine. Under that directory you can find the *Logs/ VBox.log* file.

On Windows, this is the easiest way to view the file:

```
jorhett@windows MINGW64 ~/learning-puppet4 (master)
$ notepad ../VirtualBox*/*/Logs/VBox.log
```

If the client machine never gets past `Connection timeout. Retrying...`, it might be because VT-x or AMD-V virtualization is not enabled on your system. Check the log file for warning messages, as shown here:

```
$ grep WARN ../VirtualBox*/*/Logs/VBox.log
00:00:00.278293 WARNING! 64-bit guest type selected
    but the host CPU does NOT support HW virtualization.
```

Details about this can be found in the VirtualBox User Manual (*http://bit.ly/ 1XAFpy3*).

If you are using a standard Intel-based system, the settings for VT-x or AMD-V can be found in the BIOS settings available during the boot process, or in a BIOS management tool.

If you are using an older Intel-based Mac, you can find instructions for enabling it at "Intel-based Macs: Using VT-x virtualization technology" (*http://apple.co/1PgU0Jd*) on the Apple support site.

For any other issues with Vagrant machines not booting up, utilize Vagrant Community Support (*https://www.vagrantup.com/support.html*). The book *Vagrant: Up and Running* is an excellent resource, written by Mitchell Hashimoto, the creator of Vagrant.

We've started only a single machine to learn from, named *client*. There are several other machines available that we will utilize in future chapters:

```
$ vagrant status
Current machine states:

client                   running (virtualbox)
puppetmaster             not created (virtualbox)
puppetserver             not created (virtualbox)
dashboard                not created (virtualbox)
web1                     not created (virtualbox)

This environment represents multiple VMs. The VMs are all listed
above with their current state. For more information about a specific
VM, run `vagrant status NAME`.
```

You can suspend, resume, and destroy these instances quite easily:

```
$ vagrant suspend client
==> client: Saving VM state and suspending execution...

$ vagrant resume client
==> client: Resuming suspended VM...
==> client: Booting VM...
==> client: Waiting for machine to boot. This may take a few minutes...
    client: SSH address: 127.0.0.1:2222
    client: SSH username: vagrant
    client: SSH auth method: private key
    client: Warning: Connection refused. Retrying...
==> client: Machine booted and ready!

$ vagrant destroy client
    client: Are you sure you want to destroy the 'client' VM? [y/N] n
==> client: The VM 'client' will not be destroyed, since the confirmation
==> client: was declined.
```

If you do destroy the instance, just run `vagrant up client` to create a new instance and start over. We're not going to spend any more time covering Vagrant here, but remember `suspend` and `resume` when you want to stop your test environment but don't want to have to restart from scratch.

Now that this is running, let's log in to the client system and get started.

```
$ vagrant ssh client
[vagrant@client ~]$
```

If you are using Windows and a version of Vagrant below 1.7.5, it has a bug that prevents it from recognizing MinTTY properly. Upgrade to a more recent version.

If you are using Windows and not using Git Bash, you may get an error about SSH not being found. This is due to not having the Git binaries in your path. You can correct that for this command prompt like so:

```
C:\> set PATH=%PATH%;C:\Program Files (x86)\Git\bin
```

Verifying the /vagrant Filesystem

The folder *learning-puppet4* from your personal system should be mounted inside the virtual system as */vagrant*. Let's do a quick verification that it shows up here. You should see directory contents similar to this:

```
$ ls /vagrant
bin  doc  etc-puppet  LICENSE  manifests README.md  systemd-puppet  Vagrantfile
```

If you don't see that, read back in your terminal to see if there was an error message about being unable to mount the /vagrant filesystem.

```
/sbin/mount.vboxsf: mounting failed with the error: No such device
```

Unfortunately this isn't a book about VirtualBox, so I feel obliged to send you to the VirtualBox support forum (*https://forums.virtualbox.org/*) for a solution.

 The vast majority of these problems are solved by installing the vagrant-vbguest plugin as shown in "Install the Vagrant vbguest Plugin" on page 19, followed by halting and restarting the virtual machine.

Initializing Non-Vagrant Systems

If you are using a virtual machine of your own choice, we'll need to take a couple of steps so that you can follow the instructions in this book. If possible, mount the *learning-puppet4/* directory to the virtual machine as */vagrant/*. If you're not sure how to do this, you can simulate it with the following commands:

```
$ git clone https://github.com/jorhett/learning-puppet4
...
$ sudo ln -s /home/username/learning-puppet4 /vagrant
```

Throughout this book, you will see the following prompt shown in the examples:

```
[vagrant@client ~]$
```

You'll need to mentally replace this with whatever your virtual node's shell prompt is. If you wish to ensure it looks the same, you can use the following environment variable to sync them up:

```
$ export PS1='[vagrant@client \W]\$ '
```

Installing Some Helpful Utilities

I recommend installing the following helpful utilities on the virtual machine, as we'll be using them in subsequent chapters:

```
[vagrant@client ~]$ sudo yum install rsync git
```

Choosing a Text Editor

Before we install Puppet on your virtual system, stop and take a moment to ensure you have a good text editor available to use. There are two ways to use text editors:

Inside the virtual system
> If you are comfortable using Unix text editors such as Vim, Emacs, or Nano, you can run your editor inside the virtual system.

On your desktop
> The folder *learning-puppet4* is mounted inside the virtual system as */vagrant*. This means you can use a text editor of your choice to edit files inside this directory, and they will be visible and available to Puppet on your virtual system.

One issue for both Mac and Windows users is the handling of carriage returns and line feeds within files. Puppet and Git both work best when lines are terminated by line feeds without carriage returns, which is known as "Unix file format." It is important to select an editor that can read and write files in this format without any surprises.

Many editors on Windows open Unix format files correctly, but will quietly replace the endings with a carriage return when saving. As your target nodes may expect line-feed–terminated files, this can cause file corruption on the target host. Likewise, the opposite problem can exist: if you are editing files to be written out to Windows nodes, then you may need to preserve the carriage returns in the file. If you have a mixed environment of Unix/Linux and Windows nodes, it is essential that your editor can handle both file formats.

The following subsections provide a list of editors we recommend. I have limited this list to only include editors that handle both file formats well. If you don't have any Windows nodes, then you can use any editor you like.

On the Virtual System

There are three editors immediately available to you on the virtual system. All three of these normally create Unix format files, but can edit Windows format files without causing corruption. You can use the editors shown in Table 2-1 from the command line inside your virtual system.

Table 2-1. Text editors available on the virtual system

Text editor	Command	Notes
Nano	`sudo yum install nano`	An easy text editor for beginners—no book required!
Vim	`sudo yum install vim`	A powerful editor for experienced users; see *Learning the vi and Vim Editors* (O'Reilly).
Emacs	`sudo yum install emacs-nox`	A powerful editor for experienced users; see *Learning GNU Emacs* (O'Reilly).

 If you use Vim, I highly recommend installing the Puppet syntax highlighter, available at rodjek/vim-puppet (*http://bit.ly/1RTJbP5*). As of Puppet Agent 1.4, the syntax files are installed at */opt/puppetlabs/puppet/share/vim/puppet-vimfiles/*.

On Your Desktop

As it happens, all three of the aforementioned editors are installed on Macs by default, and available with the Cygwin package for Windows. You can get quite comfortable using these editors on your desktop.

When writing Puppet modules using a Windows system, you'll run into problems with line endings within templates and source files. Windows uses both a carriage-return character and a line-feed character to end a line, whereas Mac, Linux, and Unix systems use only the line-feed character.

If you open up the files we use in this book with the Windows Notepad editor, you will see that they show up as a single, unbroken line. WorkPad can display the file, but will change the endings when it writes out changes. None of the built-in editors on Windows—Notepad, WordPad, or Word—are safe to use with Unix format files.

For Windows users, I highly recommend Notepad++ (*http://notepad-plus-plus.org/*). It can open and write out both Unix and Windows format files without changing the line endings. It does not reformat files unless you explicitly tell it to.

For Mac users, I recommend the TextWrangler (*http://bit.ly/1Za4S2I*) and TextMate (*http://macromates.com/*) editors. The built-in TextEdit editor is minimally sufficient for Unix format files, but cannot handle files in Windows format properly.

If you are already a fan of the Unix editor Vim, you can find a GUI version of it at GVim (*http://www.vim.org/download.php#pc*) or MacVim (*https://code.google.com/p/macvim/*). Vim can safely read and write files in both formats.

If you have experience with the Eclipse IDE, the workspace editor can safely read, write, and convert upon request files in both Unix and Windows formats.

In Your Profile

Use the following command to configure your editor of choice in the environment on the virtual machine (you'll obviously need to set the editor to the one you want to use):

```
[vagrant@client ~]$ echo "EDITOR=nano" >> ~/.bashrc
```

When following the instructions in this book, any time you see the word $EDITOR in a command to type, you can either type this exactly or replace it with your editor. So, for example:

```
[vagrant@client ~]$ $EDITOR filename
```

would work exactly the same as:

```
[vagrant@client ~]$ nano filename
```

Reviewing the Learning Environment

In this chapter, you created a virtualized environment suitable for learning and testing Puppet without affecting any production or personal systems.

The default learning environment we recommended had you install the Git development tools, Vagrant, and VirtualBox to provide a virtualized CentOS system on which you can test and develop.

If you already have a virtualization platform that you prefer to work with, you are welcome to use that instead. We recommended using an operating system compatible with RedHat Enterprise Linux 6 or 7, as it is the best tested and guaranteed version for compatibility with Puppet Supported modules that we will be using throughout the book. After you feel confident in the use of Puppet, there are detailed notes for use on other platforms in Appendix A.

During the course of this chapter, you cloned a Git repository that contains Vagrant system definitions, some example manifests, and other helpful files we'll use throughout this book.

We also discussed the need for editing text files, and how you can use either an editor on the virtualized system or an editor on your desktop to create and edit Puppet manifests.

This environment is yours to keep. It will be useful as you develop and test Puppet manifests and modules during the learning process.

## CHAPTER 3

Installing Puppet

In this chapter, you will install the Puppet agent and its dependencies. We have deliberately chosen a Vagrant box that doesn't have Puppet preinstalled, so that you can go through and learn the process. You can repeat these exact steps on any test or production node to install or upgrade Puppet.

Let's get started by installing the Puppet Labs package repository.

Adding the Package Repository

Now we'll install and enable a Puppet Labs Puppet Collection repository on your fresh new system. Our first step is to check what the latest Puppet Collection is. You can find this at "Using Puppet Collections" (*http://bit.ly/1SYGS2d*) in the Puppet Labs online documents.

Get the URL for the Enterprise Linux 7 Collection (*http://bit.ly/1Un7JWH*) and install that package as described in the documentation.

For EL/CentOS versions 6 and above, you can simply use `yum install` rather than `rpm -ivh`:

```
[vagrant@client ~]$ sudo yum install -y \
    http://yum.puppetlabs.com/puppetlabs-release-pc1-el-7.noarch.rpm
```

This installs and enables a Puppet Collection package repository, which contains the Puppet 4 package. After it has finished installing, you can confirm it is enabled with the following command:

```
[vagrant@client ~]$ sudo yum repolist
Loaded plugins: fastestmirror
...snip repository checks...
repo id                    repo name                                    status
base/7/x86_64              CentOS-7 - Base                              8,652
extras/7/x86_64            CentOS-7 - Extras                              84
puppetlabs-pc1/x86_64      Puppet Labs PC1 Repository el 7 - x86_64       41
updates/7/x86_64           CentOS-7 - Updates                            355
repolist: 9,037
```

This shows you that there were (at the time this book was last updated) 41 packages in the *puppetlabs-pc1* repository.

What Is a Puppet Collection?

The Puppet ecosystem contains many tightly related and dependent packages. Puppet, Facter, MCollective, and the Ruby interpreter are all tightly related dependencies. The Puppet agent, Puppet server, and PuppetDB are self-standing but interdependent applications.

Production Puppet environments have been struggling with several conflicting needs:

- It is important to stay current with the latest improvements and security fixes.
- Upgrades would sometimes introduce problems for interdependent components of the Puppet ecosystem.
- It is difficult to support a wide variety of Ruby versions used by different platforms.

Puppet Labs has chosen to address these concerns with two related changes:

Puppet and all core dependencies are shipped together in a single package
    This change reduces the need to ensure compatibility across numerous versions of dependencies. The package includes a discrete, self-standing Ruby installation that does not conflict with the Ruby version provided with the operating system.

Components of the Puppet ecosystem will be tested and shipped together
    Any breaking changes will be introduced in a new Puppet Collection. This allows Puppet environments to safely track updates within a Puppet Collection, knowing that all versions within the Collection are guaranteed to work together.

Installing the Puppet Agent

Now let's go ahead and install the Puppet agent:

```
[vagrant@client ~]$ sudo yum install -y puppet-agent
Loaded plugins: fastestmirror
Loading mirror speeds from cached hostfile
 * base: centos.sonn.com
 * extras: mirrors.loosefoot.com
```

```
   * updates: mirrors.sonic.net
  Resolving Dependencies
  --> Running transaction check
  ---> Package puppet-agent.x86_64 0:1.4.0-1.el7 will be installed
  --> Finished Dependency Resolution

  ...snip lots of output...

  Running transaction check
  Running transaction test
  Transaction test succeeded
  Running transaction
    Installing : puppet-agent-1.4.0-1.el7.x86_64               1/1
    Verifying  : puppet-agent-1.4.0-1.el7.x86_64               1/1

  Installed:
    puppet-agent.x86_64 0:1.4.0-1.el7

  Complete!
```

Guides for installing Puppet on other platforms can be found in Appendix A.

Reviewing Dependencies

If you have installed previous versions of Puppet, you're accustomed to seeing dependency packages installed along with Puppet. Puppet 4 uses an All In One (AIO) installer, where all dependencies are installed together with Puppet. You can view these in the new installation directory:

```
[vagrant@client ~]$ ls -la /opt/puppetlabs/bin/
total 0
drwxr-xr-x 2 root root 68 Apr 6 4:41 .
drwxr-xr-x 4 root root 29 Apr 6 4:41 ..
lrwxrwxrwx 1 root root 33 Apr 6 4:41 facter -> /opt/puppetlabs/puppet/bin/facter
lrwxrwxrwx 1 root root 32 Apr 6 4:41 hiera -> /opt/puppetlabs/puppet/bin/hiera
lrwxrwxrwx 1 root root 30 Apr 6 4:41 mco -> /opt/puppetlabs/puppet/bin/mco
lrwxrwxrwx 1 root root 33 Apr 6 4:41 puppet -> /opt/puppetlabs/puppet/bin/puppet
```

Unlike previous versions, the Puppet commands are not installed in */usr/bin*, and won't be available in your default path. This puppet-agent package adds the file */etc/profile.d/puppet-agent.sh*, which will add */opt/puppetlabs/bin* to your path. This file is automatically included by the Bash shell.

If you reset $PATH in your shell configuration files, remember to add source /etc/profile.d/puppet-agent.sh after that point.

Let's review the other programs you see in this directory besides Puppet:

Facter

Facter is a program that evaluates a system and provides a number of *facts* about it. These facts include node-specific information (e.g., architecture, hostname, and IP address), in addition to custom information from plugins provided by Puppet modules. For a sneak preview, run the command `facter` right now and look at all the information it has.

We'll be covering how to make use of Facter facts in Chapter 5, and how to create custom facts in Part II.

Hiera

Hiera is a component we'll use to load in the data used by Puppet manifests and modules. Hiera allows you to provide default values and then override or expand them through a customizable hierarchy. This may sound complex, but Hiera's beauty and elegance comes from its simplicity.

You'll learn how to use Hiera in Part II, and after its introduction, you will see Hiera used in every subsequent example in the book.

Marionette Collective

Marionette Collective, or MCollective, is an orchestration framework tightly integrated with Puppet.

You'll learn how to use it in Part IV, where we'll use the `mco` client to manipulate the Puppet agent.

Reviewing Puppet 4 Changes

If you have installed previous versions of Puppet, you'll notice that the installation packages and the configuration file paths have all changed.

 If you are new to Puppet, you can skim lightly through this section; we'll review each path again as we teach you how to use Puppet.

Linux and Unix

For Unix and Linux systems, the following changes have taken place:

Puppet is now installed using a new All-in-One (AIO) `puppet-agent` package

This AIO package includes private versions of Facter, Hiera, MCollective, and Ruby.

Executables are in /opt/puppetlabs/bin/
All executables have been moved to */opt/puppetlabs/puppet/bin*. A subset of executables has symlinks in */opt/puppetlabs/bin*, which has been added to your path. (You may need to restart your shell.)

A private copy of Ruby is installed in /opt/puppetlabs/puppet
Ruby and supporting commands such as `gem` are installed in */opt/puppetlabs/ puppet*, to avoid them being accidentally called by users.

The configuration directory stored in `$confdir` *is now /etc/puppetlabs/puppet*
Puppet Open Source now uses the same configuration directory as Puppet Enterprise. Files in */etc/puppet* will be ignored.

The `$ssldir` *directory is inside* `$confdir`
On many platforms, Puppet previously put TLS keys and certificates in */var/lib/ puppet/ssl*. With Puppet 4, TLS files will be installed inside the *confdir/ssl/* directory on all platforms.

 Even though SSL is now named TLS, the directory and variable names have not yet been updated.

The MCollective configuration directory is now /etc/puppetlabs/mcollective
Files in */etc/mcollective* will be checked if the former directory doesn't exist.

The `$vardir` *for Puppet is now /opt/puppetlabs/puppet/cache/*
This new directory is used only by `puppet agent` and `puppet apply`. You can change this by setting `$vardir` in the Puppet config file.

The `$rundir` *for Puppet agent is now /var/run/puppetlabs*
This directory stores PID files only. Changing this directory will cause difficulty with the installed systemd and init service scripts.

Modules, manifests, and the Hiera config file have a new directory: /etc/puppetlabs/code
Puppet code and data has moved from `$confdir` to a new directory `$codedir`. This directory contains:

- The *environments* directory for `$environmentpath`
- The *modules* directory for `$basemodulepath`
- The *hiera.yaml* config file for `$hiera_config`

Windows

On Windows, very little has changed. The Puppet package has always been an AIO installer. The package now includes MCollective. Executables remain in the same location, and the MSI package still adds Puppet's tools to the PATH. The $confdir and $rundir have not changed.

For review, the file locations are:

$confdir
COMMON_APPDATA defaults to *C:\ProgramData\PuppetLabs\puppet\etc*

$codedir
C:\ProgramData\PuppetLabs\code

$vardir
C:\ProgramData\PuppetLabs\puppet\cache

$rundir
C:\ProgramData\PuppetLabs\puppet\var\run

Making Tests Convenient

Throughout this book, you'll edit files and make changes within the Puppet configuration directory. Normally, this would require you to type sudo every time you want to change a file.

I have found that most people prefer the following change to create an easier-to-use environment for learning (this command will make the vagrant user the owner of all files in that directory):

```
[vagrant@client ~]$ sudo chown -R vagrant /etc/puppetlabs
```

The remainder of this book assumes you have made this change. If you decide to continue using sudo, you'll need to add it to any command involving files in */etc/puppetlabs*.

Obviously you won't be using the vagrant user in a production environment. However, it is not uncommon to see something like the following done to give write access to all members of a certain group:

```
[vagrant@client ~]$ sudo chgrp -R sysadmin /etc/puppetlabs
[vagrant@client ~]$ sudo chmod -R g+w /etc/puppetlabs
```

One reason you may not want to change the ownership of this directory would be if your Puppet deployment was managed by continuous integration tools, and you want to ensure that everybody uses the tools. That won't be a problem when using this book, and `chown -R vagrant /etc/puppetlabs` is highly recommended for the lessons here.

Running Puppet Without sudo

When you run Puppet with `sudo`, it uses the system-level configuration files, like so:

```
[vagrant@client ~]$ sudo puppet config print |grep dir
confdir = /etc/puppetlabs/puppet
codedir = /etc/puppetlabs/code
vardir = /opt/puppetlabs/puppet/cache
logdir = /var/log/puppetlabs/puppet
...etc...
```

When you run Puppet without `sudo`, it will use paths in your home directory for configuration files. This can be useful when you are writing and testing small manifests:

```
[vagrant@client ~]$ puppet config print |grep dir
confdir = /home/vagrant/.puppetlabs/etc/puppet
codedir = /home/vagrant/.puppetlabs/etc/code
vardir = /home/vagrant/.puppetlabs/opt/puppet/cache
logdir = /home/vagrant/.puppetlabs/var/log
...etc...
```

 Continue reading to learn why you may not see the same results if you run this command.

Most people don't want to be constantly migrating changes back and forth between two different directory structures. There are two ways to resolve this dilemma:

Use sudo *every time you run Puppet*
> While this is an easy-to-remember way of working, I find myself less comfortable with this option. There are many manifests that can be tested without root access, and many Puppet commands that perform simple lookups for which root access is not required.

Set up a configuration file to use the system-level paths
> Modify your personal Puppet configuration to use the system-level paths. This allows you to run Puppet commands that read the same modules and configuration data, but without always invoking root-level access.

I much prefer the second approach, and I recommend it for daily use. For this reason, we have preinstalled the *~/.puppetlabs/etc/puppet/puppet.conf* configuration file on all Vagrant configurations, which enables this for you. Check it out:

```
[vagrant@client ~]$ cat ~/.puppetlabs/etc/puppet/puppet.conf
# Allow "puppet hiera" and "puppet module" commands without sudo
[main]
    logdest = console
    confdir = /etc/puppetlabs/puppet
    codedir = /etc/puppetlabs/code
```

If you don't like this setup, you are welcome to remove this file. Just remember to use sudo with every Puppet command, or it will use a different configuration file than you expect.

 If you are running Puppet on a host other than the ones built by the *learning-puppet4* GitHub repository, you'll have to create this file yourself.

Running Puppet with sudo

On most systems, the sudo command resets the user search path to a list of known safe directories. Unfortunately, this does not include the Puppet directory. You can see the effect of this change with the following command:

```
[vagrant@client vagrant]$ env |grep PATH
PATH=/usr/local/bin:/usr/bin:/usr/local/sbin:/usr/sbin:/opt/puppetlabs/bin:
  /home/vagrant/.local/bin:/home/vagrant/bin

[vagrant@client vagrant]$ sudo env |grep PATH
PATH=/usr/local/bin:/sbin:/bin:/usr/sbin:/usr/bin
```

If you want to run Puppet with sudo, you'll need to add the */opt/puppetlabs/bin* directory to sudo's secure_path default. The following command will get the current secure_path from the *sudoers* file, and create a *sudoers.d/* config extension that appends */opt/puppetlabs/bin*:

```
$ sudo grep secure_path /etc/sudoers \
    | sed -e 's#$#:/opt/puppetlabs/bin#' \
    | sudo tee /etc/sudoers.d/puppet-securepath

$ sudo env |grep PATH
PATH=/usr/local/bin:/sbin:/bin:/usr/sbin:/usr/bin:/opt/puppetlabs/bin
```

 You won't need to do this on the Vagrant machines provided by the *learning-puppet4* repository. This step was performed automatically during provisioning.

Reviewing Puppet Installation

During the course of this chapter, you did the following:

- Enabled the Puppet Yum repository on your system.
- Installed Puppet and its dependencies from this repository.
- Learned the dependencies that support Puppet.
- Reviewed the changed paths used by Puppet 4 on Unix/Linux systems.

Best of all, none of this was done with magic helper scripts that hid the details from you. You can repeat these exact steps on any test or production node to install or upgrade Puppet.

## CHAPTER 4

Writing Manifests

The very first concept we want to introduce you to is the Puppet *manifest*. A manifest is a file containing Puppet configuration language that describes how resources should be configured. The manifest is the closest thing to what one might consider a Puppet *program*. It uses resources to define a policy to be enforced on a node. It is therefore the base component for Puppet configuration policy, and a building block for complex Puppet modules.

This chapter will focus on how to write configuration policies for Puppet 4 manifests. Writing manifests well is the single most important part of building Puppet policies.

Let's get started with the smallest component within a manifest.

Implementing Resources

Resources are the smallest building block of the Puppet configuration language. They represent a singular element that you wish to evaluate, create, or remove. Puppet comes with many built-in resource types. The stock resource types manipulate system components that you are already familiar with, including:

- Users
- Groups
- Files
- Host file entries
- Packages
- Services

Furthermore, you can create your own resources. However, we'll begin with one of the simplest resources—the notify resource. Let's start with the standard first program written in every language:

```
notify { 'greeting':
  message => 'Hello, world!'
}
```

This code declares a `notify` resource with a title of `greeting`. It has a single attribute, `message`, which is assigned the value we'd expect in our first program. Attributes are separated from their values by a *hash rocket* (also called a *fat comma*), which is a very common way to identify key/value pairs in Perl, Ruby, and PHP scripting languages.

This tiny bit of code is a fully functional and valid manifest. This manifest (with one single resource) does only one thing, which is to output that greeting message every time it is called. Let's go ahead and use Puppet to evaluate this manifest:

```
[vagrant@client ~]$ cat /vagrant/manifests/helloworld.pp

notify { 'greeting':
  message => 'Hello, world!'
}
```

 As part of the definition of your virtual system, we have preinstalled some Puppet manifests in the */vagrant/manifests/* directory for use in this class. We'll refer to these throughout the book.

As you can see from this example, manifests are text files named with a *.pp* file extension—they describe resources using the Puppet configuration language. You can create or modify a Puppet manifest using any text editor.

Applying a Manifest

One of Puppet's best features is the ease of testing your code. Puppet does not require you to set up complicated testing environments to evaluate Puppet manifests. It is easy—nay, downright trivial—to test a Puppet manifest.

Let's go ahead and apply this manifest. We will do this using the `puppet apply` command, which tells Puppet to apply a single Puppet manifest:

```
[vagrant@client ~]$ puppet apply /vagrant/manifests/helloworld.pp
Notice: Compiled catalog for client.example.com in environment production
Notice: Hello, world!
Notice: /Stage[main]/Main/Notify[greeting]/message:
  defined 'message' as 'Hello, world!'
Notice: Finished catalog run in 0.01 seconds
```

As you can see, Puppet has applied the manifest. It does this in several steps:

1. Builds (compiles) a *Puppet catalog* from the manifest.

2. Uses dependency and ordering information (covered soon) to determine evaluation order.
3. Evaluates the target resource on the node to determine if changes should be applied.
4. Creates, modifies, or removes the resource—a notification message is created.
5. Provides verbose feedback about the catalog application.

Don't worry about memorizing these steps at this point in the learning process. For now, it's just important that you have a general idea of the process—we'll discuss these concepts in increasing depth throughout this book. We'll cover the catalog build and evaluation process in great detail at the end of Part I.

For now, just remember that you'll use `puppet apply` to apply Puppet manifests. It will provide you verbose feedback on actions Puppet took to bring the target resources into alignment with the declared policy.

Declaring Resources

There are only a few rules to remember when declaring resources. The format is always the same:

```
resource_type { 'resource_title':
  ensure     => present,          # usually 'present' or 'absent'
  attribute1 => 1234,             # number
  attribute2 => 'value',          # string
  attribute3 => ['red','blue'],   # array
  noop       => false,            # boolean
}
```

 Don't get hung up analyzing the data types shown in this example. We will cover the different data types of Puppet 4 exhaustively in Chapter 5.

The most important rule for resources is: *there can be only one*. Within a manifest or set of manifests being applied together (the *catalog* for a node), a resource of a given type can only be declared once with a given title. Every resource of that type must have a unique title.

For example, the following manifest will fail because the same title is used for both file resources:

```
[vagrant@client ~]$ cat myfile.pp
file { 'my_file':
  ensure => present,
  path   => 'my_file.txt',
}
```

```
file { 'my_file':
  ensure => present,
  path   => 'my_file.csv',
}

notify { 'my_file':
  message => "My file is present",
}

[vagrant@client ~]$ puppet apply myfile.pp
Error: Evaluation Error: Error while evaluating a Resource Statement,
  Duplicate declaration: File[my_file] is already declared in file
  /home/vagrant/myfile.pp:1; cannot redeclare at /home/vagrant/myfile.pp:6
```

You'll notice that no complaint was given for the notify resource with the same title. This is not a conflict. Only resources of the same type cannot utilize the same title. Naming the preceding files with their full paths ensures no conflicts:

```
file { '/home/vagrant/my_file.txt':
  ensure => present,
  path   => '/home/vagrant/my_file.txt',
}

file { '/home/vagrant/my_file.csv':
  ensure => present,
  path   => '/home/vagrant/my_file.csv',
}
```

Viewing Resources

Puppet can show you an existing resource written out in the Puppet configuration language. This makes it easy to generate code based on existing configurations. Let's demonstrate how to view a resource with an email alias:

```
[vagrant@client ~]$ puppet resource mailalias postmaster
mailalias { 'postmaster':
  ensure    => 'present',
  recipient => ['root'],
  target    => '/etc/aliases',
}
```

The puppet resource command queries the node using the exact same code used by Puppet to compare and alter the system state. The output gives you the exact structure, syntax, and attributes to declare this alias resource in a Puppet manifest. You can add this to a manifest file, change the recipient, and then use puppet apply to change the postmaster alias on this node.

Let's examine another resource—the user you are logged in as:

```
[vagrant@client ~]$ puppet resource user vagrant
Error: Could not run: undefined method 'exists?' for nil:NilClass
```

This somewhat confusing error message means that you don't have the privileges to view that resource—so let's escalate our privileges to complete this command with sudo:

```
[vagrant@client ~]$ sudo puppet resource user vagrant
user { 'vagrant':
  ensure           => 'present',
  gid              => '500',
  groups           => ['wheel'],
  home             => '/home/vagrant',
  password         => '$1$sC3NqLSG$FsXVyW7azpoh76edOfAWm1',
  password_max_age => '99999',
  password_min_age => '0',
  shell            => '/bin/bash',
  uid              => '500',
}
```

If you look at the resource, you'll see why root access was necessary. The user resource contains the user's password hash, which required root privilege to read from the shadow file. As with the previous alias, you could write this user resource to a file, replace the password hash, and use sudo puppet apply to change the root password.

 Some resources output by the puppet resource command include read-only attributes that cannot be set in a manifest. You'll receive a clear is read-only error message if you attempt to set one. Refer to the resource's documentation to learn which attributes cannot be set.

Executing Programs

Let's examine a resource type that executes commands. Use the exec resource to execute programs as part of your manifest:

```
exec { 'echo-holy-cow':
  path      => ['/bin'],
  cwd       => '/tmp',
  command   => 'echo "holy cow!" > testfile.txt',
  creates   => '/tmp/testfile.txt',
  returns   => [0],
  logoutput => on_failure,
}
```

Now when you apply this manifest, it will create the *testfile.txt* file. Notice that we use single quotes to encapsulate the values given to the attributes.

Best Practice

Use single quotes for any value that does not contain a variable. This protects against accidental interpolation of a variable. Use double quotes with strings containing variables.

The `exec` resource just defined uses the `creates` attribute. This attribute defines the expected result of the command execution. When the named file exists, the command is not executed. This means the manifest can be run repeatedly and nothing will change after the file is initially created. Let's test this out here:

```
[vagrant@client ~]$ puppet apply /vagrant/manifests/tmp-testfile.pp
Notice: Compiled catalog for client.example.com in environment production
Notice: /Stage[main]/Main/Exec[echo-holy-cow]/returns: executed successfully
Notice: Finished catalog run in 0.07 seconds

[vagrant@client ~]$ puppet apply /vagrant/manifests/tmp-testfile.pp
Notice: Compiled catalog for client.example.com in environment production
Notice: Finished catalog run in 0.01 seconds
```

There are a wide variety of attributes you can use to control whether or not an `exec` resource will be executed, and which exit codes indicate success or failure. This is a complex and feature-rich resource. Whenever you create an `exec` resource, test carefully and refer to "Puppet Type Reference: exec" (*http://bit.ly/1RpsKzA*) on the Puppet docs site.

Was That Idempotent?

I must beg your forgiveness: I have deliberately led you astray to teach you a common mistake for newcomers to declarative programming. While `exec` is an essential resource type, it is best to avoid using it whenever possible. We'll apply the exact same result with a more appropriate `file` resource next.

If you examine the preceding `exec` resource, you'll note that we had to declare *how* to make the change, and also *whether* or not to make the change. This is very similar to imperative programming, and can be very difficult to maintain.

This resource would be idempotent because it used the `creates` attribute to test whether the file already existed. However, if the contents of the file were changed, this resource would not repair the contents. We would need to add more tests to validate the file contents.

It is generally difficult to write declarative code using an `exec` resource. There is a tendency to revert to an imperative programming style. Except in circumstances where no other method is possible, use of an exec is generally an indication of a poorly written manifest. In fact, at several companies where I have worked, the presence of an exec resource within a commit caused it to be flagged for a mandatory code review.

Best Practice

Find or create an idempotent Puppet resource type to apply the change.

Managing Files

How else could we create this file? We could have used the file resource. Let's examine one now:

```
file { '/tmp/testfile.txt':
  ensure  => present,
  mode    => '0644',
  replace => true,
  content => 'holy cow!',
}
```

This is a properly declarative policy. We declare that the file should exist, and what the contents of the file should be. We do not need to concern ourselves with how, or when to make changes to the file. Furthermore, we were able to ensure the contents of the file remained consistent, which is not possible within an echo command.

Notice that the declarative manifest used fewer lines of text, and guaranteed a more consistent output.

Let's apply this policy now:

```
[vagrant@client ~]$ puppet apply /vagrant/manifests/file-testfile.pp
Notice: Compiled catalog for client.example.com in environment production
Notice: /Stage[main]/Main/File[/tmp/testfile.txt]/content: content changed
  '{md5}0eb429526e5e170cd9ed4f84c24e4' to '{md5}3d508c8566858d8a168a290dd709c'
Notice: /Stage[main]/Main/File[/tmp/testfile.txt]/mode:
  mode changed '0664' to '0644'
Notice: Finished catalog run in 0.03 seconds

[vagrant@client ~]$ puppet apply /vagrant/manifests/file-testfile.pp
Notice: Compiled catalog for client.example.com in environment production
Notice: Finished catalog run in 0.02 seconds
```

Unlike with the previous `exec` resource, Puppet observed that the contents were different and changed the file to match. Now, you're probably thinking to yourself, "Aren't the file contents the same in both?" Nope. It's not obvious in the `exec` declaration, but `echo` appends a trailing newline to the text. As you can see here, the file contents don't include a newline:

```
[vagrant@client ~]$ cat /tmp/testfile.txt
holy cow![vagrant@client ~]$
```

You can easily adjust the file contents to include as many newline characters as you want. Because the newline character is interpreted, you'll need to use double quotes around the contents.

You could also change the `replace` attribute from `true` to `false` if you want to initially create a missing file, but not replace one that has been changed.

```
file { '/tmp/testfile.txt':
  ensure  => present,
  mode    => '0644',
  replace => false,
  content => "holy cow!\n",
}
```

You can find complete details of the many attributes available for the `file` resource at "Puppet Type Resource: file" (*http://bit.ly/1MeZJoa*) on the Puppet docs site.

Finding File Backups

Every file changed by a Puppet `file` resource is backed up on the node in a directory specified by the `$clientbucketdir` configuration setting. Unfortunately, the file backups are stored in directories indexed by a hash of the file contents, which makes them quite tricky to find.

Which Bucket Are We in Now?

Up through at least version 4.3.6, Puppet subcommands are inconsistent about whether they use `$clientbucketdir` or `$bucketdir`. The commands default to expecting that they are in the bucket directory used on a Puppet master. On a node, add the following to your *puppet.conf* to allow the commands to work seamlessly:

```
[user]
    bucketdir = $clientbucketdir
```

Puppet Labs has agreed that this situation is confusing and the directories should be consolidated. The issue is being tracked in PUP-5206 (*https://tickets.puppetlabs.com/browse/PUP-5206*). Hopefully it will be fixed soon.

You can back up a file to this storage any time you want, like so:

```
$ sudo puppet filebucket --local backup /tmp/testfile.txt
Info: Computing checksum on file /tmp/testfile.txt
/tmp/testfile.txt: 3d508c856685853ed8a168a290dd709c
```

Use this command to get a list of every file backed up. Here you can see the backup performed by `puppet apply` when it changed the file, as well as your manual backup a few minutes later:

```
$ sudo puppet filebucket --local list
0eb429526e5e170cd9ed4f84c24e442b 2015-11-19 08:18:06 /tmp/testfile.txt
3d508c856685853ed8a168a290dd709c 2015-11-19 08:23:42 /tmp/testfile.txt
```

Restoring Files

Use the hash associated with a specific file version to view the contents of the file at that point in time:

```
$ sudo puppet filebucket --local get 0eb429526e5e170cd9ed4f84c24e442b
Info: FileBucket read 0eb429526e5e170cd9ed4f84c24e442b
holy cow!
```

You can compare an installed file to a backup version, or compare two backup versions, using the `filebucket diff` command:

```
$ sudo puppet filebucket --local diff \
    0eb429526e5e170cd9ed4f84c24e442b /tmp/testfile.txt
Info: Comparing 0eb429526e5e170cd9ed4f84c24e442b   /tmp/testfile.txt
Info: Computing checksum on file /tmp/diff20151119-4940-1h3dwn9
Info: FileBucket read 0eb429526e5e170cd9ed4f84c24e442b
Info: Computing checksum on string
--- /tmp/diff20151119-4940-1h3dwn9      2015-11-19 08:20:59.994974403 +0000
+++ /tmp/testfile.txt   2015-11-19 08:18:06.162104809 +0000
@@ -1 +1 @@
-holy cow!
+holy cow!
\ No newline at end of file
```

You can restore a backup file to the original location or another path:

```
$ sudo puppet filebucket --local restore \
    /tmp/testfile.txt 0eb429526e5e170cd9ed4f84c24e442b
```

This command gives no output unless there is an error, so you should find the file has been restored as requested.

Avoiding Imperative Manifests

In the previous section, we established that it is best practice to avoid using `exec` resources. To understand the reason for this, let's return to our previous discussion of the word *declarative*.

If the code tells the interpreter what to do, when to do it, and how to do it, then it is functioning in an imperative manner. If the code tells the interpreter what it wants the result to be, then the code is declarative.

 It is common to see newcomers attempt to write imperative Puppet manifests. They struggle to instruct Puppet on exactly how to do something. It can take months before they grasp the value and simplicity of declarative configuration. Learn this properly now, and get a head start on becoming a Puppet expert.

Yes, the `exec` resource will let you write imperative manifests in Puppet. However, as we discussed in Chapter 1, you'll find that it takes more effort, is harder to maintain, and is less likely to produce consistent results.

Rob Nelson provided us with the perfect metaphor:[1]

> If you try hard enough, you can make it act like an imperative language. That would be akin to ripping the bottom out of your car, dressing in a leopard-print toga and a ratty blue tie, and driving to work with your feet. Is that something you really want to do, or just watch on Boomerang?

The reason I advocate so strongly to not use `exec` is fairly simple. The `exec` resource executes the command, but it doesn't really know what the command does. That command could modify the node state in any form, and Puppet wouldn't be aware of it. This creates a *fire and forget* situation, where the only piece of information returned to Puppet is the exit code from the command:

```
Notice: /Stage[main]/Main/Exec[echo-holy-cow]/returns: executed successfully
```

All you know is that the command here returned an exit code you expected (0 by default, which is the Unix convention for success). You don't really know what the command did. If someone wrote a Puppet manifest last week, and then removed it from the execution this week, you have to compare backups (if you have any) to determine what the command did.

When you declare the desired state using resources specific to what has been changed, then Puppet logs each and every change made. Files that are changed are backed up, and can be restored if necessary. For example, let's examine what happened when we applied the `file` resource:

```
Notice: /Stage[main]/Main/File[/tmp/testfile.txt]/content: content changed
  '{md5}0eb429526e5e170cd9ed4f84c24e44' to '{md5}3d508c856685853ed8a168a290dd70'
Notice: /Stage[main]/Main/File[/tmp/testfile.txt]/mode:
  mode changed '0664' to '0644'
```

---

1 *http://rnelson0.com/2015/03/26/why-not-puppet/*

Without having access to read the original Puppet manifest, you know that the file mode and the file contents were changed. You can validate the file contents later to match the md5 hash, or restore a copy of the file as it was before this change was made.

Using the `file` resource is more concise, easier to read, and more consistent in application. Best of all, it creates a detailed log of which changes were made. I have found this is true of every situation where you can replace an `exec` resource with a native resource. Use an `exec` resource only when no other choice is available.

Testing Yourself

Let's pause for a second and utilize what you have learned to build a Puppet manifest:

1. Use `puppet resource` to create a new manifest from the file */tmp/testfile.txt*.
2. Remove the `type` attribute, which is redundant with the resource name.
3. Change the file `mode` to be group writable (either `0664` or `ug=rw,o=r`).
4. Change the content to say something that amuses you.
5. Run `puppet apply` *yourmanifest.pp* and observe the changes.
6. Confirm the changes with the `ls -la /tmp` and `cat /tmp/testfile.txt` commands.
7. Run `puppet apply` again and see what happens.

You won't need to use `sudo` to make any of these changes, as you are the owner of this file.

Reviewing Writing Manifests

In this chapter, you learned about manifests, single files that contain Puppet resources to be evaluated and, if necessary, applied on the node. Manifests are the closest thing that could be called a *program* in the conventional sense.

You learned how to create and apply resources, the smallest building blocks of a Puppet manifest. You learned the common syntax of a resource, and how to retrieve the details of an existing resource on a system in the Puppet configuration language.

In addition, you learned how to instruct the Puppet agent to output messages during application of the manifest for debugging purposes.

Finally, you learned how to execute programs in the policy, as well as why this can be bad design. You learned how using a more declarative style uses less code, and works more consistently in all situations.

## CHAPTER 5

Using the Puppet Configuration Language

Now that you've been introduced to the Puppet manifest and the resource building block, you are ready to meet the Puppet configuration language.

This chapter will introduce you to the data types, operators, conditionals, and iterations that can be used to build manifests for Puppet 4. Writing manifests well is the single most important part of using Puppet. You'll find yourself returning to this chapter again and again as you develop your own manifests.

 Don't stop here if you don't understand how or why to use one piece of the language just yet. Just take in what is possible, and refer to this chapter as you build and grow your skills.

Consider this chapter a reference for the Puppet configuration language. The reasoning behind why and when to use particular bits of the language will become clear as specific implementations are discussed later in the book.

Defining Variables

Puppet makes use of *variables* (named storage of data) much like any other language you've learned to write code in.

Like many scripting languages, variables are prefaced with a $ in Puppet. The variable name must start with a lowercase letter or underscore, and may contain lowercase letters, numbers, and underscores. Let's take a look at a few examples of both valid and invalid variable names:

```
$myvar          # valid
$MyVar          # invalid

$my_var         # valid
$my-var         # invalid

$my3numbers     # valid
$3numbers       # invalid
```

 Previous versions of Puppet allowed uppercase letters, periods, and dashes with inconsistent results. Puppet 4 has improved reliability by enforcing these standards.

Variables starting with underscores should only be used within the local scope (we'll cover variable scope in "Understanding Variable Scope" on page 197):

```
$_myvar         # valid inside a local scope
$prog::_myvar   # deprecated: no underscore-prefixed variables out of scope
```

Variables are assigned values with an equals sign. Every value has a data type. The most common types are `Boolean`, `Numeric`, and `String`. As I'm sure you've seen these data types many times before, we'll jump straight to some examples:

```
$my_name      = 'Jo'        # string
$num_tokens   = 115         # numeric
$not_true     = false       # boolean
```

 Anything after the # (comment mark) is ignored by the interpreter.

A variable that has not been initialized will evaluate as undefined, or `undef`. You can also explicitly assign `undef` to a variable:

```
$notdefined = undef
```

The `puppetlabs/stdlib` module provides a function you can use to see a variable's type:

```
include stdlib
$nametype = type_of( $my_name )    # String
$numtype  = type_of( $num_tokens ) # Integer
```

Defining Numbers

In Puppet 4, unquoted numerals are evaluated as a Numeric data type. Numbers are assigned specific numeric types based on the characters at the start of or within the number:

- Decimal numbers start with 1 through 9.
- Floating-point numbers contain a single period.
- Octal numbers (most commonly used for file modes) start with a 0.
- Hexadecimal numbers (used for memory locations or colors) start with 0x.

 In previous versions of Puppet, bare numbers were evaluated as strings. Best practice as of Puppet 3 was to quote all numbers to ensure they were evaluated as a `String`. This was preparation for Puppet 4, where unquoted numbers are the `Numeric` data type, and validation is performed on the value.

Any time an unquoted word starts with numbers, it will be validated as a Numeric type.

```
$decimal     = 1234     # valid Integer decimal assignment
$decimal     = 12.34    # valid Float decimal assignment
$octal       = 0775     # valid Integer octal assignment
$hexadecimal = 0xFFAA   # valid Integer hexadecimal assignment
$string      = '001234' # string containing a number with leading zeros
```

Always quote numbers that need to be represented intact, such as decimals with leading zeros.

Creating Arrays and Hashes

It is possible to declare an Array (ordered list) that contains many values. As I'm sure you've used arrays in other languages, we'll jump straight to some examples:

```
$my_list  = [1,3,5,7,11]         # array of Numeric values
$my_names = ['Amy','Sam','Jen']  # array of String values
$mixed_up = ['Alice',3,true]     # String, Number, Boolean
$trailing = [4,5,6,]             # trailing commas OK, unlike JSON
$embedded = [4,5,['a','b']]      # number, number, array of strings
```

Array-to-array assignment works if there are equal variables and values:

```
[$first,$middle,$last] = ['Jo',undef,'Rhett']  # good
[$first,$middle,$last] = ['Jo','Rhett']        # error
```

Some functions require a list of input values, instead of an array. In a function call, the splat operator (*) operator will convert an Array into a comma-separated list of values:

```
myfunction( *$Array_of_arguments ) { ... }
```

This provides a concise, readable way to pass a list of unknown size to a function.

Mapping Hash Keys and Values

You can also create an unordered, random-access hash where member values are associated with a key value. At assignment time, the key and value should be separated by a *hash rocket* (=>), as shown here:

```
# small hash of user home directories
$homes = { 'Jack' => '/home/jack', 'Jill' => '/home/jill', }

# Multiline definition
$user = {
  'username' => 'Jill',  # String value
  'uid'      => 1001,    # Integer value
  'create'   => true,    # Boolean value
}
```

Hash keys must be Scalar (string or number), but values can be any data type. This means that the value assigned to a key could be a nested Array or Hash.

Using Variables in Strings

Strings with pure data should be surrounded by single quotes:

```
$my_name = 'Dr. Evil'
$how_much = '100 million'
```

Use double quotes when interpolating variables into strings, as shown here:

```
notice( "Hello ${username}, glad to see you today!" )
```

For very large blocks of text, you may want to use the *heredoc* multiline format. Start the block with an end tag surrounded by a @( ) start tag:

```
$message_text = @(END)
This is a very long message,
which will be composed over
many lines of text.
END
```

By default, heredoc syntax is not interpolated, so this is the same as a single-quoted block of text. You can have the block be interpolated for variables by placing the end tag within double quotes. For example, the following contains variables to customize the message:

```
$message_text = @("END")
Dear ${user},
  Your password is ${password}.

  Please login at ${site_url} to continue.
END
```

Many common shell and programming escape sequences are available for you to use within interpolated strings:

Sequence	Expands to
\n	Line feed (end of line terminator)
\r	Carriage return (necessary in Windows files)
\s	Space
\t	Tab character

Using Braces to Limit Problems

As with most scripting languages, curly braces should be used to delineate variable boundaries:

```
$the_greeting = "Hello ${myname}, you have received ${num_tokens} tokens!"

notice( "The second value in the list is ${my_list[1]}" )
```

Best Practice

Use curly braces to delineate the beginning and end of a variable name within a string.

Use curly braces any time you use a variable within a string, but not when using the variable by itself. As shown here, the variables are used directly by the resource without interpolation, so it reads easier without braces:

```
# This time we define the strings in advance
$file_name = "/tmp/testfile2-${my_name}.txt"
$the_greeting = "Hello ${myname}, you have received ${num_tokens} tokens!"

# Don't use braces for variables that stand alone
file { $file_name:
  ensure  => present,
  mode    => '0644',
  replace => true,
  content => $the_greeting,
}
```

In particular, the following array index will not resolve correctly:

```
notice( "The second value in the list is $my_list[1]" )
```

This will actually output every value in the array, followed by the string [1]. To interpolate a specific array index or hash key within a string, you must enclose the array and index or hash and key both inside curly braces, like so:

```
# Output value from an array index 1
notice( "The second value in the list is ${my_list[1]}" )

# Output value stored in hash key alpha
notice( "The value stored with key alpha is ${my_hash['alpha']}" )
```

Preventing Interpolation

You will sometimes want to utilize characters that generally have special meaning within your strings, such as dollar signs and quotes. The simplest way is to place the entire string within single quotes, but at times you need to use the special characters in combination with interpolation.

In most cases, you can simply preface the character with the escape character (a backslash or \) to avoid interpolation. Interpolation happens only once, even if a string is used within another string:

```
# Work around the need for both types of quotes in a variable
$the_greeting = "we need 'single quotes' and \"double quotes\" here."

# Place backslashes before special characters to avoid interpolation
$describe = "\$user uses a \$ dollar sign and a \\ backslash"

# Previously interpolated values won't be interpolated again
$inform = "${describe}, and resolves to the value '${user}'."
```

Using single quotes avoids the need for backslashes:

```
$num_tokens = '$100 million'    # dollars, not a variable
$cifs_share = '\\server\drive'  # windows share, not escape chars
```

Using Unicode Characters

You can safely assign Unicode characters to strings utilizing \u followed by either their UTF-16 four-digit number or the UTF-8 hex value in curly braces. Here is a very small sample of Unicode characters and the way to represent them in Puppet:

Character	Description	UTF-16	UTF-8 hex
€	Euro currency	\u20AC	\u{E282AC}
¥	Yen currency	\u00A5	\u{C2A5}
Ä	Umlaut A	\u00C4	\u{C384}
©	Copyright sign	\u00A9	\u{C2A9}

Unicode is documented at length at *www.unicode.org*; however, the site doesn't have an easy search mechanism. You can find many UTF-16 Unicode numbers at Wikipedia's "List of Unicode Characters" (*http://bit.ly/22sa0Bf*). Micha Köllerwirth maintains a more comprehensive list along with the UTF-8 equivalents (*http://bit.ly/1MrUSKV*), and you can also check out the character search (*http://bit.ly/22saaZD*) available on FileFormat.info.

Avoiding Redefinition

Variables may not be redefined in Puppet within a given namespace or scope. We'll cover the intricacies of scope in Part II, "Creating Puppet Modules", but understand that a manifest has a single namespace, and a variable cannot receive a new value within that namespace.

This is one of the hardest things for experienced programmers to grow accustomed to. However, if you consider the nature of declarative programming, it makes a lot of sense.

In imperative programming, you have a specific order of events and an expected state of change as you pass through the code:

```
myvariable = 10
print myvariable   # prints 10
myvariable = 20
print myvariable   # prints 20
```

In a declarative language, the interpreter handles variable assignment independently of usage within resources. Which assignment would be performed prior to the resource application? This can change as more resources are added to manifests, and more manifests are applied to a node. Likewise, it would change for each node that did or did not have certain resources applied to it. This means that the value could change from one node to the other, or even from one evaluation to another on the same node.

To avoid this problem, Puppet kicks out an error if you attempt to change a variable's value:

```
[vagrant@client ~]$ cat double-assign.pp
$myvar = 5
$myvar = 10

[vagrant@client ~]$ puppet apply double-assign.pp
Error: Cannot reassign variable myvar at double-assign.pp:2
```

This is simply part of the learning process for thinking declaratively.

Avoiding Reserved Words

As mentioned previously, variables may be assigned string values as bare words, without quotes. A bare word that begins with a letter is usually evaluated the same as if it were single-quoted.

There are a number of reserved words that have special meaning for the interpreter, and must be quoted when used as string values. These are all fairly obvious words that are reserved within many other programming languages:

```
and       elsif     node
attr      false     private
case      function  or
class     if        true
default   in        type
define    import    undef
else      inherits  unless
```

There really aren't any surprises in this list. Any language primitive (as just shown), resource type (e.g., file, exec), or function name cannot be used as a bare word string.

You can find a complete list of all reserved words at "Language: Reserved Words and Acceptable Names" (*http://bit.ly/1XAERZ3*) on the Puppet docs site.

 Previously working unquoted strings can yield surprising results when functions or resource types with the same name are added to the catalog. Make code future-proof by quoting string values every time:

```
$my_variable = somestring    # valid
$my_variable = 'somestring'  # best practice
```

Learning More

You can find more details about using variables at the Puppet docs site:

- Language: Variables (*http://bit.ly/1nUXjzj*)
- Language: About Values and Data Types (*http://bit.ly/1Rrhmx0*)

Some specific data types worth reading about in more detail on the Puppet docs site include the following:

- Data Types: Numbers (*http://bit.ly/1TUokRJ*)
- Data Types: Arrays (*http://bit.ly/1XAEZId*)
- Data Types: Hashes (*http://bit.ly/1MrV9gW*)

Finding Facts

Speaking of variables, Facter provides many variables for you containing node-specific information. These are always available for use in your manifests. Go ahead and run facter and look at the output:

```
[vagrant@client ~]$ facter
architecture => x86_64
augeasversion => 1.0.0
blockdevice_sda_model => VBOX HARDDISK
blockdevice_sda_size => 10632560640
blockdevice_sda_vendor => ATA
blockdevices => sda
domain => example.com
facterversion => 3.1.2
filesystems => ext4,iso9660
fqdn => client.example.com
gid => vagrant
hardwareisa => x86_64
```

```
hardwaremodel => x86_64
hostname => client
id => vagrant
interfaces => eth0,eth1,lo
ipaddress => 10.0.2.15
...etc
```

As you can see, Facter produces a significant number of useful facts about the system, from facts that won't change over the lifetime of a system (e.g., platform and architecture) to information that can change from moment to moment (e.g., free memory). Try the following commands to find some of the more variable fact information provided:

```
[vagrant@client ~]$ facter | grep version
```

```
[vagrant@client ~]$ facter | grep mb
```

```
[vagrant@client ~]$ facter | grep free
```

Puppet adds several facts for use within Puppet modules. You can run the following command to see all facts used by Puppet, and installed on the node from Puppet modules:

```
[vagrant@client ~]$ facter --puppet
```

Puppet always adds the following facts above and beyond system facts provided by Facter:

`$facts['clientcert']`
> The client-reported value of the node's `certname` configuration value.

`$facts['clientversion']`
> The client-reported version of Puppet running on the node.

`$facts['clientnoop']`
> The client-reported value of whether `noop` was enabled in the configuration or on the command line to perform the comparison without actually making changes.

`$facts['agent_specified_environment']`
> The environment requested by the client. When using a Puppet server, the server could override the environment selection. This value contains the requested value. If this value is blank, the *production* environment is used by default.

All of these facts can be found in the `$facts` hash.

 Puppet servers provide server-validated or *trusted facts* in a `$trusted` hash that is more reliable than the information provided by the client. You'll find information about trusted facts in Part III.

You can also use Puppet to list out Puppet facts in JSON format:

```
[vagrant@client ~]$ puppet facts find
$ puppet facts find
{
  "name": "client.example.com",
  "values": {
    "puppetversion": "4.4.0",
    "virtual": "virtualbox",
    "is_virtual": true,
    "architecture": "x86_64",
    "augeasversion": "1.4.0",
    "kernel": "Linux",
    "domain": "example.com",
    "hardwaremodel": "x86_64",
    "operatingsystem": "CentOS",
```

Facter can provide the data in different formats, useful for passing to other programs. The following options output Facter data in the common YAML and JSON formats:

```
[vagrant@client ~]$ facter --yaml
[vagrant@client ~]$ puppet facts --render-as yaml

[vagrant@client ~]$ facter --json
[vagrant@client ~]$ puppet facts --render-as json
```

Calling Functions in Manifests

A *function* is executable code that may accept input parameters, and may output a return value. A function that returns a value can be used to provide a value to a variable:

```
$zero_or_one = bool2num( $facts['is_virtual'] );
```

The function can also be used in place of a value, or interpolated into a string:

```
# md5() function provides the value for the message attribute
notify { 'md5_hash':
  message => md5( $facts['fqdn'] )
}

# Include the MD5 hash in the result string
$result = "The MD5 hash for the node name is ${md5( $facts['fqdn'] )}"
```

Functions can also take action without returning a value. Previous examples used the notice() function, which sends a message at notice log level but does not return a value. In fact, there is a function for logging a message at each level, including:

- debug(*message*)
- info(*message*)
- notice(*message*)

- warning(*message*)
- err(*message*)

Puppet executes functions when building the catalog; thus, functions can change the catalog. Some of the more common uses for this level of power are:

- Look up data from external sources
- Add, modify, or remove items from the catalog
- Dynamically generate and execute code segments

Functions can be written in the common prefix format or in the Ruby-style chained format. The following two calls will return the same result:

```
# Common prefix format
notice( 'this' )

# Ruby-style chained format
'this'.notice()
```

As always, use the form that is easier to read where it is used in the code.

Using Variables in Resources

Now let's cover how to use variables in resources. Each data type has different methods, and sometimes different rules, about how to access its values.

Constant strings without variables in them should be surrounded by single quotes. Strings containing variables to be interpolated should be surrounded by double quotes. No other type should be quoted. Here's an example:

```
notice( 'Beginning the program.' )
notice( "Hello, ${username}" )
notice( 1000000 )
notice( true )
```

You can access specific items within an Array by using a 0-based array index within square brackets. Two indices can be specified to retrieve a range of items:

```
$first_item = $my_list[1]
$four_items = $my_list[3,6]
```

You can access specific items within a Hash by using the hash key within square brackets as follows:

```
$username = $my_hash['username']
```

Use curly braces when interpolating variables into a double-quoted string. The curly braces must surround both the variable name and the index or key (within square brackets) when accessing hash keys or array indexes:

```
notice( "The user's name is ${username}" )
notice( "The second value in my list is ${my_list[1]}" )
notice( "The login username is ${my_hash['username']}" )
```

Array variables and their index, and hash variables with a key, must be surrounded with curly braces for interpolation in strings.

Curly braces are only necessary when you're interpolating a variable within a string. Do not use braces or quotes when using the variable by itself. Here is an example of using predefined variables properly:

```
file { $filename:
  ensure  => present,
  mode    => '0644',
  replace => $replace_bool,
  content => $file['content'],
}
```

Best Practice

Don't surround standalone variables with curly braces or quotes.

Retrieve specific values from a Hash by assigning to an Array of variables named for the keys you'd like to retrieve. Read that sentence carefully—the name of the variable in the array identifies the hash key to get the value from:

```
[$Jack] = $homes             # identical to $Jack = $homes['Jack']
[$username,$uid] = $user     # gets the values assigned to keys "username" and "uid"
$Jill = $user                # oops, got the entire Hash!
```

The facts provided by Facter can be referenced like any other variable. The facts are available in a $facts hash. For example, to customize the message shown on login to each node, use a file resource like this:

```
file { '/etc/motd':
  ensure  => present,
  mode    => '0644',
  replace => true,
  content => "${facts['hostname']} runs ${facts['os']['release']['full']}",
}
```

Older Puppet manifests refer to facts using just the fact name as a variable, such as $factname. This is dangerous, as the fact could be overwritten either deliberately or accidentally within the scope in which the code is operating. A slight improvement is to refer to the fact explicitly in the top scope with $::factname. However, the variable could be overridden there as well. Finally, neither of these options informs a code reviewer whether the value was defined in a manifest, or by a fact.

Best Practice

Refer explicitly to a fact using the $facts[] hash. This ensures access to unaltered values supplied by Facter, and tells the reader where the value came from.

You can receive Evaluation Error exceptions when Puppet tries to use a variable that has never been defined by enabling the strict_variables configuration setting in */etc/puppetlabs/puppet/puppet.conf*:

```
[main]
    strict_variables = true
```

This will not cause an error when a variable has been explicitly set to undef. It will only throw an exception if the variable has never been declared:

```
$ puppet apply --strict_variables /vagrant/manifests/undefined.pp
Notice: Scope(Class[main]):
Error: Evaluation Error: Unknown variable: 'never_defined'.
  at /vagrant/manifests/undefined.pp:4:9 on node client.example.com
```

Defining Attributes with a Hash

It is also possible to pass a hash of attribute names and values in to a resource definition. You do this with an attribute name of * (called a *splat*) with a value of the hash.

Here's an example:

```
$resource_attributes = {
  ensure    => present,
  owner     => 'root',
  group     => 'root',
  'mode'    => '0644',
  'replace' => true,
}

file { '/etc/config/first.cfg':
  source => 'first.cfg',
  *      => $resource_attributes,
}

file { '/etc/config/second.cfg':
  source => 'config.cfg',
  *      => $resource_attributes,
}
```

The splat operator allows you to utilize a common set of values across many resources without repeating the same declaration. This is an essential strategy for *don't repeat yourself* (*DRY*) development.

Declaring Multiple Resource Titles

It is possible to declare multiple resources within a single declaration. The first way you can do so is by supplying an array of titles with the same resource body. The following example works because the file's name defaults to the title if not supplied as an attribute:

```
file { ['/tmp/file_one.txt','/tmp/file_two.txt']:
  ensure => present,
  owner  => 'vagrant',
}
```

This definition creates two different file resources in the same declaration by providing two different titles. This only works successfully when the title is reused as a parameter that makes the resource unique.

Declaring Multiple Resource Bodies

The title and attributes of a resource are called the *resource body*. A single resource declaration can have multiple resource bodies separated by semicolons. Here's an example of two `file` resources within a single resource declaration:

```
file {
  'file_one':
    ensure => present,
    owner  => 'vagrant',
    path   => 'file_one.txt',
  ;

  'file_two':
    ensure => present,
    owner  => 'vagrant',
    path   => 'file_two.txt',
  ;
}
```

 It is common to use a different indentation style in multiple resource declaration to improve readability.

This format would create two resources, exactly as if these were done in two different resource declarations. As this is not necessarily easier to read, the single resource per declaration is considered a better practice, except when using default values.

If one of the resource bodies has the title `default`, it is not used to create a resource. Instead, it defines defaults for the other resource bodies. Here is an example where the preceding definition becomes shorter and easier to maintain:

```
file {
  default:
    ensure => present,
    owner  => 'vagrant',
  ;

  'file_one': path => 'file_one.txt';
  'file_two': path => 'file_two.txt';
}
```

Any of the resources can provide an override for an attribute, in which case the default value is ignored.

Modifying with Operators

You can use all of the standard arithmetic operators for variable assignment or evaluation. As before, we're going to provide examples and skip an explanation you've likely gotten many times in your life:

```
$added       = 10 + 5     # 15
$subtracted  = 10 - 5     # 5
$multiplied  = 10 * 5     # 50
$divided     = 10 / 5     # 2
$remainder   = 10 % 5     # 0
$two_bits_l  = 2 << 2     # 8
$two_bits_r  = 64 >> 2    # 16
```

 If bit-shifting operators aren't something you're accustomed to, you can safely ignore them. You won't need the bit-shift operators unless you enjoy playing in binary.

We'll cover the comparison operators in the next section about conditionals.

Adding to Arrays and Hashes

New in Puppet 4, you can add items to arrays and hashes. You might remember these structured data types we defined in the previous section:

```
$my_list = [1,4,7]
$bigger_list = $my_list + [14,17]   # equals [1,4,7,14,17]

$key_pairs = {name => 'Joe', uid => 1001}
$user_definition = $key_pairs + { gid => 500 }   # hash now has name, uid, gid...
```

The expression returns a new value from the operands; it does not change the existing data.

You can also append single values to arrays with the << operator. Watch out, as an array appended to an array creates a single entry in the array containing an array in the last position:

```
$longer_list = $my_list << 33      # equals [1,4,7,33]
$unintended = $my_list << [33,35]  # equals [1,4,7,[33,35]]
```

Concatenation and append are new operators in Puppet 4; they are not available in earlier versions of Puppet.

Removing from Arrays and Hashes

New in Puppet 4, you can remove values from arrays and hashes with the removal operator (-). The following examples return a new array without the values on the righthand side:

```
# Remove a single value
$names = ['jill','james','sally','sam','tigger']
$no_tigger = $names - 'tigger'

# Remove multiple values
$no_boys = $names - ['james','sam']
```

The expression returns a new value from the operands; it does not change the existing data.

Each of the following examples returns a hash without the keys listed on the right side:

```
# Remove a single key
$user = {name => 'Jo', uid => 1001, gid => 500 }
$no_name = $user - 'name'

# Remove multiple keys
$user = {name => 'Jo', uid => 1001, gid => 500 }
$only_name = $user - ['uid','gid']

# Remove all matching keys from another hash
$compare = {name => 'Jo', uid => 1001, home => '/home/jo' }
$difference = $user - $compare
```

 Removing values from arrays and hashes was only previously possible by using functions from the stdlib library.

Order of Operations

The operators have the precedence used by standard math and all other programming languages. If you find this statement vague, it is because I intended it to be. Very few people know all the rules for precedence.

Do yourself and whoever has to read your code a favor: use parentheses to make the ordering explicit. Explicit ordering is more readable and self-documenting:

```
# you don't need to know operator precedence to understand this
$myvar = 5 * (10 + $my_var)
```

If you are stuck reading code that was written by someone who didn't use parentheses, the implicit order of operations is documented at "Language: Expressions and Operators" (*http://bit.ly/1RrhI6T*) on the Puppet docs site.

Using Comparison Operators

If you have any experience programming, you'll find Puppet's comparison operators familiar and easy to understand. Any expression using comparison operations will evaluate to boolean true or false. First, let's discuss all the ways to evaluate statements. Then we'll review how to use the boolean results.

Number comparisons operate much as you might expect:

```
4 != 4.1              # number comparisons are simple equality match
$how_many_cups < 4    # any number less than 4.0 is true
$how_many_cups >= 3   # any number larger than or equal to 3.0 is true
```

String operators are a bit inconsistent. String equality comparisons are case insensitive, while substring matches are case sensitive:

```
coffee  == 'coffee'     # bare word string is equivalent to quoted single word
'Coffee' == 'coffee'    # string comparisons are case insensitive

'tea' !in 'coffee'      # you can't find tea in coffee
'Fee' !in 'coffee'      # substring matches are case sensitive
'fee'  in 'coffee'      # you can pay your daily barista fee
```

Array and hash comparisons match only with complete equality of both length and value. The in comparison looks for value matches in arrays, and key matches in hashes:

```
[1,2,5] != [1,2]            # array matching tests for identical arrays
5 in [1,2,5]                # value found in array

{name => 'Joe'} != {name => 'Jo'}        # hashes aren't identical
'Jo' !in {fname => 'Jo', lname => 'Rhett'} # Jo is a value and doesn't match
```

You can also compare values to data types, like so:

```
$not_true =~ Boolean    # true if true or false
$num_tokens =~ Integer  # true if an integer
$my_name !~ String      # true if not a string
```

As this feature has the most benefit for input validation in Puppet modules, we cover this topic extensively in "Validating Input with Data Types" on page 181. For now, just be aware that it is possible.

When doing comparisons you'll find the standard boolean operators and, or, and ! (not) work exactly as you might expect:

```
true and true       # true
true and false      # false
true or false       # true
true and !false     # true
true and !true      # false
```

 These same operators (except in) can be used by the odd people who enjoy Backus–Naur form. Yes, you, we know about you. And no, I'm not going to initiate any innocents into your ranks. Enjoy your innocence if you don't know Backus–Naur. Just be aware that they work, should you need that particular perversion.

You can find a complete list of all operands and operators with example uses at "Language: Expressions and Operators" (*http://bit.ly/1RrhI6T*) on the Puppet docs site.

Evaluating Conditional Expressions

Now, let's use these expressions you've learned with conditional statements. You have four different ways to utilize the boolean results of a comparison:

- `if/elsif/else` statements
- `unless/else` statements
- `case` statements
- Selectors

As you'd expect, there's always the basic conditional form I'm sure you know and love:

```
if ($coffee != 'drunk') {
  notify { 'best-to-avoid': }
}
elsif ('scotch' == 'drunk') {
  notify { 'party-time': }
}
else {
  notify { 'party-time': }
}
```

There's also `unless` to reverse comparisons for readability purposes:

```
unless $facts['kernel'] == Linux {
  notify { 'You are on an older machine.': }
}
else {
  notify { 'We got you covered.': }
}
```

 The use of `else` with `unless` is new to Puppet 4.

While `unless` is considered bad form by some, I recommend sticking with the most readable form. The following example shows why `unless` can be tricky reading with an `else` clause:

```
# The $id fact tells us who is running the Puppet agent
unless( $facts['id'] == 'root' ) {
  notify { 'needsroot':
    message => "This manifest must be executed as root.",
  }
}
else {
  notify { 'isroot':
    message => "Running as root.",
```

```
        }
    }
```

The case operator can be used to do numerous evaluations, avoiding a long string of multiple elsif(s). You can test explicit values, match against another variable, use regular expressions, or evaluate the results of a function. The first successful match will execute the code within the block following a colon:

```
case $what_she_drank {
    'wine':               { include state::california }
    $stumptown:           { include state::portland  }
    /(scotch|whisky)/:    { include state::scotland  }
    is_tea( $drink ):     { include state::england   }
    default:              {}
}
```

Always include a default: option when using case statements, even if the default does nothing, as shown in the preceding example.

Statements with selectors are similar to case statements, except they return a value instead of executing a block of code. This can be useful when you are defining variables. A selector looks like a normal assignment, but the value to be compared is followed by a question mark and a block of comparisons with fat commas identifying the matching values:

```
$native_of = $what_he_drinks ? {
    'wine'              => 'california',
    $stumptown          => 'portland',
    /(scotch|whisky)/   => 'scotland',
    is_tea( $drink )    => 'england',
    default             => 'unknown',
}
```

As a value must be returned in an assignment operation, a match is required. Always include a bare word default option with a value.

So the drinking comparisons have been fun, but let's examine some practical comparisons that you may actually use in a real manifest. Here's a long if/then/else chain:

```
# Explicit comparison
if( $facts['osfamily'] == 'redhat' ) {
    include yum
}
# Do a substring match
elsif( $facts['osfamily'] in 'debian-ubuntu' ) {
    include apt
}
# New package manager available with FreeBSD 9 and above
elsif( $facts['operatingsystem'] =~ /?i:freebsd/ )
    and ( $facts['os']['release']['major'] >= 9 ) {
    include pkgng
}
```

The same result can be had in a more compact `case` statement:

```
case $facts['osfamily'] {
  'redhat':                                             { include yum   }
  'debian', 'ubuntu':                                   { include apt   }
  'freebsd' and ($facts['os']['release']['major'] >= 9) { include pkgng }
  default: {}
}
```

Selectors are also useful for handling heterogenous environments:

```
$libdir = $facts['osfamily'] ? {
  /(?i-mx:centos|fedora|redhat)/ => '/usr/libexec/mcollective',
  /(?i-mx:ubuntu|debian)/        => '/usr/share/mcollective/plugins',
  /(?i-mx:freebsd)/              => '/usr/local/share',
}
```

The splat operator (`*`) can turn an array of values into a list of choices. This can be very useful in `case` or `select` statements, as shown here:

```
$redhat_based = ['RedHat','Fedora','CentOS','Scientific','Oracle','Amazon']
$libdir = $facts['osfamily'] ? {
  *$redhat_based => '/usr/libexec/mcollective',
```

You can find a complete list of all conditional statements with more example uses at "Language: Conditional Statements and Expressions" (*http://bit.ly/21zsTQo*) on the Puppet docs site.

Matching Regular Expressions

Puppet supports standard Ruby regular expressions, as defined in the Ruby Regexp (*http://www.ruby-doc.org/core/Regexp.html*) docs. The match operator (=~) requires a `String` value on the left, and a `Regexp` expression on the right:

```
$what_did_you_drink =~ /tea/      # likely true if English
$what_did_you_drink !~ /coffee/   # likely false if up late
$what_did_you_drink !~ "^coffee$" # uses a string value for regexp
```

The value on the left must be a string. The value on the right can be a /`Regexp`/ definition within slashes, or a string value within double quotes. The use of a string allows variable interpolation to be performed prior to conversion into a `Regexp`.

You can use regular expressions in four places:

- Conditional statements: `if` and `unless`
- `case` statements
- Selectors
- Node definitions (deprecated)

As regular expressions are well documented in numerous places, we won't spend time covering how to use them here, other than to provide some examples:

```
unless $facts['operatingsystem'] !~ /(?i-mx:centos|fedora|redhat)/ {
        include yum
}

case $facts['hostname'] {
  /^web\d/: { include role::webserver  }
  /^mail/ : { include role::mailserver }
  default : { include role::base       }
}

$package_name = $facts['operatingsystem'] ? {
  /(?i-mx:centos|fedora|redhat)/ => 'mcollective',
  /(?i-mx:ubuntu|debian)/        => 'mcollective',
  /(?i-mx:freebsd)/              => 'sysutils/mcollective',
}
```

You may find Tony Stubblebine's *Regular Expressions Pocket Reference* (O'Reilly) handy for day-to-day work with Regexps. To truly master regular expressions, there is no better book than, well, Jeffrey E.F. Friedl's *Mastering Regular Expressions* (O'Reilly).

Building Lambda Blocks

A *lambda* is a block of code that allows parameters to be passed in. You can think of them as functions without a name. You will use lambdas with the iterator functions (such as each(), introduced in the next section) to perform a set of instructions on multiple values. If you are experienced with Ruby lambdas, you'll find the syntax similar.

 Lambdas are a new, advanced feature of Puppet 4 not available in any previous version of Puppet.

A lambda begins with one or more variable names between pipe operators | |. These name the variables that will contain the values passed into the block of code:

```
| $firstvalue, $secondvalue | {
  block of code that operates on these values.
}
```

The lambda has its own variable scope. This means that the variables named between the pipes exist only within the block of code. You can name these variables any name you want, as they will be filled by the values passed by the function into the lambda on each iteration. Other variables within the context of the lambda are also available, such as local variables or node facts.

The following example will output a list of disk partitions from the hash provided by Facter. Within the loop, we refer to the hostname fact on each iteration. The device name and a hash of values about each device are stored in the $name and $device variables during each loop:

```
$ cat /vagrant/manifests/mountpoints.pp
each( $facts['partitions'] ) |$name, $device| {
  notice( "${facts['hostname']} has device ${name} with size ${device['size']}" )
}
```

```
$ puppet apply /vagrant/manifests/mountpoints.pp
Notice: Scope(Class[main]): Host geode has device sda1 with size 524288
Notice: Scope(Class[main]): Host geode has device sda2 with size 3906502656
Notice: Scope(Class[main]): Host geode has device sdb1 with size 524288
Notice: Scope(Class[main]): Host geode has device sdb2 with size 3906502656
```

 As shown here, you must enclose both the variable name and the array or hash index (in square brackets) within curly braces to ensure they are interpolated together. Otherwise, the output will contain the entire array or hash, followed by the index as literal text in square brackets.

Next, we'll cover each of the functions that can iterate over values and pass them to a lambda.

Looping Through Iterations

In this section, we're going to introduce powerful new functions for iterating over sets of data. You can use iteration to evaluate many items within an array or hash of data using a single block of code (a lambda, described on the previous page).

 Iterations are a new feature of Puppet 4.

Here are some practical examples available to you from the basic facts provided by Facter (you can use iteration with any data point that can be presented as an array or a hash):

- Going through all IP addresses assigned to a node to see if any meet a specific condition.
- Going through all users on a node to find ones that match a certain criteria.

- Going through all mounted partitions to determine the total space available to the node.

There are five functions that iterate over a set of values and pass each one to a lambda for processing. The lambda will process each input and return a single response containing the processed values. Here are the five functions, what they do to provide input to the lambda, and what they expect the lambda to return as a response:

- `each()` acts on each entry in an array, or each key/value pair in a hash.
- `filter()` returns a subset of the array or hash that were matched by the lambda.
- `map()` returns a new array or hash from the results of the lambda.
- `reduce()` combines array or hash values using code in the lambda.
- `slice()` creates small chunks of an array or hash and passes it to the lambda.

The following examples show how these functions can be invoked. They can be invoked in traditional prefix style:

```
each( $facts['partitions'] ) |$name, $device| {
  notice( "${facts['hostname']} has device $name with size ${device['size']}" )
}
```

Or you can chain function calls to the values they operate on, which is a common usage within Ruby:

```
$facts['partitions'].each() |$name, $device| {
  notice( "${facts['hostname']} has device $name with size ${device['size']}" )
}
```

Finally, new to Puppet 4 is the ability to use a hash or array literal instead of a variable. The following example demonstrates iteration over a literal array of names:

```
['sally','joe','nancy','kevin'].each() | $name | {
  notice( "$name wants to learn more about Puppet." )
}
```

Now let's review each of the functions that can utilize a lambda.

each()

The `each()` function invokes a lambda once for each entry in an array, or each key/value pair in a hash. The lambda can do anything with the input value, as no response is expected. `each()` is most commonly used to process a list of items:

```
# Output a list of interfaces that have IPs
split( $facts['interfaces'], ',' ).each |$interface| {
  if( $facts["ipaddress_${interface}"] != '' ) {
    notice( sprintf( "Interface %s has IPv4 address %s",
      $interface, $facts["ipaddress_${interface}"] )
    )
  }
}
```

```
  if( $facts["ipaddress6_${interface}"] != '' ) {
    notice( sprintf( "Interface %s has IPv6 address %s",
      $interface, $facts["ipaddress6_${interface}"] )
    )
  }
}
```

When you apply this manifest, you'll get a list of interfaces and each IP they have:

```
[vagrant@client puppet]$ puppet apply /vagrant/manifests/interface_ips.pp
Notice: Scope(Class[main]): Interface enp0s3 has IPv4 address 10.0.2.15
Notice: Scope(Class[main]): Interface enp0s3 has IPv6 address fe80::a0:27:feb:2b2
Notice: Scope(Class[main]): Interface enp0s8 has IPv4 address 192.168.250.10
Notice: Scope(Class[main]): Interface enp0s8 has IPv6 address fe80::a0:27:fec:d78
Notice: Scope(Class[main]): Interface lo has IPv4 address 127.0.0.1
Notice: Scope(Class[main]): Interface lo has IPv6 address ::1
```

If you want a counter for the values, providing an array with two entries gives you an index on the first one. For example, creating a list of all the interfaces on a system thats hosts virtualization clients yields the following:

```
$ cat /vagrant/manifests/interfaces.pp
split( $facts['interfaces'], ',' ).each |$index, $interface| {
  notice( "Interface #${index} is ${interface}" )
}

$ puppet apply /vagrant/manifests/interfaces.pp
Notice: Scope(Class[main]): Interface #0 is enp0s3
Notice: Scope(Class[main]): Interface #1 is enp0s8
Notice: Scope(Class[main]): Interface #2 is lo
```

 Be aware that the index is placed in the first variable, and the array entry in the second. This is the opposite of the same concept used in Ruby and ERB templates provided by each_with_index, where the array entry comes in the first variable and the index in the second.

You can also use each() on hashes. If you provide a single variable you'll get an array with two entries. If you provide two variables you'll have the key in the first one, and the value in the second one:

```
$ cat /vagrant/manifests/uptime.pp
each( $facts['system_uptime'] ) |$type, $value| {
  notice( "System has been up ${value} ${type}" )
}

$ puppet apply /vagrant/manifests/uptime.pp
Notice: Scope(Class[main]): System has been up 23:04 hours uptime
Notice: Scope(Class[main]): System has been up 83044 seconds
Notice: Scope(Class[main]): System has been up 23 hours
Notice: Scope(Class[main]): System has been up 0 days
```

The following manifest would provide the exact same results:

```
each( $facts['system_uptime'] ) |$uptime| {
    notice( "System has been up $uptime[1] $uptime[0]" )
}
```

The each() function returns the result of the last operation performed. In most cases, you'll use it to process each entry and you won't care about the return; however, the result could be useful if the value of the last entry has some meaning for you. While you might consider calculating an aggregate value from the operations, that is exactly what the reduce() function is for.

reverse_each()

The reverse_each() function (new in Puppet 4.4) invokes a lambda once for each entry in an array or hash in reverse order. It is otherwise identical to each().

step()

The step(N) function (new in Puppet 4.4) invokes a lambda once for each Nth entry after the first one in an array or hash. It is otherwise identical to each().

filter()

The filter() function returns a filtered subset of an array or hash containing only entries that were matched by the lambda. The lambda block evaluates each entry and returns a positive result if the item matches.

For an extended example, let's examine all interfaces and find all RFC1918 IPv4 and RFC4291 IPv6 internal-only addresses. We do this with multiple steps:

1. Filter all facts to find those containing IP addresses.
2. Filter the first results to return interfaces with RFC1918 or IPv6 link-local addresses.
3. Iterate over the second results to extract the interface name for each address.

Here's a sample code block that does this:

```
$ips = $facts.filter |$key,$value| {
  $key =~ /^ipaddress6?_/
}
$private_ips = $ips.filter |$interface, $address| {
  $address =~ /^(10|172\.(?:1[6-9]|2[0-9]|3[0-1])|192\.168)\./
    or $address =~ /^fe80::/
}
$private_ips.each |$ip_interface,$address| {
  $interface = regsubst( $ip_interface, '^ipaddress6?_(\w+)', '\1' )
  notice( "interface $interface has private IP $address" )
}
```

If you apply this on a node, you'll see results like this:

```
$ puppet apply /vagrant/manifests/ipaddresses.pp
Notice: Scope(Class[main]): interface enp0s3 has private IP fe80::a0:27:feb:2b28
Notice: Scope(Class[main]): interface enp0s8 has private IP fe80::a0:27:fec:d78c
Notice: Scope(Class[main]): interface enp0s3 has private IP 10.0.2.15
Notice: Scope(Class[main]): interface enp0s8 has private IP 192.168.250.10
```

map()

The map() method returns an Array from the results of the lambda. You call map() on an array or hash, and it returns a new array containing the results. The lambda's final statement should result in a value that will be added to the array of results.

Here's an example where we create an array of IPv4 addresses. We pass in an array of interface names. We use the interface name to look for an IP address associated with that interface name in the ipaddress_ facts.

As with filter(), when you pass in an array, the named variable contains the array value:

```
$ips = split( $facts['interfaces'], ',' ).map |$interface| {
  $facts["ipaddress_${interface}"]
}
```

If you pass in a hash, the named variable will contain an array with the key in the first position and the value in the second. The following example uses filter() to create a hash of interfaces that have IP addresses. Then it uses map() to create separate arrays of the interfaces, and the IPs:

```
$ints_with_ips = $facts.filter |$key,$value| {
  $key =~ /^ipaddress_/
}

# Create an array of ints with IPv4 addresses
$ints = $ints_with_ips.map |$intip| {
  $intip[0] # key
}

# Create an array of IPv4 addresses
$ips  = $ints_with_ips.map |$intip| {
  $intip[1] # value
}
```

reduce()

The reduce() function processes an array or hash and returns only a single value. It takes two arguments: an array or hash and an initial seed value. If the initial seed value is not supplied, it will use the first entry in the array or hash as the initial seed value. The lambda should be written to perform aggregation, addition, or some other function that will operate on many values and return a single value.

 The way reduce() utilizes the first entry in the array could have unintended consequences if the entry is not the appropriate data type for the output. As this is a common source of confusion, we'll show you an example of this problem.

In the following example, we pass the hash of partitions in to add together all of their sizes. As with all other functions, each hash entry is passed in as a small array of [key,value]:

```
$ cat /vagrant/manifests/partitions.pp
$total_disk_space = $facts['partitions'].reduce |$total, $partition| {
    notice( "partition $partition[0] is size $partition[1]['size']" )
    $total + $partition[1]['size']
}
notice( "Total disk space = ${total_disk_space}" )
```

```
$ puppet apply /vagrant/manifests/partitions.pp
Notice: Scope(Class[main]): partition sdb2 is size 3906502656
Notice: Scope(Class[main]): partition sda1 is size 524288
Notice: Scope(Class[main]): partition sda2 is size 3906502656
Notice: Scope(Class[main]): Total disk space = 7814053888
Total disk space = [sdb1, {filesystem => linux_raid_member, size => 524288},
    3906502656, 524288, 3906502656]
```

As we didn't supply an initial value, the first entry of the array contains the hash of values for the first partition (sdb1). It then added the remaining partition sizes to the array.

To resolve this situation, you should seed the initial value with the appropriate data type (integer 0, in this case). The first hash entry is then processed by the block, adding the integer size to the seed value and creating the output we were looking for:

```
$ cat /vagrant/manifests/partitions.pp
$total_disk_space = $facts['partitions'].reduce(0) |$total, $partition| {
    notice( "partition $partition[0] is size $partition[1]['size']" )
    $total + $partition[1]['size']
}
notice( "Total disk space = ${total_disk_space}" )
```

```
$ puppet apply /vagrant/manifests/partitions.pp
Notice: Scope(Class[main]): partition sdb1 is size  524288
Notice: Scope(Class[main]): partition sdb2 is size 3906502656
Notice: Scope(Class[main]): partition sda1 is size 524288
Notice: Scope(Class[main]): partition sda2 is size 3906502656
Notice: Scope(Class[main]): Total disk space = 7814053888
```

slice()

The slice() function creates small chunks of a specified size from an array or hash. Of the available functions, this is perhaps one of the subtlest and trickiest to use, as the output changes depending on how you invoke it.

If you invoke slice() with a single parameter specified between the pipe operators, the value passed into the lambda will be an array containing the number of items specified by the slice size. The following example should make this clear:

```
[vagrant@client ~]$ cat /vagrant/manifests/slices.pp
[1,2,3,4,5,6].slice(2) |$item| {
    notice( "\$item[0] = ${item[0]}" )
    notice( "\$item[1] = ${item[1]}" )
}

[vagrant@client ~]$ puppet apply /vagrant/manifests/slices.pp
Notice: Scope(Class[main]): $item[0] = 1
Notice: Scope(Class[main]): $item[1] = 2
Notice: Scope(Class[main]): $item[0] = 3
Notice: Scope(Class[main]): $item[1] = 4
Notice: Scope(Class[main]): $item[0] = 5
Notice: Scope(Class[main]): $item[1] = 6
```

If you invoke slice() with the same number of parameters as the slice size, each variable will contain one entry from the slice. The following manifest would return exactly the same results as the previous example:

```
[vagrant@client ~]$ cat /vagrant/manifests/slices.pp
[1,2,3,4,5,6].slice(2) |$one, $two| {
    notice( "\$one == ${one}" )
    notice( "\$two == ${two}" )
}

[vagrant@client ~]$ puppet apply /vagrant/manifests/slices.pp
Notice: Scope(Class[main]): $one == 1
Notice: Scope(Class[main]): $two == 2
Notice: Scope(Class[main]): $one == 3
Notice: Scope(Class[main]): $two == 4
Notice: Scope(Class[main]): $one == 5
Notice: Scope(Class[main]): $two == 6
```

Unlike the other functions, hash entries are always passed in as a small array of [key,value], no matter how many parameters you use. So if you have a slice of size 2 from a hash, the lambda will receive two arrays, each containing two values: the key and the value from the hash entry. Here's an example that demonstrates the idea.

```
$facts['partitions'].slice(2) |$part1, $part2| {
    notice( "partition names in this slice are $part1[0] and $part2[0]" )
}
```

Similar to each(), most invocations of slice do not return a value and thus the result can be ignored.

with()

The with() function invokes a lambda exactly one time, passing the variables provided as parameters. The lambda can do anything with the input values, as no response is expected.

You might point out that this function doesn't iterate and thus doesn't belong in this section of the book. You're quite right, but I've included it here because it behaves exactly like these other iterators, and can be very useful for testing:

```
with( 'austin', 'powers', 'secret agent' ) |$first,$last,$title| {
  notice( "A person named ${first} ${last}, ${title} is here to see you." )
}
```

The with() function is most commonly used to isolate variables to a private scope, unavailable in the main scope's namespace.

Capturing Extra Parameters

Most of the functions only produce one or two parameters for input to a lambda; however, slice() and with() can send an arbitrary number of parameters to a lambda. For ease of definition, you can prefix the final parameter with the splat operator (*) to indicate that it will accept all remaining arguments (called *captures-rest*). Even if only one value is supplied, the final item's data type will be Array.

> The splat operator will also turn an array into a list of comma-separated values when necessary.

In the following example, we'll use the splat operator to transform the input array into comma-separated values for with(), and then use splat again to catch all remaining input values for the lambda. This example parses lines from */etc/hosts* and returns an single entry with an array of aliases:

```
# hosts line example:
#   192.168.250.6    puppetserver.example.com puppet.example.com puppetserver
$host = $hosts_line.split(' ')
with( $host* ) |$ipaddr, $hostname, *$aliases| {
  notice( "Host ${hostname} has IP ${ipaddr} and aliases ${aliases}" )
}
```

Test it out by running puppet apply /vagrant/manifests/hostsfile_lines.pp.

Iteration Wrap-Up

As you have seen in this section, the functions that iterate over arrays and hashes provide a tremendous amount of power not available in any previous version of Puppet.

You can invoke these functions like traditional functions or by chaining the functions to the data they are processing.

You can find more information about iteration and lambdas at "Language: Iteration and Loops" (*http://bit.ly/1RpsHUG*) on the Puppet docs site.

Reviewing Puppet Configuration Language

This chapter introduced many of the components of the Puppet configuration language. Specifically, you learned the following:

- Variables provide named storage of data.
- All data has a type: `String`, `Numeric`, `Boolean`, `Array`, `Hash`, and others.
- Operators add, subtract, multiply, divide, concatenate, and merge values.
- Conditional operators compare data for equality and inclusion.
- Regular expressions match ranges of values or substrings within a value.
- Conditional expressions such as `if` and `unless` allow you to limit application.
- `case` and `select` evaluate a value to select an action or result.
- Lambdas are unnamed functions intended to process values passed in by iteration functions.
- Iterations pass each entry in an array or hash to a lambda block for evaluation.

These are the data types and functions available for evaluating and operating on data for use in Resource definitions within a Puppet manifest.

## CHAPTER 6

Controlling Resource Processing

You can control how Puppet utilizes and acts upon resources with *metaparameters*. Metaparameters are common attributes that can be used with any resource, including both built-in and custom resource types. Metaparameters control how Puppet deals with the resource.

You can find all metaparameters documented at "Metaparameter Reference" (*https:// docs.puppetlabs.com/references/latest/metaparameter.html*) on the Puppet docs site.

Adding Aliases

As previously mentioned, every resource in the Puppet manifest must refer to a unique resource. Each resource has one attribute (called *namevar*) that identifies the unique resource on the node. If the *namevar* attribute is not set, it defaults to the title as a value. You've already seen this in previous examples:

```
file { '/tmp/testfile.txt':
  ensure  => present,
  path    => '/tmp/testfile.txt',   # this was implicit in earlier example
  content => "holy cow!\n",
}
```

The *namevar* attribute uniquely identifies the resource manifestation (e.g., the file on disk in this example), therefore it differs for each resource. Refer to the "Resource Type Reference" (*http://bit.ly/259ffYL*) on the Puppet docs site to find the *namevar* for a given resource.

To simplify references to resources, you can add an `alias` or "friendly name" to the resource name. This is an essential technique when the resource's name or location on disk might change from one node to the other. There are two ways to create an alias.

Specifying an Alias by Title

The first way to provide an alias for a resource is to supply a different value in the title than in the *namevar* attribute:

```
file { 'the-testfile':
  ensure  => present,
  path     => '/tmp/testfile.txt',
  content => "holy cow!\n",
}
```

This implicitly creates an alias that can be used as an alternate name for the resource.

Adding an Alias Metaparameter

The `alias` attribute provides an explicit way to provide a friendly name to a resource. This usage may be more readable to a Puppet novice unaware of implicit aliasing:

```
file { '/tmp/testfile.txt':
  ensure  => present,
  alias    => 'the-testfile'
  content => "holy cow!\n",
}
```

Preventing Action

The *no operation* (noop) attribute allows a resource to be evaluated, but prevents a change from being applied during convergence. This can be useful for auditing purposes, or to identify what would change during convergence. For example, to determine if a newer version of the `puppet-agent` package is available without performing the update, set the attribute to true:

```
package { 'puppet-agent':
  ensure  => latest,
  noop     => true,
}
```

When this manifest is processed, if a new package version is available it will report what it would have done:

```
[vagrant@client ~]$ sudo puppet apply /vagrant/manifests/puppet-agent.pp
Notice: Compiled catalog for client.example.com in environment production
Notice: /Stage[main]/Main/Package[puppet-agent]/ensure:
  current_value 1.3.6-1.el7, should be 0:1.4.0-1.el7 (noop)
Notice: Class[Main]: Would have triggered 'refresh' from 1 events
Notice: Stage[main]: Would have triggered 'refresh' from 1 events
Notice: Applied catalog in 0.37 seconds
```

You can get the same behavior by using the --noop command-line flag on a manifest that doesn't have the attribute defined:

```
[vagrant@client ~]$ puppet apply --noop /vagrant/manifests/tmp-testfile.pp
Notice: Compiled catalog for client.example.com in environment production
Notice: /Stage[main]/Main/Exec[echo-holy-cow]/returns:
  current_value notrun, should be 0 (noop)
Notice: Class[Main]: Would have triggered 'refresh' from 1 events
Notice: Stage[main]: Would have triggered 'refresh' from 1 events
Notice: Applied catalog in 0.01 seconds
```

There is no way to override the noop resource attribute with a command-line flag, as the resource attribute has a higher priority than the global option. However, you can place noop = true as a configuration option in the Puppet configuration file, and override that with a command-line flag.

Auditing Changes

The audit attribute defines a list of attributes that you want to track changes to. Define this attribute with an array of attribute names that you wish to track, or the value all. Changes to any of these values will log a message during a puppet apply or puppet inspect run. This could be useful if you don't want to manage the content of a file, but do want to know every time the content changes:

```
file { '/etc/hosts':
  audit => ['content','owner'],
}
file { '/etc/passwd':
  audit => 'all',
}
```

This attribute is generally used on resources that Puppet does not manage the values for. If you define this attribute on a resource Puppet manages, you will receive a log notice that Puppet has changed the resource, followed by the audit noticing that Puppet made a change.

Here's how the preceding manifest would work on the first run:

```
[vagrant@client ~]$ puppet apply /vagrant/manifests/audit.pp
Notice: Compiled catalog for client.example.com in environment production
Notice: /Stage[main]/Main/File[/etc/hosts]/content:
  audit change: newly-recorded value {md5}e2b06541983600068fff455f8c11861a
Notice: /Stage[main]/Main/File[/etc/hosts]/owner:
  audit change: newly-recorded value 0
Notice: /Stage[main]/Main/File[/etc/hosts]/group:
  audit change: newly-recorded value 0
Notice: Applied catalog in 0.01 seconds
```

Now let's modify the file, and rerun the audit:

```
[vagrant@client ~]$ echo "# adding junk" | sudo tee -a /etc/hosts
# adding junk
[vagrant@client ~]$ puppet apply /vagrant/manifests/audit.pp
Notice: Compiled catalog for client.example.com in environment production
Notice: /Stage[main]/Main/File[/etc/hosts]/content: audit change:
  previously recorded value {md5}e2b06541983600068fff455f8c11861a
  has been changed to {md5}28c9f9f5a3d060a500d4b57f9875ba32
Notice: Applied catalog in 0.02 seconds
```

Defining Log Level

The `loglevel` attribute allows you to identify the level at which changes to the resource should be logged. The log levels are similar to syslog log levels, and map to those on Unix and Linux systems:

- debug
- info (also called verbose)
- notice
- warning
- err
- alert
- emerg
- crit

For example, log at `warning` level whenever the `puppet-agent` package is upgraded:

```
package { 'puppet-agent':
  ensure  => latest,
  loglevel  => warning,
}
```

Filtering with Tags

Tags can be used for selective enforcement of resources—that is, applying only part of a policy, such as adding packages, without applying other parts of the policy, such as restarting or stopping services. Let's look at an example of this.

Tags can be added to resources as a single string, or as an array of strings. The following policy will tag both the package and the service with the `puppet` tag, and put an additional `package` tag on the package resource:

```
package { 'puppet-agent':
  ensure => present,
  tag    => ['package','puppet'],
}

service { 'puppet':
  ensure => running,
  enable => true,
  tag    => 'puppet',
}
```

If you run this manifest it will start the Puppet agent, which perhaps isn't desirable right now. So you can apply the policy and limit action to resources marked with the package tag:

```
[vagrant@client ~]$ cd /vagrant/manifests
[vagrant@client ~]$ sudo puppet apply packagetag.pp --tags package
Notice: Compiled catalog for client.example.com in environment production
Notice: Finished catalog run in 0.26 seconds

[vagrant@client ~]$ puppet resource service puppet
service { 'puppet':
  ensure => 'stopped',
  enable => 'false',
}
```

As you can see, the policy was applied, but the Puppet service was not started. This demonstrates the power of tags in limiting policy evaluation on demand.

 It wasn't necessary to add a tag package to the package resource. Puppet automatically adds a tag of the resource type to every resource. We could have applied this manifest with --tags ser vice to affect only the service, even though the service tag isn't shown in the preceding declaration.

The --tags command-line option can accept multiple comma-separated tags. So you could apply the same manifest with --tags package,service to process both of them.

Skipping Tags

As of Puppet 4.4, tags can be used to selectively skip over tagged resources—that is, applying only the parts of the policy that don't match a tag, such as restarting or stopping services. Let's look at an example of this:

```
[vagrant@client ~]$ sudo puppet apply packagetag.pp --skip_tags service
Notice: Compiled catalog for client.example.com in environment production
Notice: Finished catalog run in 0.23 seconds

[vagrant@client ~]$ puppet resource service puppet
service { 'puppet':
  ensure => 'stopped',
  enable => 'false',
}
```

As you can see, the policy was applied, but the Puppet service was not started. This had the same effect as our previous run, but can be more useful when trying to isolate a smaller set of resources that should be excluded.

 You can use both options together. The `--skip_tags` configuration option will be applied before `--tags`, which makes it possible to exclude a set of resources from a larger set of included resources.

Limiting to a Schedule

The `schedule` metaparameter can be used to limit when Puppet will make changes to a resource. You can define how many times (`repeat`) within a given hour, day, or week (`period`) a resource is applied on the node:

```
schedule { 'twice-daily':
  period  => daily,
  repeat  => 2,      # apply twice within the period
}
```

You can also limit application to specific hours or days of the week, using the `range` and `weekday` attributes:

```
schedule { 'business-hours':
  period  => hourly,
  repeat  => 1,                             # apply once per hour
  range   => '08:00 - 17:00',               # between 8 a.m. and 5 p.m.
  weekday => ['Mon','Tue','Wed','Thu','Fri'], # on weekdays
}

schedule { 'after-working-hours':
  period      => daily,
  range       => '17:00 - 08:00',           # between 5 p.m. and 8 a.m.
}
```

The period can be any of the following values:

- `hourly`
- `daily`

- weekly
- monthly
- never

The repeat attribute limits how many times it will be applied within the period. The default is 1. The range attribute defines hours and minutes in a 24-hour period. week day should be an array whose items are either a number, the three-letter name, or the full English name for a weekday. The following example is valid, albeit confusing:

```
schedule { 'odd-days':
  weekday => ['Mon','3','Friday'],
}
```

If the range crosses the midnight boundary and the weekday attribute is defined, then the weekday applies to the start of the time period, not when it ends. For example, a resource with the following schedule could be applied any time between Sunday night and Monday morning:

```
schedule { 'sunday-night':
  range   => '20:00 - 06:00',
  weekday => ['Sunday'],
}
```

Add the schedule metaparameter to a resource to limit when the resource is applied. For example, if we want to limit upgrades of Puppet until after the normal working day has ended, we might declare it this way:

```
package { 'puppet-agent':
  ensure => latest,
  schedule  => 'after-working-hours',
}
```

The value of the schedule metaparameter must be the name of a schedule resource you've declared.

 A schedule's only function is to prevent a resource from being applied outside of the specified range. You have to run Puppet during the range specified for the resource to be applied. If the timing of the Puppet runs and the allowable range never intersect, the resource will never be applied.

You can find the complete documentation for the schedule resource at "Puppet Types: Schedule" (*http://bit.ly/1nUWRBn*) on the Puppet docs site.

Utilizing periodmatch

The schedule resource has an additional (and somewhat confusing) attribute named periodmatch. The current documentation in the Puppet type reference is vague about the meaning of this parameter, so I'm going to spell this one out. `periodmatch` takes only two values:

`distance` *(default)*

This value prevents application of the resource until the `period` (hourly, daily, weekly, monthly) time has passed. If the `repeat` attribute is specified, the `period`/ `repeat` distance (e.g., four times in a day) is used.

`number`

This value prevents application of a resource in the same period (hour, day, week, or month) by the number of the period. That would be the 5th hour of the day, the 3rd day of the week, the 17th week of the year, and so on.

 When `periodmatch` is set to `number`, the `repeat` attribute cannot be greater than 1.

The effect of this parameter is not intuitive, and you may find yourself coming back to reread this section. Let's provide some concrete examples. Imagine that you ran `puppet apply` on a manifest with a file resource at 01:57. Then you deleted the file it created. Say you had a schedule like the following:

```
schedule { 'once-every-hour':
  period      => hourly,
  periodmatch => distance,
}
file { '/tmp/test.txt':
  ensure   => file,
  schedule => 'once-every-hour',
}
```

If you ran Puppet every minute with a schedule like this, it would be 02:57, or 60 minutes before the file was re-created.

A `periodmatch` of `number` means that the resource is evaluated once within the same number—for example, the second hour. Say you used a schedule like the following and ran it once at 1:57, before deleting the file:

```
schedule { 'once-in-an-hour':
  period      => hourly,
  periodmatch => number,
}
file { '/tmp/test.txt':
  ensure   => file,
  schedule => 'once-in-an-hour',
}
```

In this case, the file would be re-created in the first minute of the second hour, only three minutes later!

```
[vagrant@client ~]$ while true; do date; rm -f /tmp/test.txt;
     puppet apply /vagrant/manifests/schedule.pp ; sleep 60;
  done
Sun Sep 20 03:57:10 UTC 2015
Notice: Compiled catalog for client.example.com in environment production
Notice: /Stage[main]/Main/File[/tmp/test.txt]/ensure: created
Notice: Applied catalog in 0.01 seconds

Sun Sep 20 03:58:12 UTC 2015
Notice: Compiled catalog for client.example.com in environment production
Notice: Applied catalog in 0.02 seconds

Sun Sep 20 03:59:13 UTC 2015
Notice: Compiled catalog for client.example.com in environment production
Notice: Applied catalog in 0.02 seconds

Sun Sep 20 04:00:15 UTC 2015
Notice: Compiled catalog for client.example.com in environment production
Notice: /Stage[main]/Main/File[/tmp/test.txt]/ensure: created
Notice: Applied catalog in 0.01 seconds
```

When you use the default distance value with a repeat greater than 1, the period is divided evenly by the value of repeat. With a period of daily and a repeat of 4, the resource will be reapplied no sooner than six hours after the last application.

 Keep in mind that the schedule only defines when the resource won't be applied. It does not schedule anything to update the resource at that time. The first Puppet run after the period expires will apply the resource again.

If you run Puppet every 30 minutes (default config), then an hourly schedule will cause the resource to be updated every other standard run. Using an hourly period with a repeat of 2 will only prevent ad hoc runs in between the normal runs from affecting the resource.

The manifest */vagrant/manifests/schedule.pp* defines three hourly schedules and three files using those schedules. To see this in action, apply this manifest in a loop as follows and examine the results:

```
[vagrant@client ~]$ while true; do date;
     puppet apply /vagrant/manifests/schedule.pp; sleep 60; done
```

Avoiding Dependency Failures

There is a "feature" of Puppet that may surprise you. A resource that is not applied because it falls outside the configured schedule will succeed for the purposes of dependency evaluation. This means that if the resource creates something that a later resource utilizes, like a configuration file, the dependent resource will fail.

Here's an example:

```
schedule { 'workhours':
  range => '08:00 - 17:00',
}

file { '/tmp/workhours.txt':
  ensure   => file,
  content  => 'Open for business',
  schedule => 'workhours',
}

exec { 'use file':
  path    => '/bin:/usr/bin',
  command => 'cat /tmp/workhours.txt',
  require => File['/tmp/workhours.txt'],
}
```

If we apply this manifest outside of work hours, the file is not created because it falls outside the schedule. The following exec resource then fails because a file it needs doesn't exist:

```
[vagrant@client ~]$ puppet apply /vagrant/manifests/unscheduled.pp
Notice: Compiled catalog for client.example.com in environment production
Notice: /Stage[main]/Main/Exec[use file]/returns:
  cat: /tmp/workhours.txt: No such file or directory
Error: cat /tmp/workhours.txt returned 1 instead of one of [0]
Error: /Stage[main]/Main/Exec[use file]/returns: change from notrun to 0 failed:
  cat /tmp/workhours.txt returned 1 instead of one of [0]
Notice: Applied catalog in 0.02 seconds
```

There are a few ways to avoid this problem.

- Assign the same schedule to both resources.
- Use onlyif to check if the file exists first (only works with exec resources).
- Run Puppet with --ignoreschedules to ensure that all resources are created.

The final suggestion is perhaps the single best option. The first time you run Puppet to initialize a new node, you may want to enable ignoreschedules to ensure that every resource is created. The schedule will prevent further changes to those resources until the specified range of time.

Declaring Resource Defaults

You can declare defaults for all resources of a given type. If a resource declaration of the same type does not explicitly declare the attribute, then the attribute value from the resource default will be used.

Resource defaults are declared with a capitalized resource type and no title. For example, the following resource definition would make all packages be applied after working hours:

```
Package {
  schedule => 'after-working-hours',
}
```

Defaults can be defined multiple times, causing confusion for the people who have to debug the code. A default specified later in the manifest affects resources above it. Avoid this whenever possible.

Best Practice

Declare resource defaults at the top of the manifest for easy reading purposes.

Resource defaults also bleed into other code that is called or declared within the manifest scope. This can have surprising consequences. A more readable and maintainable method is to place the default attribute values into a hash, and add it to resources with the splat operator, as shown in "Defining Attributes with a Hash" on page 62.

The problems with resource defaults and variable scope are explained in "Understanding Variable Scope" on page 197.

Reviewing Resource Processing

This chapter introduced you to attributes that control how resources are processed:

- `alias` provides friendly names for resources with complicated or variable titles.
- `noop` prevents changes to the resource.
- `audit` logs changes to a resource outside of Puppet.
- `loglevel` controls log output on a per-resource basis.
- `tags` identifies resources to be evaluated on a filtered Puppet run.
- `schedule` limits when or how often changes to a resource are permitted.
- An uppercase first letter on a resource declaration assigns default attribute values.

Using these attributes provides fine-grained control over how and when your resources are updated.

## CHAPTER 7

Expressing Relationships

This chapter focuses on metaparameters that create and manage relationships between resources.

After parsing all of the Puppet manifests, Puppet builds a dependency graph used to structure the application of changes. Relationships between resources control the order in which resources are evaluated.

Resource relationships and ordering are perhaps the most confusing topics for newcomers to Puppet. Most people are familiar with linear processing, controlled by the order expressed within the file. Puppet provides metaparameters to define dependencies to be handled within and between manifests. This is significantly more powerful than rigid, linear ordering for the following reasons:

- Linear ordering is easy to write once, but difficult to maintain over time.
- Linear ordering prevents code from easily extending common or shared code.
- Targeted relationships allow for multiple dependencies beyond strict ordering.
- Many-to-one relationships are considerably more powerful, albeit harder to learn.
- Loose ordering allows isolation of dependences for failed resources.

You will appreciate the power and flexibility of Puppet's resource ordering when you build a module that extends (or "wraps") a community-provided module. For now, simply keep in mind that Puppet will process the resources by evaluating the dependency graph created from the metaparameters introduced in this chapter.

Managing Dependencies

There are situations where avoiding implicit dependencies of linear ordering can provide significant value.

In a linear ordering dependency evaluation, every succeeding statement is assumed to depend on the statement before it. In that case, nothing following in that script should be processed, as it is assumed to depend on the statement that failed.

In a scenario where the manifest has six operations listed in the order A → B → C → D → E → F, if A fails then should B through F not happen?

This would be undesirable if a resource early in the manifest was not essential to other resources in the manifest. By allowing you to explicitly declare dependencies, Puppet can enforce significantly more of the catalog. In the example just cited, it may be that only step F depends on A, so resources B through E can be processed.

During convergence, Puppet will evaluate the dependencies for each resource. If a dependency for a resource fails, neither it nor any resource that depends on it will be applied by Puppet. This is generally desirable behavior.

Puppet's explicit dependency metaparameters provide for complex and powerful dependency management. Let's show you how to use them.

Referring to Resources

As shown throughout all previous examples, a resource is declared using the resource type in lowercase, with the definition enclosed in curly braces:

```
package { 'puppet-agent':
  ensure => present,
}
```

Once the resource has been given a unique title, it is possible to refer to that resource by name. This is called a *resource reference*. In this chapter, we're going to refer to specific resources quite often, so let's describe how to do it. To create a resource reference, capitalize the first letter of the resource type and enclose the title in square brackets. For example, when referring to the preceding package resource, you'd use Package['puppet-agent']. Here's an example that creates a service to run the Puppet agent:

```
service { 'puppet':
  ensure  => running,
  enabled => true,
  require => Package['puppet-agent'],
}
```

Remember: create a resource with the lowercase type, and refer to an existing resource with a capitalized first letter.

An easy way to remember this is the common name versus proper name rule of English. A park is a resource type, but Golden Gate Park is a specific instance—that is, a proper noun, the first letter of which is always capitalized.

Ordering Resources

In many situations, some resources must be applied before others. For example, you cannot start a service until after you install the package that contains the application. Here we will show you the `before` and `require` metaparameters you can use to ensure the package is installed before the service is started:

```
package { 'puppet':
  ensure  => present,
  before  => Service['puppet'],
}

service { 'puppet':
  ensure  => running,
  enable  => true,
  require => Package['puppet'],
}
```

The `before` and `require` metaparameters are redundant in this case. Either one would work by itself. Use the one that fits your manifest and is easiest to read. Belt-and-suspenders people like myself often use both when possible.

 Ordering resources can be a trap. Many Puppet novices try to order every resource into a strict pattern, no matter whether the resources are truly dependent or not. This makes an implementation fragile. Adopt a *less is more* approach, and list only the necessary dependencies.

Assuming Implicit Dependencies

Many Puppet types define `autorequire` dependencies on other Puppet resources. For example, a directory will have implicit dependencies on a parent directory:

```
file { '/var/log':
  ensure  => directory,
}

file { '/var/log/puppet':
  ensure  => directory,
  autorequire => File['/var/log'],    # implicit dependencies
  autorequire => File['/var'],        # added by Puppet
}
```

The autorequire lines are not in the manifest; Puppet adds them automatically. However, unlike an explicit dependency, this dependency is *soft*, meaning that it only exists if the other resource is found within the catalog. If you haven't explicitly defined a File['/var/log'] or File['/var'] resource, then no dependency will be added.

File resources also autorequire the user resource of the user who owns the file or directory:

```
user { 'jill':
  ensure => present,
  shell  => '/bin/bash',
}

file { '/home/jill':
  ensure => directory,
  owner  => 'jill',
  require => User['jill'], # implicit dependency added by Puppet
}
```

In this situation, Puppet will always order the application of user jill before it tries to create the directory owned by her. You don't need to set this dependency explicitly. If the user jill were not defined by a resource, then the file resource would not have a dependency and would blindly attempt to change the file ownership, with the assumption that the node already has an account for Jill.

Triggering Refresh Events

The before and require metaparameters ensure that dependencies are processed before resources that require them. However, these parameters do not link or provide data to the other resource.

The notify and subscribe metaparameters operate in a similar manner, but will also send a *refresh event* to the dependent resource if the dependency is changed. The dependent resource will take a resource-specific action. For example, a service would restart after the configuration file has been changed.

Let's modify our previous policy to upgrade the Puppet package whenever a newer version is available:

```
package { 'puppet-agent':
  ensure => latest,
  notify => Service['puppet'],
}

service { 'puppet':
  ensure => running,
  enable => true,
  subscribe => Package['puppet-agent'],
}
```

If a newer version of Puppet is available, then the `puppet-agent` package will be upgraded. Any time this package is installed or upgraded, the `puppet` service will be restarted.

As noted previously, the `notify` and `subscribe` metaparameters are redundant. Either one would send the refresh event without the other. However, there is no harm in applying a belt-and-suspenders approach.

The refresh event has special meaning for `exec` resources with the attribute `refreshonly` set to `true`. These resources will not be applied unless it receives a refresh event. In the following example, we will update the *facts.yaml* file for MCollective only after Puppet has been upgraded:

```
Package { 'puppet-agent':
  ensure => latest,
  notify => Exec['update-facts'],
}

exec { 'update-facts':
  path       => ['/bin','/usr/bin'],
  command    => 'facter --puppet --yaml > /etc/mcollective/facts.yaml',
  refreshonly => true,
}
```

Under normal conditions, this `exec` resource will not execute. However, if the `puppet-agent` package is installed or upgraded, the `notify` attribute will send a refresh event and the command will be run.

Chaining Resources with Arrows

You can also order related resources using *chaining arrows*. Place the required resource on the left, and a dependent resource on the right, linked together with ->. For example, to install Puppet before starting the service, you could declare it like so:

```
Package['puppet-agent'] -> Service['puppet']
```

You can use ~> to also send a refresh event, like `notify` does. For example, this will restart the Puppet service after the package is upgraded:

```
Package['puppet'] ~> Service['puppet']
```

The chaining arrow syntax is harder to read than the metaparameters, and should be avoided when possible. In particular, right-to-left relationships are harder to read and explicitly against the Puppet Language Style Guide (*http://bit.ly/1pQT89r*):

```
# Don't do this. Order it left -> right instead.
Service['puppet'] <~ Package['puppet']
```

Processing with Collectors

A *collector* is a grouping of many resources together. You can use collectors to affect many resources at once.

For this reason, we often refer to collectors as "agents of unintended consequences." Use collectors sparingly and carefully.

A collector is declared by the capitalized type followed by <|, an optional attribute comparison, and |>. Let's examine some collectors:

```
User <||>                        # every user declared in a manifest
User <| groups == 'wheel' |>     # users in the wheel group
Package <||>                     # every package declared in a manifest
Package <| tag == 'yum' |>       # packages tagged with 'yum' tag
Service <||>                     # every service declared in a manifest
Service <| enabled == true |>    # services set to start at boot time
```

Search expressions may be grouped with parentheses and combined, as shown here:

```
# Services running OR set to start at boot time
Service <| ( ensure == running ) or ( enabled == true ) |>

# Services other than Puppet set to be running
Service <| ( ensure == running ) and ( title != 'puppet' ) |>
```

Note the phrase "declared in a manifest." The User collector in the second example would only match users who are declared in a manifest to be within the wheel group, and not a user added to the group outside of Puppet. Collectors act on resources in the catalog; they do not inspect the system for undeclared resources.

One scenario where chaining arrows have proven very useful is processing many resources with collectors. By combining chaining arrows with collectors, you can set dependencies for every resource of one type.

For example, you could have our previous **exec** update *facts.yaml* whenever a package is added or removed:

```
# Regenerate the facts whenever a package is added, upgraded, or removed
Package <||> ~> Exec['update-facts']
```

Likewise, you could ensure that the Puppet Labs Yum repository is installed before any packages tagged with puppet or mcollective:

```
Yumrepo['puppetlabs'] -> Package <| tag == 'puppet' |>
Yumrepo['puppetlabs'] -> Package <| tag == 'mcollective' |>
```

 Best Practice

Limit use of collectors to clearly scoped and limited effect. A collector that matches all resources of a given type will affect a resource another person adds to the catalog, unaware that your collector will affect it. The best usage of collectors affects only the resources within the same manifest.

You can find more details about collectors at "Language: Resource Collectors" (*http://bit.ly/1UHn6bq*) on the Puppet docs site.

Understanding Puppet Ordering

During the catalog build, prior to applying any resources, Puppet creates a dependency graph using the Directed Acyclic Graph (DAG) model, which ensures no loop in the pathways. Each catalog resource is a vertex in the graph. The directed edges between vertices are created from the implicit dependencies of related resources, followed by dependencies declared using the metaparameters and chaining arrows discussed in this chapter. Puppet uses this non-looping directed graph to order the resource evaluation.

Resources without explicit ordering parameters are not guaranteed to be ordered in any specific way. In versions of Puppet greater than 2.6, unrelated resources were evaluated in an order that was apparently random, but was consistent from run to run. (In versions of Puppet prior to 2.6, it was not consistent from node to node or run to run.) The only way to ensure that one resource was evaluated before another was to define dependencies explicitly.

The ordering configuration option was introduced in Puppet 3.3 to allow control of ordering for unrelated resources. This configuration option accepts three values:

title-hash (*default in all previous versions of Puppet*)
    Orders unrelated resources randomly but consistently between runs.

manifest (*default in Puppet 4*)
    Orders unrelated resources by the order they are declared in the manifest.

random
    Orders resources randomly and changes the order on each run. This is useful for identifying missing dependencies in a manifest.

Although resources in a manifest will generally be evaluated in the order defined, never count upon implicit dependencies. Always define all dependencies explicitly. This is especially important when you are extending another manifest or module, or when your manifest or module could be extended by someone else. This happens more than you might expect.

Best Practice

State all dependencies explicitly.

You can flush out missing dependencies by testing your manifests with the `random` ordering option. Each time you run the following, the resources will be ordered differently. This almost always causes failures for any resources missing necessary dependencies:

```
$ puppet apply --ordering=random testmanifest.pp
```

Debugging Dependency Cycles

It is necessary to avoid loops in dependencies, where two things each depend on the other being created first. The first time you run into this you may realize that many of the expressed dependencies aren't really essential. Many newcomers to Puppet try to order every resource into a strict pattern, no matter whether the resources are truly dependent or not. This will make dependency cycle problems show up far more often than necessary:

```
[vagrant@client ~]$ puppet apply /vagrant/manifests/depcycle.pp
Notice: Compiled catalog for client.example.com in environment production
Error: Failed to apply catalog: Found 1 dependency cycle:
(Cron[check-exists] => File[/tmp/file-exists.txt] => Cron[check-exists])
Try the '--graph' option and opening the resulting '.dot' file
    in OmniGraffle or GraphViz
```

Puppet will tell you about the dependency cycle, and the output for this simple example is obvious and easy to read. You could edit this manifest and fix this cycle within a minute.

As the amount of Puppet code in use grows, avoiding this problem can take a fairly significant effort. If different teams are all writing their own modules with their own dependencies, you may find a situation where only one group of nodes sees a dependency loop that doesn't affect hundreds of other cluster configurations. It all depends on which resources are included in the node's catalog.

When you're dealing with a large catalog of interdependent modules, that analysis can be very difficult. Thankfully, Puppet will show you the DAG-model dependency graph of the generated Puppet catalog, so that you can evaluate it visually.

```
[vagrant@client ~]$ puppet apply /vagrant/manifests/depcycle.pp --graph
Notice: Compiled catalog for client.example.com in environment production
Error: Failed to apply catalog: Found 1 dependency cycle:
(Cron[check-exists] => File[/tmp/file-exists.txt] => Cron[check-exists])
Cycle graph written to
   /home/vagrant/.puppetlabs/opt/puppet/cache/state/graphs/cycles.dot.
```

After you have created the *cycles.dot* file you can load it up in a viewer. Here are some suggestions:

- I'm a big fan of OmniGraffle (*https://www.omnigroup.com/omniGraffle/*) and it works great for this. There's a free 14-day trial period.
- You can download GraphViz (*http://www.graphviz.org/*) to convert the files, and ZGRViewer (*http://zvtm.sourceforge.net/zgrviewer.html*) to view them graphically.
- You can copy and paste the contents of *cycles.dot* into a web resource like WebGraphviz (*http://www.webgraphviz.com/*) to see an online rendering.

The graphical representation can be very useful for people who think in a visual manner. When working with a big team, it can be helpful to print it out in very large form, hang it on the wall, and discuss potential solutions with pins and markers.

Avoiding the Root User Trap

There is a very common dependency cycle trap that nearly every Puppet user falls smack into at least once. High up in the dependency graph are always several basic systems management resources owned by the root user that must be installed before anything else is done—for example, configuring authentication and name service ordering.

Farther down the dependency graph are things like mounting NFS volumes, creating users, and so on. Seems reasonable, yeah? You could declare a small dependency set such as the following to create users and ensure their home directories are mounted:

```
file { '/home':
  ensure => directory,
  owner  => 'root',
}

mount { '/home':
  ensure  => 'mounted',
  fstype  => 'nfs',
  device  => 'netapp:/home',
  require => File['/home'],
}
```

```
$users.each |$user,$config| {
  user { $user:
    uid      => $config['uid'],
    password => $config['passwd'],
    home     => $config['home'],
    shell    => $config['shell'],
    require  => Mount['/home'],
  }
}
```

And if your users are *jack, jill, tina,* and *mike,* then this recipe will work perfectly. Then one day you add the *root* user to the list, so that you can centrally manage the root password:

```
[vagrant@client ~]$ puppet apply /vagrant/manifests/depcycle2.pp
Notice: Compiled catalog for client.example.com in environment production
Error: Failed to apply catalog: Found 1 dependency cycle:
(File[/home] => Mount[/home] => User[root] => File[/home])
Try the '--graph' option and opening the resulting '.dot' file
  in OmniGraffle or GraphViz
```

At this point you're saying, "Wait, what? There have been no code changes, how could data break a manifest dependency?" This is where you learn an important lesson; *the dependency graph only tracks resources in the catalog.*

Yesterday the root user wasn't in the catalog. The file resource defined a soft autore quire upon the user, but this resource wasn't defined so the dependency was ignored. In this situation, the file resource will blindly attempt to chown the file or directory to the named user.

However, when you add the root user to the Puppet catalog, the autorequire matches and a dependency is created. This creates a dependency loop that didn't exist yesterday.

There are several simple ways to get out of this scenario:

- Avoid creating a root user resource in the catalog. Create an alternate root account if necessary for root login.
- Create the root user (and other users necessary for critical dependencies) early in a separate manifest.
- Utilize numeric uid => 0 and gid => 0 attribute values to avoid creating the implicit root user dependency.

All of these solutions have drawbacks. You'll have to figure out which one best suits your needs.

Utilizing Stages

Stage resources allow you to break up the Puppet run into *stages* to ensure that some things happen before other things. You create a stage and define the order of staging using the ordering metaparameters:

```
stage { 'initialize':
  before => Stage['main'],
}
stage { 'finalize': }
  after => Stage['main'],
}
```

Then you could assign classes to stages using the `stage` metaparameter.

 We haven't covered Puppet classes yet, but topically this is the best time to discuss catalog ordering. (This book has a dependency cycle!) Just know that Puppet classes are named blocks of Puppet code.

In theory, this sounds great. In practice, I've been forced to remove `stage` from every place I've tried to use it, due to the overwhelming limitations of this approach:

- It becomes even harder to sort out dependency cycles, as the assignment of a class to a stage prevents resolving conflicts with dependencies in a different stage.
- You cannot `notify` or `subscribe` to resources across stage boundaries.
- You cannot assign classes to stages using Hiera data, which forces you back to inflexible old-style class resource declarations (covered in Part II).

Stages are effectively unusable except for small corner cases where a very small manifest with no dependencies needs to run first or last. Even then it's usually easier to set this up with class ordering metaparameters.

Reviewing Resource Relationships

Puppet evaluates resources in a manifest according to a dependency graph created from the following explicit dependency controls:

- `before` metaparameter and the -> chaining arrow
- `notify` metaparameter and the ~> chaining arrow
- `require` metaparameter
- `subscribes` metaparameter

Puppet 4 will evaluate resources not listed in the dependency graph in the order in which they are declared. You can change this ordering using the `ordering` configuration option. Never depend on the manifest ordering; instead, declare all relationships explicitly.

The `random` ordering option is useful for testing manifests for missing dependencies.

## CHAPTER 8

Upgrading Puppet 3 Manifests

The upgraded parser used in Puppet 4 makes several changes to the Puppet language. This chapter covers changes from Puppet 3.

If you are new to Puppet, you can safely skip this chapter for now. Refer back to it if you must update someone else's older Puppet code.

Replacing Deprecated Features

There are features that were necessary in the Puppet 2 days that have been deprecated in Puppet 3 and are completely gone from Puppet 4. All of these have been known for years, so there should be no surprises here.

The following pages include the deprecations and how to replace them.

Junking the Ruby DSL

Puppet 2.6 introduced the Ruby DSL to allow Puppet resources to be declare in pure Ruby. This was intended to allow Ruby developers to utilize Ruby control features, such as iteration, that weren't available in the Puppet configuration language at the time.

 As the Ruby DSL really never worked well, you are very unlikely to find this in use anywhere.

The Ruby DSL was very limited in what could be expressed. There was a development attempt to make it more powerful, but the result was unstable and likely to hang the

Puppet process. As the limited Ruby subset didn't provide significant functionality, Puppet Labs instead added iteration to the Puppet language.

The Ruby DSL was deprecated in Puppet 3, and has been completely removed in Puppet 4.

Upgrade Action

Search for manifests that have the *.rb* extension and rewrite them in the Puppet configuration language.

Upgrading Config Environments

Unless you are dealing with an ancient Puppet environment, I doubt you have *configuration file environments*. These were environments defined by sections in the Puppet configuration file (usually */etc/puppet/puppet.conf*):

```
[test]
    settings for test environment

[dev]
    settings for dev environment
```

These have been deprecated for many years, and won't work at all in Puppet 4. Replace these with the much more flexible *directory environments* by following this process:

1. `mkdir -p /etc/puppetlabs/code/environments/production`.
2. Add `environmentpath = /etc/puppetlabs/code/environments` to the `[main]` section of *puppet.conf*.
3. Create a directory for each environment in the preceding path.
4. Move module path settings from *puppet.conf* to an *environment.conf* file in each environment's directory.
5. Copy manifests used by each environment to the *manifests/* directory of the environment.
6. Move modules used by specific environments to the *modules/* directory of the environment.
7. Move modules used by all environments to the `$confdir`/*modules/* directory, or a directory specified with the `basemodulepath` configuration option.

This may not cover every situation, but it will get you most of the way.

Chapter 29 covers the setup and usage of directory environments in greater detail.

Removing Node Inheritence

The only way to apply a list of classes to similar nodes in Puppet 2 was via explicit node assignments in the *manifests/site.pp/* file. To avoid repeating common definitions required creating node assignments that inherited from other node assignments:

```
node default {
  class { 'ntp': }
  class { 'puppet::agent': }
}
node 'webserver' inherits default {
  class { 'apache': }
}
```

The ability to assign classes using *external node classifiers* (*ENCs*) and Hiera data provides significantly more flexible solutions. Node assignment remains possible in Puppet 4, but node inheritance has been completely removed.

You'll learn to flexibly group class assignments to nodes in "Assigning Modules to Nodes" on page 153.

Disabling puppet kick

The limited and broken `puppet kick` is gone, replaced by the significantly more powerful MCollective agent for Puppet.

If you have been using `puppet kick`, you should disable the network service that listens on the port, as follows:

1. Remove `listen = true` from the *puppet.conf* configuration file.
2. Remove any firewall configuration that allowed connections to tcp port 8139.
3. Remove permissions for `/run` from the *auth.conf* file.

You'll learn the powerful new way to kick off Puppet runs in Chapter 30.

Qualifying Relative Class Names

Previous versions of Puppet would sometimes resolve class names using the current context. For example, the following statement could be "intercepted":

```
class mymodule {
  include ntp
}
```

If the class or defined type `mymodule::ntp` existed, it would be used instead of the global class `::ntp`. This code dates far back to when Puppet modules were first being developed, and has always confused people.

Upgrade Action

Replace relative type or class declarations with their fully qualified names: `include mymodule::ntp:`

Losing the Search Function

Relative namespace problems were made even more confusing by the use of the `search()` function to add lookup paths.

Upgrade Action

Remove the `search()` function call, and adjust all class declarations with their fully qualified name.

Replacing Import

The `import` statement has been removed:

```
# this won't work with Puppet 4
import commonfunctions.pp
```

This was previously used to pull in another manifest within the current code context. This was never a good idea.

Place the code you were importing in a module class, and `include` the class.

Upgrade Action

Move the imported manifests into a Puppet module, and include the module class instead: `include commonlib::functions`.

You'll learn to create Puppet modules in Chapter 13.

Upgrade Action

Remove the irrelevant `ignoreimport` setting from your configuration files.

Documenting Modules with Puppet Strings

The `puppet doc` command now only documents Puppet commands. Module documentation once provided by `puppet doc` has been replaced by `puppetlabs-strings`, which generates a complete documentation tree for the module in Markdown format.

You'll learn the powerful new features available for documentation in Chapter 16.

Installing the Tagmail Report Processor

The `tagmail` Puppet report processor is no longer included by default. Instructions for installing this report processor with the optional Puppet module can be found in "Processing Puppet Node Reports" on page 338.

Querying PuppetDB

Some features have been removed from Puppet and migrated to the PuppetDB service. These include:

- The ActiveRecord `storeconfigs`
- The `inventory` service
- The `puppet facts upload` command (which utilized the inventory service)
- The `puppet facts find --terminus rest` command (which utilized the inventory service)

Adjust manifests that need these features to use the PuppetDB API: Facts Endpoint (*http://bit.ly/1PgSred*).

PuppetDB is a full-featured product worthy of its own book. At this time, the best available documentation can be found at "PuppetDB Overview" (*https://docs.puppet labs.com/puppetdb/*) on the Puppet docs site.

Preparing for the Upgrade

Many of the language changes can be safely made on an existing Puppet 3 environment.

The improved parser in Puppet 4 has cleaned up many consistency issues from previously unclear documentation. If you are writing manifests, you should adopt these practices immediately to avoid upgrade problems. If you maintain older manifests, you should review them and address these issues before testing the manifests with Puppet 4.

Every change mentioned in this section is backward compatible with Puppet 3.

Validating Variable Names

Variable names are now limited to lowercase letters, numbers, and underscores. Variable names must contain at least one letter, and start with a lowercase letter or underscore:

```
$5 = 'hello'            # invalid
$5letters = 'hello'     # invalid
$five_letters = 'hello' # valid

Error: Illegal numeric variable name,
    The given name '5letters' must be a decimal value if it starts with a digit 0-9
```

Parameters in classes and defined resource types have the same limitations:

```
define mytype( $21, $32 ) {          # invalid
define mytype( $twenty1, $thirty2 ) { # valid
```

Upgrade Action

Adjust all variable and parameter names to start with lowercase letters or underscores.

Quoting Strings

Bare word strings must start with a letter. Older Puppet code contains fairly common usage of unquoted values (present, true, etc.). Previous versions of Puppet would treat these as unquoted strings, but Puppet 4 supports many data types. It is best to quote all string values to ensure they are handled properly:

```
$myvar = fourguys    # assumed to be String
$myvar = 42          # assumed to be Numeric (Integer)
$myvar = true        # assumed to be Boolean
$myvar = '4guys'     # quotes ensure String data type
```

Upgrade Action

Quote all strings to avoid misinterpretation.

Preventing Numeric Assignment

In previous versions of Puppet, numbers were really just strings. Unquoted numbers were unquoted strings, which happened to work. Documented best practice in Puppet 3 was to quote all numbers to ensure they were explicitly strings, but a lot of modules have unquoted numbers in them.

In Puppet 4, unquoted numerals are the Numeric data type. Numbers are validated as part of the catalog build, and an invalid number will cause the catalog build to fail:

```
Error: Could not parse for environment production: Illegal number '4guys'
```

To avoid catalog build failures, quote strings that may be misinterpreted as numbers. Some data uses hex or octal values with suffixes specific to the application. The following are situations where unquoted numbers would work in Puppet 3 but cause errors in Puppet 4:

```
# leading 0x causes evaluation as hexidecimal
$address =  0x1AH      # 'H' is not a valid hex number
$address = '0x1AH'     # safe as quoted string

# leading zeros cause numbers to evaluated as octal
$leadingzero =  0119   # ERROR octal has 8 bits, 0-7
$leadingzero = '0119'  # safe as quoted string

# mixed letters and numbers
$mixed_chars = 1x2x3    # will be mistaken for decimal and raise error
$mixed_chars = '1x2x3' # safe as quoted string.
```

Any unquoted string that starts with a number will be validated as if it were a number, and may cause a catalog build failure.

The easiest way to avoid confusion is to always quote strings. As you can pass a string containing a number as input to anything that will accept a number, it is safest to quote numbers that may be misinterpreted.

Upgrade Action

Quote all numbers used in attributes or assigned to variables to match the older code's expectations.

File mode is not Numeric

Although it would be fantastic to use the new number validation with file modes, an unfortunate decision[1] was made to require all file modes to be strings.

This decision means that modules that had unquoted numbers for the mode will throw errors, rather than apply an unexpected file rights set. I understand the reasoning, but I would have liked to use the automatic number validation for file modes in Puppet 4.

You must use a string value containing the octal number for file modes, like so:

```
file '/tmp/testfile.txt' {
    mode => '0644',
}
```

---

1 The comments on Ticket PUP-2156 (*https://tickets.puppetlabs.com/browse/PUP-2156*) explain the decision to force file modes to be strings

Testing Boolean Facts

In previous versions of Puppet, boolean values were internally converted to the strings `true` and `false`. You could compare either the bare word or the quoted string value successfully.

Puppet 4 introduced the `Boolean` data type, which does not compare equally with a `String` value. This comparison will fail without warning:

```
if $is_virtual == "true" {
```

Search through the Puppet code for instances of quoted boolean values. Check the data source to confirm if the value is `Boolean` or `String`. For example, the `is_vir tual` fact is now `Boolean`, so the check should be rewritten like so:

```
if $facts['is_virtual'] == true {
```

Empty strings evaluate to boolean `true`. This can trip you up if you had code that depended on a `false` evaluation:

```
# replace this
if ! $empty_string {

# with this
if $empty_string == '' {
```

Upgrade Action

Check each instance of `true` or `false` to determine if it should be tested as a string, or boolean.

Qualifying Defined Types

In previous versions of Puppet, it was possible and somewhat common to place defined types in the top namespace:

```
# modules/users/manifests/createuser.pp
define createuser(
...
```

This defined type could be declared exactly like a global resource type:

```
# any manifest
createuser{ 'jo':
  ensure => present,
  uid    => 1001,
...
```

This won't work with Puppet 4, and will instead yield a nonintuitive error:

```
Error: Could not retrieve catalog from remote server: Error 400 on SERVER:
  Error while evaluating a Resource Statement, Invalid resource type createuser
```

This message simply means that defined types created in modules need to be prefixed with the module name:

```
# modules/users/manifests/createuser.pp
define users::createuser( $name, $uid, $gid ) {
  ...
}
```

Upgrade Action

Adjust the declaration of defined types to include their module name.

```
# any manifest
users::create{ 'jo':
  ensure => present,
  uid    => 1001,
  ...
```

It remains possible to create top-level defined types in the *manifests/* directory of an environment, but this support may be removed in a future version.

Adding Declarative Permissions

In previous versions of Puppet, if the following attributes were not defined, they were copied from the source file on the Puppet master's filesystem:

- owner
- group
- mode

This is not very declarative, as the final state of the file depends on attributes in the filesystem you can't read from the manifest.

Upgrade Action

Add specific owner, group, and mode attributes to all file resources.

If this is not possible or practical for one reason or another, add the following attribute to the resource to implement the nondeclarative behavior:

```
file { filename:
  source_permissions => use,
}
```

Removing Cron Purge

In previous versions of Puppet, the following would remove unmanaged cron entries from only the user that Puppet was running as (root):

```
resource { 'cron':
  purge => true,
}
```

This differed from most other resource purges. In Puppet 4, this will now purge unknown cron entries for every user.

Upgrade Action

Disable cron purge until cron resources for every user have been added to the catalog.

Replacing MSI Package Provider

Puppet 3 deprecated the msi Windows package provider with an improved windows provider.

Upgrade Action

Replace every explicit assignment of the msi provider to windows.

The following query can find all the right files for you:

```
$ grep -rlE 'provider\s*=>\s*[^\w]?msi[^\w]?' /etc/puppet /etc/puppetlabs
```

Adjusting Networking Facts

With the latest version of Facter, many of the network-related facts have been restructured into hashes that allow much more intelligent retrieval and analysis of interfaces.

You may have some logic like this in existing manifests:

```
if( $ipaddress_eth0 =~ /^10\./ ) {
  $has_rfc1918address = true
}
```

You'll need to replace that with something much clearer. For example:

```
if( $facts['networking']['interfaces']['ip'] =~ /^10\./ )
  $has_rfc1918address = true
}
```

The new facts are in iterable hashes, thus allowing easy methods to check every interface:

```
$net10ints = $facts['networking']['interfaces'].filter |$interface,$config| {
  $config['ip'] =~ /^10\./ )
}
```

Testing with the Future Parser

You can test the new language features on an existing Puppet 3 environment by making the following changes to the Puppet configuration:

- Upgrade all Puppet clients and masters to the latest Puppet 3 version.
- Disable `stringify_facts` in the Puppet configuration.
- Set `parser = future` in the Puppet configuration.

Upgrade Puppet on all nodes to the latest version of Puppet 3—currently 3.8.6. Development of Puppet 3 has ceased except for critical security updates. This version is very stable and well tested. Furthermore, it will provide deprecation warnings to help you identify upgrade concerns.

Add the following line to the Puppet configuration file (usually */etc/puppet/ puppet.conf*) on the master and any nodes used for testing. The following change disables the conversion of all facts to strings (default in Puppet 3 and earlier):

```
[main]
  stringify_facts = false
```

This change must be made on your Puppet master and any clients you are using to test the manifests.

Enable the *future parser*, which provides most of the language improvements that are standard in Puppet 4. Choose one of the ways outlined in the following subsections to enable the future parser for testing.

Using Directory Environments

If directory environments are enabled, you can test module upgrades in place. Create an environment named `upgrade` environment with a complete copy of `production`. This may be as simple as the following:

```
$ cd /etc/puppet/environments
$ cp -r production upgrade
```

Add the following line to the *${environmentpath}/upgrade/environment.conf* file.

```
parser = future
```

Then you can test out individual clients by changing the environment on the command line, as follows:

```
$ puppet apply upgrade/manifests/site.pp --environment=future --noop
```

or on a client of a Puppet master:

```
$ puppet agent --test --environment=future --noop
```

Duplicating a Master or Node

If directory environments are not available, then an alternative is to clone a Puppet master or a node that uses `puppet apply`. Then make the following change to the Puppet configuration file (usually */etc/puppet/puppet.conf*):

```
[main]
  parser = future
```

You would test this with the same commands shown in the preceding section.

Enhancing Older Manifests

After the future parser is enabled and catalogs are building and being applied successfully, you may want to refactor modules to take advantage of improvements in the Puppet configuration language.

Adding else to unless

You can now use `else` with `unless`:

```
unless ( $somevalue > 10 ) {
    # do this
}
else {
    # do that
}
```

It is generally better to use `if/else` than `unless/else` for readability, but readable code is the most important thing. Use whichever reads more naturally.

Calling Functions in Strings

You can now call functions from within a double-quoted string by wrapping them in curly braces exactly as if they were variables. For all intents and purposes, the function call is a short-lived, unnamed variable:

```
notify { 'need_coffee':
  message => "I need a cup of coffee. Remind me in ${fqdn_rand(10)} minutes.",
}
```

This may allow you to remove some single-use variable assignments.

Matching String Regexps

You can now match against regular expressions defined by strings:

```
$what_did_you_drink !~ "^coffee$"        # uses a string value for regexp
```

The quoted string on the right is converted to a Regexp before matching against the left String variable. This can provide flexibility by allowing interpolated variables in a regular expression:

```
$you_drank =~ "^${drink_du_jour}$"       # uses a variable for matching in Regexp
```

Letting Expressions Stand Alone

Previous versions of Puppet required the results of all expressions to be assigned. In Puppet 4, an expression can stand alone. If it is the last expression in a lambda or a function, the result will be returned. Otherwise, the value will be discarded.

The following rather simple lambda returns the result of the last expression within the lambda block:

```
$tenfold = with( $input_number ) |$number| {
  $number * 10
}
```

Blocks of code (lambdas and functions) always return the result of their last expression. You do not need an explicit return.

 In Puppet 4, you can safely call a function without using the returned value. Earlier versions of Puppet would raise errors in this situation.

If the returned value is not used, the result is silently discarded:

```
# the resulting value is ignored
with( $input_number ) |$number| {
  $number * 10
}
```

Chaining Assignments

You can now change multiple assignments in the same expression. You can chain both equality and addition operations, like so:

```
$security_deposit = 100
$first = 250
$last = 250
$down_payment = $first + $security_deposit

# could be rewritten as
$first = $last = 250
$down_payment = $first + ( $security_deposit = 100 )
```

As chained assignments have low precedence, you must use parentheses to ensure proper ordering.

Best Practice

Chained assignments are rarely more readable than the expanded version. Avoid them to improve comprehension for the reader.

Chaining Expressions with a Semicolon

You can now use a semicolon to concatenate two expressions together:

```
$fname = 'Jo'; $lname = 'Rhett'
```

The semicolon can be used to prevent the last statement of a block from being returned as the value:

```
{
  $fname = 'Jo'; $lname = 'Rhett'; 1     # returns 1 for success
}
```

Best Practice

Using a semicolon to change operations never makes code more readable. Leave this for special cases where you must execute several commands on a single line.

Using Hash and Array Literals

Older versions of Puppet required you to assign arrays and hashes to variables before using them in resources or functions. Puppet 4 allows you to use literal arrays and hashes more naturally in a Puppet manifest:

```
notify { "(['one','two','three'][1] )": }     # produces the output "two"
```

New in Puppet 4, you can concatenate arrays and merge hashes with +:

```
$my_list = [1,4,7]
$bigger_list = $my_list + [14,17]                 # equals [1,4,7,14,17]

$key_pairs       = {name => 'Jo', uid => 1001}
$user_definition = $key_pairs + { gid => 500 }   # hash now has name, uid, gid...
```

Also new in Puppet 4, you can append to arrays with <<. Watch out, as anything appended to an array is added as a single entry. This means that an array appended to an array adds an array, not multiple values, in the last position:

```
$my_list << 33            # equals [1,4,7,33]
$my_list << [33,35]       # equals [1,4,7,[33,35]]
```

Configuring Error Reporting

Error reports are much improved with Puppet 4. You'll generally see the following improvements:

Most errors now show character position on line
Errors from manifest parsing use the format *filename:line_number:charac ter_number* when reporting where an error was found:

```
Error: Illegal numeric variable name,
    The given name '5words' must be a decimal value
    if it starts with a digit 0-9 at /vagrant/manifests/broken.pp:2:1
```

Many block and token parsing errors have been improved
In previous versions, the message would often indicate something completely unhelpful to diagnose the error. A concerted effort was made in Puppet 4 to clean those up and improve clarity.

The maximum warnings or errors Puppet will display is configurable
The following settings in *puppet.conf* can be used to override the defaults of showing 10 of each type:

```
[main]
  max_errors = 3
  max_warnings = 3
  max_deprecations = 20
```

No matter what the limits are configured to show, a final error line provides the total error and warning count:

```
Error: Found 4 errors. Giving up
```

## CHAPTER 9

Wrap-Up of Puppet Basics

In this part, you've created a safe, risk-free learning environment you can utilize to write and test Puppet manifests. You've learned the following things about Puppet:

- Puppet policies are written in manifests.
- Manifests contain one or more resource declarations.
- Resources create, alter, or remove their types: `user`, `group`, `file`, and so on.
- Facter provides data about the node useful for local customization.

You have learned each part of the Puppet configuration language and how to utilize it to create manifests. You've used Puppet to apply the manifest on your test system. `puppet apply` does the following:

- Parses a manifest file and reports any errors.
- Utilizes facts about the system as variables for customization.
- Executes immediately on the local system.
- Provides verbose output informing you of what it has done.

 While many people utilize `puppet apply` only for testing manifest changes, it can be used at broad scale if a method of synchronizing manifests to each node is available. We'll discuss the pros and cons of this approach in Part IV.

Best Practices for Writing Manifests

Before moving on to the next chapter, I'd like to remind you of best practices for writing Puppet manifests:

- Quote all unquoted string values.
- `ensure` should be the first attribute in a resource block.
- Align the arrows for attributes within a resource block.
- Enable the `strict_variables` configuration setting to catch errors while testing.
- Group resources by their relationship with each other.
- Don't use conditionals within resource declarations.
- Provide defaults for `case` and `select` statements.
- When something can be done multiple ways, always use the most readable option.

You can find the Puppet Style Guide at *https://docs.puppetlabs.com/guides/ style_guide.html*. All of the examples in this book have been compliant with the style guide.

Learning More About Puppet Manifests

To expand on what you have learned in this chapter, investigate the built-in resource types provided by Puppet. There are more than we have discussed in this chapter, and you'll find many of them immediately useful. Here are just a few we didn't mention previously:

`augeas`	A programatic API for managing configuration files
`cron`	Cron scheduler entries
`host`	Host file entries
`interface`	Networking
`mailalias`	Mail aliases
`mount`	Filesystem mount points
`nagios_*`	Types to manage Nagios host, service, contact entries
`router`	Manages a connected router
`sshkey`	SSH key management
`yumrepo`	Package repository

The complete list of built-in resource types can be found at "Resource Type Reference" (*http://bit.ly/259dLhf*) on the Puppet docs site.

## PART II

Creating Puppet Modules

Puppet modules are bundles of Puppet code, files, templates, and data. Well-written Puppet modules provide a clean interface for sharing reusable code between different teams either within your organization or throughout the global community.

Puppet modules provide several benefits. For example, they:

- Organize code and data within the module's namespace.
- Contain manifests that evaluate, install, configure, or remove something.
- Provide files, templates, tests, functions, and plugins for use in other modules.

In this part, we'll discuss how to find and use Puppet modules that other people have made available for you. We'll show you how to provide data to these modules such that you can use them without modifying the module code.

While you may find old examples of Puppet manifests used independently, it has been best practice for many years now for all manifests to reside within modules. We will go through the process of turning the manifests built in Part I into fully formed and well-built Puppet modules.

## CHAPTER 10

Creating a Test Environment

Puppet provides the ability to serve clients different versions of modules and data using *environments*. You can use environments to provide unique catalogs to different groups of machines, which can be very useful in large projects with many teams. However, a primary usage of environments is to enable testing of changes to Puppet policy without breaking production environments.

Puppet environments have proven so necessary and useful for code testing and deployment that they are enabled by default in Puppet 4. So before we go on to install Puppet modules, let's configure the *production* and *test* environments.

Verifying the Production Environment

The default environment used by Puppet clients is named `production`. The Puppet installation creates the `production` environment during the installation of Puppet. You should find that this already exists:

```
[vagrant@client ~]$ ls -l /etc/puppetlabs/code/environments/production
total 4
-rw-r--r-- 1 root root 879 Mar 26 19:27 environment.conf
drwxr-xr-x 2 root root   6 Mar 26 19:38 hieradata
drwxr-xr-x 2 root root   6 Mar 26 19:38 manifests
drwxr-xr-x 2 root root   6 Mar 26 19:38 modules
```

The `default` environment is prepared with an environment configuration file, and directories for Hiera data, modules, and manifests.

Creating the Test Environment

Now let's create a *test* environment you can use to test out new modules or changes to modules prior to implementing them in production. Create the environment like so:

```
[vagrant@client ~]$ mkdir -p /etc/puppetlabs/code/environments/test/modules
[vagrant@client ~]$ cd /etc/puppetlabs/code/environments/test
[vagrant@client test]$ mkdir hieradata
```

This gives us a place to test module changes without breaking any production nodes. Let's also enable a reminder that we are using the testing environment:

```
[vagrant@client test]$ mkdir manifests
[vagrant@client test]$ $EDITOR manifests/site.pp
```

The contents of this file should be something like this:

```
notify { 'UsingTest':
  message => "Processing catalog from the Test environment.",
}
```

This will give you a warning any time you use this environment, which can be a helpful reminder to move a node back to the production environment when testing is complete.

Changing the Base Module Path

The Puppet configuration has a convenience setting that allows you to share modules between all environments. The following can be specified in */etc/puppetlabs/puppet/puppet.conf*:

```
[main]
  # these are both default values
  environmentpath = /etc/puppetlabs/code/environments
  basemodulepath = /etc/puppetlabs/code/modules
```

The environmentpath variable contains a path under which a directory for each environment will be created.

The basemodulepath variable contains a directory that will be used as a fallback location for modules not found in the environment's *modules/* directory. This allows you to place common and well-tested modules in a single location shared by all environments.

Both of the directory names shown are the default values, and do not need to be specified in the configuration file unless you wish to change them.

Skipping Ahead

While there are many things you can fine-tune and customize with Puppet environments, many of them wouldn't make much sense at this point in our learning process. These environments are ready for us to use.

We'll come back to cover environments in much greater detail in Chapter 29.

## CHAPTER 11

Separating Data from Code

When using modules, it's important to separate the code from the input data. A module written for a single target node may work fine with explicit data within the code; however, it won't be usable on other systems without changes to the code.

If the data resides within the code, you'll find yourself constantly going back to hack `if/else` conditions into the code for each necessary difference. I'm sure you've done this before, or may even have to do this now to maintain scripts you use today. This chapter will introduce a better way.

Moving the data (values) out of the code (manifest) creates reusable blocks of code that can implement configurable, data-driven policy.

Introducing Hiera

Hiera is a key/value lookup tool for configuration data. Puppet uses Hiera to dynamically look up configuration data for Puppet manifests.

Hiera allows you to provide node-specific data to a Puppet module to create a customized policy for the node. Hiera utilizes a configurable hierarchy of information that allows you to tune Hiera appropriately for how information is structured within your organization.

For example, at a small company, you may organize your data in this way:

1. Company-wide common data
2. Operating system–specific changes
3. Site-specific information

A much larger organization might have a hierarchy such as the following:

1. Enterprise-level common data
2. Company specifics
3. Division overrides
4. Production/staging/QA/development
5. Region (US, EU, Asia)-specific changes
6. Operating system–specific configurations
7. Cluster-specific changes
8. Application-specific details

The multilevel hierarchy can be used to merge common data with node and environment-specific overrides, making it easy to utilize the same shared code throughout a diverse organization.

Creating Hiera Backends

Hiera has two built-in data file backends: YAML and JSON. Both support five data types:

- `String`
- `Number`
- `Boolean` (true/false)
- `Array`
- `Hash`

Let's review how to utilize these data types in each backend.

Hiera Data in YAML

The easiest and most common way to provide data to Hiera is utilizing the YAML file format. Files must have a *.yaml* file extension.

Files in YAML format always start with three dashes by themselves on the first line. The YAML format utilizes indentation to indicate the relationships between data. YAML should always be written using spaces for indentation (do not use tabs).

Here are some examples of strings, boolean, arrays, and hashes in YAML:

```
# string
agent_running: 'running'

# boolean
agent_atboot: true

# array
puppet_components:
```

```
  - facter
  - puppet

# a hash of values
puppet:
  ensure: 'present'
  version: '4.4.0'

# A variable lookup
hostname: %{facts.hostname}
```

As this data is all about managing the Puppet agent, why don't we organize this within a single hash? That could look as simple as this:

```
puppet:
  ensure: 'present'
  version: '4.4.0'
  agent:
    running: 'running'
    atboot: true
  components:
    - 'facter'
    - 'puppet'
```

As you can see, YAML provides a clean, readable way to provide data without too much syntax. You can find out more about YAML at the "Yaml Cookbook for Ruby" site (*http://bit.ly/1XAD1Yd*).

 It is not always necessary to quote strings in YAML. The words `running`, `facter`, and `puppet` in the preceding example would be correctly interpreted as strings without the quotes. However, the rules for when to quote strings in YAML are many and often subtle. It's better to be safe than sorry.

Hiera Data in JSON

You can also provide data to Hiera with the JSON file format. Files must have a *.json* file extension.

As is common with almost every use of JSON, the root of each data source must be a single hash. Each key within the hash names a piece of configuration data. Each value within the hash can be any valid JSON data type.

Our previous example rewritten in JSON format would look like the following (this example shows values of a string, a boolean, and an array of strings):

```
{
  "puppet": {
    "ensure": "present",
    "version": "4.4.0",
```

```
      "agent": {
        "running": "running",
        "atboot": true
      },
      "components": [
        "facter",
        "puppet"
      ]
    }
  }
}
```

 JSON requires that the final entry in any data structure does not end in a comma. This is different from Puppet, where a final comma presents no difficulty.

You can find complete details of the JSON data format at the "Introducing JSON" site (*http://www.json.org/*).

Puppet Variable and Function Lookup

You can look up Puppet variables or execute functions to interpolate data within a Hiera value. Interpolation is performed on any value prefixed by % and surrounded by curly braces {}.

To return the value of a Puppet variable, place the variable name within the braces—for example: `%{facts.hostname}`.

Functions can be invoked within the interpolation braces as well: `%{ split([1,2,3]) }`.

Configuring Hiera

Puppet looks for a Hiera configuration file at the location specified by the `hiera_con fig` configuration variable. By default, this is *${codedir}/hiera.yaml*, or */etc/puppet-labs/code/hiera.yaml* in Puppet.

The Hiera configuration file is a YAML hash. Items at the top are called *global* settings. Each global setting is a Ruby symbol prefaced with a colon. Valid symbol names are alphanumeric with an underscore, but not containing dashes.

All settings are optional and fall back to default values. Let's review these settings now.

Backends

The configuration key `:backends` should provide an array that lists the backend data providers that Hiera should use. As we've discussed, there are two built-in backends, YAML and JSON.

If you wish to utilize both built-in file types, you could configure Hiera as follows:

```
:backends:
  - yaml
  - json
```

> Custom backends can be added to Hiera, but that is beyond the scope of this book.

The `:backends:` configuration option defaults to YAML if not included. We will only be utilizing YAML within this book.

Backend Configuration

For each backend data provider you name in the `backends` array, you should create a global setting with the name of the provider. Provide a hash of configuration data for each backend

The only configuration key necessary for the built-in backends is `:datadir`, which identifies the directory in which the data files reside. The following shows the default values if not overridden in the Hiera configuration file:

```
# default values for datadir
:yaml:
  :datadir: /etc/puppetlabs/code/environments/%{::environment}/hieradata
:json:
  :datadir: /etc/puppetlabs/code/environments/%{::environment}/hieradata
```

As the files read by each backend must be named with different file extensions, you can use the same data directory for both data sources as shown.

This configuration uses the top-scope `::environment` variable (defined by a Puppet server or agent) to allow different environment data in each environment. It allows use of the *hieradata/* directory we created for the `test` environment in Chapter 10.

Logger

By default, Hiera command line tools log warning and debug messages to `STDOUT`. You can change this using the `:logger` configuration value. Valid values are:

---

console

Emit warnings and debug on STDERR (default)

puppet

Send messages to Puppet's logging system

noop

Don't emit messages

name

Utilize the Ruby class Hiera::*name*_logger, which must provide warn and debug class methods that expect a single string argument

Note that this value is only used for Hiera command line-tools. Puppet overrides the value and logs Hiera messages utilizing the Puppet internal logger.

Hierarchy

The final mandatory parameter is :hierarchy. The hierarchy defines the priority order for lookup of configuration data. For single values, Hiera will proceed through the hierarchy until it finds a value (at which point, it will stop). For arrays and hashes Hiera will merge data from each level of the hierarchy, as configured by the merge strategy selected for that lookup key.

There are two types of data sources: static and dynamic. Static data sources are files explicitly named in the hierarchy that contain data. Dynamic data sources are files that are named using interpolation of local configuration data, such as the hostname or operating system of the node.

In a larger enterprise, the data lookup hierarchy could be quite complex; however, I recommend the following for a good starting point:

1. Put default values in a file named *common.yaml*.
2. Put all operating system–specific information in a file named for the OS family as returned by Facter (e.g., *RedHat.yaml*, *Debian.yaml*, *FreeBSD.yaml*)
3. Put information specific to a single node within a file named the fully qualified domain name with a *.yaml* extension.

You would implement this hierarchy using the following configuration syntax (as you can see, we are interpolating data provided by Facter to choose which files will be read):

```
:hierarchy:
  - "fqdn/%{facts.fqdn}"
  - "os/%{facts.osfamily}"
  - common
```

Naturally you can extend this hierarchy to use information such as the domain name of the node or any other Facter-provided node value. For example, given our small list of nodes in *example.com*, we can save some typing by using the shorter hostname instead:

```
:hierarchy:
  - "hostname/%{facts.hostname}"
  - "os/%{facts.osfamily}"
  - common
```

If you have multiple backends configured, Hiera will evaluate the entire hierarchy for the first configured backend, then evaluate the entire hierarchy in order for the second configured backend, and so on.

Merge Strategy

In previous versions of Puppet, you could only set merge strategy globally, using the `:merge_behavior` configuration parameter in *hiera.yaml*. This was not flexible enough for even basic use cases, and is thus ignored by the more powerful Puppet lookup mechanism.

The following merge strategies are supported:

`first` *(default)—formerly known as* `priority`
> Returns the first value found, with no merging. Keys found at the higher priority will return the value from that priority level without any recursion.

`hash`—*formerly known as* `native`
> Merge keys only. The values from the higher priority match will be used exclusively, without any values from lower priority keys.

`deep`—*formerly known as* `deeper`
> Recursively merge array and hash values. If a key exists at multiple levels, the lower-priority values that don't conflict will be merged with the higher-priority values.

`unique`—*formerly known as* `array`
> Flatten array and scalar values from all priority levels into a single list. Duplicate values will be dropped. Hashes will cause an error.

Puppet allows setting the merge strategy on a per-key basis, using the following two methods:

An entry in the `lookup_options` *hash*
> A key the `lookup_options` hash named for the value can be defined in global (Hiera), environment, or module data. The hash of values assigned to the key will provide the lookup options, including the merge strategy.

Options provided in the lookup() *function*

Any options used in a lookup() fuction call will override the lookup_options provided in the data.

We'll provide examples of using both methods in "Looking Up Hiera Data" on page 134.

Complete Example

Following is a complete example of a Hiera configuration file. This example is what we will use for the rest of testing code within this book. It enables YAML data input from */etc/puppetlabs/code/hieradata*, which allows us to share the same Hiera data across all environments.

When the environments are distinct only to test code, use a shared Hiera path for ease of data management.

The following hierarchy prioritizes host-specific values, followed by operating system values, and defaulting to the lowest priority values common to every host:

```
---
:backends:
  - yaml
:hierarchy:
  - "hostname/%{facts.hostname}"
  - "os/%{facts.osfamily}"
  - common
:yaml:
  :datadir: /etc/puppetlabs/code/hieradata
```

Let's go ahead and add this file now to your Puppet code directory:

```
[vagrant@client ~]$ cp /vagrant/etc-puppet/hiera.yaml /etc/puppetlabs/code/
```

Looking Up Hiera Data

There are several ways to validate that your data is defined correctly in Hiera. For the following tests, create a Hiera data file containing values to control the Puppet service (this will be much like the Puppet manifest we created in Part I):

```
$ mkdir /etc/puppetlabs/code/hieradata
$ $EDITOR /etc/puppetlabs/code/hieradata/common.yaml
```

Within this file, place the following values:

```
---
puppet::status: 'running'
puppet::enabled: true
```

Now, let's set up an override for this host. Create a file in the */etc/puppetlabs/code/hieradata/hostname/* directory with the name of the node:

```
$ mkdir /etc/puppetlabs/code/hieradata/hostname
$ facter hostname
client
$ $EDITOR /etc/puppetlabs/code/hieradata/hostname/client.yaml
```

In this file, place the following values:

```
---
puppet::status: 'stopped'
puppet::enabled: false
```

Checking Hiera Values from the Command Line

You can utilize the `hiera` command-line tool to test lookups of Hiera data. Unfortunately, this tool doesn't retrieve values in the same manner as Puppet:

```
[vagrant@client ~]$ hiera puppet::enabled
true
[vagrant@client ~]$ hiera puppet::status
running
```

Wait, weren't these values changed for the client host? Yes, they were. But the `hiera` command-line tool doesn't have facts and other configuration data available from Puppet. As a result, it didn't properly interpret the hierarchy that uses filenames derived from facts. Thus, it has returned the only values it knows to find: the default values from the *common.yaml* file.

For this reason, it is significantly easier and more accurate to test Hiera values by using the `lookup()` function to query Hiera data, as follows:

```
[vagrant@client ~]$ puppet apply -e "notice(lookup('puppet::enabled'))"
Notice: Scope(Class[main]): false
Notice: Compiled catalog for client.example.com in environment production
Notice: Applied catalog in 0.01 seconds
```

Better yet, it is possible to test Puppet lookups directly from the command line without evaluating code:

```
[vagrant@client code]$ puppet lookup puppet::status
--- stopped
...
```

If you don't get the values back that you expect, it may be because you don't have the personal configuration file installed that points at the system `$confdir` and `$codedir` directories. Rerun with sudo and compare.

Performing Hiera Lookups in a Manifest

Let's modify one of our manifests to utilize Hiera data. First, create a manifest that contains variables for the configuration of the Puppet agent service. Name it something like *hierasample.pp*:

```
# Always set a default value when performing a Hiera lookup
$status = lookup({ name => 'puppet::status',  default_value => 'running' })
$enabled = lookup({ name => 'puppet::enabled', default_value => true })

# Now the same code can be used regardless of the value
service { 'puppet':
  ensure => $status,
  enable => $enabled,
}
```

Execute this manifest utilizing the Hiera data we created:

```
[vagrant@client ~]$ sudo puppet apply /vagrant/manifests/hierasample.pp
Notice: Compiled catalog for client.example.com in environment production
Notice: /Stage/Main/Service[puppet]/ensure: ensure changed 'running' to 'stopped'
Notice: /Stage/Main/Service[puppet]/enable: enable changed 'true' to 'false'
Notice: Applied catalog in 0.07 seconds
```

This has stopped the Puppet service, and prevented it from starting at boot, due to the overrides we added for this specific hostname.

Now let's comment out the host-specific override in *hostname/client.yaml*, and reapply the manifest:

```
[vagrant@client ~]$ rm /etc/puppetlabs/code/hieradata/hostname/client.yaml
[vagrant@client ~]$ sudo puppet apply hierasample.pp
Notice: Compiled catalog for client.example.com in environment production
Notice: /Stage/Main/Service[puppet]/ensure: ensure changed 'stopped' to 'running'
Notice: /Stage/Main/Service[puppet]/enable: enable changed 'false' to 'true'
Notice: Applied catalog in 0.07 seconds
```

Now that the host-specific override has been removed, the default values we placed in *common.yaml* are applied.

Testing Merge Strategy

For a more complex example, let's test how data in hashes can be merged together. Using the example Hiera configuration we created in the previous section, define some users in the global *common.yaml* file, like so:

```
# common.yaml
users:
  jill:
    uid: 1000
    home: '/home/jill'
  jack:
    uid: 1001
    home: '/home/jack'
```

Let's query this data source and confirm the global values. The following are the results for any system without any higher-priority overrides:

```
[vagrant@client ~]$ puppet lookup users
---
jill:
  uid: 1000
  home: "/home/jill"
jack:
  uid: 1001
  home: "/home/jack"
```

On the client system, we actually want home directories in */homes/* for some strange reason. In addition, we have a special local user, Jane. As we only want to change the user's home directories, we might create a higher-priority *hostname/clients.yaml* file with just the differences:

```
# hostname/client.yaml
users:
  jill:
    home: '/homes/jill'
  jack:
    home: '/homes/jack'
  jane:
    uid : 999
    home: '/homes/jane'
```

So let's test this out now with a command-line lookup() query. We'll compare the results for a default match with a match for the client machine, as shown here:

```
[vagrant@client ~]$ puppet lookup --node default users
---
jill:
  uid: 1000
  home: "/home/jill"
jack:
  uid: 1001
  home: "/home/jack"

[vagrant@client ~]$ puppet lookup users
---
jill:
  home: "/homes/jill"
jack:
```

```
    home: "/homes/jack"
jane:
    uid: 999
    home: "/homes/jane"
```

What happened to the user's UIDs when run on the local client node? When searching for users, it found the jill and jack user keys in the *hostname/client.yaml* file. It accepted the value associated with that key, and ignored the unique sub-keys in the lower-priority global file. To get the same results with first or hash merging, you'd have to repeat all keys in the higher-priority file.

 The --node option causes lookup to request the facts from PuppetDB, which we haven't discussed yet. Without PuppetDB the query for puppet lookup --node client.example.com won't return the same results, as the Hiera hierarchy depends on fact values. Leave off the --node option to use the local node's facts in the hierarchy.

Let's try a query that performs a recursive merge through both hashes and find unique keys at each level:

```
[vagrant@client ~]$ puppet lookup users --merge deep
---
jill:
    uid: 1000
    home: "/homes/jill"
jack:
    uid: 1001
    home: "/homes/jack"
jane:
    uid: 999
    home: "/homes/jane"
```

As you can see, this result merged hash keys from all levels in the hierarchy. When keys matched ("home" for instance) it chose the higher-priority value.

As we know that users should be merged from all levels in the hierarchy, let's set the merge strategy using the lookup_options hash in *common.yaml*, as shown here:

```
# common.yaml
lookup_options:
    users:
        merge: deep
```

By placing this configuration in the data, the deep merge strategy will be used by default for lookups of the users key:

```
[vagrant@client ~]$ puppet lookup users
---
jill:
  uid: 1000
  home: "/homes/jill"
jack:
  uid: 1001
  home: "/homes/jack"
jane:
  uid: 999
  home: "/homes/jane"
```

Best Practice

Use the deep merge strategy for Don't Repeat Yourself (DRY) data
management.

Providing Global Data

In this chapter, you created a global data repository that can provide data to customize the catalog of a node. You have configured this to use YAML data files from the
global directory */etc/puppetlabs/code/hieradata*, independent of the node's environment.

This configuration is easy to maintain, and works well for nodes using puppet apply.
It also provides a source for global data parameters common to all environments.

In Chapter 29, you will learn how to create environment-specific Hiera data hierarchies.

## CHAPTER 12

Using Modules

One of the most powerful benefits of using Puppet is having access to the shared community of module developers. While Puppet enables you to create modules to do nearly anything, it is quite possible that somebody has already written the module you need. You may be able to use it intact, or use it as a starting point for further development.

In this chapter, you'll learn how to find, evaluate, install, and use modules provided by Puppet Labs and the global community.

Finding Modules

There are several places to find Puppet modules you can use. Let's review each of them in turn.

Puppet Forge

The single largest repository of Puppet modules is the Puppet Forge (*https:// forge.puppetlabs.com/*).

The Puppet Forge provides an easy-to-use interface to search for and find Puppet modules provided by others. It is also the default repository used by the `puppet mod ule` command. Let's take a look at how to use it.

Start by opening a browser and going to *https://forge.puppetlabs.com/*. The very first thing you'll see is the search interface, as shown in Figure 12-1.

Figure 12-1. Puppet Forge search

Enter the name of an application you wish to manage with Puppet into the search interface, and you'll receive a list of modules that may do what you are looking for. For example, enter **apache** into the search query to see what modules exist to manage the Apache HTTPd server.

You can also search the Puppet Forge from the command line. For example, the following search will provide the same results:

```
$ puppet module search apache
Notice: Searching https://forgeapi.puppetlabs.com ...
NAME                DESCRIPTION                      AUTHOR
puppetlabs-apache   Installs, configures, and manages  ...  @puppetlabs
example42-apache    Puppet module for apache         @example42
evenup-apache       Manages apache including ajp proxy ...  @evenup
theforeman-apache   Apache HTTP server configuration   @theforeman
snip many other results
```

I have personally found the Puppet module command-line search useful when I am trying to remember the name of a module that I have already researched. However, the web interface provides a lot of useful information not available in the command-line output.

Public GitHub Repositories

Many people share their Puppet modules on GitHub. The following GitHub search will show you a significant number of modules that may not be found in the Puppet Forge: Search for "puppet" on GitHub (*https://github.com/search?q=puppet*).

A great many of the modules available on the Puppet Forge are also available on GitHub. If you click on the Project URL or Report Issues links in the Puppet Forge, the vast majority of the time you will find yourself on the GitHub repository for the module in question. If you need to report a problem or suggest an improvement to the module, you'll find yourself using GitHub extensively.

There are a number of reasons why authors may not have published modules available on GitHub to the Puppet Forge:

- They haven't prepared and documented the module appropriately for the Puppet Forge.
- They do not feel the module is appropriate or ready for general use.

- The module does not meet the licensing requirements for publication on the Puppet Forge. Be careful to read the license file provided by any module on GitHub!

Internal Repositories

If you work within a larger organization, you may also have an internal repository of modules. Depending on the software used to provide the forge, the web search interface will vary. However, you can use the stock `puppet module` command with any forge:

```
$ puppet module search --module_repository=http://forge.example.org/ apache
```

If you always or exclusively use the internal forge, you can add this parameter to your *puppet.conf* file to simplify command-line searches:

```
[main]
  module_repository = http://forge.example.org/
```

Evaluating Module Quality

While there are many high-quality modules on the Puppet Forge or GitHub, not all modules are created equal. It is best to examine the modules carefully before using them in your environment.

The Puppet Forge indicates some information about each entry on the right side of the page. It shows the results of both automated tests of the code base, and community feedback on the module (see Figure 12-2).

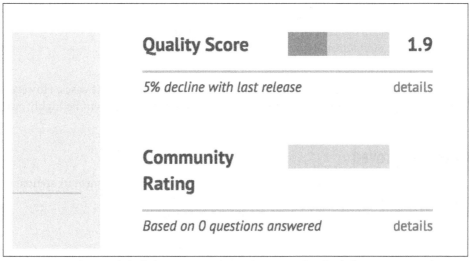

Figure 12-2. This module fails many automated tests, and nobody has commented on it

Let's review some ways to identify high-quality modules.

Puppet Supported

Puppet Supported modules are written and officially supported by Puppet Labs (see Figure 12-3).

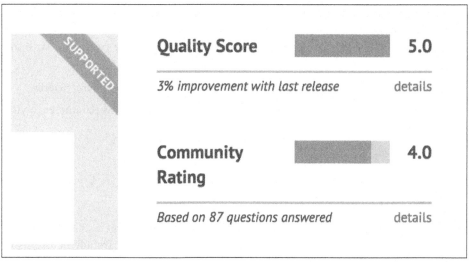

Figure 12-3. This module is fully supported by Puppet Labs

From "Puppet Supported Modules" (*http://bit.ly/1SYDnbR*) at the Puppet Forge:

> *Puppet Labs guarantees that each supported module:*
> - *has been tested with Puppet Enterprise*
> - *is subject to official Puppet Labs Puppet Enterprise support*
> - *will be maintained with bug or security patches as necessary*
> - *is tested on and ensured compatible with multiple platforms*

From personal experience, these modules work very well for base use cases. However, there are not very many Supported modules, and they tend not to handle highly customized situations.

Puppet Approved

Puppet Approved modules have been reviewed by Puppet Labs, and meet its standards for quality (see Figure 12-4).

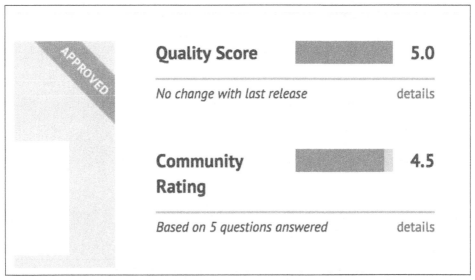

Figure 12-4. This module has been reviewed and approved by Puppet Labs

From "Puppet Approved Modules" (*http://bit.ly/1XACsOc*) at the Puppet Forge:

> *Puppet Labs ensures that Puppet Approved modules:*
>
> - *Solve a discrete automation challenge*
> - *Are developed in accordance with module best practices*
> - *Adhere to Puppet Labs' standards for style and design*
> - *Have accurate and thorough documentation to help you get started quickly*
> - *Are regularly maintained and versioned according to SemVer rules*
> - *Provide metadata including license, issues URL, and where to find source code*
> - *Do not deliberately inject malicious code or otherwise harm the system they're used with*

In my personal experience, all Puppet Approved modules have been high-quality modules. They have all been actively maintained, such that I have been consistently able to get minor problems fixed in a reasonable amount of time.

Quality Score

The *quality score* of a module, as shown in Figure 12-5, is the result of automated review and testing of the module.

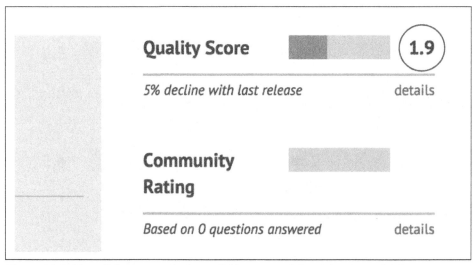

Figure 12-5. You might want to look carefully at a module with a score this low

You can see the test results by clicking on the "details" link, which is located underneath the rating (see Figure 12-6).

As you can see, the quality score is broken down into three tests:

- Code quality
- Puppet compatibility
- Metadata quality

README   Types   **Scores**

Have questions or feedback about our module scoring s

Quality Score: 4.0

Code Quality

Lint Results: 0 errors, 4 warnings, and 0 notices.

View full Code Quality results...

Puppet Compatibility

Syntax Checking: 0 errors, 0 warnings, and 4 notices.

View full Puppet Compatibility results...

Metadata Quality

Metadata Quality: 1 error, 2 warnings, and 2 notices.

View full Metadata Quality results...

Figure 12-6. A breakdown of the quality test results

Clicking on the "details" link may not produce a visible effect on small screens. Scroll down the page to see Scores displayed farther down the page on a laptop or mobile device.

The score breakdown provides you with a review of the issues found by each test, and a link to see detailed test results.

Community Rating

The final piece of data provided to you about a module is the *community rating* (see Figure 12-7). This provides feedback about what other users thought of the module.

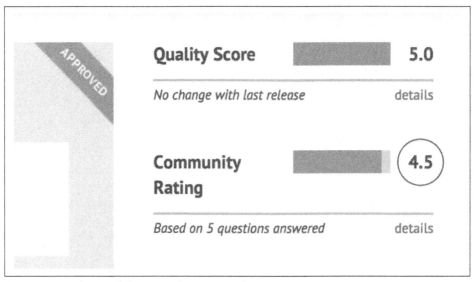

Figure 12-7. This module received a 4.5 out of 5 community rating

You can see details of the community rating by clicking on the "details" link. You can also scroll down and click Scores just below the module version. You'll find the community rating at the bottom, below the quality score (see Figure 12-8).

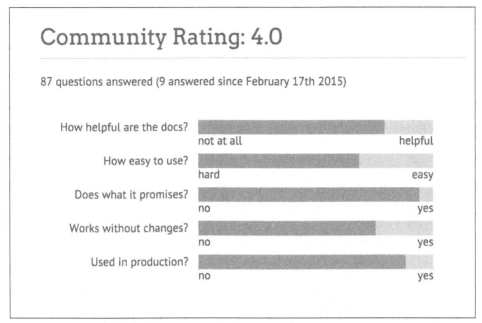

Community Rating: 4.0

87 questions answered (9 answered since February 17th 2015)

How helpful are the docs?
not at all   helpful

How easy to use?
hard   easy

Does what it promises?
no   yes

Works without changes?
no   yes

Used in production?
no   yes

Figure 12-8. Breakdown of community rating

As with the quality score, clicking on the "details" link may not produce a visible change on a smaller display. Scroll down to see the changes.

Installing Modules

You can install modules from the Puppet Forge, a private internal forge, or directly from the developer's code repository.

Installing from a Puppet Forge

The process for installing a module from the Puppet Forge (or an internal forge of your choice) is very simple. Let's go ahead and do this to install a very useful module that many other modules depend upon: the Puppet Supported `stdlib` module:

```
[vagrant@client ~]$ puppet module install puppetlabs-stdlib
Notice: Preparing to install into
  /etc/puppetlabs/code/environments/production/modules ...
Notice: Downloading from https://forgeapi.puppetlabs.com ...
Notice: Installing -- do not interrupt ...
/etc/puppetlabs/code/environments/production/modules
└── puppetlabs-stdlib (v4.8.0)
```

As you'll note, this command installed the module into the production environment. When testing this out, you should install it in the test environment instead:

```
[vagrant@client ~]$ puppet module install puppetlabs-stdlib --environment test
Notice: Preparing to install into
    /etc/puppetlabs/code/environments/test/modules ...
Notice: Downloading from https://forgeapi.puppetlabs.com ...
Notice: Installing -- do not interrupt ...
/etc/puppetlabs/code/environments/test/modules
└── puppetlabs-stdlib (v4.8.0)
```

 If you didn't set up the personal configuration file as discussed in "Running Puppet Without sudo" on page 33, then it will install the module in your personal ~/.puppetlabs/etc/code/modules directory. Add the --modulepath command-line option to place it in the system directory.

The test environment is an excellent place for you to examine the module and determine if it meets your needs. You can run tests to see if the module meets your needs, yet avoid the consequences of breaking production systems.

Once you decide that a module will do what you need, you can install this module in another environment by rerunning the puppet module command with the new environment, or simply moving the directory to that environment:

```
$ cd /etc/puppetlabs/code/environments
$ mv test/modules/stdlib production/modules/
```

Installing from GitHub

Sometimes you will find a module you'd like to use on GitHub, or perhaps you need to test bleeding-edge changes to the module without waiting for the author to update the Puppet Forge. If that's the case, then going straight to their source tree may be your best bet.

If you haven't installed Git already, you should do that now:

```
[vagrant@client ~]$ sudo yum install -y git
...snip...
Installed:
  git.x86_64 0:1.8.3.1-4.el7

Dependency Installed:
  libgnome-keyring.x86_64 0:3.8.0-3.el7   perl-Error.noarch 1:0.17020-2.el7
  perl-Git.noarch 0:1.8.3.1-4.el7         perl-TermReadKey.x86_64 0:2.30-20.el7
  rsync.x86_64 0:3.0.9-15.el7

Complete!
```

This allows us to pull directly from any Puppet module available in a Git repository. For example, if you'd like to get the latest changes to my MCollective module, you can install it from GitHub like so:

```
$ cd /etc/puppetlabs/code/environments/test/modules
$ git clone https://github.com/jorhett/puppet-mcollective mcollective
Initialized empty Git repository in
    /etc/puppetlabs/code/environments/test/modules/mcollective/.git/
remote: Counting objects: 183, done.
Receiving objects: 100% (183/183), 51.13 KiB, done.
remote: Total 183 (delta 0), reused 0 (delta 0), pack-reused 183
Resolving deltas: 100% (98/98), done.
```

Do read the instructions that come with the module. Some modules published on GitHub require steps to be taken before the module can be used successfully, and this module is no exception. Better yet, set it aside for now, as all of Chapter 30 is devoted to this module.

Testing a Single Module

To test a module, you will need to follow the instructions on the page where you found the module. In most situations, you will need to:

1. Declare the module's classes in the node definition.
2. Define Hiera data keys under the module's name.

Let's go through this process now. Start by installing and configuring the `puppetlabs-ntp` module. As this module will change system files, we'll need to run this as root so we must install the module in the systemwide module path:

```
[vagrant@client ~]$ cd /etc/puppetlabs/code/environments/test/modules
[vagrant@client modules]$ puppet module install --modulepath=. puppetlabs-ntp
Notice: Preparing to install into /etc/puppetlabs/code/environments/
    test/modules ...
Notice: Downloading from https://forgeapi.puppetlabs.com ...
Notice: Installing -- do not interrupt ...
/etc/puppetlabs/code/environments/test/modules
└─┬ puppetlabs-ntp (v3.3.0)
  └── puppetlabs-stdlib (v4.5.1)
```

If you look in the */etc/puppetlabs/code/environments/test/modules* directory now, you'll find both `ntp` and `stdlib` modules installed. The `puppet module install` command automatically installs all dependencies listed in the module's metadata.

Looking at the documentation at *puppetlabs/ntp* (*http://bit.ly/1XACRQt*) on the Puppet Forge, you'll find that this module can operate without any input data. It will define the configuration using module defaults. Let's try that out now:

```
$ sudo puppet apply --environment test --execute 'include ntp'
Notice: Compiled catalog for client.example.com in environment test
```

```
Notice: /Stage[main]/Ntp::Install/Package[ntp]/ensure: created
Notice: /Stage[main]/Ntp::Config/File[/etc/ntp.conf]/content: content changed
  '{md5}dc9e5754ad2bb6f6c32b954c04431d' to '{md5}ff26b20aa0c9fed35515afbcbf7190'
Notice: /Stage[main]/Ntp::Service/Service[ntp]/ensure:
  ensure changed 'stopped' to 'running'
Notice: Applied catalog in 11.77 seconds
```

As you can see, the module has modified the NTP configuration and started the NTP service. The module works!

Defining Config with Hiera

Now, let's say that you want to change the NTP configuration that the module generated. For instance, the NTP service was configured to only allow connections from localhost. Let's say we want to expand that to allow connections from other systems on the same LAN.

At this point, you need to define some test data in Hiera. Let's go ahead and open up the *common.yaml* file in the *hieradata/* directory:

```
[vagrant@client ~]$ $EDITOR /etc/puppetlabs/code/hieradata/common.yaml
```

Looking at the documentation at *puppetlabs/ntp* (*http://bit.ly/1XACRQt*) on the Puppet Forge, you'll find that this module's security can be changed by the restrict and interface parameters.

To provide data for a module's input, the data must be named modulename::param name. So start by defining the restrict and interface options in the YAML file:

```
---
ntp::interfaces:
ntp::restrict:
```

The documentation says that both of these parameters expect array values. Based on what you learned in "Configuring Hiera" on page 130, use leading dashes to indicate array values. Use single quotes to surround unparsed strings. So the input data for the ntp module would look like this:

```
---
# Data for the puppetlabs NTP module
#   which interfaces will accept connections
ntp::interfaces:
  - '127.0.0.1'
#   which nodes can connect
ntp::restrict:
  - 'default kod nomodify notrap nopeer noquery'
  - '-6 default kod nomodify notrap nopeer noquery'
  - '127.0.0.1'
  - '-6 ::1'
  - '192.168.250.0/24'
  - '-6 fe80::'
```

Let's make use of our host-level overrides and add some values specific to the *client* host. Add the following values to the */etc/puppetlabs/code/hieradata/hostname/client.yaml* file:

```
---
# Data for the puppetlabs NTP module
#   which interfaces will accept connections
ntp::interfaces:
  - '127.0.0.1'
  - '192.168.250.10'
```

Now that you've defined the input data, rerun Puppet to implement the changes:

```
$ sudo puppet apply --environment test --execute 'include ntp'
Notice: Compiled catalog for client.example.com in environment test
Notice: /Stage[main]/Ntp::Config/File[/etc/ntp.conf]/content: content changed
  '{md5}ff26b20aa0c9fed35515afbcbf7190' to '{md5}b751b9441d5057a503c13f5f5da3f1'
Notice: /Stage[main]/Ntp::Service/Service[ntp]: Triggered 'refresh' from 1 events
Notice: Applied catalog in 0.13 seconds
```

As you can see, Puppet has updated the configuration file and restarted the service. You can validate the changes by examining the revised */etc/ntp.conf*:

```
[vagrant@client ~]$ grep 192.168.250 /etc/ntp.conf
restrict 192.168.250.0/24
interface listen 192.168.250.10

[vagrant@client ~]$ grep listen /etc/ntp.conf
interface listen 127.0.0.1
interface listen 192.168.250.10
```

As this outputs shows, the array values from the hostname-specific file were used instead of the values from the common file to produce the list of interfaces that would accept connections.

Assigning Modules to Nodes

The modern, best-practice way to assign module classes to a node's run list is to define the classes within Hiera. This takes advantage of the Hiera hierarchy to customize the load list. Back in Chapter 10, we set up a manifest in each environment to load classes from Hiera, like so:

```
[vagrant@client modules]$ cat ../manifests/site.pp
# Look up all classes defined in Hiera and other data sources
lookup('classes', Array[String], 'unique').include
```

Using Hiera for Module Assignment

We should configure each environment to assign Puppet modules to your nodes from Hiera data.

To do this, we will create a simple manifest in each environment's *manifests/* directory. In older versions of Puppet, this file had to be named *manifests/site.pp*, but in Puppet 4 this can be any filename. I often name the file *manifests/hieraclasses.pp*, for example. We'll use the most common name for the following examples:

```
[vagrant@client ~]$ cd /etc/puppetlabs/code/environments
[vagrant@client ~]$ $EDITOR test/manifests/site.pp
```

Within this file, we are going to add a `lookup` of `classes` to be assigned to nodes:

```
notify { 'UsingTest':
  message => "Processing catalog from the Test environment.",
}

# Lookup all classes defined in Hiera and other data sources
lookup('classes', Array[String], 'unique').include
```

This statement will do a lookup in Hiera for module classes to be assigned to the node. Let's go ahead and add the same to the `production` environment:

```
[vagrant@client ~]$ cd /etc/puppetlabs/code/environments
[vagrant@client ~]$ $EDITOR production/manifests/site.pp
```

The entire contents of this file should be:

```
# Look up all classes defined in Hiera and other data sources
lookup('classes', Array[String], 'unique').include
```

Now that we have done this, we can assign classes using Hiera data.

Assigning Classes to Every Node

To assign the `ntp` module to be applied by Puppet to every node, edit the *common.yaml* file in the *hieradata/* directory:

```
[vagrant@client modules]$ $EDITOR /etc/puppetlabs/code/hieradata/common.yaml
```

Within this file, create a top-level key named `classes`. The first entry in that array should be the name of the class we want the node to apply:

```
---
classes:
  - 'ntp'
```

Now that the `ntp` module is listed in the class list, you can test the module by applying a manifest that includes Hiera classes, such as the one we just created:

```
[vagrant@client modules]$ sudo puppet apply --environment test ../manifests/
Notice: Compiled catalog for client.example.com in environment test
Notice: Finished catalog run in 0.14 seconds
```

Wait, what happened? This time it didn't do anything. That's because the module is properly *idempotent*. The configuration hasn't changed and the service is still running, so no changes were necessary.

Let's give the ntp module something to do by stopping the service:

```
[vagrant@client modules]$ sudo systemctl stop ntpd
[vagrant@client modules]$ sudo puppet apply --environment test ../manifests/
Notice: Compiled catalog for client.example.com in environment test
Notice: /Stage[main]/Ntp::Service/Service[ntp]/ensure:
    ensure changed 'stopped' to 'running'
```

Altering the Class List per Node

You may want to run Puppet agent on every node, but only run the Puppet server on the puppetserver node. For that you would define your Hiera data as follows.

Place the following classes in the */etc/puppetlabs/code/hieradata/common.yaml* file:

```
---
classes:
  - ntp
  - puppet::agent
```

Now, let's set up an override for the puppetserver node. Create the file */etc/puppet-labs/code/hieradata/hostname/puppetserver.yaml* with the following:

```
---
classes:
  - puppet::server
```

Class assignment is always done as an array merge, so every value in the classes array will be merged together from each level of the hierarchy.

With this configuration, every node will apply the ntp and puppet::agent classes, while the puppetserver node will also apply the puppet::server class.

Avoiding Node Assignments in Manifests

If you used Puppet version 2 or older, you had no choice but to create explicit node assignments in the *manifests/site.pp* file. If you wanted to apply a list of classes to similar nodes, you were forced to create node assignments that inherited from other node assignments:

```
node 'puppetserver' inherits default {
  class { 'puppet::server': }
}
node 'webserver' inherits default {
  class { 'apache': }
```

```
  }
node default {
  class { 'ntp': }
  class { 'puppet::agent': }
}
```

If you have managed a diverse group of nodes, you know exactly how convoluted and confusing those inherited relationships could easily become. These inheritances were linear top to bottom, which meant that duplicate data was required for any slight variance in configuration:

```
node 'webserver' inherits 'web-server' {
  class { 'apache':
    'modules' => 'fail2ban'
  }
}
node 'passenger-host' inherits 'web-server' {
  class { 'apache':
    'modules' => 'passenger'
  }
}
```

With a single parameter difference, we have eight lines of code in node assignments. In large environments, this quickly devolved into a maintenance nightmare of node assignments and inheritance. When combined with altering the modules available in different environments, managing module assignment consistently went from impractical to implausible.

The ability to look up classes from data has completely solved that problem. You can now assign classes to nodes based on lookups of the class list from a flexible data hierarchy.

Classic node assignment and inheritance were still supported but deprecated with warnings in Puppet 3. Node assignment remains possible in Puppet 4, but node inheritance has been completely removed. There is simply no reason to use the preceding nightmare syntax when you can completely replace it with something as simple as a Hiera file loaded by all web servers:

```
classes:
  - apache

apache::modules:
  - passenger
```

Upgrading from Puppet 2 or 3

If you have one of these nightmare *site.pp/* files, you may be wondering how to do the upgrade. There's no simple conversation script, but I have some advice for how to do this.

 If you don't have older versions of Pupppet installed, you can skip this section and go straight to "Examining a Module" on page 158.

Take apart each block of your node assignments and create a separate file for each one in the *hieradata/* directory, using the following strategy:

1. Place everything from the *default* node into *common.yaml*.
2. Place everything that matched only a single host into a file named for that node, such as *hostname/web01.yaml* or *fqdn/web01.example.com.yaml*.
3. Place everything that was applied to a group of nodes into a unique file for that role, such as *role/frontend.yaml* and *role/passengerhost.yaml*.

It is best to utilize node facts or configuration values that will properly identify a node. This will work the best and be the easiest to maintain. But if you have to do it based on node name, either of the following changes to your manifest will work.

If your nodes are named such that you can derive a role from their name, set a variable based on their name and use that to include the right file. For example, if servers are uniformly named by their role and a number (e.g., *frontend01*), the following regex can derive the role name for you:

```
# manifests/site.pp
if( $facts['hostname'] =~ /^/^([a-z]+)(\d+)/ ) {/ {
  $node_role = $1
  $node_number = $2
}

# Lookup all classes defined in Hiera and other data sources
lookup('classes', Array[String], 'unique').include
```

Alter your Hiera hierarchy to load the appropriate files for each role, like so:

```
:hierarchy:
  - "hostname/%{facts.hostname}"
  - "role/%{::node_role}"
  - "os/%{facts.osfamily}"
  - common
```

If the assignment isn't so straightforward, you can set the role with if/else assignments, like so:

```
# manifests/site.pp
if( $facts['hostname'] =~ /^web/ {
  $node_role = 'frontend'
}
elsif( $facts['hostname'] =~ /^rails/ {
  $node_role = 'passengerhost'
}

# Look up all classes defined in Hiera and other data sources
lookup('classes', Array[String], 'unique').include
```

 if/else is a hack. It's a quick slash-burn to help you upgrade fast. Once you get past the initial need, develop more intelligent node classification using node facts.

These examples will grant all the advantages of the Hiera hierarchy for parameters. This allows you to remove many lines of redundant parameter assignments.

As you learn more about module development, you'll learn how to create and utilize facts based on node data. With good definitions of custom facts for your nodes, you can avoid this if/else nonsense entirely.

Examining a Module

Regardless of the quality score or community rating given to a module, it is always best to examine modules carefully to ensure they will work well in your environment. Badly written modules can create unintended chaos when put into use within your existing module space.

Here is a short list of items to check in the code base to determine if the module will work well for you:

OS support
    May not support your operating system properly.

Module namespace
    May require dependency modules named the same as modules you use.

Environment assumptions
    May enforce local assumptions that won't work in your environment.

Sloppy code
    Could require or overwrite global variables.

Resource namespace

    Could use simple resource titles that conflict with others used already.

Greedy collectors

    Could utilize collectors that accidentally grab unrelated resources.

You should also utilize the preceding list when building your own modules.

Reviewing Modules

In this chapter, we have reviewed the installation, configuration, testing, and execution of a module from the Puppet Forge. You have now completed all of these steps:

1. Set up the directory environments `test` and `production`.
2. Installed the `puppetlabs-ntp` module and its dependency into the `test` environment.
3. Configured the `ntp` module using Hiera configuration data based on instructions from the module.
4. Applied the module to configure and run the NTP service on our system.

In summary, you have done everything necessary to install, evaluate, and use a module from the Puppet Forge.

## CHAPTER 13

Designing a Custom Module

In this chapter, we will review the process of creating a custom module. We will cover each step from the beginning, including:

1. Naming a module properly
2. Generating an empty module skeleton
3. Writing the base manifest
4. Identifying files to be copied to the node
5. Creating templates to customize files on the node
6. Testing that the module works as expected

Let's get started.

Choosing a Module Name

A module can have any name that begins with a letter and contains only lowercase letters, numbers, underscores. A hyphen is not allowed within a module name. Here are some valid and invalid module names:

```
mymodule      Valid
3files        Invalid
busy_people   Valid
busy-people   Invalid
```

It is important to choose your module name carefully to avoid conflicts with other modules. As each module creates its own namespace, only one module may exist within a Puppet catalog with a given name at the same time. For most intents and purposes, this means that you can never use two modules with the same name.

When naming modules, I try to avoid naming the module anything that conflicts with a module name available in the Puppet Forge. I never know when another team might utilize that module for its project, or when a module I download might use the Puppet Forge module as a dependency.

 It's possible to manage conflicting module names by utilizing them within separate environments. We'll cover how to do this in Chapter 29.

Avoiding Reserved Names

Some namespaces are internal to and used by Puppet itself. For this reason, you can never create a module with these names:

`main`   This class contains any resources not contained by any other class.

`facts`   This namespace contains facts provided by the node's Puppet agent.

`server_facts`   This namespace contains server-side facts supplied by the Puppet server.

`settings`   This namespace contains the Puppet configuration settings.

`trusted`   This namespace contains facts taken from the client's certificate, as signed by the Puppet certificate authority.

Generating a Module Skeleton

Puppet will generate an empty skeleton for you with the `puppet module generate` command. As mentioned at the start of the book, your first module will manage the Puppet agent itself. Let's create that now. Use your own name or organization name instead of *myorg*.

When you generate a module, it will ask you a number of questions. Default values used if you just press Enter are included in square brackets after each question:

```
$ puppet module generate myorg-puppet
We need to create a metadata.json file for this module.  Please answer the
following questions; if the question is not applicable to this module, feel free
to leave it blank.

Puppet uses Semantic Versioning (semver.org) to version modules.
What version is this module?  [0.1.0]
-->
```

After you have answered all of the questions, it will generate the module in your current directory:

```
Notice: Generating module at /home/vagrant/puppet...
Notice: Populating templates...
Finished; module generated in puppet.
puppet/manifests
puppet/manifests/init.pp
puppet/spec
puppet/spec/classes
puppet/spec/classes/init_spec.rb
puppet/spec/spec_helper.rb
puppet/tests
puppet/tests/init.pp
puppet/Gemfile
puppet/Rakefile
puppet/README.md
puppet/metadata.json
```

If you prefer to skip the questions and edit the file yourself, add `--skip-interview` to the command line.

Modifying the Default Skeleton

After you've been creating modules for a while, you may want to tune the default module skeleton to add things you want in your modules. You do so by placing your revised skeleton in the *~/.puppetlabs/opt/puppet/cache/puppet-module/skeleton* directory.

Previous versions of Puppet used the *~/.puppet/var/puppet-module/skeleton* directory. You'll need to copy any existing skeleton to the new directory:

```
$ mkdir -p ~/.puppetlabs/opt/puppet/cache/puppet-module/
$ cd ~/.puppetlabs/opt/puppet/cache/puppet-module/
$ cp -r ~/.puppet/var/puppet-module/skeleton ./
```

You can also find enhanced module skeletons that others have created. There are skeletons that include better test suites, and skeletons that include common examples for different application environments. You can find Puppet module skeletons by searching for "puppet skeleton" on GitHub (*http://bit.ly/1R4Q8iL*).

You can install multiple skeletons in a directory of your choice, and select one for the module you will be building like so:

```
$ puppet module --module_skeleton_dir=~/skels/rails-app generate myorg-railsapp
```

Understanding Module Structure

Let's review the files and directories created in your new module. All of the following files are fixed, unchangeable paths built into Puppet's expectations and utilization of modules:

manifests/	Directory where code manifests (classes) are read.
files/	Directory containing files served by your module.
templates/	Directory containing templates parsed for custom files.
lib/	Directory containing Ruby facts or functions.
specs/	Directory containing unit tests to validate the manifests.
tests/	Directory containing system tests to validate the manifests.
facts.d/	Directory containing external facts to be distributed.
metadata.json	File containing version and module dependencies.

Installing the Module

To test the module, we'll have to place it somewhere that Puppet can find it. While developing a new module, it is easiest to simply move the directory into a test environment's $modulepath:

```
[vagrant@client ~]$ cd /etc/puppetlabs/code/environments/test/modules
[vagrant@client modules]$ mv ~/puppet ./
```

Now that the module is in place, add it to classes for the host you are going to test it on:

```
[vagrant@client ~]$ $EDITOR /etc/puppetlabs/code/hieradata/hostname/client.yaml
```

Add this file to the classes loaded by your test node:

```
---
classes:
  - puppet
```

When you apply the test environment to the *client* node, this class will be included. This allows for testing the module in isolation.

Creating a Class Manifest

Let's start within the *manifests/* directory of your module. In this directory, you will find a single file named *init.pp*. This file must exist within every Puppet module, and it must contain the definition for the *base class*. The base class is a class with the same name as the module. Let's take a look at that now:

```
[vagrant@client modules]$ cd puppet/manifests
[vagrant@client manifests]$ cat init.pp
class puppet {

}
```

Right now this class has no definition. That is an acceptable situation—the class must be defined, but it doesn't have to do anything. We'll flesh it out in the very next section, after we discuss the difference between a class and a manifest.

You will observe that the file contains a documentation template above this class definition. Ignore this for now. We'll cover creating and updating module documentation in Chapter 16.

What Is a Class?

In Part I of the book, you created and applied Puppet manifests. Here's a brief summary to refresh your memory:

- Manifests use Puppet configuration language to define configuration policy
- Manifests contain resources that describe how their target type should be configured
- Manifests execute immediately with the `puppet apply` command

The good news for you is that a *class* is a manifest with special properties. It uses Puppet configuration language to declare resources exactly the same as in a manifest. This means that if you know how to write a manifest, then you know how to write a class.

Before we get started, let's quickly review the special properties that make a class different from a manifest. A class is different in the following ways:

- A class is a manifest that can be called by name.
- A class has a *namespace* or variable scope of the same name.
- A class is not used until called by name.
- A class may include or be included by other modules.
- A class may be passed parameters when called.

Declaring Class Resources

As we mentioned previously, class manifests are almost exactly like the manifests you used with `puppet apply`. I am sure that you remember (if not, flip back to "Referring to Resources" on page 94) the resources declared to install a package and start a service. Go ahead and fill in the class manifest with those resources right now.

The manifest should look something like this:

```
class puppet {
  # Install the Puppet agent
  package { 'puppet-agent':
    ensure => 'latest',
    notify => Service['puppet'],
  }

  # Manage the Puppet service
  service { 'puppet':
    ensure    => 'running',
    enable    => true,
    subscribe => Package['puppet-agent'],
  }
}
```

This is very similar to the package and service manifest built out earlier in the book. As per best practice, we have defined dependencies to ensure that the service is restarted if the package is updated.

Let's apply the test environment to the node now for our first test of the module:

```
[vagrant@client modules]$ puppet apply --environment test ../manifests/
Notice: Compiled catalog for client.example.com in environment test
Notice: Applied catalog in 0.02 seconds
```

Accepting Input

Let's define parameters your Puppet module will accept. Adjust the *init.pp* file to look something like this:

```
class puppet(
  # input parameters and default values for the class
  $version = 'latest',
  $status  = 'running',
  $enabled,                # required parameter
) {

  # echo the input provided
  notice("Install the $version version of Puppet,
    ensure it's $status, and set boot time start $enabled.")
}
```

Here we have declared three input parameters. Two of them have default values, which will only be used if input is not provided when the class is called. The third value enabled is required, and will generate an error if a value is not provided.

Puppet 4.3 introduced a tiered, pluggable approach to data access called *Puppet Lookup*. Classes can now receive parameter input from three possible places. If the data is not available in the first place, it looks in the next according to the following flow:

Parameter values can be explicitly passed when the class is declared
> You can define parameters to pass when declaring classes in a manifest, or the output of an external node classifier (ENC). Using resource definitions to declare classes in manifests was the only available method prior to data lookups from Hiera, and dominates the older documentation available on the Internet.

Parameter values will be looked up in the data providers (Hiera, environment, module)
> This is the most practical way to assign values. The key will be searched for in the global data provider (Hiera v3) followed by the environment and module data providers (if defined). The results from the first data source that contains the key will be returned.

Default values can be supplied in the class definition
> The Puppet Style Guide requires that every class should include default values that provide the most common use case.

Let's go ahead and test our new module to ensure the default values work as expected:

```
$ puppet apply --environment test ../manifests/
Error: Evaluation Error: Error while evaluating a Function Call,
  Must pass enabled to Class[Puppet]
  at /etc/puppetlabs/code/environments/test/manifests/site.pp:2:1
```

Whoops! That's right, we made the `enabled` parameter required. However, we have not provided a value for this key in any data provider (Hiera is the only one enabled by default). This is one of the reasons that the Puppet Style Guide recommends supplying defaults for all parameters.

Best Practice

Provide every parameter with a default value that will implement the most common use case.

Adjust the module to provide a default value and try again:

```
class puppet(
  $version = 'latest',
  $status  = 'running',
  $enabled = true,

$ puppet apply --environment test ../manifests/
Notice: Scope(Class[Puppet]): Install the latest version of Puppet,
    ensure it's running, and set boot time start true.
Notice: Compiled catalog for client.example.com in environment test
Notice: Applied catalog in 0.02 seconds
```

As you can see, the module will apply properly without any parameters provided.

Sharing Files

You're probably thinking that this manifest isn't sufficient. One can't generally install and run software without configuring it. I agree. Let's add a configuration file.

The first step is to create a directory in which to store files. A module's files must reside in a *files/* directory within the module. You can add subdirectories to organize files:

```
$ cd /etc/puppetlabs/code/environments/test/modules/puppet
$ mkdir files
```

Let's copy our existing *puppet.conf* configuration file to that directory to test out the concept:

```
$ cp /etc/puppetlabs/puppet/puppet.conf files/
$ $EDITOR files/puppet.conf
```

Let's make a small change to Puppet's configuration. Add the following line to make the logging a bit more verbose:

```
[main]
    log_level = notice
```

Now we'll add a `file` resource to the class manifest. Instead of using the `content` attribute, we'll use a `source` attribute. Files specified by this attribute are copied intact to the node. Add the resource to *manifests/init.pp*:

```
file { '/etc/puppetlabs/puppet/puppet.conf':
  ensure => file,
  owner  => 'root',
  group  => 'wheel',
  mode   => '0644',
  source => 'puppet:///modules/puppet/puppet.conf',
}
```

There are three valid URIs for use as file sources:

- `puppet:///modules/module_name/filename`
- `file:///path/to/file/on/local/system`
- `http:` or `https://web-server/filename` (new in Puppet 4.4)

> Downloading files over http/https only works well if you add this attribute to the file resource, as remote web servers don't provide file checksums:
>
> ```
> checksum => 'mtime'
> ```

The best practice is to store all files used by a module within the module, and use the preceding `puppet:///` URI pattern. Leaving the server field in the URI blank indicates to download the file from the Puppet server the agent is currently talking to. This same URI also works seamlessly with `puppet apply` to get the module files from `modulepath` on the local system.

The path */modules/puppet* is a special path that maps to the *files/* directory in the puppet module.

Best Practice

Avoid specifying an explicit Puppet server in the URI source for a file, as the module will fail if any node doesn't have direct access to that server. Synchronize the dependent files to all Puppet servers that serve the module.

You can specify an array of file sources. Puppet will go through the array of sources and use the first file it finds.

It is possible to source files that are not within a module from the Puppet server. However, this practice is deprecated and not recommended for many good reasons, so I am not going to cover it.

Best Practice

Place files in the same module as the manifests that use the files.

Testing File Synchronization

Let's stop and test the file copy feature before we proceed. You should see something like this:

```
[vagrant@client test]$ sudo puppet apply --environment test manifests/
Notice: Compiled catalog for client.example.com in environment test
Notice: /Stage[main]/Puppet/File[/etc/puppetlabs/puppet/puppet.conf]/content:
  content changed '{md5}2c15ae72acdbd8878a6550275bc15fef'
            to '{md5}b0547c4cf4cc5a5cb7aee439765f82a4'
Notice: /Stage[main]/Puppet/File[/etc/puppetlabs/puppet/puppet.conf]/owner:
  owner changed 'vagrant' to 'root'
Notice: /Stage[main]/Puppet/File[/etc/puppetlabs/puppet/puppet.conf]/group:
  group changed 'vagrant' to 'wheel'
Notice: Applied catalog in 0.37 seconds
```

View the contents of the file, and you'll find that it has copied the file exactly.

One of the things changed by our `file` resource was the permissions of the file. You may want to change them back for convenience while learning:

```
$ chown vagrant:vagrant /etc/puppetlabs/puppet/puppet.conf
$ chmod 0664 /etc/puppetlabs/puppet/puppet.conf
```

Alternatively, you could change the owner and group attributes and run Puppet again.

You can use `puppet filebucket` to restore the file. First, query the filename to get the most recent hash, and then supply the hash to the `restore` command:

```
$ sudo puppet filebucket -l list | grep puppet.conf
c15ae72acdbd8878a6550275bc 2015-09-07 03:58:51 /etc/puppetlabs/puppet/puppet.conf
8c1fd25aed09e7b2c8cfc3b0eb 2015-09-07 08:36:39 /etc/puppetlabs/puppet/puppet.conf
bc1a4e205b7e2ec921fee7380d 2015-09-07 08:50:34 /etc/puppetlabs/puppet/puppet.conf

$ sudo puppet filebucket restore \
    /etc/puppetlabs/puppet/puppet.conf c15ae72acdbd8878a6550275bc
```

Synchronizing Directories

The file resource has optional `recurse` and `purge` attributes that make it possible to synchronize a directory of files:

```
file { '/tmp/sync/':
  ensure  => directory,
  owner   => 'root',
  group   => 'wheel',
  mode    => '0444',
  recurse => true,   # go into subdirectories
  replace => true,   # replace any files that already exist
  purge   => false,  # don't remove files that we don't have
  links   => follow, # follow symbolic links and modify the link target
  force   => false,
  source  => 'puppet:///modules/puppet/sync/',
}
```

As you can see, there are many parameters for controlling how files are installed, and under what situations they will replace other files. You can find detailed explanations for these attributes at "Puppet 4 Type Reference: file" (*http://bit.ly/1UmYB4r*) on the Puppet docs site.

Avoid Synchronizing Large Files

In my experience, Puppet is not well suited for synchronizing very large files or directories. It works well for small trees of configuration or data files. It can be painfully slow for synchronizing large directories or files greater than 100 megabytes.

Synchronize large files and directories using utilities designed for efficiency. Tools like `rsync`, `unison`, `wget --mirror`, and for some purposes `git` can be significantly faster.

Parsing Templates

I imagine you're saying to yourself, "Not every system will get the same configuration." Good point! Let's build a customized template for this configuration file.

Create a directory in which to store templates. Like files, templates have their own directory in the module structure:

```
$ cd /etc/puppetlabs/code/environments/test/modules/puppet
$ mkdir templates
```

The template we are going to build will utilize four variables. Let's build a manifest that supplies those variables. First, let's modify the module input to set default values for each of these variables:

```
class puppet(
  $version          = 'latest',
  $status           = 'running',
  $enabled          = true,
  $server           = 'puppet.example.com',
  $common_loglevel = 'warning',
  $agent_loglevel  = undef,
  $apply_loglevel  = undef,
) {
```

With this declaration, we now have seven parameters in our class that we can use in a template. You'll notice that we explicitly set the agent and apply log levels to an undefined value. We'll use these only if values are passed in when the class is declared. (If we left out a default value, then the parameters would be required, which is the opposite of our intention.)

There are two different template parsers within Puppet:

- Puppet EPP templates use Puppet variables and Puppet functions.
- Ruby ERB templates use Ruby language and functions.

It doesn't matter which one you use, so we'll teach you to use each of these.

Common Syntax

Both Puppet EPP and Ruby ERB files are plain-text files that contain some common syntax and template tags. Outside of these tags is normal, unprocessed text. Within the tags are Puppet or Ruby variables and code:

`<%= variable or code %>`	This tag is replaced with the value of the variable, or result of the code.
`<% code block %>`	The code is executed. Nothing is returned unless the code prints output.
`<%# a comment %>`	This tag is removed from the output.
`<% code block -%>`	Immediately trailing newlines or whitespace is removed. Use to prevent blank lines.

`<%- code block %>`	Leading newlines or whitespace is removed. Use when indenting template tags.
`<%= variable or code -%>`	Removes trailing whitespace after the result of the code. (There is no option for trimming leading whitespace.)
`<%%` `%%>`	Double percent signs are replaced with a single percent sign. Use to prevent interpolation.

Don't worry about memorizing these patterns. These tags will be used extensively in the next few pages, and you'll get to see them applied in context.

Using Puppet EPP Templates

Adjust the file declaration from the previous section to remove the `source` attribute and replace it with a `content` attribute. The content will be provided by the `epp()` function:

```
file { '/etc/puppetlabs/puppet/puppet.conf':
  ensure  => ensure,
  owner   => 'root',
  group   => 'wheel',
  mode    => '0644',
  content => epp('puppet/puppet.conf.epp'),
}
```

The `epp()` function takes a two arguments:

URI of the Puppet EPP template
> The format of that URI is always `puppet:///modulename/filename.epp`. The file should be placed in the *templates/* directory of the module. Puppet EPP templates should end with the *.epp* extension to indicate that the file contains tags for the Puppet EPP template processor.

A hash of parameters for input
> An optional hash of input parameters for the template, described in "Providing parameters" on page 173.

Let's create a template file. From within the module directory, invoke your editor like so:

```
[vagrant@client puppet]$ $EDITOR templates/puppet.conf.epp
```

The template should look something like this:

```
# Generated by Puppet EPP template processor
[master]
    log_level = <%= $::puppet::common_loglevel %>

# This is used by "puppet agent"
[agent]
<% if $puppet::agent_loglevel != undef { -%>
    log_level = <%= $::puppet::agent_loglevel %>
```

```
<% } -%>
    server = <%= $::puppet::server %>

# This is used for "puppet apply"
[user]
<% if $puppet::apply_loglevel != undef { -%>
    log_level = <%= $::puppet::apply_loglevel %>
<% } -%>
```

This example utilizes four variables. Each instance of `<%= $::class::variable %>` is replaced with the Puppet variable from that class. We added those variables to the manifest as our very first step.

In this declaration, the `epp()` function processes the EPP template and provides the content to be placed in the file. It does this by replacing the variable lookups in the file we created with variables from the current variable scope (within this class).

Go ahead and test this change right now with `puppet apply`. You will see the contents of the Puppet configuration file get updated:

```
[vagrant@client test]$ sudo puppet apply --environment test manifests/
Info: Applying configuration version '1441617320'
Info: Computing checksum on file /etc/puppetlabs/puppet/puppet.conf
Info: /Stage[main]/Puppet/File[/etc/puppetlabs/puppet/puppet.conf]: Filebucketed
  /etc/puppetlabs/puppet/puppet.conf to puppet with sum 1698e7d7bfb88eace241ca
Notice: /Stage[main]/Puppet/File[/etc/puppetlabs/puppet/puppet.conf]/content:
  changed '{md5}1698e7d7bfb88eace241ca' to '{md5}ae81b356db7fcf0846901d'
Notice: Applied catalog in 0.35 seconds
```

EPP templates can do far more than variable replacement. You can put any Puppet function within `<% ... %>` tags without the equals sign. Here's an example that uses conditional evaluation to limit duplicate assignment of log levels that aren't different:

```
[user]
<% if $::puppet::apply_loglevel != undef and
      $::puppet::apply_loglevel != $::puppet::common_loglevel { -%>
    log_level = <%= $::puppet::apply_loglevel %>
<% } -%>
```

By placing this line of output within the Puppet `if` condition, we ensure that the line will only be output if both conditions match. This will avoid outputting the configuration line if the log level matches the main log level, thus simplifying the configuration file.

Providing parameters

It was pretty annoying to have to list the fully qualified name of each variable, wasn't it? You can simplify the variable naming by providing a hash of input parameters for the template. This is very useful when the Puppet variable names don't match the variable names used in the template. For example:

```
content => epp('puppet:///puppet/puppet.conf.epp', {
  'server'          => $server,
  'common_loglevel' => $common_loglevel,
  'agent_loglevel'  => $agent_loglevel,
  'apply_loglevel'  => $apply_loglevel,
}),
```

When providing parameter input, make sure the very first line of the template contains the following special syntax for accepting the variables:

```
<%- | String $server,
      String $common_loglevel,
      Optional['String'] $agent_loglevel = undef,
      Optional['String'] $apply_loglevel = undef,
| -%>
```

This input format exactly matches the input assignments used for class parameters, where the `server` and `common_loglevel` values are required to be provided, while the other log-level parameters are optional.

The hash of values passed to a template must match the definition at the top of the template. If it doesn't supply all required values, an error will be issued. If it supplies too many values, a different error will be issued.

 Best Practice

Always place the parameters you will use in the template at the top, and send them explicitly when declaring the template file in your manifest. This ensures the greatest readability. A reader can identify the origin of all template values from the manifest source.

Iterating over values with EPP

You can use any Puppet function within the template tags. By far the most common operation to perform within a template is to iterate through some values.

Here's an example where we use the `reduce()` function to iterate through an array of tags used to limit the resources applied. This example uses the `sprintf()` function creatively to add commas between values:

```
[agent]
    tags = <%= $taglist.reduce |$tags,$tagname| {
      sprintf("%s,%s", $tags, $tagname)
    } -%>
```

This iteration function was used as shown in "Looping Through Iterations" on page 72.

Learning more about EPP

EPP templates are new and thus only modules designed for Puppet 4 will use them.

Complete documentation for EPP templates is available at "Puppet Functions: epp" (*http://bit.ly/1TUkQyL*) on the Puppet docs site.

Using Ruby ERB Templates

Although EPP modules are superior, modules that provide backward compatibility for earlier versions of Puppet may need to utilize ERB templates.

Remove the epp() function and replace it with a template() function. Rename the file to use an *.erb* extension:

```
file { '/etc/puppetlabs/puppet/puppet.conf':
  ensure  => ensure,
  owner   => 'root',
  group   => 'wheel',
  mode    => '0644',
  content => template('puppet/puppet.conf.erb'),
}
```

Similar to the epp() function, the template() function takes a single argument: the URI of the ERB template.

Let's create the ERB template file. The template should be placed in the *templates/* directory of the module. ERB templates should end with the *.erb* extension to indicate that the file contains tags for the ERB template processor:

```
[vagrant@client puppet]$ $EDITOR templates/puppet.conf.erb
```

Accessing Puppet variables with ERB

Similar to the EPP example, we'll utilize the values of Puppet variables to customize the file. Each instance of <%= @variable %> is replaced with the value of the Puppet variable named after the @ sign. Unlike EPP, there is not an explicit list of variables for the template. The variables accessed with the @ prefix must exist in the same scope (e.g., within the module class) as the template declaration.

The contents of the file should look like this:

```
# Generated by Puppet ERB template processor
[main]
    log_level = <%= @common_loglevel %>

# This is used by "puppet agent"
[agent]
<% if @agent_loglevel -%>
    log_level = <%= @agent_loglevel %>
```

```
<% end -%>
    server = <%= @server -%>

# This is used for "puppet apply"
[user]
<% if @apply_loglevel -%>
    log_level = <%= @apply_loglevel %>
<% end -%>
```

Look up variables from another class using the `scope.lookupvar()` function, or use `scope[]` as if it were a hash. For example, if we wanted to look up the log level used by MCollective, either of the following would work:

```
loglevel = <%= scope.lookupvar('mcollective::loglevel') -%>
loglevel = <%= scope['::mcollective::loglevel'] -%>
```

Best Practice

Avoid looking up data outside the module within a template, as it hides the external dependency from a code review of the manifest. Instead, lookup the data within the manifest and provide the data to the template in variables.

Call Puppet functions using `scope.function_puppet_function()`. For example, you could call the `fqdn_rand()` function to produce a random number based on the node's hostname:

```
server = <%= scope.function_fqdn_rand( 3600 ) -%>
```

As ERB templates were intended for inline Ruby development, you can put any Ruby statement within `<% ... %>` tags without the equals sign. Here's an example that would limit duplicate assignment of the same log level:

```
[user]
<% if @apply_loglevel != @loglevel -%>
  log_level = <%= @apply_loglevel %>
<% end -%>
```

By wrapping this line of the template within the Ruby block, it will skip the output line if the log level matches the main log level, thus simplifying the configuration file output.

Go ahead and test this change right now with `puppet apply`. You will see the contents of the Puppet configuration file get updated.

Iterating over values with ERB

Here's an example where we use the Ruby `each()` function to iterate through an array of tags, which can be used to limit the resources evaluated. This example uses the dash creatively to suppress line feeds and output tags as a single comma-separated value:

```
[agent]
    tags = <%= tags = ''; @taglist.each do |tagname|
        tags += tagname + ','
      end
      tags.chop # remove trailing comma
    %>
```

You'll note that we don't put an @ sign before the variable name. That is because we are not referencing a variable in the Puppet module class, but instead from the local loop shown in this example.

Learning more about ERB

More documentation for using ERB templates with Puppet can be found at "Embedded Ruby (ERB) Template Syntax" (*http://bit.ly/1SYDfct*) on the Puppet docs site.

ERB is commonly used by Ruby in many other situations, so you can find advice and help for using ERB syntax with any search engine.

Creating Readable Templates

Notice that both the original template and the preceding block sometimes utilize a leading dash in the closure: -%>. The dash tells the interpreter to suppress an immediately following line feed. This is commonly used to keep comments or Ruby statements from adding blank lines to the output, but can also be used to concatenate two sequential lines.

You want to avoid trimming whitespace with the dash if that is the end of the line, or two lines will be joined together.

Best Practice

Use Puppet EPP templates with Puppet configuration language in both the manifests and the templates. Specify parameters for the template explicitly for clarity and readability.

I cannot emphasize the preceding suggestion strongly enough. I can't tell you how many hours I have spent searching through manifests to determine where a variable used in a template was sourced from.

Testing the Module

Now that we have created the resources, and defined our Hiera data, it's time to test the module. We expect to see all the resources change status:

```
$ puppet apply --environment test ../manifests/
Notice: Compiled catalog for client.example.com in environment test
Notice: /Stage[main]/Puppet/Service[puppet]/ensure:
  ensure changed 'running' to 'stopped'
Notice: /Stage[main]/Puppet/Service[puppet]/enable:
  enable changed 'true' to 'false'
Notice: Applied catalog in 31.98 seconds
```

If you don't see any of the above, it could be that the services are already configured that way (no changes) or that the values weren't defined in Hiera correctly.

You can easily test this by changing the Hiera file and observing the change in output. For example, if you set `enabled` to `true`, you should get the following output when reapplying the class:

```
$ puppet apply --environment test ../manifests/
Notice: Compiled catalog for client.example.com in environment test
Notice: /Stage[main]/Puppet/Service[puppet]/enable:
  enable changed 'false' to 'true'
Notice: Applied catalog in 0.35 seconds
```

Peeking Beneath the Hood

In this section, we're going to talk about peeking beneath the hood: looking at variables and resources in other classes.

 Best Practice

Don't use the techniques described here for anything other than debugging.

Environments are strict. You cannot see data or code that is not loaded in your active environment.

Within an environment, class boundaries are not enforced. You can access both variables and resources in other classes. Here's an example:

```
class other_class( $idea = 'games!' ) {
  $sentence = "an idea: ${idea}"
  notify { 'announcement': message => "I have ${sentence}" }
}

class my_class {
  # I can see the other class parameter
  notice( "The idea was: ${Class['other_class']['idea']}" )

  # I can see the other class variables
  notice( "The sentence was: ${::other_class::sentence}" )
```

```
    # I can see parameters of resources in another class
    notice( "Entire message was: ${Notify['announcement']['message']}" )
}
```

Given an idea of *games!* you'd see output like this:

```
$ puppet apply /vagrant/manifests/peek.pp
Notice: Scope(Class[My_class]): The idea was: games!
Notice: Scope(Class[My_class]): The sentence was: an idea: games!
Notice: Scope(Class[My_class]): Entire message was: I have an idea: games!
```

Best Practices for Module Design

Let's review some of the best practices for module development we covered in this chapter:

- Create a module skeleton that implements your organization's standards for module design.
- Declare a class with the module name in *manifests/init.pp*.
- Assign default parameter values that reflect the most likely use case.
- Use EPP templates with explicitly provided parameter values to improve readability.
- Don't access external data within a template. Assign the external data to a variable in the manifest, where the dependency is visible during code review.

You can find more detailed guidelines in the Puppet Labs Style Guide (*https://docs.puppetlabs.com/guides/style_guide.html*).

Reviewing Custom Modules

Modules provide an independent namespace for reusable blocks of code that configure or maintain something. A module provides new resource types that can be independently used by others.

In this chapter, we discussed how to:

- Select an appropriate module name.
- Generate an empty module skeleton.
- Create the default class manifest.
- Synchronize files and directories to nodes.
- Customize files from templates and node data.

This chapter covered the required pieces of modules, and their most common use cases. In the next chapter, we're going to look at expert features and improved functionality you can utilize within your module.

## CHAPTER 14

Improving the Module

There is a tremendous amount of additional features that can be utilized in a module. This chapter will cover the following features:

- Validating input data to ensure it conforms to expectations
- Providing data to modules using Hiera
- Classes and subclasses within the module
- Definitions that can be reused for processing multiple items
- Utilizing other modules within your own
- Documenting modules

Let's get started.

Validating Input with Data Types

Puppet 4 introduced a new type system that can validate input parameters. This improves code quality and readability.

In older versions of Puppet, it was common to perform input validation like this:

```
class puppet(
  # input parameters and default values for the class
  $version = 'latest',
  $status  = 'running',
  $enabled,
) {
  validate_string( $version )
  validate_string( $status )
  validate_bool( $enabled )
...resources defined below...
```

While this looks easy with three variables, it could consume pages of code if there are a lot of input variables. In my experience with larger modules, it wasn't uncommon for the first resource defined in a manifest to be down below line 180.

Puppet 4 allows you to define the type when declaring the parameter now, which both shortens the code and improves its readability. When declaring the parameter, simply add the type before the variable name. This declares the parameter and adds validation for the input on a single line.

I think you'll agree the following is significantly more readable:

```
class puppet(
  # input parameters and default values for the class
  String $version = 'latest',
  Enum['running','stopped'] $status  = 'running',
  Boolean $enabled = true,
) {
...class resources...
}
```

It is not necessary for you to declare a type. If you are passing in something that can contain multiple types of data, simply leave the definition without a type as shown in the previous chapter. A parameter without an explicit type defaults to a type named Any.

Best Practice

Use explicit data types for all input parameters. Avoid accepting ambiguous values that must be introspected before use.

You can (and should) also declare types for lambda block parameters:

```
split( $facts['interfaces'] ).each |String $interface| {
  ...lambda block...
}
```

Valid Types

The type system is hierarchical, where you can allow multiple types to match by defining at a higher level in the tree. If you are familiar with Ruby object types, this will look very familiar:

- Data accepts any of:
  - Scalar accepts any of:
    - Boolean (true or false)
    - String (ASCII and UTF8 characters)

— Enum (a specified list of String values)

— Pattern (a subset of strings that match a given Regexp)

— Numeric accepts either:

— Float (numbers with periods; fractions)

— Integer (whole numbers without periods)

— Regexp (a regular expression)

— Undef (a special type that only accepts undefined values)

- Collection accepts any of:

— Array (list containing Data data types)

— Hash (Scalar keys associated with Data values)

- Catalogentry accepts any of:

— Resource (built-in, custom, and defined resources)

— Class (named manifests that are not executed until called)

As almost every common data value falls under Data, use it to accept any of these types. When you are testing types, $type =~ Data will also match a Collection that contains only Scalar values.

There are a few special types that can match multiple values:

Variant
A special type that matches any of a specified list of types

Optional
A special type that matches a specific type, or no value

NotUndef
A special type that will match any type, but not an undefined value

Tuple
An Array with specific data types in specified positions

Struct
A Hash with specified types for the key/value pairs

Iterable
A special type that matches any Type or Collection that can be iterated over (new in Puppet 4.4)

Iterator
A special type that produces a single value of an Iterable type, used by chained iterator functions to act on elements individually instead of copying the entire Iterable type (new in Puppet 4.4)

There are a few types you will likely never use, but you might see them in error messages.

Default
> A special type to match `default:` key in `case` and `select` statements

Callable
> A special type that holds a lambda block

Runtime
> Refers to the running interpreter (e.g., Ruby)

All of these types are considered type Any. There's no point in declaring this type because you'd be saying that it accepts anything, when most of the time you want Data.

 Best Practice

Even when variables may contain multiple data types, in most circumstances you are expecting a `Scalar` data type, rather than one of the internal objects. Use `Scalar` for parameters where the values can be multiple types.

Validating Values

The type system allows for validation of not only the parameter type, but also of the values within structured data types. For example:

```
Integer[13,19]          # teenage years
Array[Float]            # an array containing only Float numbers
Array[ Array[String] ]  # an array containing only Arrays of String values
Array[ Numeric[-10,10] ] # an array of Integer or Float values between -10 and 10
```

For structured data types, the range parameters indicate the size of the structured type, rather than a value comparison. You can check both the type and size of a Collection (Array or Hash) using two values—the type and an array with the size parameters:

```
Array[String,0,10]      # an array of 0 to 10 string values
Hash[String,Any,2,4] ]  # a hash with 2 to 4 pairs of string keys with any value
```

For even more specificity about key and value types for a hash, a `Struct` specifies exactly which data types are valid for the keys and values.

```
# This is a Hash with short string keys and floating-point values
Struct[{
  day => String[1,8],      # keys are 1-8 characters in length
  temp => Float[-100,100], # values are floating-point Celsius
}]
```

```
# This is a hash that accepts only three well-known ducks as key names
Struct[{
  duck  => enum['Huey','Dewey','Louie'],
  loved => Boolean,
}]
```

Like what a Struct does for a Hash, you can specify types of data for an Array using the Tuple type. The tuple can list specific types in specific positions, along with a specified minimum and optional maximum number of entries:

```
# an array with three integers followed by one string (explicit)
Tuple[Integer,Integer,Integer,String]

# an array with two integers followed by 0-2 strings (length 2-4)
Tuple[Integer,Integer,String,2,4]

# an array with 1-3 integers, and 0-5 strings
Tuple[Integer,Integer,Integer,String,1,8]
```

That last one is pretty hard to understand, so let's break it down:

- Integer in position 1 (required minimum).
- Integers in positions 2–3 are optional (above minimum length).
- String in position 4 is optional (above minimum length).
- The final type (String) may be added 4 times up to the maximum 8 entries.

As you can see, the ability to be specific for many positions in an Array makes Tuple a powerful type for well-structured data.

The Variant and Optional types allow you to specify valid alternatives:

```
Variant[Integer,Float]          # the same as Numeric type
Variant[String,Array[String]]   # a string or an array of strings
Variant[String,undef]           # a string or nothing
Optional[String]                # same as the previous line
Optional[String,Integer]        # string, integer, or nada
```

You can also check the size of the value of a given type:

```
String[12]          # a String at least 12 characters long
String[1,40]        # a String between 1 and 40 characters long
Array[Integer,3]    # an Array of at least 3 integers
Array[String,1,5]   # an Array with 1 to 5 strings
```

You can use all of these together in combination:

```
# An array of thumbs up or thumbs down values
Array[ Enum['thumbsup','thumbsdown'] ]

# An array of thumbs up, thumbs down, or integer from 1 to 5 values
Array[ Variant[ Integer[1,5], Enum['thumbsup','thumbsdown'] ] ]
```

Testing Values

In addition to defining the type of parameters passed into a class, defined type, or lambda, you can perform explicit tests against values in a manifest. Use the =~ operator to compare a value against a type to determine if the value matches the type declaration. For instance, if a value could be one of several types, you could determine the exact type so as to process it correctly:

```
if( $input_value =~ String ) {
  notice( "Received string ${input_value}" )
}
elsif( $input_value =~ Integer ) {
  notice( "Received integer ${input_value}" )
}
```

The match operator can inform you if a variable can be iterated over:

```
if( $variable =~ Iterable ) {
  $variable.each() |$value| {
    notice( $value )
  }
}
else {
  notice( $variable )
}
```

You can also determine if a type is available within a Collection with the in operator:

```
if( String in $array_of_values ) {
  notice('Found a string in the list of values.')
}
else {
  notice('No strings found in the list of values.')
}
```

The with() function can be useful for type checking as well:

```
with($password) |String[12] $secret| {
  notice( "The secret '${secret}' is a sufficiently long password." )
}
```

You can likewise test value types using case and selector expressions:

```
case $input_value: {
  Integer: { notice('Input plus ten equals ' + ($input_value+10) ) }
  String:  { notice('Input was a string, unable to add ten.') }
}
```

You can test against Variant and Optional types as well:

```
if( $input =~ Variant[ String, Array[String] ] ) {
  notice( 'Values are strings.' )
}
```

```
if( $input =~ Optional[Integer] ) {
  notice( 'Values is a whole number or undefined.' )
}
```

A type compares successfully against its exact type, and parents of its type, so the following statements will all return true:

```
'text' =~ String  # exact
'text' =~ Scalar  # Strings are children of Scalar type
'text' =~ Data    # Scalars are a valid Data type
'text' =~ Any     # all types are children of Any
```

If you don't like the default messages displayed when the catalog build fails due to a type mismatch, you can customize your own by using the `assert_type()` function with a lambda block:

```
assert_type(String[12], $password) |$expected, $actual| {
  fail "Passwords less than 12 chars are easily cracked. (provided: ${actual})"
}
```

Comparing Strings with Regular Expressions

You can evaluate strings against regular expressions to determine if they match using the same =~ operator. For instance, if you are evaluating filenames to determine which ones are Puppet manifests, the following example would be useful:

```
$manifests = ${filenames}.filter |$filename| {
  $filename =~ /\.pp$/
}
```

Puppet uses the Ruby core Regexp (*http://ruby-doc.org/core-2.1.8/Regexp.html*) class for matching purposes. The following options are supported:

i *(case insensitive)*
> Ignore upper/lowercase when matching strings.

m *(multiline mode)*
> Allow matching newlines with the . wildcard.

x *(free spacing)*
> Ignore whitespace and comments in the pattern.

Puppet doesn't support options after the final slash—instead, use the (? <options>:<pattern>) syntax to set options:

```
$input =~ /(?i:food)/        # will match Food, FOOD, etc.
$input =~ /(?m:fire.flood)/  # will match "fire\nflood"
$input =~ /(?x:fo \w $)/     # will match fog but not food or "fo g"
$input =~ /(?imx:fire . flood)/ # will match "Fire\nFlood"
```

You can match against multiple exact strings and regular expressions with the Pattern type:

```
$placeholder_names = $victims.filter |$name| {
  $name =~ Pattern['alice','bob','eve','^(?i:j.* doe)',/^(?i:j.* roe)/]
}
```

A `String` on the righthand side of the matching operator is converted to a `Regexp`. This allows you to use interpolated variables in the regular expression:

```
$drink_du_jour = 'coffee'
$you_drank =~ "^${drink_du_jour}$"        # true if they drank coffee
```

Matching a Regular Expression

You can also compare to determine if something is a `Regexp` type:

```
/foo/ =~ Regexp     # true
'foo' =~ Regexp     # false
```

This allows for input validation:

```
if $input =~ Regexp {
  notify { 'Input was a regular expression': }
}
```

You can compare to see if the regular expressions are an identical match:

```
/foo/ =~ Regexp[/foo/]   # true
/foo/ =~ Regexp[/foo$/]  # false
```

The `Regexp` type can use variable interpolation, by placing another variable within a string that is converted to the regular expression to match. Because this string requires interpolation, backslashes must be escaped:

```
$nameregexp =~ Regexp["${first_name} [\\w\\-]+"]
}
```

The preceding example returns `true` if $nameregexp is a regular expression that looks for the first name input followed by another word.

Revising the Module

Now that you've taken a tour of data type validation, let's take a look at how the Puppet module could be revised to validate each parameter:

```
class puppet(
  String $server                        = 'puppet.example.com',
  String $version                       = 'latest',
  Enum['running','stopped'] $status     = 'running',
  Boolean $enabled                      = true,
  String $common_loglevel               = 'warning',
  Optional[String] $agent_loglevel      = undef,
  Optional[String] $apply_loglevel      = undef,
) {
```

As written, each parameter value is now tested to ensure it contains the expected data type.

 Instead of type String, it would be more specific to use the following for each log level:

```
Enum['debug','info','notice','warning','err','alert',
    'emerg','crit','verbose']
```

I didn't do this here due to page formatting reasons.

Looking Up Input from Hiera

As discussed in Chapter 11, Hiera provides a configurable, hierarchical mechanism to look up input data for use in manifests.

Retrieve Hiera data values using the lookup() function call, like so:

```
$version = lookup('puppet::version')
```

One of the special features of Puppet classes is *automatic parameter lookup*. Explicit hiera() or lookup() function calls are unnecessary. Instead, list the parameters in Hiera within the module's namespace.

As we are still testing our module, let's go ahead and define those values now in data for this one node at */etc/puppetlabs/code/hieradata/hostname/client.yaml*:

```
--
classes:
  - puppet

puppet::version = 'latest'
puppet::status  = 'stopped'
puppet::enabled = false
```

Without any function calls, these values will be provided to the puppet module as parameter input, overriding the default values provided in the class declaration.

Naming Parameters Keys Correctly

Given that Hiera uses the :: separator to define the data hierarchy, you might think that it would be easier to define the input parameters as hash entries underneath the module. And yes, I agree that the following looks very clean:

```
puppet:
  version = 'latest'
  status  = 'stopped'
  enabled = false
```

Unfortunately, it does not work. The key for an input parameter must match the complete string of the module namespace plus the parameter name. You must write the file using the example shown immediately before this section.

 You cannot define input parameters as hash keys under the module name.

Using Array and Hash Merges

By default, automatic parameter lookup will use the *first* strategy for lookup of Hiera data, meaning that the first value found will be returned. There are two ways to retrieve merged results of arrays and hashes from the entire hierarchy of Hiera data:

- Define a default merge strategy for the value with the lookup_option hash from the module data provider.
- Use the merge parameter of lookup() to override the default strategy.

An explicit lookup() function call will override the merge strategy specified in the module data. We will cover how to adjust the merge policy for module lookups in "Binding Data Providers in Modules" on page 242. This section will document how to perform explicit lookup calls.

In order to retrieve merged results of arrays or hashes from the entire hierarchy of Hiera data, utilize the lookup() function with the merge parameter. A complete example of the function with merge, default value, and value type checking parameters is shown as follows:

```
$userlist = lookup({
    name          => 'users::users2add',
    value_type    => Array[String],
    default_value => [],
    merge         => 'unique',
})
```

The following merge strategies are currently supported:

first
   Returns the first value found in priority order (called priority in older Hiera versions).

unique
   Returns a flattened array of all unique values found (called array in older Hiera versions).

hash

Returns a hash containing the highest priority key and its values (called `native` in older Hiera versions). Ignores unique values of lower-priority keys.

deep

Returns a hash containing every key and all values from every level of the hierarchy. Merges the values of unique lower-priority keys with higher-priority values.

Understanding Lookup Merge

The `lookup()` function will merge values from multiple levels of the Hiera hierarchy. For example, a `users` module for creating user accounts might expect data laid out like so:

```
users::home_path: '/home'
users::default_shell: '/bin/bash'
users::users2add:
  - jill
  - jack
  - jane
```

If you wanted to add one user to a given host, you could create an override file for that host with just the user's name:

```
users::users2add:
  - jo
```

By default the automatic parameter lookup would find this entry and return it, making *jo* be the only user created on the system:

```
[vagrant@client hieradata]$ puppet lookup users::users2add
---
jo
```

To merge all the answers together, you could instead look up all unique Hiera values, as shown here:

```
[vagrant@client hieradata]$ puppet lookup --merge unique users::users2add
---
jo
jill
jack
jane
```

Apply this same merge option in the Puppet manifest to create an array of all users, as shown here:

```
class users(
  # input parameters and default values for the class
  $home_path     = '/home',
  $default_shell = '/bin/bash',
) {

  $userlist = lookup({ name => 'users::users2add', merge => 'unique' })
```

The $userlist variable will be assigned a unique, flattened array of values from all priority levels.

Specifying Merge Strategy in Data

The unfortunate aspect of the previous example is that you have to split out the parameter assignment to an explicit lookup() call, which doesn't read well.

It is possible to specify the default merge strategy on a per-parameter basis. Do this by creating a lookup_options hash in your data source with the full parameter name as a key. The value should be a hash of lookup options, exactly the same as used in the lookup() call shown in "Using Array and Hash Merges" on page 190.

```
lookup_options:
  users::userlist:
    merge: unique
```

This allows you to simplify the class parameter lookup shown in the preceding section back to a single location:

```
class users(
  # input parameters and default values for the class
  $home_path    = '/home',
  $default_shell = '/bin/bash',
  $userlist     = [],
) {
```

Adding a lookup_options hash to the data allows module authors to set a default merge strategy and other options for automatic parameter lookup. The user of the module can override the module author by declaring a lookup_options hash key in the global or environment data, which are evaluated at a higher priority.

You cannot do a lookup() query to retrieve the lookup_options hash. It is accessible only to the lookup() function and automatic parameter lookup.

Replacing Direct Hiera Calls

Direct Hiera queries utilize only the original (global) lookup scope. Replace all hiera() queries with lookup() queries to make use of environment and module data providers.

If a module does direct Hiera queries, such as this:

```
# Format: hiera( key, default )
$status = hiera('specialapp::status', 'running')
```

replace them with one of the following two variants, depending on whether extra options like default values and type checking are necessary. The simplest form is identical to the original `hiera()` function with a single parameter.

```
# Format: lookup( key )
# Simple example assumes type Data (anything), no default value
$status = lookup('specialapp::status')
```

The more complex form allows you to pass in a hash with optional attributes that define how the data is retrieved and validated. Here are some examples:

```
# Perform type checking on the value
# Provide a default value if the lookup doesn't succeed
$status = lookup({
  name          => 'specialapp::status',
  value_type    => Enum['running','stopped'],
  default_value => 'running',
}
```

Here is another example, which performs an array merge of all values from every level of the hierarchy:

```
$userlist = lookup({
  name          => 'users2add',
  value_type    => Array[String],
  merge         => 'unique',
})
```

Here are some example replacements for the older Hiera functions:

```
# replaces hiera_array('specialapp::id', [])
lookup({
  name          => 'specialapp::id',
  merge         => 'unique'
  default_value => [],
  value_type    => Array[Data],
})
```

```
# replaces hiera_hash('specialapp::users', {})
lookup({
  name          => 'specialapp::users',
  merge         => 'hash'
  default_value => {},
  value_type    => Hash[Data],
})
```

The `lookup()` function will accept an array of attribute names. Each name will be looked up in order until a value is found. Only the result for the first name found is returned, although that result could contain merged values:

```
lookup( ['specialapp::users', 'specialapp::usernames', 'specialapp::users2add'], {
  merge => 'unique'
})
```

The lookup() function can also pass names to a lambda and return the result it provides, as shown here:

```
# Create a default value on request
$salt = lookup('security::salt') |$key| {
  # ignore key; generate a random salt every time
  rand(2**256).to_s(24)
}
```

Building Subclasses

When building a module you may find yourself with several different related components, some of which may not be utilized on every system. For example, our Puppet class should be able to configure both the Puppet agent and a Puppet server. In situations like this, it is best to break your module up with subclasses.

Each subclass is named within the scope of the parent class. For example, it would make sense to use puppet::agent as the name for the class that configures the Puppet agent.

Each subclass should be a separate manifest file, stored in the *manifests* directory of the module, and named for the subclass followed by the *.pp* extension. For example, our Puppet module could be expanded to have the following classes:

Class name	Filename
puppet	*manifests/init.pp*
puppet::agent	*manifests/agent.pp*
puppet::server	*manifests/server.pp*

As our module currently only configures the Puppet agent, let's go ahead and move all resources from the puppet class into the puppet::agent class. When we are done, the files might look like this:

```
# manifests/init.pp
class puppet(
  # common variables for all Puppet classes
  String $version  = 'latest',
  String $loglevel = 'warning',
) {
  # no resources in this class
}

# manifests/agent.pp
class puppet::agent(
  # input parameters specific to agent subclass
  Enum['running','stopped'] $status  = 'running',
  Boolean $enabled,              # required parameter
)
```

```
inherits puppet {

  all of the resources previously defined
}

# manifests/server.pp
class puppet::server() {
  # we'll write this in Part III of the book
}
```

Best Practice

Any time you would need an if/then block in a module to handle different needs for different nodes, use subclasses instead for improved readability.

One last change will be to adjust Hiera to reflect the revised class name:

```
# /etc/puppetlabs/code/hieradata/common.yaml
classes:
  - puppet::agent

puppet::common_loglevel: 'info'
puppet::version: 'latest'
puppet::agent::status: 'stopped'
puppet::agent::enabled: false
puppet::agent::server: 'puppetmaster.example.com'
```

With these small changes we have now made it possible for a node to have the Puppet agent configured, or the Puppet server configured, or both.

Remember that module parameters must be supplied with the entire module class. You cannot define parameters as hash keys under the module name.

Creating New Resource Types

Puppet classes are what's known as *singletons*. No matter how many places they are called with include or require() functions, only one copy of the class exists in memory. Only one set of parameters is used, and only one set of scoped variables exists.

There will be times that you may want to declare Puppet resources multiple times with different input parameters each time. For that purpose, create a *defined resource type*. Defined resource types are implemented by manifests that look almost exactly like subclasses:

- They are placed in the *manifests/* directory of a module.
- They are named within the module namespace exactly like subclasses.
- The filename should match the type name, and end with the *.pp* suffix.
- They begin with parentheses that define parameters that are accepted.

Like the core Puppet resources, and unlike classes, defined resource types can be called over and over again. This makes them suitable for use within the lambda block of an iterator. We'll use an iterator in our `puppet` class in the next section. To demonstrate the idea now, here's an example from a `users` class.

```
# modules/users/manifests/create.pp
define users::create(
  String $comment,
  Integer $uid,
  Optional[Integer] $gid = undef,
) {
  user { $title:
    uid     => $uid,
    gid     => $gid || $uid,
    comment => $comment,
  }
}

# modules/users/manifests/init.pp
class users( Array[Hash] $userlist = [] ) {
  userlist.each |$user| {
    users::create { $user['name']:
      uid     => $user['uid'],
      comment => $user['comment'],
    }
  }
}
```

The `create` defined type will be declared once for every user in the array provided to the `users` module. Unlike a class, the defined type sees fresh input parameters each time it is called.

You might notice that this defined type utilizes a variable that wasn't listed in the parameters. Just like a core resource, a defined resource type receives two parameters that aren't named in the parameter list:

`$title`
:   The resource title used when the defined resource was declared.

`$name`
:   Defaults to `$title` but can be overridden in the declaration.

These attributes should be declared exactly the same way as any core Puppet resource.

Defined resource types are also called *defined types*, or just plain *defines* in many places.

Understanding Variable Scope

Modules may only declare variables within the module's namespace (also called *scope*). This is very important to remember when using subclasses within a module, as each subclass has its own scope.

```
class puppet::agent {
    # these two definitions are the same and will produce an error
    $status = 'running'
    $::puppet::agent::status = 'running'
```

A module may not create variables within the top scope or another module's scope. Any of the following declarations will cause a build error:

```
class puppet {
    # FAIL: can't declare top-scope variables
    $::version = '1.0.1'

    # FAIL: Can't declare variables in another class
    $::mcollective::version = '1.0.1'

    # FAIL: no, not even in the parent class
    $::puppet::version = '1.0.1'
```

Variables can be prefaced with an underscore to indicate that they should not be accessed externally:

```
# variable that shouldn't be accessed outside the current scope
$_internalvar = 'something'

# deprecated: don't access underscore-prefaced variables out of scope
notice( $::mymodule::_internalvar )
```

This is currently polite behavior rather than enforced; however, external access to internal variables will be removed in a future version of Puppet.

Using Out-of-Scope Variables

While you cannot change variables in other scopes, you can use them within the current scope:

```
notify( $variable )                 # from current, parent, node, or top scope
notify( $::variable )               # from top scope
notify( $::othermodule::variable )  # from a specific scope
```

The first invocation could return a value from an in-scope variable, or the same variable name defined in the parent scope, the node scope, or the top scope. A person would have to search the module to be certain a local scope variable wasn't defined. Furthermore, a declaration added to the manifest above this could assign a value different from what you intended to use. The latter forms are explicit and clear about the source.

Best Practice

Always refer to out-of-scope variables with the explicit $:: root prefix for clarity.

Understanding Top Scope

Top-scope variables are defined from the following crazy mishmash of places, which can confuse and baffle you when you're trying to debug problems in a module:

- Facts submitted by the node
- Variables declared in manifests outside of a module
- Variables declared in the parameters block of an ENC's result
- Variables declared at top scope within Hiera
- Variables set by the Puppet agent or Puppet server

In my own perfect world, top-scope variables would cease to exist and be replaced entirely by hashes of data from each source. That said, top-scope variables are used in many places, and many Forge modules, and some of them have no other location from which to gather the data. If you are debugging a module, you'll have to evaluate all of these sources to determine where a value came from.

Follow these rules to simplify debugging within your environment:

- Always use client-supplied facts from the facts[] hash.
- When using a Puppet server, enable trusted_server_facts and use the server-validated facts available in the $server_facts[] and $trusted[] hashes.

By following these rules you can safely assume that any top-level variable was set by Hiera or an ENC's results.

Best Practice

Avoid defining top-scope variables. Declare all variables in a module or role namespace.

Understanding Node Scope

Node scope is a special type of scope where variables could be defined that look like top-scope variables but are specific to a node assignment.

As discussed in "Assigning Modules to Nodes" on page 153, it was previously common to declare classes within node blocks. It was possible to declare variables within the node block, which would override top-scope variables if you were using the variable name without the $:: prefix.

It is generally considered best practice to avoid node blocks entirely and to assign classes to nodes using Hiera data, as documented in the section mentioned. However, it remains possible in Puppet 4 to declare node definitions, and to declare variables within the node definitions. These variables would be accessible as $*variable*, and hide the values defined in the top scope.

Best Practice

Avoid using node-scope variables. It's never fun to debug a module when you have to comb through the entire environment to determine where a value is being declared from.

Understanding Parent Scope

Parent scope for variables is the scope of the class which the current class inherits (for example, when a subclass inherits from the base class, as shown in "Building Subclasses" on page 194):

```
class puppet::agent() inherits puppet {
  ...
}
```

Previous versions of Puppet would use the class that declared the current class as the parent class. This caused significant confusion and inconsistent results when multiple modules/classes would declare a common class dependency.

Tracking Resource Defaults Scope

As discussed in Chapter 6, it is possible to declare attribute defaults for a resource type.

It can be useful to change those defaults within a module or a class. To change them within a class scope, define the default within the class. To change them for every class in a module, define them in a `defaults` class and inherit it from every class in the module.

It's not uncommon to place module defaults in the `params` class, as it is inherited by every class of the module to provide default values:

```
class puppet::params() {
  # Default values
  $attribute = 'default value'

  # Resource defaults
  Package {
    install_options => '--enable-repo=epel',
  }
}
```

As with variables, if a resource default is not declared in the class, it will use a default declared in the parent scope, the node scope, or the top scope. Unlike variables, parent scope is selected through dynamic scoping rules. This means that the parent class *will be the class which declared this class if the class does not inherit from another class.* Read that sentence twice, carefully.

- If a class is declared within another class, then the parent scope is the calling class.
- If a class inherits from another class, then the parent scope is the inherited class.

As classes are singletons and thus instantiated only once, this means the parent scope changes depending on which class declares this class first. This can change as you add and remove modules from your environment.

 Make all classes with resources inherit from another class in the module to ensure that no resource defaults bleed in from another module. This defensive technique prevents unexpected attribute values from being applied to the module's resources.

Avoiding Resource Default Bleed

Puppet 4 provides the ability to implement named resource defaults which never bleed to other modules. It involves combining two techniques together:

- A resource can accept multiple attributes from a hash containing attribute keys, as documented in "Defining Attributes with a Hash" on page 62.
- A resource declaration with a *default* resource body can provide default attributes, as documented in "Declaring Multiple Resource Bodies" on page 63.

By combining these techniques together, you can create resource defaults that can be applied by name. Let's use this technique with the same default values shown in the previous section:

```
$package_defaults = {
  'ensure'         => 'present',
  'install_options' => '--enable-repo=epel',
}

# Resource defaults
package {
  default:
    * => $package_defaults
  ;

  'puppet-agent':
    ensure => 'latest'
  ;
}
```

This works exactly as if a `Package {}` default was created, but it will apply only to the resources that specifically use that hash for the defaults. This allows you to have multiple resource defaults, and select the appropriate one by name.

Best Practice

Use the `default:` resource title to set resource defaults based upon a hash of attribute values. This is more readable, less surprising, and will never bleed over to something you didn't expect.

Redefining Variables

In previous versions of Puppet, you could also use `$sumtotal += 10` to declare a local variable based on a computation of variable in a parent, node, or top scope. This reads an awful lot like a redefinition of a variable, which as you might recall is not possible within Puppet. This was removed in Puppet 4 to be more consistent.

This kind of redeclaration is now handled with straightforward assignment like so:

```
$sumtotal = $sumtotal + 10
```

This appears to be a variable redefinition. However, the = operator actually creates a variable in the local scope with a value computed from the higher scope variable as modified by the operands.

To avoid confusion, I won't use this syntax. I always use one of the following forms instead:

```
# clearly access top-scope variable
$sumtotal = $::sumtotal + 10

# clearly access parent-scope variable
$sumtotal = $::parent::sumtotal + 10
```

```
# even more clear by not using the same name
$local_sumtotal = $::sumtotal + 10
```

 Node-scope variables can only be accessed using the unqualified variable name and dynamic scope lookup. This is an excellent reason to avoid node-scope variables.

Calling Other Modules

In "Building Subclasses" on page 194, we split up the module into separate subclasses for the Puppet agent and Puppet server. A complication of this split is that both the Puppet agent and Puppet server read the same configuration file, *puppet.conf*. Both classes would modify this file, and restart their services if the configuration changes.

Let's review two different ways to deal with this complication. Both solutions have classes depend on another module to handle configuration changes. Each presents different ways to deal with the complications of module dependencies, and thus we cover both solutions to demonstrate different tactics.

Sourcing a Common Dependency

One way to solve this problem would be to create a third subclass named `config`. This module would contain a template for populating the configuration file with settings for both the agent and server. In this scenario, each of the classes could include the `config` class. This would work as shown here:

```
# manifests/_config.pp
class puppet::_config(
  Hash $common = {},  #   [main] params empty if not available in Hiera
  Hash $agent  = {},  #  [agent] params empty if not available in Hiera
  Hash $user   = {},  #   [user] params empty if not available in Hiera
  Hash $server = {},  # [master] params empty if not available in Hiera
) {
  file { 'puppet.conf':
    ensure  => ensure,
    path    => '/etc/puppetlabs/puppet/puppet.conf',
    owner   => 'root',
    group   => 'wheel',
    mode    => '0644',
    content => epp(
      'puppet:///puppet/puppet.conf.epp',          # template file
      { 'agent' => $agent, 'server' => $server } # hash of config params
    ),
  }
}
```

This example shows a common practice of naming classes that are used internally by a module with a leading underscore.

Best Practice

Name classes, variables, and types that should not be called directly by other modules with a leading underscore.

You may notice that the file resource doesn't `require` the agent or server packages, nor `notify` the Puppet agent or Puppet server services. This is because a Puppet agent and server are separate classes. One or the other may not be declared for a given node.[1] Don't define relationships with resources that might not exist in the catalog.

It is only safe to depend on resources from classes that are guaranteed to be available in the catalog.

Instead, we'll modify the `agent` class to include the `config` class, and depend on the `file` resource it provides:

```
# manifests/agent.pp
class puppet::agent(
  String $status = 'running',
  Boolean $enabled,
) {
  # Include the class that defines the config
  include puppet::_config

  # Install the Puppet agent
  package { 'puppet-agent':
    version => $version,
    before  => File['puppet.conf'],
    notify  => Service['puppet'],
  }

  # Manage the Puppet service
  service { 'puppet':
    ensure    => $status,
    enable    => $enabled,
    subscribe => [ Package['puppet-agent'], File['puppet.conf'] ],
  }
```

---

1 The astute reader might point out that Puppet couldn't possibly configure the Puppet server if the Puppet agent isn't installed—a unique situation for only a Puppet module. This concept would be valid for any other module that handles both the client and server configurations.

Create a server class with the same dependency structure. As you might remember from the preceding section, each class is a singleton: the configuration class will be called only once, even though it is included by both classes. If the `puppet::server` class is defined with the same dependencies as the `puppet::agent` class, the `before` and `subscribe` attributes shown will ensure that resource evaluation will happen in the following order on a node that utilizes either or both classes:

1. Packages will be installed:

   `puppet::agent`
   : The Puppet agent package would be installed.

   `puppet::server`
   : The Puppet server package would be installed.

2. `puppet::_config`: The Puppet configuration file would be written out.

3. The services will be started:

   `puppet::agent`
   : The Puppet agent service would be started.

   `puppet::server`
   : The Puppet server service would be started.

Avoiding Circular Dependencies

You might think `require` would be more appropriate than `include` for the `_config` class. However, `require` defines a complete dependency where every resource in the class depends on the other class. As we want the packages to be installed before the configuration file is modified, this would introduce a circular dependency. It is best to include the class and use per-resource dependencies.

Using a Different Module

The previous example showed a way to solve a problem within a single Puppet module, where you control each of the classes that manages a common dependency. Sometimes there will be a common dependency shared across Puppet modules maintained by different groups, or perhaps even sometimes entirely outside of Puppet.

The use of templates requires the ability to manage the entire file. Even when using modules that can build a file from multiple parts, such as *puppetlabs/concat* (*http://bit.ly/1Vk5anP*) on the Puppet Forge, you must define the entirety of the file within the Puppet catalog.

The following alternative approach utilizes a module to make individual line or section changes to a file without any knowledge of the remainder of the file:

```
# manifests/agent.pp
class puppet::agent(
  String $status  = 'running',
  Boolean $enabled = true,
  Hash $config    = {},
) {
  # Write each agent configuration option to the puppet.conf file
  $config.each |$setting,$value| {
    ini_setting { "agent $setting":
      ensure  => present,
      path    => '/etc/puppetlabs/puppet/puppet.conf',
      section => 'agent',
      setting => $setting,
      value   => $value,
      require => Package['puppet-agent'],
    }
  }
}
```

This shorter, simpler definition uses a third-party module to update the Puppet configuration file in a nonexclusive manner. In my opinion, this is significantly more flexible than the common dependency module shown in the previous example.

Ordering Dependencies

When using other modules, it will be necessary to use ordering metaparameters to ensure that the dependencies are fulfilled before resources that require those dependencies are evaluated. Some tricky problems come about when you try to utilize ordering metaparameters between classes maintained by different people.

In this section, we'll cover strategies for safe ordering of dependencies between modules.

Depending on Entire Classes

A primary problem with writing classes that depend on resources in other classes comes from this requirement:

> You must know the name of the resource(s).

If you are using a module that depends on an explicitly named resource in another module, you are at risk of breaking when the dependency module is refactored and resource titles are changed.

As discussed in "Understanding Variable Scope" on page 197, classes and defined types has their own unique scope. Each instance of a class or defined type becomes a container for the variables and resources declared within it. This means you can set dependencies on the entire container.

Best Practice

Whenever possible, treat other modules as black boxes and depend on the entire class, rather than "peeking in" to depend on specific resources.

If a resource defines a dependency with a class or type, it will form the same relationship with every resource inside the container. For example, say that we want the Puppet service to be started after the rsyslog daemon is already up and running. As you might imagine, the `rsyslog` module has a similar set of resources as our `puppet::client` module:

```
class rsyslog {
  package { ... }
  file { ... }
  service { ... }
}
```

Rather than setting a dependency on one of these resources, we can set a dependency on the entire class:

```
# Manage the Puppet service
service { 'puppet':
  ensure    => $status,
  enable    => $enabled,
  subscribe => Package['puppet-agent'],
  after     => Class['rsyslog'],
}
```

With the preceding configuration, someone can refactor and change the `rsyslog` module without breaking this module.

Placing Dependencies Within Optional Classes

There is another difficulty with ordering dependencies that you may run into:

The resource you `notify` or `subscribe` to must exist in the catalog.

This obviously comes into play when you are writing a module that may be used with or without certain other modules. It's easy if the requirement is absolute: you simply `include` or `require` the dependency class. But if not having the class is a valid configuration, then it becomes tricky.

Let's use, for example, the `puppet` module you are building. It is entirely valid for a user to install Puppet server with it, but not to run or even configure the Puppet agent. If you use a `puppet::config` class, the `file['puppet.conf']` resource cannot safely notify `service['puppet']` because that service won't be available in the catalog if the `puppet::agent` class wasn't included. The catalog build will abort, and animals will scatter in fright.

You could explicity declare the `puppet::agent` class, and force everyone who doesn't want to run the agent to define settings to disable it. However, a more flexible approach would be to have the optional service `subscribe` to the `file` resource, which is always included:

```
# Manage the Puppet service
service { 'puppet':
  ensure    => $status,
  enable    => $enabled,
  subscribe => File['puppet.conf'],
}
```

By placing the notification dependency within the optional class, you have solved the problem of ensuring that the resources exist in the catalog. If the `puppet::agent` class is not included on a node, the dependency doesn't exist, and no animals were harmed when Puppet applied the resources.

Notifying Dependencies from Dynamic Resources

The same rule discussed before has a much trickier application when ordering dependencies of dynamic resources:

> You must know the name of the resource(s).

This comes into play when you are writing a module that depends on resources that are dynamically generated. The use of `puppetlabs::inifile` to modify the configuration file defines each configuration setting as a unique resource within the class:

```
# Write each agent configuration option to the puppet.conf file
$config.each |$setting,$value| {
  ini_setting { "agent $setting":
    ensure  => present,
    ...
  }
}
```

Because each setting is a unique resource, the `package` and `service` resources can't use `before` or `subscribe` attributes, as the config settings list can change. In this case, it is best to reverse the logic. Use the dynamic resource's `require` and `notify` attributes to require the package and notify the service resources.

Here's an example that places ordering metaparameters on the dynamic INI file resources for the Puppet configuration file:

```
# Write each agent configuration option to the puppet.conf file
$config.each |$setting,$value| {
  ini_setting { "agent $setting":
    ensure  => present,
    path    => '/etc/puppetlabs/puppet/puppet.conf',
    section => 'agent',
    setting => $setting,
    value   => $value,
    require => Package['puppet-agent'],
    notify  => Service['puppet'],
  }
}
```

In this form, we've moved the ordering attributes into the dynamic resources to target the well-known resources. The service no longer needs to know in advance the list of resources that modify the configuration file. If any of the settings are changed in the file, it will notify the service.

Solving Unknown Resource Dependencies

The really tricky problems come about when you are facing all of these problems together:

> You must know the name of the resource(s).
> The resource you notify or subscribe to must exist in the catalog.

This obviously comes into play when you are writing a module that depends on resources dynamically generated by a different class. If that class can be used without your dependent class, then it cannot send a notify event, as your resource may not exist in the catalog.

> Likewise, if your class depends on a module from the Puppet Forge, you can't modify their class without having to maintain patches to that module going forward.

The solution is what I call an *escrow refresh resource*, which is a well-known static resource that will always be available to notify and subscribe to.

Let's return to the Puppet module you are building for an example. It is entirely valid for a user to install Puppet with it, but not to run or configure the Puppet agent. Changes to the Puppet configuration file can happen within the agent class. As the agent service is defined in the same class, it can safely notify the service.

However, changes to the Puppet configuration file can happen in the main puppet class and modify the configuration parameters in [main]. As these parameters will affect the Puppet agent service, the Puppet agent will need to reload the configuration file.

However, the base `puppet` class can be used without the `puppet::agent` subclass, so the `inifile` configuration resources cannot notify the agent service, as that service might not exist in the catalog. Likewise, the Puppet agent service cannot depend on a dynamically generated set of configuration parameters.

In this situation, the base `puppet` class creates an escrow refresh resource to which it will submit notifications that the Puppet configuration file has changed. With this combination of resource definitions, the following sequence takes place:

1. Each dynamic resource notifies the escrow refresh if it changes the file.
2. On receiving a refresh event, the escrow resource does something negligible.
3. Services that subscribe to the escrow resource receive refresh events.

Implement this by creating a resource which does something that succeeds. It need not do anything in particular, as it only serves as a well-known relay for refresh events:

```
# refresh escrow that optional resources can subscribe to
Exec { 'puppet-configuration-has-changed':
  command    => '/bin/true',
  refreshonly => true,
}
```

Adjust the dynamic resources to notify the escrow resource if they change the configuration file:

```
# Write each main configuration option to the puppet.conf file
$config.each |$setting,$value| {
  ini_setting { "main $setting":
    ensure  => present,
    path    => '/etc/puppetlabs/puppet/puppet.conf',
    section => 'main',
    setting => $setting,
    value   => $value,
    require => Package['puppet-agent'],
    notify  => Exec['puppet-configuration-has-changed'],
  }
}
```

Declare the agent service to subscribe to the escrow refresh resource:

```
# Manage the Puppet service
service { 'puppet':
  ensure    => $status,
  enable    => $enabled,
  subscribe => Exec['puppet-configuration-has-changed'],
}
```

The only difficulty with this pattern is that the escrow resource must be defined by the class on which the optional classes depend. This may require you to submit a request to the maintainer of a Forge module to add in an escrow resource for you to subscribe to.

Best Practice

If you maintain a module that manages a configuration file upon which other services may depend, or for which plugins or add-ons exist, create an escrow resource to which wrapper modules can subscribe.

Containing Classes

In most situations, each class declaration stands independent. While a class can include another class, the class is defined at an equal level as the calling class—they are both instances of the Class type. Ordering metaparameters are used to control which classes are processed in which order.

As classes are peers, no class contains any other class. In almost every case, this is exactly how you want class declaration to work. This allows freedom for any class to set dependencies and ordering against any other class.

However, there is also a balance where one class should not be tightly tied to the internals of another class. It can be useful to allow other classes to declare ordering metaparameters that refer to the parent class, yet ensure that any necessary subclasses are processed at the same time.

For example, a module may have a base class that declares only common variables. All resources might be declared in package and service subclasses. A module that sets a dependency on the base class would not achieve the intended goal of being evaluated after the service is started:

```
service 'dependency' {
  ensure => running,
  after  => Class['only_has_variables']
}
```

Rather than require the module to set dependencies on each subclass of the module, declare that each of the subclasses is contained within the main class:

```
class application(
  Hash[String] $globalvars = {},
) {
  # Ensure that ordering includes subclasses
  contain application::package
  contain application::service
}
```

With this definition, any class that references the `application` class need not be aware of the subclasses it contains.

Creating Reusable Modules

In this section, we'll talk about ways to ensure your module can be used successfully by others, and even yourself in different situations. Even if you don't plan to share your modules with anyone, the ideas in this section will help you build better modules that you won't kick yourself for later.

Avoiding Fixed Values in Attribute Values

Many, many examples in this book have placed hard values in resources in the name of simplicity, to make the resource language easy to read for learning purposes. Unfortunately, this is a terrible idea when building manifests for production use. You'll find yourself changing paths, changing values, and adding `if`/`else` sequences as the code is deployed in more places.

Best Practice

Use variables for resource attribute values. Set the values in a `params` class, Hiera, or another data source.

To give you a clear example, visualize a module that installs and configures the Apache httpd server. The following would be a valid definition for a virtualhost configuration file on CentOS 7:

```
file { '/etc/httpd/conf.d/virtualhost.conf':
  ensure  => file,
  owner   => 'apache',
  group   => 'apache',
  mode    => '0644',
  source  => 'puppet:///modules/apache_vhost/virtualhost.conf',
  require => Package['httpd'],
  notify  => Service['httpd'],
}
```

Then someone wants to use that module on an Ubuntu server. The problem is, nearly everything in that definition is wrong. The package name, the service name, the file location, and the file owners are all different on Ubuntu. It's much better to write that resource as follows:

```
package 'apache-httpd-package' {
  ensure => present,
  name   => $apache_httpd::package_name,
}
```

```
file { 'virtualhost.conf':
  ensure => file,
  path   => "${apache_httpd::sites_directory}/virtualhost.conf",
  owner  => $apache_httpd::username,
  group  => $apache_httpd::groupname,
  mode   => '0644',
  source => 'puppet:///modules/apache_vhost/virtualhost.conf',
  require => Package['apache-httpd-package'],
  notify => Service['apache-httpd-service'],
}

service 'apache-httpd-service' {
  name   => $apache_httpd::service_name,
  ensure => 'running',
}
```

Then utilize your Hiera hierarchy and place the following variables in the *os/redhat.yaml* file:

```
apache_httpd::username: apache
apache_httpd::groupname: apache
apache_httpd::package_name: httpd
apache_httpd::service_name: httpd
```

If this service is ever deployed on Ubuntu, you can redefine those variables for that platform in the *os/debian.yaml* file—zero code changes to your module:

```
apache_httpd::username: httpd
apache_httpd::groupname: httpd
apache_httpd::package_name: apache2
apache_httpd::service_name: apache2
```

Likewise, if you find yourself using the module for an Apache instance installed in an alternate location, you can simply override those values for that particular hostname in your Hiera hierarchy, such as *hostname/abitoddthisone.yaml*.

Ensuring Fixed Values for Resource Names

If you were looking carefully at the preceding section, you might have noticed that I didn't take advantage of the resource's ability to take the resource name from the title. Here, have another look:

```
package 'apache-httpd-package' {
  ensure => present,
  name   => "apache_httpd::package_name",
}
```

Wouldn't it be much easier and less code to inherit the value like this?

```
package $apache::httpd::package_name {
  ensure => present,
}
```

It would be simpler, but *only the first time I used this class*. The resource's name would vary from operating system to operating system. If I ever created a wrapper class for this, or depended on it in another class, I'd have to look up which value contains the resource and where it was defined. And then I'm scattering variable names from this class throughout another class.

Here's an example of what a class that needs to install its configuration files before the Apache service starts would have to put within its own manifest:

```
# poor innocent class with no knowledge of Apache setup
file 'config-file-for-other-service' {
 ...
 require => Package[ $apache_httpd::package_name ],
 notify  => Service[ $apache_httpd::service_name ],
}
```

Worse, if you refactor the Apache class and rename the variables, it will break every module that referred to this resource.

Best Practice

Use static names for resources to which wrapper classes may need to refer with ordering metaparameters.

In this situation, it's much better to explicitly define a static title for the resource, and declare the package or service name by passing a variable to the name attribute. Then wrapper and dependent classes can safely depend on the resource name:

```
# poor innocent class with no knowledge of Apache setup
file 'config-file-for-other-service' {
 ...
 require => Package['apache-httpd-package'],
 notify  => Service['apache-httpd-service'],
}
```

Defining Defaults in a Params Manifest

As discussed previously in this book, parameters can be declared in the class definition with a default value. Continuing with our Apache module example, you might define the base class like so:

```
class apache_httpd (
  String $package_name = 'httpd',
  String $service_name = 'httpd',
```

Then you could define the default values in Hiera operating system overrides. However, this would require everyone who uses your module to install Hiera data to use your module. To avoid that, you'd have to muddy up the class with case blocks or selector expressions:

```
String $package_name = $osfamily ? {
    /redhat/  => 'httpd',
    /debian/  => 'apache2',
    default   => 'apache',
}
String $service_name = $osfamily ? { ... }
String $user_name = $osfamily ? { ... }
```

A much cleaner design is to place all conditions on platform-dependent values in another manifest named *params.pp*.

Best Practice

Place all conditional statements around operating system and similar data in a params class. Inherit from the params class and refer to it for all default values.

Here's an example:

```
class apache_httpd (
    String $package_name = $apache_httpd::params::package_name,
    String $service_name = $apache_httpd::params::service_name,
    String $user_name    = $apache_httpd::params::user_name,
) inherits apache_httpd::params {
```

This makes your class clear and easy to read, hiding away all the messy per-OS value selection. Furthermore, this design allows Hiera values to override the OS-specific values if desired.

In many cases, the params manifest can be replaced with data in modules, as described in "Binding Data Providers in Modules" on page 242.

Best Practices for Module Improvements

Let's review some of the best practices for module development we covered in this chapter:

- Declare parameters with explicit types for data validation.
- Validate each parameter for expected values in the manifest.
- Place each subclass and defined type in a separate manifest file.
- Avoid using top or node scope variables.

- Use the `contain()` function to wrap subclasses for simple dependency management.
- Use variables instead of fixed values for resource attributes.
- Use static names for resources which other modules may depend on.
- Create escrow resources for wrapper and extension modules to subscribe to.

You can find more detailed guidelines in the Puppet Labs Style Guide (*https://docs.puppetlabs.com/guides/style_guide.html*).

Reviewing Module Improvements

Modules provide an independent namespace for reusable blocks of code that configure or maintain something. A module can create new resource types that can be independently used in other modules.

In this chapter, we have covered how to configure a module to:

- Create reusable Puppet manifests that accept external data
- Provide data to modules using Hiera
- Validate input data to ensure it conforms to expectations
- Utilize other modules to provide dependencies
- Share new types and subclasses with discrete functionality
- Relay refresh events through escrow resources to wrapper modules

This chapter has reviewed the features and functionality you can utilize within modules. The next chapter will discuss how to create plugins that extend modules with less common functionality.

## CHAPTER 15

Extending Modules with Plugins

This chapter covers adding plugins to Puppet modules. Plugins are used to provide new facts, functions, and module-specific data that can be used in the Puppet catalog.

This chapter will explain how to extend a module to:

- Provide new customized facts that can be used within your module.
  - Facts can be supplied by a program that outputs one fact per line.
  - Facts can be supplied by Ruby functions.
  - Facts can be read from YAML, JSON, or text file formats.
- Provide new functions that extend the Puppet configuration language.
  - Facts can be written in either Puppet or Ruby languages.
- Provide data lookups that are environment- or module-specific.
  - Custom data sources are written in Ruby.

Nothing in this chapter is required to build a working module, and there are thousands of modules that don't use plugins. You can safely skip this chapter and return to it after you are comfortable building the common features of modules.

 Many of the extensions in this chapter are written in Ruby. To build Ruby plugins, you'll need knowledge of the Ruby programming language. I recommend Michael Fitzgerald's *Learning Ruby* as an excellent reference.

Adding Custom Facts

One of the most useful plugins a module can provide is custom facts. Custom facts extend the built-in facts that Facter provides with node-specific values useful for the module. Module facts are synced from the module to the agent, and their values are available for use when the catalog is built.

Previous versions of Puppet could only supply string values for facts. In Puppet 4, custom facts can return any of the `Scalar` data types (e.g., `String`, `Numeric`, `Boolean`, etc.) in addition to any of the `Collection` types (`Array`, `Hash`, `Struct`, etc.).

There are two ways to provide custom facts: using Ruby functions, or through external data. Let's go over how to build new facts using both methods.

External Facts

Would you like to provide facts without writing Ruby? This is now possible with *external facts*. There are two ways to provide external facts:

- Write fact data out in YAML, JSON, or text format.
- Provide a program or script to output fact names and values.

The program or script can be written in Bash, Python, Java, whatever... it's only necessary that it can be executed by the Puppet agent. Let's go over how to use these.

Structured data

You can place structured data files in the *facts.d/* directory of your module with values to assign to facts. Structured data files must be in a known format, and must be named with the appropriate file extension for their format. At the time this book was written, the formats shown in Table 15-1 were supported.

Table 15-1. Supported formats for structured data files containing facts

Type	Extension	Description
YAML	*.yaml*	Facts in YAML format
JSON	*.json*	Facts in JSON format
Text	*.txt*	Facts in *key=value* format

We introduced YAML format back in Chapter 11. Following is a simplified YAML example that sets three facts:

```
# three_simple_facts.yaml
---
my_fact: 'myvalue'
my_effort: 'easy'
is_dynamic: 'false'
```

The text format uses a single *key=value* pair on each line of the file. This only works for string values; arrays and hashes are not supported. Here is the same example in text format:

```
# three_simple_facts.txt
my_fact=myvalue
my_effort=easy
is_dyanamic=false
```

Programs

You can place any executables program or script in the *facts.d/* directory of your module to create new facts.

The script or program must have the execute bit set for root (or the user that you are running Puppet as). The script must output each fact as *key=value* on a line by itself. Following is a simplified example that sets three facts:

```
#!/bin/bash
echo "my_fact=myvalue"
echo "my_effort=easy"
echo "is_dynamic=false"
```

Install this in the directory and test it:

```
$ $EDITOR facts.d/three_simple_facts.sh
$ chmod 0755 facts.d/three_simple_facts.sh
$ facts.d/three_simple_facts.sh
my_fact=myvalue
my_effort=easy
is_dynamic=false
```

Facts on Windows. Executable facts on Windows work exactly the same, and require the same execute permissions and output format. However, the program or script must be named with a known extension. At the time this book was written, the following extensions were supported:

.com, .exe
: Binary executables to be executed directly

.psl PowerShell scripts
: Scripts to be run by the PowerShell interpreter

.cmd, .bat command-shell scripts
: ASCII or UTF8 batch scripts to be processed by `cmd.exe`

Following is the same example from earlier, rewritten as a PowerShell script:

```
Write-Host "my_fact=myvalue"
Write-Host "my_effort=easy"
Write-Host "is_dyanamic=false"
```

You should be able to save and execute this PowerShell script on the command line.

Custom (Ruby) Facts

To create new facts in Ruby for Facter to use, simply create the following directory in your module:

```
$ mkdir -p lib/facter
```

Ruby programs in this directory will be synced to the node at the start of the Puppet run. The node will evaluate these facts, and provide them for use in building the catalog.

Within this directory, create a Ruby script ending in *.rb*. The script can contain any normal Ruby code, but the code that defines a custom fact is implemented by two calls:

- A Ruby code block starting with `Facter.add('`*fact_name*`')`
- Inside the Facter code block, a `setcode` block that returns the fact's value

For an easy example, let's assume that hosts in a cluster have the same name. Unique numbers are added to each node to keep them distinct. This results in a common pattern with hostnames like:

- `webserver01`
- `webserver02`
- `webserver03`
- `mailserver01`
- `mailserver02`

You'd like to define Hiera data based on the cluster name. Right away, you might think to use the `hostname` command to acquire the node name. Facter provides a helper function to execute shell commands: `Facter::Core::Execution.exec()`.

 Keep in mind that you are passing a Ruby `String` to a Ruby function. You must escape metacharacters as required by Ruby, rather than the more permissive rules of Puppet.

The code to derive a node's cluster name from the `hostname` command could look like this:

```
# cluster_name.rb
Facter.add('cluster_name') do
  setcode do
    Facter::Core::Execution.exec("/bin/hostname -s | /usr/bin/sed -e 's/\d//g'")
  end
end
```

This new fact will be available as $facts['cluster_name'] for use in manifests and templates.

 The value passed to exec should be a command to execute. Pipe (|) and redirection (>) operators work as you might expect, but shell commands like if or for do not work.

It is best to run the smallest command possible to acquire a value, and then manipulate the value using native Ruby code. Here's an example using Ruby native libraries to acquire the hostname, and then manipulate the value to remove the domain and numbers:

```
# cluster_name.rb
require 'socket'
Facter.add('cluster_name') do
  setcode do
    hostname = Socket.gethostname
    hostname.sub!(/\..*$/, '') # remove the first period and everything after it
    hostname.gsub(/[0-9]/, '') # remove every number and return revised name
  end
end
```

For more optimization, you could simply use the hostname fact. You can acquire the value of an existing fact using Facter.value('*factname*'). Here is a simpler example starting with the existing fact:

```
# cluster_name.rb
Facter.add('cluster_name') do
  setcode do
    hostname = Facter.value(:hostname).sub(/\..*$/, '')
    hostname.gsub(/[0-9]/, '')
  end
end
```

Plugins including facts are synced from the modules to the node (*pluginsync*) during Puppet's initial configuration phase, prior to the catalog being built. This makes the fact available for immediate use in manifests and templates.

You can run puppet facts to see all facts, including those that have been distributed via pluginsync:

```
[vagrant@client facter]$ puppet facts find |grep cluster_name
    "cluster_name": "client",
```

Avoiding delay

To limit problems with code that may run long or hang, use the timeout property of Facter.add() to define how many seconds the code should complete within. This causes the `setcode` block to halt if the timeout is exceeded. The facts evaluation will move on without an error, but also without a value for the fact. This is preferable to a hung Puppet client.

Returning to our example of calling a shell command, modify it as follows:

```
# cluster_name.rb
Facter.add('cluster_name', :sleep, :timeout => 5) do
  setcode do
    Facter::Core::Execution.exec("/bin/hostname -s |/usr/bin/sed -e 's/\d//g'")
  end
end
```

Best Practice

Define a timeout for any fact that calls a program or connects to a dependency, to avoid hanging the Puppet agent during initialization.

Confining facts

Some facts are inappropriate for certain systems, would not work, or simply wouldn't provide any useful information. To limit which nodes attempt to execute the fact code, utilize a `confine` statement. This statement lists another fact name and valid values. For example, to ensure that only hosts in a certain domain provide this fact, you could use the following:

```
# cluster_name.rb
Facter.add('cluster_name') do
  confine 'domain' => 'example.com'
  setcode do
ruby code which provides the value...
```

You can use multiple `confine` statements to enforce multiple conditions, all of which must be true. Finally, you can also test against multiple values by providing an array of values. If you are looking for a fact only available on Debian-based systems, you could use this:

```
# debian_fact.rb
Facter.add('debian_fact') do
  confine 'operatingsystem' => %w{ Debian Ubuntu }
  setcode do
ruby code which provides the value...
```

Ordering by precedence

You can define multiple methods, or *resolutions*, to acquire a fact's value. Facter will utilize the highest precedence resolution that returns a value. To provide multiple resolutions, simply add another `Facter` code block with the same fact name.

This is a common technique used for facts where the source of data differs on each operating system.

The order in which Facter evaluates possible resolutions is as follows:

1. Facter discards any resolutions where the confine statements do not match.
2. Facter tries each resolution in descending order of weight.
3. Whenever a value is returned, no further code resolutions are tried.

You can define a weight for a resolution using the has_weight statement. If no weight is defined, the weight is equal to the number of confine statements in the block. This ensures that more specific resolutions are tried first.

Following is an example that attempts to acquire the hostname from two different system configuration files:

```
# configured_hostname.rb
Facter.add('configured_hostname') do
  has_weight 10
  setcode do
    if File.exist? '/etc/hostname'
      File.open('/etc/hostname') do |fh|
        return fh.gets
      end
    end
  end
end

Facter.add('configured_hostname') do
  confine "os['family']" => 'RedHat'
  has_weight 5
  setcode do
    if File.exist? '/etc/sysconfig/network'
      File.open('/etc/sysconfig/network').each do |line|
        if line.match(/^HOSTNAME=(.*)$/)
          return line.match(/^HOSTNAME=(.*)$/)[0]
        end
      end
    end
  end
end
```

Aggregating results

The data provided by a fact could be created from multiple data sources. You can then aggregate the results from all data sources together into a single result.

An aggregate fact is defined differently than a normal fact:

1. `Facter.add()` must be invoked with a property `:type => :aggregate`.
2. Each discrete data source is defined in a chunk code block.
3. The chunks object will contain the results of all chunks.
4. An `aggregate` code block should evaluate chunks to provide the final fact value (instead of `setcode`).

Here's a simple prototype of an aggregate fact that returns an array of results:

```
Facter.add('fact_name', :type => :aggregate) do
  chunk('any-name-one') do
    ruby code
  end

  chunk('any-name-two') do
    different ruby code
  end

  aggregate do |chunks|
    results = Array.new
    chunks.each_value do |partial|
      results.push(partial)
    end
    return results
  end
end
```

The `aggregate` block is optional if all of the chunks return arrays or hashes. Facter will automatically merge the results into a single array or hash in that case. For any other resolution, you should define the `aggregate` block to create the final result.

For more examples of aggregate resolutions, see "Writing Facts with Aggregate Resolutions" (*http://bit.ly/1PgQTAJ*) on the Puppet docs site.

Best Practice

Place values from discrete data sources in their own facts, rather than creating facts with complex data structures.

Debugging

Your new fact will not appear in the output of `facter`. Use `puppet facts find` to see the values of custom Puppet facts.

To test the output of your fact, run `puppet facts find --debug` to see verbose details of where facts are being loaded from:

```
$ puppet facts find --debug
...
Debug: Loading facts from modules/stdlib/lib/facter/facter_dot_d.rb
Debug: Loading facts from modules/stdlib/lib/facter/pe_version.rb
Debug: Loading facts from modules/stdlib/lib/facter/puppet_vardir.rb
Debug: Loading facts from modules/puppet/facts.d/three_simple_facts.txt
```

If the output from your custom fact wasn't in the proper format, you'll get errors like this:

```
Fact file facts.d/python_sample.py was parsed but returned an empty data set
```

In those situations, run the program by hand and examine the output. Here's the example I used to generate the preceding complaint:

```
$ /etc/puppetlabs/code/environment/testing/modules/puppet
$ facts.d/python_sample.py
fact1=this
fact2
fact3=that
```

 External facts obsolete and supersede the facter-dot-d functionality provided by the stdlib module for older Puppet versions. Instead of installing facts in the global *facter/facts.d/* directory, place them in an appropriate module's *facts.d/* directory.

Understanding Implementation Issues

There are a few things to understand about how the Puppet agent utilizes facts:

- External facts are evaluated first, and thus cannot reference or use Facter or Ruby facts.
- Ruby facts are evaluated later and can use values from external facts.
- External executable facts are forked instead of executed within the same process. This can have performance implications if thousands of external fact programs are used.

Outside of these considerations, the facts created by these programs are equal and indistinguishable.

Defining Functions

You can create your own functions to extend and enhance the Puppet language. These functions will be executed during the catalog build process. Functions can be written in either the Puppet configuration language or in Ruby.

Puppet Functions

New to Puppet 4 is the ability to write functions in the Puppet configuration language. This gives you the freedom to write functions for use in your manifests entirely in the Puppet language.

Each function should be declared in a separate file stored in the *functions/* directory of a module. The file should be named for the function name followed by the *.pp* extension. Each function defined in a module must be qualified within the module's namespace.

A function placed in an environment's *manifests/* directory should be qualified with the environment:: namespace.

At this time, it is possible to write a function that patches (by masking) a broken function from another module. I expect that future changes will enforce the qualified naming standards, and prevent that usage.

For an example, we'll create a function called make_boolean() that accepts many types of input and returns a Boolean value. Much like the str2boolean and num2boolean functions from the puppetlabs/stdlib library, this function will accept either strings (yes/no/y/n/on/off/true/false) or numbers. Unlike the stdlib functions, it will handle either input type, and also accept Boolean input without raising an error.

The function should be placed in a file named *functions/make_boolean.pp* in the module directory. The function must be named with the qualified scope of the module. For our example, the function would be declared like so:

```
# functions/make_boolean.pp
function puppet::make_boolean( Variant[String,Numeric,Boolean] $inputvalue ) {
  case $inputvalue {
    Undef:   { false }
    Boolean: { $inputvalue }
    Numeric: {
      case $inputvalue {
        0:      { false }
        default: { true }
      }
    }
    String: {
      case $inputvalue {
        /^(?i:off|false|no|n|'')$/: { false }
        default: { true }
      }
    }
  }
}
```

Functions written in the Puppet language can only take actions possible within the Puppet language. Ruby functions remain significantly more powerful.

Ruby Functions

Each Ruby function should be declared in a separate file, stored in the *lib/puppet/functions/modulename/* directory of the module, and named for the function followed by the *.rb* extension.

Define the function by calling `Puppet::Functions.create_function()` with the name of the new function as a Ruby symbol for the only parameter. The code for the function should be defined within a method of the same name.

Our `make_boolean()` function from the previous section could look like this:

```
Puppet::Functions.create_function(:'puppet::make_boolean') do
  def make_boolean( value )
    if [true, false].include? value
      return value
    elsif value.nil?
      return false
    elsif value.is_a? Integer
      return value == 0 ? false : true
    elsif value.is_a? String
      case value
      when /^\s*(?i:false|no|n|off)\s*$/
        return false
      when ''
        return false
      when /^\s*0+\s*$/
        return false
      else
        return true
      end
    end
  end
end
```

Accepting varied input with dispatch

The Puppet 4 API supports Puppet type validation inside Ruby functions with the dispatch method. The API supports multiple dispatch, allowing the selection of method based on the input type(s). dispatch will select the first method that has parameters matching the Puppet type (not Ruby type!) and call the named method with the parameters:

```
Puppet::Functions.create_function(:'puppet::make_boolean') do
  dispatch :make_boolean_from_string do
    param 'String', :value
  end
```

```
    dispatch :make_boolean_from_integer do
      param 'Integer', :value
    end

    dispatch :return_value do
      param 'Boolean', :value
    end

    dispatch :return_false do
      param 'Undef', :false
    end

    def return_value( value )
      return value
    end

    def return_false( value )
      return false
    end

    def make_boolean_from_integer( value )
      return value == 0 ? false : true
    end

    def make_boolean_from_string( value )
      case value
      when /^\s*(?i:false|no|n|off)\s*$/
        return false
      when ''
        return false
      when /^\s*0+\s*$/
        return false
      else
        return true
      end
    end
  end
```

It's possible to accept a range or unlimited values as well. Here are dispatchers for when two values are supplied, and for all other (e.g., unlimited) amounts of values:

```
Puppet::Functions.create_function(:'puppet::find_largest') do
  dispatch :compare_two_values do
    required_param 'Integer', :first
    optional_param 'Integer', :second
  end

  dispatch :compare_unlimited_values do
    repeated_param 'Integer', :values
  end

  def compare_two_values( first, second )
```

```
    ...
  end

  def compare_unlimited_values( *values )
    ...
  end
```

Accessing facts and values

In older versions of Puppet, Ruby functions could access facts and values. In Puppet 4, any values that are needed by the function should be passed as a parameter to the function. For example, here's a function that calculates the subnet for the primary network interface:

```
require 'ipaddr'
# @param [String] address - an IPv4 or IPv6 address
# @param [String] netmask - a netmask
Puppet::Functions.create_function(:'puppet::get_subnet') do
  def get_subnet( address, netmask )
    if !address.nil?
      ip = IPAddr.new( address )
      return ip.mask( netmask ).to_s
    end
  end
end
```

Call this function with the necessary facts as input parameters:

```
puppet::get_subnet( $facts['networking']['ip'], $facts['networking']['netmask'] )
```

Calling other functions

You can invoke a custom Puppet function from another custom Puppet function using the `call_function()` method. This function scans the scope of where the function was invoked to find and load the other function.

All values after the name of the other function are passed as parameters to the other function:

```
Puppet::Functions.create_function(:'mymodule::outer_function') do
  def outer_function( host_name )
    call_function('process_value', 'hostname', host_name )
  end
end
```

Sending back errors

To send an error response back to Puppet (which will cause the Puppet catalog build to fail), `raise` an error of type `Puppet::ParseError`. Here's an example:

```
Puppet::Functions.create_function(:'mymodule::outer_function') do
```

```
    def outer_function( fact_value )
      raise Puppet::ParseError, 'Fact not available!' if fact_value.nil?
      ...things you do if the fact is available...
    end
  end
```

Whenever possible, it is preferred to simply return nil or some other failure value when a function doesn't succeed. This allows the code that called the function to determine what action to take. This is generally better practice than causing the entire Puppet catalog build to fail.

Learning more about functions

The Puppet Functions API has changed dramatically in Puppet 4, and new features are being introduced in each new version in the 4.x releases. You can find the very latest details at "Puppet::Functions" (*http://bit.ly/1PgQWN0*) on the Puppet docs site.

Using Custom Functions

Whether your function was written in Puppet or Ruby, you can use a function you've created the same way as a function built into Puppet. For example, we could use the make_boolean() function we've defined to ensure that a service receives a Boolean value for enable, no matter what type of value was passed to it:

```
service { 'puppet':
  ensure    => $status,
  enable    => puppet::make_boolean( $enabled ),
  subscribe => Package['puppet-agent'],
}
```

Within Puppet templates, all functions are methods of the scope object. To call a custom function within a Puppet template, prepend function_ to the function name as a method of the scope object. This is because, as you might guess, templates are parsed within the scope of the Ruby function template(). Use square brackets around the input variables to create a single array of parameters:

```
<%= if scope.function_puppet::make_boolean( [input_variable] ) -%>
```

Creating Puppet Types

One way to create a *type* in Puppet is using the Puppet configuration language, as described in "Creating New Resource Types" on page 195. A more powerful way to create new types in Puppet is to create them in a Ruby class.

For an example, we will create a somewhat ridiculous elephant type that generates an elephant resource. A resource using our type would look something like this:

```
elephant { 'horton':
  ensure   => present,
  color    => 'grey',
  motto    => 'After all, a person is a person, no matter how small',
}
```

Each Puppet type should be declared in a separate file, stored in the *lib/puppet/type/* directory of the module, and named for the type followed by the *.rb* extension. For our example, the filename will be *lib/puppet/type/elephant.rb*.

Define the type by calling `Puppet::Type.newtype()` with the name of the type as a Ruby symbol for the only parameter. The Ruby code that evaluates the type should be defined within the following block:

```
Puppet::Type.newtype( :elephant ) do
  @doc = %q{Manages elephants on the node
    @example
      elephant { 'horton':
        ensure   => present,
        color    => 'grey',
        motto    => 'After all, a person is a person, no matter how small',
      }
  }
end
```

Place Markdown within the value of the `@doc` tag to provide an example of how to utilize the resource. You can safely indent underneath the value, as the common amount of leading whitespace on following lines is removed when the documentation is rendered.

Defining Ensurable

Most types are `ensurable`, meaning that we compare the current state of the type to determine what changes are necessary. Add the method `ensurable` to the type:

```
Puppet::Type.newtype( :elephant ) do
  ensurable
end
```

The provider for the type is required to define three methods to create the resource, verify if it exists, and destroy it.

Accepting Params and Properties

There are two types of values that can be passed into a type with an attribute. `params` are values used by the type but not stored or verifiable on the resource's manifestation.

Every type must have a *namevar* parameter, which is how the resource is uniquely identified on the system. For user resources this would be the uid, while file resources use path. For our example, the unique identifier is the elephant's name:

```
newparam( :name, :namevar => true ) do
  desc "The elephant's name"
end
```

A property is different in that we can retrieve the property from the resource and compare the values:

```
newproperty( :color ) do
  desc "The color of the elephant"
  defaulto 'grey'
end

newproperty( :motto ) do
  desc "The elephant's motto"
end
```

The preceding example defines the properties and sets a default value for the color.

Validating Input Values

You can perform input validation on each param or property provided to the type. For example, we need to ensure that the color is a known elephant color:

```
newproperty( :color ) do
  desc "The color of the elephant"
  defaulto 'gray'

  validate do |value|
    unless ['grey','brown','red','white'].include? value
      raise ArgumentError, "No elephants are colored #{value}"
    end
  end
end
```

There's a newvalues() method that provides this kind of test, albeit without the more informative message. If a clear error message is not required, it's much shorter to write:

```
newproperty( :color ) do
  desc "The color of the elephant"
  defaulto 'grey'
  newvalues('grey','brown','red','white')
end

newproperty( :motto ) do
  desc "The elephant's motto"
  newvalues(/^[\w\s\'\.]$/)
end
```

The latter form used a `Regexp` to accept any string that contained only alphanumeric letters, spaces, single quotes, and periods.

 You can also define default values as symbols, but this requires your provider to translate symbols to strings in some cases, and it gets messy. Use strings consistently and avoid type conversions entirely.

You can munge values to provide clean mapping for local inconsistencies:

```
newproperty( :color ) do
  desc "The color of the elephant"
  defaulto 'grey'
  newvalues('grey','brown','red','white')
  munge do |value|
    case value
    when 'gray'
      'grey'
    else
        super
    end
  end
end
```

You can perform input validation for the entire type using a global `validate` method. The input values are available as attributes of `self`:

```
Puppet::Type.newtype( :elephant ) do
  ...

  validate do |value|
    if self[:motto].nil? and self[:color].nil?
      raise ArgumentError, "Both a color and a motto are required input."
    end
  end
end
```

You can define a `pre_run_check` method, which will run the code for each instance added to the catalog just before attempting to apply the catalog on the node. Every instance that generates an error will be output as an error by Puppet, and the Puppet run will be aborted.

Keep in mind the difference in the placement of these methods in the run cycle:

- The `validate` method is called each time a resource of this type is added to the catalog. Other resources and types may not yet be parsed and available in the catalog yet.

- The `pre_run_check` method is called after the entire catalog is built, and every instance should exist within the catalog. This is the only valid place to check that requirements for this type exist within the catalog.

Defining Implicit Dependencies

As you might recall from Chapter 7, many Puppet types will `autorequire` other items in the catalog upon which they depend. For example, a `file` resource will `autorequire` the user who owns the file. If the user exists in the catalog, that file resource will depend on that user resource.

You can `autorequire` dependent resources for your type as shown here:

```
Puppet::Type.newtype( :elephant ) do

autorequire(:file) do
  '/tmp/elephants'
end
autorequire(:file) do
  '/tmp'
end
```

As our elephant exists in the */tmp/elephants* directory, we autorequire the `File['/tmp']` resource. If that resource exists in the catalog, we will depend on it. If it is not defined, then the dependency will not be set.

In addition to `autorequire`, you can use the same syntax for `autobefore`, `autonotify`, and `autosubscribe`. These create soft dependencies and refresh events in the same manner as the ordering metaparameters without *auto* in their name.

Learning More About Puppet Types

One of the most informative ways to debug issues with Puppet types is to run Puppet with the `--debug` argument. The debugging shows the loading of custom types and selection of the provider.

The best book to learn more about Puppet types is Dan Bode and Nan Liu's *Puppet Types and Providers*. That book covers this topic much more exhaustively than this quick introduction.

The Puppet::Type documentation (*http://bit.ly/1XAC2Hu*) provides a detailed reference to all methods available.

The Custom Types documentation (*http://bit.ly/1R3xN6V*) provides some prescriptive guidance.

Adding New Providers

Puppet *providers* are Ruby classes that do the detailed work of evaluating a resource. The provider handles all operating system–specific dependencies. For example, there are `yum`, `apt`, `pkgng`, and `chocolatey` providers for installing packages on RedHat, Debian, FreeBSD, and Windows systems, respectively. There are more than 20 different providers for the `package` type due to the wide variety of package managers in use.

For an example, we will create a `posix` provider for our `elephant` type that generates an elephant resource on a POSIX-compliant system (e.g., Linux, Solaris, FreeBSD, etc.).

Providers for Puppet types are always written in Ruby. Each provider should be declared in a separate file, stored in a subdirectory of *lib/puppet/provider/* named for the type. The file should be named for the provider followed by the *.rb* extension. For our example, the filename will be *lib/puppet/provider/elephant/posix.rb*.

Define the provider by calling `Puppet::Type.type()` method with the name of the type, followed by the `provide()` method with the following three inputs:

- The provider name as a Ruby symbol
- Optional `:parent` that identifies a provider from which to inherit methods
- Optional `:source` that identifies a different provider that manages the same resources

The Ruby code that implements the provider should be defined within a following block:

```
Puppet::Type.type( :elephant ).provide( :posix ) do
  desc "Manages elephants on POSIX-compliant nodes."
end
```

Always include a description of what the provider does. You would create an alternate provider for Windows nodes with the following definition in the *lib/puppet/provider/elephant/windows.rb* file:

```
Puppet::Type.type( :elephant ).provide( :windows ) do
  desc "Manages elephants on Windows nodes."
end
```

Determining Provider Suitability

Each provider needs to define ways that Puppet can determine if the provider is suitable to manage that resource on a given node.

There are a wide variety of suitability tests. Following are some examples with comments about their use:

```
Puppet::Type.type( :elephant ).provide( :posix ) do
  # Test the operating system family fact
  confine :osfamily => ['redhat','debian','freebsd','solaris']

  # Test true/false comparisons
  confine :true     => /^4/.match( clientversion )

  # A directory for /tmp must exist
  confine :exists => '/tmp'

  # Ensure that the 'posix' feature is available on this target
  confine :feature => 'posix'
end
```

Check Your Features at the Door

To know what features are available on a node, you can run the interactive Ruby interpreter and ask the Puppet library directly:

```
[vagrant@client ~]$ /opt/puppetlabs/puppet/bin/irb
irb(main):001:0> require 'puppet'
=> true
irb(main):002:0> Puppet.features.posix?
=> true
irb(main):003:0> Puppet.features.root?
=> false
irb(main):004:0> Puppet.features.instance_variable_get(:@results)
=> {:syslog=>true, :posix=>true, :microsoft_windows=>nil,
    :root=>false, :manages_symlinks=>true}
```

As you can see, the syslog, posix, and manages_symlinks features are available on this node. The root feature wasn't enabled because I ran the command without sudo.

Assigning a Default Provider

At times, multiple providers can manage the same resource on a given node. For example, the yum and rpm providers can both manage packages on a CentOS node.

You can declare the provider suitable to be the default provider for a given platform by using defaultfor method and passing it a fact name as a symbol, and an array of suitable values:

```
# Test the operating system family fact
defaultfor :osfamily => ['redhat','debian','freebsd','solaris']
```

Defining Commands for Use

The `commands` method lets you test for the existence of a file, and sets up an instance method you can use to call the program. If the command cannot be found, then the provider is not suitable for this resource:

```
# The echo command must be within /bin
commands :echo => '/bin/echo'

# the ls command must be found in Puppet's path
commands :ls  => 'ls'
```

The `commands` method also defines a new method named for the command that invokes the command, passing all arguments as space-separated command-line options. The method puts the command invocation in the Puppet debug output, and it automatically traps nonzero exit codes and raises `Puppet::ExecutionFailure` for you.

This is significantly better than using Ruby's built-in command execution methods, and having to write the exception handling yourself.

Ensure the Resource State

Most types are `ensurable`, meaning that the provider must validate the existence of the resource and determine what changes are necessary. Define three methods to create the resource, verify its existence, and destroy it:

```
Puppet::Type.type( :elephant ).provide( :posix ) do
  # where elephants can be found
  filename = '/etc/elephants/' + resource['name']

  # commands we need.
  commands :echo => 'echo'
  commands :ls  => 'ls'
  commands :rm  => 'rm'

  # ensurable requires these methods
  def create
    echo("color = #{resource['color']}",'>',filename)
    echo("motto = #{resource['motto']}",'>>',filename)
  end

  def exists?
    begin
      ls(filename)
    rescue Puppet::ExecutionFailure => e
      false
    end
  end
end
```

```
def destroy
  rm(filename)
end
```

These three methods are used to handle transition from *present* to *absent* and vice versa. The type calls the `exists?` method and then determines whether to call `create` or `destroy` in order to meet the state defined by `ensure`.

 We could implement the same features in pure Ruby. I'm using the command-line variant because more information is provided in debug output, and to demonstrate the technique.

Adjusting Properties

For each property with a value that needs to be compared to the resource, you'll need to define two methods—a *getter* and a *setter* for each attribute:

```
# where elephants can be found
filename = '/etc/elephants/' + resource['name']

# commands we need.
commands :sed => 'sed'

def color
  sed('-e','s/^color = \(.*\)$/\1/',filename)
end

def color=(value)
  sed('-i','-e','s/^color = /color = #{value}/',filename)
end
```

The first method retrieves the current value for the property `color`, and the second method changes the elephant's color on the node. The definition for `motto` would be nearly identical.

If there are many attributes that change values, you may want to cache up the changes and write them out at once. After calling any setter methods, a resource will call the `flush` method if defined:

```
def color=(value)
  true
end

def flush
  echo("color = #{resource['color']}",'>',filename)
  echo("motto = #{resource['motto']}",'>>',filename)
  @property_hash = resource.to_hash
end
```

If the resource was modified through a long command line of values (e.g., `usermod`), you could track which values were changed and build a customized command invocation with only those values. Because this resource is only two lines of text, it's significantly easier to just write the file out again.

The final line caches the current values of the resource into an instance variable. Let's talk about what can be done with caching now.

Providing a List of Instances

If it is low impact to read in the resources, you can implement an `instances` class method that will load all instances into memory. This can improve performance in comparison to loading each one separately and modifying it.

Resource providers can make use of that data—for example, when someone uses the following command:

```
$ puppet resource elephant
```

 Do not implement anything in this section if the work required to read the state of all instances would be a drain on resources. For example, the file resource does not implement `instances` because reading the information about every file on the node would be very costly.

To disable preloading of instance data, define it with an empty array.

```
self.instances
  []
end
```

To preload instance data, we simply need to construct the method to output each file in the directory and create a new object with the values:

```
commands :ls  => 'ls'
commands :cat => 'cat'

self.instances
  elephants = ls('/tmp/elephants/)
  # For each elephant...
  elephants.split("\n").collect do |elephant|
    attrs = Hash.new
    output = cat("/tmp/elephants/#{elephant}")
    # for each line in the file
    output.split("\n").collect do |line|
      name, value = line.split(' = ', 2)
      # store the attribute
      attrs[name] = value
    end
    # add the name and its status and then create the resource type
```

```
    attrs[:name] = elephant
    attrs[:ensure] = :present
    new( attrs )
  end
end
```

The preceding code reads each assignment in the elephant file, and assigns the value to the name in a hash. It adds the elephant's name to the hash, and sets `ensure` to `present`. Voilà, we have built this resource in memory! This preloads every instance of the resource, and makes the data available in the `@property_hash` instance variable.

When the `instances` method is available, `puppet agent` and `puppet apply` will load all instances in this manner, and then match up resources in the database to the provider that returned their values.

Taking Advantage of Caching

If all of your instances are cached in memory, then you don't need to read from disk every time. This means you can rewrite your `exists` method to simply...

```
def exists?
  @property_hash[:ensure] == 'present'
end
```

Although in the same sense, you need to ensure that any resources created or deleted are updated in memory:

```
def create
  echo("color = #{resource['color']}",'>',filename)
  echo("motto = #{resource['motto']}",'>>',filename)
  @property_hash[:ensure] = :present
end

def destroy
  rm(filename)
  @property_hash[:ensure] = 'absent'
end
```

Finally, how about each of those instance setter and getter methods? These would each be identical, as they would be just setting or reading from the hash. There is a convenience method, `mk_resource_methods`, which would define all resource attribute methods as follows:

```
def color
  @property_hash[:color] || :absent
end
def color=(value)
  @property_hash[:color] = value
end
```

Place the `mk_resource_methods` invocation near the top of the provider. You can then override any one or more of the default methods it creates. On a resource type with 20 or more attributes, this convenience method will save you a lot of typing!

However, now that you are only saving the changes back to a hash, you must define a `flush()` method to write the changes out to disk as described in "Adjusting Properties" on page 238.

Learning More About Puppet Providers

One of the most informative ways to debug issues with Puppet types is to run Puppet with the `--debug` argument. The debugging shows the selection and execution of the provider for a given node.

The best book to learn more about Puppet providers is Dan Bode and Nan Liu's *Puppet Types and Providers*. That book covers providers much more exhaustively than this quick introduction.

The Puppet::Provider (*http://bit.ly/1RppJPU*) documentation provides a detailed reference to all methods available.

The Provider Development (*http://bit.ly/1MeVetG*) documentation includes many details of creating providers.

Identifying New Features

Puppet *features* are Ruby classes that determine if a specific feature is available on the target node. For an example, we will create an `elephant` feature that is activated if the node has elephants installed.

Features for Puppet are always written in Ruby. Each feature should be declared in a separate file, stored in the module's *lib/puppet/feature/* directory. The file should be named for the feature followed by the *.rb* extension. For our example, the filename will be *elephant.rb*.

Always start by requiring the `puppet/util/feature` library.

Define the feature by calling `Puppet.features.add()` method with the name of the feature as a Ruby symbol. The code that validates if the feature is available should be defined within a following block:

```
require 'puppet/util/feature'

Puppet.features.add( :elephant ) do
  Dir.exist?('/tmp') and
  Dir.exist?('/tmp/elephants') and
  !Dir.glob?('/tmp/elephants/*').empty?
end
```

You can simplify the expression of features that validate whether a certain library is installed by adding an optional :libs argument to the feature definition:

```
require 'puppet/util/feature'

Puppet.features.add( :openssl, :libs => %{openssl} )
```

Binding Data Providers in Modules

Until Puppet 4, data for a module was provided in only three ways:

- Provided as an attribute to the class declaration
- Automatically looked up in Hiera, the only data provider available
- Statically defined within the module itself

Puppet 4 has introduced independent data providers for environments and modules. The lookup() function and automatic parameter lookup in classes use the following sources for data:

- The global data provider (Hiera v3) configured in *${codedir}/hiera.yaml*
- The environment data provider specified in *environment.conf*
- The module data provider specified in *metadata.json*

There are only two steps to providing a data source specific to a module:

1. Define data_provider in the module's *metadata.json* file.
2. Create a function or a Hiera configuration file as the data source for the module.

 Data providers in modules can replace the use of a params class for providing default data values.

Let's take a look at how to create each of them.

Using Data from a Function

As described in "Defining Functions" on page 225, create a Ruby function named data inside your module's namespace. If your module is named specialapp, then the function must be named specialapp::data().

The function can be a Puppet language function defined in *functions/data.pp*, or it can be a Ruby function defined in *lib/puppet/functions/specialapp/data.rb*.

A Ruby function should look something like the following. Replace this simple example function with your own:

```
Puppet::Functions.create_function(:'specialapp::data') do
  def data()
    # the following is just example code to be replaced
    # Return a hash with parameter name to value mapping for the user class
    return {
      'specialapp::user::id'   => 'Value for parameter $id',
      'specialapp::user::name' => 'Value for parameter $name',
    }
  end
end
```

Whether the function is defined in Puppet or Ruby, the function must return a hash that contains keys within the class namespace, exactly the same as how keys must be defined in the Hiera data.

Finally, modify the *metadata.json* in the module's directory to indicate `"data_pro vider": "function"`. The `specialapp::data()` function is now the module data source for the `specialapp` module.

Using Data from Hiera

Create a module data configuration file that defines the Hiera hierarchy. The file should be named *hiera.yaml*, much like the global Hiera configuration file, but it uses a v4 configuration format.

The file must contain a `version` key with value 4, and a `datadir`, which is a path relative to and contained within the module root. The `hierarchy` in the file must be an array of hashes. An example file is shown here:

```
---
version: 4
datadir: data
hierarchy:
  - name: "OS family"
    backend: json
    path: "os/%{facts.os.family}

  - name: "common"
    backend: yaml
```

Create the *data/* directory indicated in the file, and populate Hiera data files with data specific to this module.

To enable the Hiera data source for your module, modify the *metadata.json* file in the module's directory to indicate `"data_provider": "hiera"`. The *hiera.yaml* file in the module's root directory will be used to configure the Hiera data provider for the `specialapp` module.

Performing Lookup Queries

For the example `specialapp` module, the new lookup strategy of global, then environment, then module data providers, would be queried as follows if you used the *function* data source for the module:

```
class specialapp(
  Integer $id,  # will check global Hiera, then environment data provider,
  String $user, # then call specialapp::data() to get all values
) {
```

If you used the *hiera* data source for the module, then parameter values would be independently looked up in each data source:

```
class specialapp(
  Integer $id,  # will check global Hiera, then environment data provider,
  String $user, # then check module Hiera data
) {
```

Requirements for Module Plugins

There were a lot of rules in this chapter around how module plugins are named and created. Let's review them:

- External fact programs should be placed in the *facts.d/* directory and be executable by the `puppet` user. Windows fact providers need to be named with a known file extension.
- External fact data should be placed in the *facts.d/* directory and have a file extension of *.yaml*, *.json*, or *.txt*.
- Functions written with the Puppet language should be placed in the *functions/* directory and be named with a *.pp* file extension.
- Ruby functions should be placed in the *lib/puppet/functions/modulename/* directory and be named the same as the function with an *.rb* file extension.
- Ruby features should be placed in the *lib/puppet/features/* directory and be named the same as the feature with a *.rb* file extension.
- Ruby functions or templates that call custom functions need to prefix the function name with `function_`.
- Ruby functions or templates that call custom functions need to pass all input parameters in a single array.

You can find more detailed guidelines in "Plugins in Modules" (*http://bit.ly/1R8Mz8U*) on the Puppet docs site.

Reviewing Module Plugins

In this chapter, we covered how to extend a module to:

- Provide new facts that will be available for any module to reference.
  - — A program can output one fact name and value per line.
  - — Facts can be written in Ruby, and use Ruby language features.
  - — Facts can be read from YAML, JSON, or text file formats.
- Provide new functions that will be available for any module to reference.
  - — Facts can be written in the Puppet language and use all Puppet features.
  - — Facts can be written in Ruby, and use all Ruby language features.
- Bind a custom function as a data lookup source.
  - — This data source will be queried after the global data provider (Hiera), and the environment data provider (if defined).

As you can see, module plugins can provide powerful new features and functionality.

## CHAPTER 16

Documenting Modules

In this chapter, we're going to discuss how to document your manifests well. Good documentation ensures that others can use your module. It also enables people to build modules that depend on yours in a manner that you can support.

Don't skimp on documentation if it's an internal module that will never be published. Your own users in the company are far more important than random people on the Internet. Give your own users the very best.

Don't forget that you are creating this module based on active needs you understand today. Make notes to remind yourself of the requirements you are trying to solve, so that you can recall what you were thinking when you come back to refactor the class a year later. You'll have a whole new set of requirements in your head, and what you did last year won't make any sense. Trust me, this happens.

Learning Markdown

Puppet is moving away from RDoc format to the widely used Markdown format. Markdown is much easier to learn than RDoc, and is utilized today by the Puppet Forge, GitHub, Sourceforge, Stack Exchange, and many other code repositories and forums.

While you should absolutely read the Markdown documentation, it is entirely possible to build a valid and working README document with just the following simple rules:

- Paragraphs should be typed as-is with no special formatting.
- Code blocks should be indented four spaces or surrounded by ``` ```.
- Headers start with one # sign for each level: #heading1 ##heading2.
- Bullet lists start with a leading asterisk, dash, or plus sign.

- Number lists start with a leading number and period.
- Use spaces to indent for list and code block hierarchy.
- Add two spaces to the end of a line to insert a line feed.
- Surround words with *single asterisks* for *italic text*.
- Surround words with **double asterisks** for **bold text**.

These nine rules provide more than enough syntax to create valid README documents.

Markdown supports a lot more syntax than this. You can find complete documentation of the format at Markdown: Syntax (*http://bit.ly/markdown-doc*).

Writing a Good README

An initial *README.md* template is generated by the `puppet module generate` command. Replace the example content with details specific to your module.

This is documentation for users of your module, so be clear and unambiguous about how to use it. A well-written README will inform a user what your module does, and how to use it without reading its manifests. In particular, make sure you include:

- A list of all dependencies required by your module
- A list of all parameters used by your module
- An example Hiera configuration for a common use case

You can find Puppet Labs' latest recommendations for style on its site at "README Style Notes" (*http://bit.ly/1pyP5ia*). These are well worth reading, and will greatly improve the usability of your module.

Documenting the Classes and Types

Each class and defined type in your module should be documented in the manifest.

Puppet 4 has deprecated RDoc syntax documentation in favor of using Markdown for class documentation. Therefore you'll need to use the formats shown in this book instead of the RDoc format you may find in older modules.

Installing YARD and Puppet Strings

Puppet 4 has moved away from RDoc in favor of Markdown format documentation for consistency. You can use Markdown format even if your module is used by Puppet 3 users, as Markdown is easy to read. Puppet 3 users can also install the `puppet-strings` module to generate HTML and PDF documentation.

puppet doc no longer generates module documentation in Puppet 4. Module documentation is generated by puppet strings, which you can make available by installing the puppetlabs-strings module.

Install the Yard gem as a gem used by the AIO puppet installation:

```
$ sudo puppet resource package yard provider=puppet_gem
Notice: /Package[yard]/ensure: created
package { 'yard':
  ensure => ['0.8.7.6'],
}
```

Install the Puppet Labs strings module. You can install this in the production environment, or within your personal Puppet directory:

```
$ puppet module install puppetlabs-strings
Notice: Preparing to install into /home/vagrant/.puppetlabs/etc/code/modules ...
Notice: Created target directory /home/vagrant/.puppetlabs/etc/code/modules
Notice: Downloading from https://forgeapi.puppetlabs.com ...
Notice: Installing -- do not interrupt ...
/home/vagrant/.puppetlabs/etc/code/modules
└── puppetlabs-strings (v0.3.0)
```

Finally, ensure that the *.yardopts* file exists in the root of each module. If you are updating older modules not generated from a recent skeleton, you may need to add this file:

```
$ echo '--markup markdown' > .yardopts
```

Fixing the Headers

At the time this book was written, the default Puppet module skeleton included headers tagged with a valid but less common Markdown header. If these don't appear as headers in your documentation, then you may be missing the aforementioned *.yardopts* file:

```
#
# Authors
# -------
```

It is also completely valid to replace those headers with the same Markdown headers used in the README file. Use the proper number of # characters for your header depth and leave no spaces before the start of the header:

```
#
##Authors
#
```

When updating an older module, change the heading for *Examples* to a comment, as Yard includes its own special heading for examples in the generated output.

Listing Parameters

Parameters are documented with the @param meta tag. Follow this tag with the name of the parameter and a description of its use. The following lines should document the default and expected values, as shown here:

```
# @param [Type] sample_parameter Description of parameter
# * `sample parameter`
# Description of the parameter
```

 If you are updating an older module, there will be no examples of @param in the manifest documentation.

I have found that it displays better if you put two spaces after the parameter bullet so the description falls on the following line. It is no longer necessary to document the type or default value, as this is shown clearly in the Parameter Summary lower on the page.

Here is an example for documenting the puppet::client class we built earlier in the book:

```
# @param [Enum['running','stopped']] status Whether Puppet runs as a daemon
# * `status`
#    Whether Puppet agent should be running as a daemon
#
# @param [Boolean] enabled Whether Puppet client should start at boot
# * `enabled`
#    Whether Puppet agent should start at boot
#
# @param [Hash] config Hash of configuration options for the [agent] section
# * `config`
#    Hash containing key/value pairs of Puppet configuration directives

class puppet::agent(
  Enum['running','stopped'] $status  = 'running',
  Boolean $enabled                   = true,
  Hash $config                       = {},
) {
```

Every parameter listed in the class invocation must be listed with a @param option, or the documentation will reflect the discrepancy with marked-out lines and (TBD) flags.

Documenting Variable References

In the Variables section of the documentation, list any variables declared by this class that are not input parameters. This can include:

- Internal variables created by the class
- Direct access of variables from other modules and classes
- Direct Hiera lookups of data not passed in as parameters

Variables are documented with the same syntax used for parameters, but without the @param tag. Follow the bullet line with a freeform description of how the variable is used. As before, adding two spaces after the bullet line provides the best display.

Here is an example for documenting the puppet::agent class we built earlier in the book:

```
##Variables
#
# * `puppet::package_version`
#    This uses the common $package_version variable provided by the base class
#
class puppet::agent(...) {
  include '::puppet'

  package { 'puppet-agent':
    version => $::puppet::package_version,
  }
```

Showing Examples

Examples are documented with the @examples meta tag. Follow this tag with the name of the parameter and a description of its use. The following lines should document how to use the module, the required values, and the most likely use case.

Here is an example for documenting how to use the puppet::agent class we built earlier in the book:

```
# Examples here (no header required)
#
# @examples Hiera data for using puppet::agent
#    classes:
#      - puppet::agent
#
#    puppet::agent::status = 'running'
#    puppet::agent::enabled = true
```

As always in Markdown, add two spaces to any empty line you wish to preserve in the output.

Listing Authors and Copyright

The Authors section of the documentation is self-explanatory. List your name and the names of your coauthors. Include an email address where they can contact you with questions. If you intend to publish this module on the Puppet Forge and don't feel comfortable giving out your email, list the address of your issue tracking system as a contact method.

Here's an example:

```
##Authors
# Jo Rhett, Net Consonance
#  - report issues at http://github.com/jorhett/puppet4-module/issues
```

For the copyright section of the documentation, identify the module copyright. If this is a module that you created for an employer, you should probably use *Employer Name*, All Rights Reserved.

If you're publishing the module with an intent for others to use it, include a reference to the license in question:

```
##Copyright
# Copyright &copy; 2015 Acme Products
# Licensed under the Apache License, Version 2.0 (the "License");
#    you may not use this module except in compliance with the License.
#    http://www.apache.org/licenses/LICENSE-2.0
```

Common Mistake

Only the copyright owner can assign rights to others, so you or your organization must retain copyright for the license to be valid. See Open Source Initiative: Frequently Asked Questions (*http://opensource.org/faq#public-domain*) for more details.

Refer to "Identifying the License" on page 254 for instructions about selecting the correct license for your needs.

Documenting Functions

Document function parameters using the @param meta tag followed by the input value type. If the function returns any values they should be defined using @returns followed by the type.

The following lines provide the format for parameter and return values:

```
# @param [Type] sample_parameter - Description of parameter
# @returns [Type] - Description of the result
# @since [String] - Description of when the function became available
```

It is not necessary to document a default value, as this is shown in the Parameter Summary lower on the page.

Here is an example for documenting the get_subnet class built earlier in the book:

```
##Function: get_subnet
#
# @param [String] address - an IP address
# @param [String] netmask - the subnet mask
# @returns [String] - the network address of the subnet
# @since 1.2.2

Puppet::Functions.create_function(:'mymodule::get_subnet') do
```

Every parameter listed in the class invocation must be listed with a @param option, or the documentation will reflect the discrepancy with marked-out lines and (TBD) markers.

Functions can include @example blocks exactly the same as Puppet classes.

If the function is private and you want to warn others against making use of it, you can mark it as such and a big warning label will be included in the documentation alerting others not to use it:

```
# @api private
Puppet::Functions.create_function(:'mymodule::get_subnet') do
```

Generating Documentation

Generate module documentation by changing into the module path and running puppet strings. strings reads each manifest and plugin, and creates the final documentation from tags in them. It places the HTML documentation in the *doc/* folder within the module.

If you run this against your Puppet module, you should see output like this:

```
$ cd /etc/puppetlabs/code/environments/test/modules/puppet
$ puppet strings
Files:           1
Modules:         0 (    0 undocumented)
Classes:         0 (    0 undocumented)
Constants:       0 (    0 undocumented)
Methods:         0 (    0 undocumented)
Puppet Classes:    3 (    0 undocumented)
Puppet Types:    1 (    0 undocumented)
 100.00% documented
true
```

If it points out that any of your classes or defined types aren't documented, you know what to do.

You can read the documentation for a module you are using by opening up the *index.html* file within the module's *doc/* directory.

You can generate documentation for all modules by running `puppet strings` from the *modules* directory:

```
$ cd /etc/puppetlabs/code/environments/test/modules
$ puppet strings
```

Updating Module Metadata

An initial *metadata.json* file is generated by the `puppet module generate` command. You should go through each of these sections and replace the example content with details specific to your module.

 As this file is standard (*picky*) JSON format, use double quotes for everything and remove trailing commas from the last entry in each item.

You can find Puppet Labs' latest recommendations for names and values at "Writing a metadata.json File" (*http://bit.ly/1pt89Oa*) on its site. However, we will review some important guidelines next.

Identifying the License

If you are publishing on the Puppet Forge, you must select a license that allows others to use the module, such as one of the following:

- Apache 2.0 License (*http://choosealicense.com/licenses/apache-2.0/*)
- LGPL 3.0 License (*http://choosealicense.com/licenses/lgpl-3.0/*)
- BSD Simplified License (*http://choosealicense.com/licenses/bsd-2-clause/*)
- BSD Revised License (*http://choosealicense.com/licenses/bsd-3-clause/*)

If you need help finding the right license for your needs, the Choose an OSS License website (*http://choosealicense.com/*) provides a choose-your-path approach to finding a license that meets your needs. Once you have chosen the license, find the appropriate identifier on the SPDX License List (*http://spdx.org/licenses/*) and use that for the value, like so:

```
"license": "Apache-2.0",
```

Generate a license for your module by following the instructions included with the license selected. This generally involves adding a copyright year, a copyright owner, and perhaps the project name to the boilerplate text provided. Place this in a file named *LICENSE*.

Promoting the Project

An important thing to get right is the `source`, `project`, and `issues` tags. These are used to create links in the Puppet Forge and private forges. They inform users how to find documentation and submit issues related to the project:

```
"source": "https://github.com/exampleorg/exampleorg-puppet",
"project_page": "https://forge.puppetlabs.com/exampleorg/puppet",
"issues_url": "https://github.com/exampleorg/exampleorg-puppet/issues",
```

Indicating Compatibility

Operating system compatibility informs the viewer which operating systems and versions your module is known to work on. This is defined as an array of hashes in the metadata. A match for any one hash indicates success.

Each hash contains two values:

`operatingsystem`
> This is the value of `$facts['os']['name']`

`operatingsystemrelease`
> An array of possible values, which are matched against either `$facts['os']['release']['major']` or `"$facts['os']['release']['major'].$facts['os']['release']['minor']"`

Here's an example of compatibility that supports recent Enterprise Linux and Debian/Ubuntu versions:

```
"operatingsystem_support": [
  {
    "operatingsystem":"RedHat",
    "operatingsystemrelease":[ "6", "7" ]
  },
  {
    "operatingsystem":"CentOS",
    "operatingsystemrelease":[ "6", "7" ]
  },
  {
    "operatingsystem":"Amazon",
    "operatingsystemrelease":[ "2016.03", "2015.09", "2015.03", "2014.09" ]
  },
  {
    "operatingsystem":"OracleLinux",
    "operatingsystemrelease":[ "6", "7" ]
  },
  {
    "operatingsystem":"Scientific",
    "operatingsystemrelease":[ "6", "7" ]
  },
  {
    "operatingsystem":"Debian",
    "operatingsystemrelease":[ "6", "7", "8" ]
  },
  {
    "operatingsystem": "Ubuntu",
    "operatingsystemrelease": [ "16.04", "15.10", "15.04", "14.10", "14.04" ]
  }
],
```

Defining Requirements

Requirements are an array of hashes, each item of which identifies a valid Puppet version. A match for any one hash indicates success:

name

This is the value of the production. At this time, I think only puppet and pe (Puppet Enterprise) are supported.

version_requirement

This is a comparison expression that can utilize both <= and >= operators:

```
"requirements": [
  { "name": "pe",     "version_requirement": ">= 2015.0.0" },
  { "name": "puppet", "version_requirement": ">= 4.0.0"    }
],
```

A module that requires Puppet 4/PE 2015 or greater might use the preceding example, whereas a module that supports only Puppet 3 might use >= 3.7.0 < 4.0.0.

 Puppet Enterprise versions use a single digit after the period, but the version_requirement attribute requires two periods in the version number. Append an extra .0 to the end of the Puppet Enterprise version number.

I wish there were a way to suggest that Puppet 3 versions that utilized the *future* parser (the prototype for Puppet 4's parsing engine) were compatible, but I've found no way to express that.

Listing Dependencies

List all modules required by this module in Dependencies. Indicate the range of acceptable versions with comparison operators. puppet module uses this information to automatically install dependencies when the module is installed:

name
: This is the name of the module as shown on the Puppet Forge, but with the prefix and the module name separated by a slash (/).

version_requirement
: This expression can utilize multiple >= and <= operators to indicate a valid range of matching versions:

```
"dependencies": [
  { "name": "puppetlabs/stdlib",  "version_requirement": ">= 3.2.0" },
  { "name": "puppetlabs/inifile", "version_requirement": ">= 1.0.2" }
],
}
```

Identifying a Module Data Source

If the module uses a data provider as documented in "Binding Data Providers in Modules" on page 242, list the data provider type (valid values are hiera or function):

```
"data_provider": "function"
```

You can leave out this variable or use none to indicate that there is no data provider specific to this module.

Updating Old Metadata

The following changes are necessary when updating on an older module:

- The types field has been obsoleted, and should be removed from the file.
- Puppet Enterprise version numbers have changed format.
    — Puppet Enterprise 3.8 was the final version based on Puppet 3.
    — Puppet Enterprise 2015.2 was the first version based on Puppet 4.

Maintaining the Change Log

The *CHANGELOG.md* file isn't generated by default. Create this file and update it with every version change in your module. For each version change, include something like this:

```
##YYYY-MM-DD - Release X.Y.Z
###Summary

This release ...

####Features
- Added new...
- Revised...

####Deprecations
- Removed support for...

####Bugfixes
- Fixed bug where...
```

Maintaining *CHANGELOG.md* will save you a tremendous amount of bug reports and frustrated users. Consider this a worthwhile investment.

Evolving and Improving

The migration to Markdown format is an evolving effort that has iterated a few times during the development of this book, and will continue after the book has gone to press.

You can find the latest updates for recommended style at the puppetlabs-strings module (*http://bit.ly/22oR6yM*) on GitHub.

It can be useful to refer to the YARD Documentation Guides and Resources (*http://yardoc.org/guides/index.html*) for how-to guides and other resources. The following tags are supported at this time:

`@example` *(http://bit.ly/1Rpprs9)*
  Show an example snippet of code for an object. The first line is an optional title.

`@param` *(http://bit.ly/1RTF7yc)*
  Documents a single function or class parameter with a given name, type, and optional description.

`@returns` *(http://bit.ly/1Z9YiJO)*
  Describes the return value and type of a function or fact.

`@since` *(http://bit.ly/1pt8ksM)*
  Lists the version in which the fact or function was first added.

Keep in mind that not all YARD tags are parsed by Puppet `strings`. The following YARD tags were not supported when this book was last updated:

`@author` *(http://bit.ly/1TUkesO)*
  Special formatting for the author of the code.

`@note` *(http://bit.ly/22oRbCo)*
  Emphasize a note about the class, type, or method.

`@options` *(http://bit.ly/1Vk4I98)*
  List valid options for a hash.

`@see` *(http://bit.ly/1TUkjwy)*
  Refer to a web page.

`@todo` *(http://bit.ly/1Z9Yqch)*
  Comment about things that need to be completed.

`@version` *(http://bit.ly/1UmXCBa)*
  Show version of the specific class, type, or function.

Best Practices for Documenting Modules

Let's review some of the best practices for module documentation covered in this chapter:

- Document every manifest using Markdown markup within the file.
- Document each input parameter's type and acceptable values.
- Update the module version for every change released.
- Update the README and CHANGELOG Markdown documents for each version of the module.

You can find more detailed guidelines in "Documenting Modules" *(http://bit.ly/1Z9YuIW)* on the Puppet docs site.

## CHAPTER 17

Testing Modules

Sad to say, but not many modules include good tests. Good tests help keep embarrassing bugs from going out. Tests can save you a lot of time, avoiding the exhaustive debugging of an issue in production that turns out to be a wrong type used, or a similar mistake.

This chapter will teach you how to add good tests to your modules. When I got started, I struggled a lot due to a lack of good examples. This chapter provides good examples of each type of test you should be doing. It's my intention that you'd be able to use the examples provided here like tinker toys, and build a good set of tests for your modules without much effort.

This chapter won't provide exhaustive documentation of `rspec` or `beaker`, the testing tools of choice for the Puppet ecosystem. However, you should be able to build a good foundation of tests from what we cover in this chapter.

Let's get started by setting up your testing tools.

Installing Dependencies

The first time you set up to do testing, you'll need to install some specific software.

Installing Ruby

You can use the Ruby version that comes with your operating system. If you are using the Vagrant testing setup documented in this book, it is easy to install Ruby into the system packages:

```
[vagrant@client ~]$ sudo yum install -y ruby-devel rubygems rake libxml2-devel
```

Guides for installing Ruby can be found in Appendix C.

Install the bundler gem for local installation of necessary dependencies:

```
$ sudo gem install bundler --no-ri --no-rdoc
Fetching: bundler-1.11.1.gem (100%)
Successfully installed bundler-1.11.1
1 gem installed
```

Adding Beaker

Add the following lines to the *Gemfile* in the module directory:

```
gem 'beaker-rspec', :require => false
gem 'pry',          :require => false
```

These lines will ensure that Beaker is installed along with the other dependencies in the next step. Beaker gem dependencies require these development libraries to compile binary extensions:

```
[vagrant@client ~]$ sudo yum install -y gcc-d++ libxml2-devel libxslt-devel
```

Bundling Dependencies

If you haven't done this already, you'll need to install the *puppetlabs_spec_helper* and other dependency gems. The best way to do this is to run the bundler install command within the module directory. bundle will read the *Gemfile* and pull in rspec, rspec-puppet, beaker, and all of their dependencies. These are testing and template creation tools that simplify test creation:

```
[vagrant@client puppet]$ bundler install
Fetching gem metadata from https://rubygems.org/..........
Fetching version metadata from https://rubygems.org/..
Resolving dependencies...
Installing rake 11.1.1
Installing CFPropertyList 2.2.8
Using diff-lcs 1.2.5
...snip a long list of gems...
Installing rspec 3.4.0
Installing puppet 4.4.0
Installing rspec-puppet 2.3.2
Installing puppetlabs_spec_helper 1.1.1
Installing beaker 2.37.0
Installing beaker-rspec 5.3.0
Bundle complete! 6 Gemfile dependencies, 95 gems now installed.
Use `bundle show [gemname]` to see where a bundled gem is installed.
```

Don't use sudo when running bundler. Its purpose is to *vendor* the gems locally in *~/.gems/*, without affecting the system gems.

Preparing Your Module

The next step is to set up your module for testing. We'll have to modify a few files to use the best tools for this.

Defining Fixtures

Create a *.fixtures.yml* file to define the testing fixtures (dependencies) and where to acquire them for testing purposes. The information in this file should duplicate the dependencies in *metadata.json*.

The top of the file should always be the same. This tells the testing frame to copy the current module from its directory:

```
fixtures:
  symlinks:
    puppet: "#{source_dir}"
```

Then define each dependency for your module and the minimum version you support. You can list their names on the Puppet Forge or their GitHub URL. The following two examples will have similar effects. From the Forge:

```
forge_modules:
  stdlib:
    repo: "puppetlabs/stdlib"
    ref: 4.5.1
```

From GitHub:

```
repositories:
  stdlib:
    repo: "git://github.com/puppetlabs/puppetlabs-stdlib"
    ref: "4.5.1"
```

If you are testing development of multiple modules, you may want to use symlinks to the source tree for each. Assuming the dependency is in the same directory structure:

```
symlinks:
  some_dependency: "#{source_dir}/../some_dependency"
```

Test that dependency setup worked properly like so:

```
$ rake spec
(in /etc/puppetlabs/code/environments/test/modules/puppet)
Notice: Preparing to install into
  /etc/puppetlabs/code/environments/test/modules/puppet/spec/fixtures/modules ...
Notice: Downloading from https://forgeapi.puppetlabs.com ...
Notice: Installing -- do not interrupt ...
/etc/puppetlabs/code/environments/test/modules/puppet/spec/fixtures/modules
└── puppetlabs-stdlib (v3.2.1)
/usr/bin/ruby -I/usr/lib/ruby/gems/1.8/gems/rspec-support-3.2.2/lib:...
No examples found.
```

```
Finished in 0.00027 seconds (files took 0.04311 seconds to load)
0 examples, 0 failures
```

This shows that all fixtures (dependencies) were installed, but no examples (tests) were available. Let's start building one now.

Defining RSpec Unit Tests

Now let's build some tests for the module. We know, few people think that building tests is fun work—but it is important work that will save you time and effort down the road.

You should follow these guidelines for creating useful tests:

- Test every input parameter.
- Test every file, package, and service name.
- Test every variation in implementation your module is designed to handle.
- Test for implicit choices based around operating system or other environmental tests.
- Test for invalid input as well as valid input.

Let's look at some examples that test each one of these situations.

Defining the Main Class

Within your module directory, change into the *spec/classes/* directory. Inside this directory, create a file named *<modulename>_spec.rb*.

```
[vagrant@client puppet]$ cd spec/classes
[vagrant@client classes]$ $EDITOR puppet_spec.rb
```

First, we will define a test where the module test builds (compiles) a catalog successfully with the default options:

```
require 'spec_helper'

describe 'puppet', :type => 'class' do

  context 'with defaults for all parameters' do
    it do
      should contain_class('puppet')
      should contain_class('puppet::params')
    end

    it do
      should compile.with_all_deps
    end
  end
end
```

Let's go ahead and run the testing suite against this very basic test:

```
[vagrant@client puppet]$ rake spec
(in /etc/puppetlabs/code/modules/puppet)
ruby -I/opt/puppetlabs/puppet/lib/ruby/gems/2.1.0/gems/rspec-support-3.2.2/lib:
..

Finished in 10.22 seconds (files took 0.56629 seconds to load)
2 examples, 0 failures
```

Check the Puppet Gem Version

If you are using an older system for testing, you may see the following error:

```
Failures:

  1) puppet with defaults for all parameters should contain Class[puppet]
```

This is because a version of the Puppet gem older than 3.7 has been loaded. Any of the following commands will solve this problem. If you are testing modules for maximum compatibility, run all of these commands. Notice the special comparison operator ~>, which will give you the latest available version for each minor version of Puppet:

```
$ gem install puppet --no-ri --no-rdoc
Fetching: puppet-4.4.0.gem (100%)
Successfully installed puppet-4.4.0
1 gem installed

$ gem install puppet --version '~> 3.8.0' --no-ri --no-rdoc
Fetching: puppet-3.8.1.gem (100%)
Successfully installed puppet-3.8.1
1 gem installed

$ gem install puppet --version '~> 3.7.0' --no-ri --no-rdoc
Fetching: puppet-3.7.5.gem (100%)
Successfully installed puppet-3.7.5
1 gem installed
```

Try running your test again, and you should see that it succeeds.

Now that our basic test passed, let's go on to start checking the input parameters.

Passing Valid Parameters

What if we expand the tests to include every possible input value? Rather than repeating each test with a different value, we use Ruby loops to iteratively build each of the tests from an array of values:

```
['1','0'].each do |repo_enabled|
  ['emerg','crit','alert','err','warning','notice','info'].each do |loglevel|
    context "with repo_enabled = #{repo_enabled}, loglevel #{loglevel}" do
      let :params do
        {
          :repo_enabled => repo_enabled,
          :loglevel     => loglevel,
        }
      end

      it do
        should contain_package('puppet-agent').with({
          'version' => '1.4.0-1'
        })
      end
    end
  end
end
```

Whoa, look at that. We added 17 lines of code and yet it's performing 36 more tests:

```
[vagrant@client puppet]$ rake spec
(in /etc/puppetlabs/code/modules/puppet)
ruby -I/opt/puppetlabs/puppet/lib/ruby/gems/2.1.0/gems/rspec-support-3.2.2/lib:

........................................

Finished in 10.53 seconds (files took 0.56829 seconds to load)
38 examples, 0 failures
```

Failing Invalid Parameters

Always test to ensure incorrect values fail. This example shows two tests that are intended to fail:

```
context 'with invalid loglevel' do
  let :params do
    {
      :loglevel => 'annoying'
    }
  end

  it do
    expect { should compile.with_all_deps }
  end
end

context 'with invalid repo_enabled' do
  let :params do
    {
      :repo_enabled => 'EPEL'
    }
  end
```

```
    it do
      expect { should compile.with_all_deps }
    end
  end
```

Run the tests to see what error messages are kicked back:

```
[vagrant@client puppet]$ rake spec
Failures:

1) puppet4 with invalid loglevel should build a catalog w/o dependency cycles
   Failure/Error: should compile.with_all_deps
     error during compilation: Parameter loglevel failed on Class[Puppet]:
       Invalid value "annoying". Valid values are debug, info, notice, warning,
       err, alert, emerg, crit, verbose.  at line 1
   # ./spec/classes/puppet_spec.rb:52:in 'block (3 levels) in <top (required)>'

2) puppet4 with invalid repo_enabled should build a catalog w/o dependency cycles
   Failure/Error: should compile.with_all_deps
     error during compilation: Expected parameter 'repo_enabled' of
       'Class[Puppet]' to have type Enum['0', '1'], got String at line 1
   # ./spec/classes/puppet_spec.rb:65:in 'block (3 levels) in <top (required)>'

Finished in 10.81 seconds (files took 0.57989 seconds to load)
40 examples, 2 failures
```

Now let's change the expect lines to accept the error we expect:

```
expect { should raise_error(Puppet::Error,
    /Invalid value "annoying". Valid values are/)
}
```

and the following for the test of repo_enabled:

```
expect { should raise_error(Puppet::Error,
    /Expected parameter 'repo_enabled' .* to have type Enum/)
}
```

Now when you run the tests, you will see the tests were successful because the invalid input produced the results expected.

Testing File Creation

You can test to ensure that a file resource is created. The simplest form is:

```
it { should contain_file('/etc/puppetlabs/puppet/puppet.conf') }
```

Now, this only checks that the file exists, and not that it was modified correctly by the module. Test resource attributes using this longer form:

```
it do
  should contain_file('/etc/puppetlabs/puppet/puppet.conf').with({
    'ensure' => 'present',
    'owner'  => 'root',
    'group'  => 'root',
    'mode'   => '0444',
  })
end
```

Finally, you can also check the content against a regular expression. Here's an example where we pass in a parameter, and then want to ensure it would be written to the file:

```
let :params do
{
  :loglevel => 'notice',
}
end

it do
  should contain_file('/etc/puppetlabs/puppet/puppet.conf').with_content({
    /^\s*loglevel\s*=\s*notice/
  })
end
```

Validating Class Inclusion

You can test to ensure that a dependent class was loaded:

```
it { should contain_class('puppet::_config') }
```

When testing a defined type, set a title for the defined type to be passed during the test:

```
let(:title) { 'mytype_testing' }
```

Using Facts in Tests

Some manifests or tests may require that certain facts are defined properly. Inside the context block, define a hash containing the fact values you want to have available in the test:

```
let :facts do
{
  :osfamily => 'RedHat',
  :os       => {
    'family' => 'RedHat',
    'release' => { 'major' => '7', 'minor' => '2' }
  },
}
end
```

By default, the `hostname`, `domain`, and `fqdn` facts are set from the fully qualified domain name of the host. To adjust the node name and these three facts for testing purposes, add this to the test:

```
let(:node) { 'webserver01.example.com' }
```

Using Hiera Input

Within your module directory, change to the *spec/fixtures/* directory. Inside this directory, create a subdirectory named *hiera*, containing a valid *hiera.yaml* file for testing:

```
[vagrant@client puppet]$ cd spec/fixtures
[vagrant@client puppet]$ mkdir hiera
[vagrant@client classes]$ $EDITOR hiera/hiera.yaml
```

You can change anything you want that is valid for Hiera in this configuration file, except for the `datadir`, which should reside within the fixtures path. Unless you desire a specific change, the following file could be used unchanged in every module:

```
# spec/fixtures/hiera/hiera.yaml
---
:backends:
  - yaml
:yaml:
  :datadir: /etc/puppetlabs/code/hieradata
:hierarchy:
  - os/"%{facts.osfamily}"
  - common
```

Now, add the following lines to a test context within one of the class spec files:

```
let(:hiera_config) { 'spec/fixtures/hiera/hiera.yaml' }
hiera = Hiera.new( :config => 'spec/fixtures/hiera/hiera.yaml' )
```

Now create your Hiera input files. The only necessary file is *spec/fixtures/hiera/common.yaml*. The others can be added only when you want to test things:

```
---
puppet::loglevel        : 'notice'
puppet::repo_enabled  : '1'
puppet::agent::status : 'running'
puppet::agent::enabled: true
```

You can use this Hiera data to configure the tests:

```
let :params do
  {
    :repo_enabled => hiera.lookup('puppet::repo_enabled',nil,nil),
    :loglevel     => hiera.lookup('puppet::loglevel',nil,nil),
  }
end
```

This configuration allows you to easily test the common method of using Hiera to supply input parameters for your modules.

Defining Parent Class Parameters

In some situations, your module will depend upon a class that requires some parameters to be provided. You cannot set parameters or use Hiera for that class, because it is out of scope for the current class and test file.

The workaround is to use a `pre_condition` block to call the parent class in resource-style format. Pass the necessary parameters for testing as parameters for the resource declaration, and this module instance will be created before your module is tested.

Here is an example from my `mcollective` module, which had to solve this exact problem:

```
describe 'mcollective::client' do
  let(:pre_condition) do
    'class { "mcollective":
      hosts            => ["middleware.example.net"],
      client_password  => "fakeTestingClientPassword",
      server_password  => "fakeTestingServerPassword",
      psk_key          => "fakeTestingPreSharedKey",
    }'
  end

  ...tests for the mcollective::client class...
```

Testing Functions

Unit tests should be created for any functions added by the module. Each function test should exist in a separate file, stored in the *spec/functions/* directory of the module, and named for the function followed by the *_spec.rb* extension.

At a bare minimum, the test should ensure that:

- The function is defined within the Puppet space (test for `function_`*function-name*).
- There aren't insufficient or too many values.
- Given an expected input, it produces an expected output.

Here is an example that should work for our `make_boolean()` example:

```
#! /usr/bin/env ruby -S rspec
require 'spec_helper'
require 'puppetlabs_spec_helper/puppetlabs_spec/puppet_internals'

describe "the make_boolean function" do
  let(:scope) { PuppetSpec::Scope }
```

```
    it "should exist" do
      expect(Puppet::Functions.function("make_boolean")).to
        eq("function_make_boolean")
    end

    it "should raise a ParseError if there is less than 1 arguments" do
      expect { scope.function_make_boolean([]) }.to(
        raise_error(Puppet::ParseError)
      )
    end

    it "should convert '0' to false"  do
      result = scope.function_make_boolean(["0"])
      expect(result).to(eq(false))
    end
  end
end
```

Adding an Agent Class

Within the *spec/classes/* directory, create a file named *agent_spec.rb*. This is an exercise for you. Build the agent class, testing every valid and invalid input just like we did for the Puppet class.

For this, we simply want to test that the package, config file, and service resources are all defined:

```
require 'spec_helper'

describe 'puppet::agent', :type => 'class' do

  context 'with defaults for all parameters' do
    it do
      should contain_package('puppet-agent').with({ 'version' => 'latest' })
      should contain_file('puppet.conf').with({ 'ensure' => 'file' })
      should contain_service('puppet').with({ 'ensure' => 'running' })
    end

    it do
      should compile.with_all_deps
    end
  end
end
```

We have demonstrated how to build tests. Now, you should build out more tests for valid and invalid input.

Testing Other Types

Every object type provided by a module can be tested. Place tests for the other types in the directories specified in Table 17-1.

Table 17-1. Directories in which to place other tests

Type	Directory
Class	*spec/classes/*
Defined resource type	*spec/defines/*
Functions	*spec/functions/*
Node differences	*spec/hosts/*

Creating Acceptance Tests

The rspec unit tests discussed earlier in this chapter validate individual features by testing the code operation in the development environment. Rspec tests provide low-cost, easy-to-implement code validation.

In contrast, the Beaker test harness spins up (virtual) machines to run platform-specific acceptance tests against Puppet modules.

Beaker creates a set of test nodes (or nodeset) running each operating system and configuration you'd like to perform system tests for. Beaker tests are significantly slower and more resource-intensive than rspec tests, but they provide a realistic environment test that goes far beyond basic code testing.

Installing Ruby for System Tests

As Beaker will need to run `vagrant` commands to create virtual machines to run the test suites on, you'll need to run Beaker on your development system rather than one of the virtual machines you've been using so far. Following are the steps to set up and appropriate testing environment on your system.

1. Follow the instructions for installing Ruby on your desktop operating system. Directions for installing Ruby on different operating systems can be found in Appendix C.
2. Use the `gem install bundler` command to install Bundler.
3. Change into the module directory and run `bundle install` to install the test dependencies.

Defining the Nodeset

Create a directory within the module to contain the nodesets used for testing:

```
[vagrant@client puppet]$ mkdir -p spec/acceptance/nodesets
```

Create a file name *default.yml* within this directory. This file should contain YAML data for nodes to be created for the test. The following example will create a test node using the same Vagrant box utilized within this book.

```
HOSTS:
  centos-7-x64:
    roles:
        - agent
    platform: el-7-x86_64
    box: puppetlabs/centos-7.2-64-nocm
    hypervisor: vagrant
    vagrant_memsize: 1024
```

Create additional nodeset files within this directory for all platforms that should be tested. Sample nodeset files for different operating systems can be found at Example Vagrant Hosts Files (*http://bit.ly/1R4hLJY*).

 Beaker is capable of using many virtualization systems. However, configuring these is beyond the scope of this book. Vagrant is sufficient for most testing purposes.

Configuring the Test Environment

Create a file named *spec/spec_helper_acceptance.rb* within the module directory. This file defines the tasks needed to prepare the test system.

The following example will ensure Puppet and the module dependencies are installed:

```
require 'beaker-rspec'
require 'pry'

step "Install Puppet on each host"
install_puppet_agent_on( hosts, { :puppet_collection => 'pc1' } )

RSpec.configure do |c|
  # Find the module directory
  module_root = File.expand_path( File.join( File.dirname(__FILE__), '..') )

  # Enable test descriptions
  c.formatter = :documentation

  # Configure all nodes in nodeset
  c.before :suite do
    # Install module and dependencies
    puppet_module_install(
      :source      => module_root,
      :module_name => 'puppet',
    )
    hosts.each do |host|
      # Install dependency modules
      on host, puppet('module', 'install', 'puppetlabs-stdlib'),
        { :acceptable_exit_codes => [0,1] }
```

```
        on host, puppet('module', 'install', 'puppetlabs-inifile'),
          { :acceptable_exit_codes => [0,1] }
      end
    end
end
```

This is generally a consistent formula you can use with any module. The adjustments specific to this module have been bolded in the preceding example.

Creating an Acceptance Test

The tests are written in rspec, like the unit tests created in the previous section. However ServerSpec tests are also available and can be used in combination with rspec tests.

For most modules that set up services, the first test should be an installation test to validate that it installs with the default options, and that the service is properly configured.

Create a file named *spec/acceptance/installation_spec.rb* within the module directory. The following example defines some basic tests to ensure that the package is installed and that the service runs without returning an error:

```
require 'spec_helper_acceptance'

describe 'puppet class' do
  context 'default parameters' do
    # Using puppet_apply as a helper
    it 'should install with no errors using default values' do
      puppetagent = <<-EOS
        class { 'puppet::agent': }
      EOS

      # Run twice to test idempotency
      expect( apply_manifest( puppetagent ).exit_code ).to_not eq(1)
      expect( apply_manifest( puppetagent ).exit_code ).to eq(0)
    end

    describe package('puppet-agent') do
      it { should be_installed }
    end

    describe file('/etc/puppetlabs/puppet/puppet.conf') do
      it { should be_a_file }
    end

    describe service('puppet') do
      it { should be_enabled }
    end

  end
end
```

You can and should create more extensive tests that utilize different input scenarios for the module. Each test should be defined as a separate file in the *spec/acceptance/* directory, with a filename ending in *_spec.rb*.

You can find more information, including details about writing good tests at the following places:

- The best documentation for Beaker can be found at puppetlabs/beaker (*http://bit.ly/1LvbR4l*) on GitHub.
- The best documentation for writing rspec tests can be found at rspec-core (*http://bit.ly/1XABjWS*) on the `rspec.info` site.
- The best documentation for writing serverspec tests can be found at serverspec resource types (*http://bit.ly/1S8sAto*) on the `serverspec.org` site.

Running Acceptance Tests

To spin up virtual machines to run the test, you'll need to run the acceptance tests from a system that has Vagrant installed. Your personal system will work perfectly fine for this purpose.

Running tests on all nodes

Let's go ahead and run the entire acceptance test suite:

```
$ bundle exec rspec spec/acceptance
Hypervisor for centos-7-x64 is vagrant
Beaker::Hypervisor, found some vagrant boxes to create
==> centos-7-x64: Forcing shutdown of VM...
==> centos-7-x64: Destroying VM and associated drives...
created Vagrantfile for VagrantHost centos-7-x64
Bringing machine 'centos-7-x64' up with 'virtualbox' provider...
==> centos-7-x64: Importing base box 'puppetlabs/centos-7.2-64-nocm'...
Progress: 100%
==> centos-7-x64: Matching MAC address for NAT networking...
```

The test will spin up a Vagrant instance for each node specified in the *spec/acceptance/nodeset/* directory. It will run the tests on each of them, and output the status to you, as shown here:

```
puppet::agent class
  default parameters

    should install with no errors using default values
    Package "puppet-agent"
      should be installed
    File "/etc/puppetlabs/puppet/puppet.conf"
      should be a file
    Service "puppet"
      should be enabled
```

```
Destroying vagrant boxes
==> centos-7-x64: Forcing shutdown of VM...
==> centos-7-x64: Destroying VM and associated drives...

Finished in 17.62 seconds (files took 1 minute 2.88 seconds to load)
4 examples, 0 failures
```

As shown, all tests have completed without any errors.

Troubleshooting Beaker failures

Test failure messages are clear and easy to read. However, they won't necessarily tell you why something isn't true. When testing this example, I got the following errors back:

```
2) puppet::agent class default parameters
     Package "puppet-agent" should be installed
   Failure/Error: it { should be_installed }
     expected Package "puppet-agent" to be installed


   # ./spec/acceptance/installation_spec.rb:17:in `block (4 levels) in <top>'
```

Beaker provides extensive debug output, showing every command and its output on the test nodes. Preserve the test system for evaluation by setting the BEAKER_destroy environment variable to no:

$ **BEAKER_destroy=no BEAKER_debug=yes bundle exec rspec spec/acceptance**

You can isolate debugging to a single host configuration. For example, if there were a nodeset in *spec/acceptance/nodeset/centos-6-x86.yml*, then the following command would run the tests in debug mode on the CentOS 6 node only:

$ **BEAKER_set=*centos-6-x86* BEAKER_debug=yes rspec spec/acceptance**

Debug output will show the complete output of every command run by Beaker on the node, like so:

```
* Install Puppet on each host

centos-7-x64 01:36:36$ rpm --replacepkgs -ivh
  Retrieving http://yum.puppetlabs.com/puppetlabs-release-el-7.noarch.rpm
  Preparing...                          ####################################
  Updating / installing...
  puppetlabs-release-7-11               ####################################
  warning: rpm-tmp.KNaXPi: Header V4 RSA/SHA1 Signature, key ID 4bd6ec30: NOKEY

centos-7-x64 executed in 0.35 seconds
```

Avoid reprovisioning the node each time when you are debugging code. The following process is a well-known debugging pattern:

---

1. Run the test but keep the node around:

   ```
   $ BEAKER_destroy=no BEAKER_debug=yes rspec spec/acceptance
   ```

2. Attempt to fix the test or the manifest.
3. Rerun the test using the existing node:

   ```
   $ BEAKER_destroy=no BEAKER_provision=no BEAKER_debug=yes \
         bundle exec rspec spec/acceptance
   ```

4. Return to step 2 until the test runs cleanly.
5. Run the test with a fresh provisioning:

   ```
   $ rspec spec/acceptance
   ```

Accessing a Beaker host console

When all else fails, access the console of a host so that you can dig around and determine what happened during the test. At the point where investigation is necessary, add binding.pry to the _spec.rb_ test file that is failing:

```
describe package('puppet-agent') do
  it { should be_installed }
end
# Access host console to debug failure
binding.pry
```

Then rerun the test:

```
$ BEAKER_destroy=no bundle exec rspec spec/acceptance
...
From: learning-puppet4/puppet4/spec/acceptance/installation_spec.rb @ line 20 :

    16:     describe package('puppet-agent') do
    17:       it { should be_installed }
    18:     end
    19:     # Make the debug console available
 => 20:     binding.pry
    21:

[1] pry(RSpec::ExampleGroups::PuppetAgentClass::DefaultParameters)>
```

Pry is a debugging shell for Ruby, similar but more powerful than IRB. Documenting all features is beyond the scope of this book, but the following commands have proven very useful to investigate host state.

You can cat and edit local files directly:

```
>> cat spec/acceptance/installation_spec.rb
>> edit spec/acceptance/installation_spec.rb
```

Enter shell-mode to be placed in a local directory. Prefix commands with a period to execute them on the local system:

```
>> shell-mode
learning-puppet4/puppet4 $ .ls spec/acceptance/
installation_spec.rb    nodesets/
```

Get a list of hosts in the text, with their index number:

```
>> hosts.each_with_index do |host,i| print "#{i} #{host.hostname()}\n"; end;
1 centos-7-x64
```

Use the host index to execute a command on the host. Add a trailing semicolon to avoid debugger verbosity:

```
>> on hosts[0], 'rpm -qa |grep puppet' ;

centos-7-x64 02:50:14$ rpm -qa |grep puppet
  puppet-3.8.4-1.el7.noarch
  puppetlabs-release-7-11.noarch
```

Whoops, the wrong version of Puppet was installed. The default is still currently to install the old open source version (Puppet v3). Changing the `type` parameter to `aio` in the nodeset solved this problem.

For more information about using this debugger, refer to Pry: Get to the Code (*http://pryrepl.org/*).

Doing more with Beaker

Beaker can test dozens of other resources, including network interfaces, system devices, logical configurations, and TLS certificates. A complete list of resource types with `should` and `expect` examples can be found at ServerSpec Resource Types (*http://serverspec.org/resource_types.html*).

Beaker is a fast-moving project with new features added constantly. Check the Beaker GitHub project (*https://github.com/puppetlabs/beaker*) for the latest documentation.

Using Skeletons with Testing Features

There are a number of Puppet module skeletons that preinstall frameworks for enhanced testing above and beyond what we've covered. You may want to tune the module skeleton you use to include testing frameworks and datasets consistent with your release process.

Place the revised skeleton in the *~/.puppetlabs/opt/puppet/cache/puppet-module/skeleton* directory, or specify it on the `puppet module generate` command line with `--module_skeleton_dir=path/to/skeleton`.

The following are skeletons I have found useful at one time or another (in their own words):

garethr/puppet-module-skeleton (http://bit.ly/1TUjmEv)
> This skeleton is very opinionated. It's going to assume you're going to start out with tests (both unit and system), that you care about the Puppet style guide, test using Travis, keep track of releases and structure your modules according to strong conventions.
>
> > —puppet-module-skeleton README

This skeleton is popular and recommended by Puppet Labs Professional Services Engineers.

jimdo/puppet-skeleton (http://bit.ly/1pyOLjs)
> The module comes with everything you need to develop infrastructure code with Puppet and feel confident about it.
>
> > —puppet-skeleton README

This skeleton includes helpers to spin up Vagrant instances and run tests on them.

ghoneycutt/puppet-module-skeleton (http://bit.ly/22oR49W)
> At the time this book was written, Garret didn't provide a README for this skeleton; however, Garret is an active and high-quality contributor to the Puppet community with numerous Puppet Approved modules.

gds-operations/puppet-skeleton (http://bit.ly/1Wwefbo)
> This is a skeleton project for Web Operations teams using Puppet. It ties together a suite of sensible defaults, best current practices, and re-usable code. The intentions of which are two-fold:
>
> - New projects can get started and bootstrapped faster without needing to collate or rewrite this material themselves.
>
> - The standardization and modularization of these materials makes it easier for ongoing improvements to be shared, in both directions, between different teams.
>
> > —puppet-skeleton README

wavesoftware/puppet-os-skeleton (http://bit.ly/1pQPxIp)
> A complete working solution with:
>
> - Puppet master and agent nodes on Puppet Open Source
>
> - Spotify Puppet Explorer and PuppetDB
>
> - Hiera configuration
>
> - Dynamic Git environments by r10k
>
> - External puppet modules installation and maintenance by r10k

- Landrush local DNS

Couple of bootstrap Puppet classes:

- `common::filebucket` - use of filebucket on all files
- `common::packages` - central packages installation from hiera
- `common::prompt` - a Bash command prompt with support for Git and Mercurial

—puppet-os-skeleton README

You can find many others by searching for "puppet skeleton" on GitHub (*http://bit.ly/ 1R4Q8iL*). In particular, you can find skeletons specialized for specific application frameworks: OpenStack, Rails, Django, and so on.

Finding Documentation

You may have found a tricky problem not covered by the examples here. At this point, it is best to refer to the original vendor documentation:

- RSpec: Behavior-Driven Development for Ruby (*http://rspec.info/*)
- The RSpec Tests for Puppet (*http://bit.ly/1PgPBFW*) extension
- Puppet Labs Spec Helper (*http://bit.ly/1SYCcco*), a set of shared spec helpers for Puppet Labs projects
- Beaker: Puppet Acceptance Testing Harness (*http://bit.ly/1LvbR4l*)
- RSpec Best Practices (*http://bit.ly/21zqd5q*)

Much of this documentation is dated, but still valid. There are open bugs to provide Puppet 4.x-specific documentation, and I will update this section as soon as it is available.

Reviewing Testing Modules

Each class and defined type should have both unit and acceptance tests defined for it. Some good rules of thumb for tests are:

- Place unit tests for each class in the *spec/classes/* directory.
- Place unit tests for defined types in the *spec/defines/* directory.
- Place unit tests for functions in the *spec/functions/* directory.
- Tests should (at minimum) validate the most common case and default parameter values.

In this chapter, we have discussed how to test modules for:

- Simple catalog build success with default values
- Minimum and acceptable values passed in as parameters
- Creating the resources they were intended to manage
- Invalid and unacceptable values
- Providing data using Hiera fixtures
- Preloading parent modules with required parameters to ensure module dependencies are valid

This has covered the necessary tests that should be included in every module. In the next chapter, we're going to look at how to publish modules on the Puppet Forge.

## CHAPTER 18

Publishing Modules

This chapter will cover how to share your module with others, both inside and outside of your organization.

This chapter makes numerous references to the Puppet Forge, but nearly every case is also true of private forges hosted internally by organizations.

Updating the Module Metadata

First, review and update the Chapter 16. In particular, make sure that the following files have been created, and are up to date:

- *README.md*, as described in "Writing a Good README" on page 248
- *CHANGELOG.md*, as described in "Maintaining the Change Log" on page 258
- *metadata.json*, as described in "Updating Module Metadata" on page 254
- *LICENSE*, as described in "Identifying the License" on page 254

Every one of these files is used by the Puppet Forge to create details for users of your module.

One feature of the metadata we didn't discuss previously was keyword tags. These are used by the Puppet Forge search engine to help users find your module.

Update the *metadata.json* file to include an array of keyword tags relevant to your project. Tags cannot contain spaces, and should not match any valid value from `$facts['operatingsystem']`.

```
"tags": [ "agent", "server" ],
```

As this file is standard (*picky*) JSON format, make sure to remove single quotes and trailing commas.

Packaging a Module

After verifying the metadata is accurate, use `puppet module build` to package the module.

```
$ puppet module build
Notice: Building jorhett-puppet for release
Module built: jorhett-puppet/pkg/jorhett-puppet-1.2.1.tar.gz
```

Note that the *pkg/* directory can become very full over time. You may want to clean that out. I recommend adding this directory to your *.gitignore* file.

Uploading a Module to the Puppet Forge

There is no API for uploading modules to the Puppet Forge. Using a web browser, follow this process to add or update a module you own:

1. Navigate to Puppet Forge (*http://forge.puppetlabs.com/*).
2. Click Login or Sign Up if necessary.
3. Click Publish in the upper-right corner beside your name (see Figure 18-1).
4. Click Choose File and select the module package you created in the previous step.
5. Click Upload.

Figure 18-1. You'll find a link to Publish modules near your name on the top right

Your module will be added to the Forge. The README and CHANGELOG from your module will be shown as the web page for your module. The results of standard tests and community feedback will be added to the page when they are available.

If this process has changed since this book was published, the revised process should be documented at "Publishing Modules on the Puppet Forge" (*http://bit.ly/1SYBxrE*).

Publishing a Module on GitHub

It is common and expected for you to have a place to accept bug reports and pull requests for your module. GitHub is by far the most common location for this. The following steps will create a GitHub repository for your module.

If you haven't installed Git already, do that now:

```
[vagrant@client ~]$ sudo yum install -y git
...snip...
Installed:
  git.x86_64 0:1.8.3.1-4.el7

Dependency Installed:
  libgnome-keyring.x86_64 0:3.8.0-3.el7  perl-Error.noarch 1:0.17020-2.el7
  perl-Git.noarch 0:1.8.3.1-4.el7        perl-TermReadKey.x86_64 0:2.30-20.el7
  rsync.x86_64 0:3.0.9-15.el7

Complete!
```

Configure the Git software with your name and email address:

```
$ git config --global user.name "Jane Doe"
$ git config --global user.email janedoe@example.com
```

If you don't already have a GitHub account, create one at *https://github.com/join*.

Create a new repository in your GitHub account at *https://github.com/new*. You will likely want to name the repository by replacing your name in the module with *puppet-*, as GitHub already organizes the repository under your name. Ignore the options below the name and click Create Repository.

Set up version tracking of your module by running the following command within your module directory:

```
$ git init
Initialized empty Git repository in
    /home/vagrant/.puppet/modules/jorhett-puppet/.git/
```

There are some files to avoid uploading to the source repository. These include:

- Binary packages of the module
- Dependency fixtures created by rspec for testing

To prevent this, create a *.gitignore* file with the following contents:

```
# .gitignore
/pkg/
/spec/fixtures/
```

Commit your module to the Git repository by running the following commands within your module directory:

```
$ git add --all

$ git commit -m "Initial commit"
[master (root-commit) e804295] initial commit
11 files changed, 197 insertions(+), 0 deletions(-)
 create mode 100644 Gemfile
 create mode 100644 README.md
 create mode 100644 CHANGELOG.md
 create mode 100644 Rakefile
 create mode 100644 manifests/init.pp
 create mode 100644 manifests/client.pp
 create mode 100644 manifests/master.pp
 create mode 100644 metadata.json
 create mode 100644 spec/classes/init_spec.rb
 create mode 100644 spec/spec_helper.rb
 create mode 100644 tests/init.pp
```

You have now committed your changes to the source tree. However, they are not yet pushed up to GitHub. Let's configure GitHub as our remote origin. *If you have a different origin and are just pushing to GitHub as a remote branch, we expect that you know how to do that.*

```
$ git remote add origin https://github.com/janedoe/modulename.git
$ git push -u origin master
Counting objects: 14, done.
Compressing objects: 100% (11/11), done.
Writing objects: 100% (14/14), 3.68 KiB | 0 bytes/s, done.
Total 14 (delta 0), reused 0 (delta 0)
To https://github.com/jorhett/puppet-systemstd.git
 * [new branch]      master -> master
Branch master set up to track remote branch master from origin.
```

Whenever you wish to publish a change to the module, make sure to update the version number and changes for the version in the following files:

- *metadata.json*
- *README.md*
- *CHANGELOG.md*

Commit these changes to the repository, and then push them up to GitHub.

```
$ git commit -a -m "Updated documentation for version X.Y"
[master a4cc6b7] Updated documentation
 Committer: jorhett vagrant@client.example.com
 3 files changed, 11 insertions(+), 2 deletions(-)
$ git push
Counting objects: 14, done.
Compressing objects: 100% (11/11), done.
 ...
```

Automating Module Publishing

There is a community-provided Ruby gem that automates the task of updating your module on the Forge. You can find documentation for this at maestrodev/puppet-blacksmith on GitHub (*http://bit.ly/1MeTIrq*).

Preparation for using this gem requires adding two lines to *Rakefile*, and placing your Puppet Forge credentials in a text file in your home directory.

If you've just made a minor fix to your module, the release process could be as simple as this:

```
$ rake module:bump:patch
$ $EDITOR CHANGELOG.md
$ rake module:tag
$ rake module:push
```

You can also use `module:bump:minor` after adding new features, or `module:bump:major` after making changes that are not backward-compatible.

> This module includes an all-in-one `release` command that combines the three `rake` commands above. I don't recommend it, as it prevents you from updating the *CHANGELOG.md* file with the new version's changes.

Getting Approved Status from Puppet Labs

At the time this book was written, the approval requirements were as follows:

- Solve a unique problem well. Puppet Labs won't approve multiple modules that solve the same problem.
- Comply with the Puppet Style Guide. No warnings can be issued by syntax checking tools like `puppet-lint`.
- Have regular updates from more than one person or organization. Have Forge updates in the last six months, and less than a one-month lag between source repo (e.g., GitHub) and the Forge.
- Provide thorough and readable documentation.
- Be licensed under Apache, MIT, or BSD licenses.
- Have every standard metadata field filled out, including Puppet version and operating system compatibility.
- Be versioned according to SemVer (*http://semver.org/*) guidelines to keep expectations consistent with regards to upgrades.
- Have rspec and acceptance tests for every manifest, and unit tests for types, providers, facts, and functions.

Given the nature of supporting a community of published modules, I feel the requirements are straightforward, easy to understand, and generally easy to apply.

You can check for updates to the approval guidelines at *https://forge.puppetlabs.com/ approved/criteria*.

To have your module marked as Puppet Approved, open an issue in the Forge Modules project at *https://tickets.puppetlabs.com/*. Request that the module be evaluated for Approved status.

## PART III

Using a Puppet Server

Puppet server authenticates and provides centralized infrastructure for Puppet agents, including the following:

- Distributes policies to nodes without file sync
- Evaluates and builds a catalog for the node
- Provides a central source for configuration data
- Collects convergence reports from Puppet agents
- Stores backups of files managed by Puppet

In this part we'll discuss how to install and configure two different servers for your Puppet nodes: the well-known Puppet master, and the fast new Puppet Server. These are two different products that perform much of the same functionality. You'll learn how to install and configure both, and why you would select one over the other.

"Puppet server" Versus "Puppet Server"

For the remainder of this book, keep the following names in mind:

Puppet master
> Refers to the Puppet server provided by the deprecated `puppet master` command, available with the base Puppet installation. This was the only server available in previous versions of Puppet.

Puppet Server
> Refers to the Puppet Server product, which is packaged separately. Puppet Server provides a high-performance, scalable replacement for the Puppet master.

Puppet server
> Refers to either the Puppet Server or Puppet master. Any statement with this capitalization would apply equally to both, as they both offer this functionality.

Obviously, the two different capitalizations will be easy to confuse, but that's OK. Those two are and should be synonymous. Any statement made about *Puppet server* with a lowercase *s* is true of the Puppet Server product.

## CHAPTER 19

Preparing for a Puppet Server

Before we start building a Puppet server, we'll stop to review some essential considerations:

- Why a Puppet server changes the catalog build process
- How to build a Puppet server that will be easy to move or upgrade
- Whether to use Puppet master or Puppet Server with your nodes

Understanding these important details will save unnecessary and time-consuming rebuilds later.

Understanding the Catalog Builder

To properly explain the functionality provided by a server for Puppet nodes, we'll start by reviewing what we have previously covered about how Puppet builds the resource catalog.

Node

A node is a discrete system that could be managed by a Puppet agent. You can probably name the conventional node types quickly:

- A physical computer system, like an Oracle Sun X5-4 or Dell PowerEdge R720
- A virtualized operating system, like RedHat Enterprise Linux, running on an VMWare ESX or OpenStack instance
- A virtualized operating system running on a public cloud provider like Amazon Web Services (AWS) or Google Compute.

There are a large number of nodes that can run Puppet agents you might not be aware of. Here's a short but incomplete list of unconventional node types:

- Routers, switches, and VPN concentrators supplied by Juniper, Cisco, Arista, and other network device vendors come with integrated Puppet agents.
- Virtualization platforms like OpenStack can use Puppet agent to configure and manage the hypervisor.
- Container technologies like Docker can be deployed and managed by Puppet agents.
- Puppet agents can be isolated under different users or paths on the same system.

In summary, any device or system that can run a Puppet agent can be a Puppet node. As more and more devices every day contain small computers and participate in the Internet of Things, more and more things will have Puppet agents.

Agent

The Puppet agent evaluates and applies Puppet resources (from the catalog) on a node. Following is a more detailed review of the Puppet evaluation process when `puppet apply` is used to evaluate resources on the node. We have presented all of this functionality in the first two parts of this book.

1. Gathers node data

   - Reads the `environment` value from the configuration file or command-line input
   - Retrieves plugins including functions and facts
   - Runs Facter to generate the node's facts—both built-in and custom facts added by Puppet modules
   - Selects the node name from the configuration file or fact data

2. Builds a catalog of resources for the node

   - Query a node terminus (if configured) to obtain node information
   - Evaluate the main manifest, node terminus, and Hiera data to create a list of classes to apply
   - Performs all variable assignment to resolve variables into values within the catalog
   - Evaluates `if`, `unless`, and other conditional attributes
   - Performs iterations to build resources or map values
   - Executes functions configured in classes to provide module-specific data
   - Executes functions configured in the environment to provide environment-specific data

3. Evaluates (or converges) the catalog on the node
   - Evaluates the `onlyif`, `creates`, and other conditional attributes to determine which resources in the catalog should be applied to the node
   - Creates a dependency graph based on ordering attributes and automatic dependencies
   - Compares the state of each resource, and makes the necessary changes to bring the resource into compliance with the policy
   - Creates a report containing all events processed during the agent run

---

Simplified

The catalog build process has been simplified for the purpose of keeping the list easy to read. I've included the parts I did to ensure that you realized that all of the Puppet configuration language has been evaluated and built into a "compiled" resource catalog to be processed by the agent.

If you create an iteration loop to process a list of 500 users, the iteration loop will declare 500 unique `user` resources that will be applied at convergence time. The Puppet agent sees 500 unique resources, not the loop you used to create those resources.

Although Puppet agent is currently a Ruby application, it is planned that many agents will become native applications and not require Ruby in the near future. At convergence time the Puppet agent processes only the Puppet catalog, and thus does not need to process Ruby source code.

Server

When you use a Puppet master or Puppet Server (both collectively referred to as a *Puppet server* for the remainder of the book), the server takes over the process of evaluating the data and compiling a catalog for the node to evaluate. This moves the core processing and policy evaluation to the server, like so:

1. The Puppet agent submits name, environment, and facts to the Puppet server.
2. The Puppet server builds a Puppet catalog for the node.
3. The Puppet agent applies the catalog's resources on the node.

This configuration is by far the most common and well-supported configuration for a Puppet deployment. Only the server requires access to the raw Puppet modules and their data sources. This provides many advantages:

- Removes the need to distribute code and data down to every node
- Reduces computational cost on the end node
- Provides auditing and controls for some security requirements
- Simplifies network access requirements for internal data sources

This doesn't mean that every environment must use a Puppet server, or that it is the correct solution for every need. In Part IV we'll discuss the pros and cons of both server and serverless Puppet environments, and why you may want to evaluate each one.

Right now, let's show you how to build your own server.

Planning for Puppet Server

This section will discuss some important considerations when you are adding a server to a Puppet environment. There are some choices that are important to get right. Many of these are subtle, and you won't feel the pain until your environment has grown a bit. So I'm going to share with you what I and many others have found to be best practices for creating a server-oriented Puppet environment.

If you are new to Puppet, read these as ways you can avoid some pain in the future. If you have an existing Puppet environment, you may already feel the pain around the early choices. Use these as suggestions for ways to improve your environment.

The Server Is Not the Node

You need to select a unique name for the Puppet server. This name will be around for the entire lifetime of this Puppet environment, so it should be easy to remember and use. If you are a small company, or use a discrete domain for the nodes you will be managing, you may want to name the service *puppet.example.com* or something equally straightforward and easy to remember.

You will choose a node or nodes on which to run Puppet server. Do not confuse the node with the Puppet Server service. Do not name the node *puppet.example.com*.

This probably seems counterintuitive at the moment, so let me share some crucial information here. When you start the Puppet server services, it will create a new certificate authority with the name you assign. Every Puppet agent that will use the service must acquire a certificate signed by this authority. This means that renaming the service later will be a huge effort, involving recertification of every node in the environment.

Puppet server is an application service that can be hosted anywhere. The node on which it runs today may change, or be replaced with a cluster of nodes. If the server is not named for a specific node, upgrades can be simple application migrations with zero changes to the end nodes.

Best Practice

Use a globally unique name for your Puppet server that can easily be moved or shared between multiple servers.

To set the globally unique name of the server, use the following configuration settings in */etc/puppetlabs/puppet/puppet.conf*.

```
[agent]
    server = puppet.example.com

[master]
    certname = puppet.example.com
```

The Node Is Not the Server

A very common mistake is to set the `certname` of the node to be the same as the name of the Puppet server. This creates a different kind of problem. Don't do this:

```
[main]
  certname = puppet.example.com   # bad idea. server and agent are distinct
```

Each node that connects to the Puppet server must have a unique name, and a unique TLS key and certificate. When the node shares the server's key and certificate, what happens when the Puppet server is migrated to a new node? You guessed it—conflict. Both of the nodes cannot use the same key. Even if the old node is shut down, the history and reports for the new node will be invalid, and could corrupt the new node by using data from the old node.

Best Practice

On the node that hosts the Puppet server, configure Puppet agent to use the node's fully qualified and unique hostname.

To configure this properly, ensure that only the Puppet server uses the certificate authority's name. Use the following configuration settings in */etc/puppetlabs/puppet/puppet.conf*:

```
[main]
    certname = $fqdn      # default value, could be left out

[agent]
    server = puppet.example.com

[master]
    certname = puppet.example.com
```

With this configuration, the node that hosts the Puppet server is a node like any other. If the server moves to another node, there is no conflict between the node identities.

Store Server Data Files Separately

The Puppet Server runs as a nonprivileged user account. I believe it is a mistake for the Puppet Server to use the same directories and paths as the Puppet agent, which is running as a privileged user on the node. Furthermore, it is easier to migrate or duplicate the Puppet Server when the service's files are in their own file hierarchy.

For reasons completely unclear to the author, Puppet Server stores TLS key and certificate data for its nodes within *etc/puppetlabs/*. For a typical managed node, which will create a single TLS key pair, this makes sense. The */etc/* directory should contain static configuration files.

In contrast, a Puppet server will create, alter, and remove files constantly to manage keys of every authorized node. In virtualized, autoscaled environments new Puppet clients come and go. Some of my environments build and destroy 9,000 test nodes in a single day. This makes the TLS directory volatile, and completely unsuitable for placement within */etc/*.

Placing the volatile TLS certificate repository within the */etc* directory on a Puppet server violates the Filesystem Hierarchy Standard (FHS)[1] and the expectations of every experienced Unix/Linux administrator.

Likewise, the default settings place the highly volatile node state and report data within the */opt/* directory or filesystem, which is likewise not expected to contain highly volatile data.

Best Practice

Configure your Puppet server to place all volatile files within the */var* filesystem.

Use the following configuration settings in *etc/puppetlabs/puppet/puppet.conf*:

```
[user]
  vardir = /var/opt/puppetlabs/server
  ssldir = $vardir/ssl
```

---

1 Bug PUP-4376 (*https://tickets.puppetlabs.com/browse/PUP-4376*) tracks this obvious mistake.

```
[master]
  vardir = /var/opt/puppetlabs/server
  ssldir = $vardir/ssl
```

 Even though SSL is now named TLS, the directory and variable names have not yet been updated.

The remainder of this book assumes that you have made this change. If you do not use these recommended settings, you'll need to remember that the default locations are as follows:

```
[master]
  vardir = /opt/puppetlabs/puppet/cache
  ssldir = /etc/puppetlabs/puppet/ssl
```

Functions Run on the Server

Functions are executed by the process that builds the catalog. When a server builds the catalog, the functions are run by the server. This has three immediate concerns:

Log messages will be in the server logs, not on the node
Log messages created by the debug(), info(), notice(), warning(), and err() functions will output to the server's logs.

Data used by the catalog must be local to the server, or supplied by facts
In most situations it is easier to centralize data on a server than to distribute it to every node. However, if migrating from a puppet apply environment, you may need to take steps to centralize the data sources.

The only method to provide local node data to the server is facts
In a puppet apply configuration it is possible to write functions that read data from the node. In a server-based environment, the only node-specific data available to the server comes from the node's facts. You must change the functions into custom facts that supply the same data.

Choosing Puppet Master Versus Puppet Server

With Puppet 4 you have two different products that can function as a Puppet server. At this point in time they provide similar feature sets. Which one should you use?

In turns out that this question is very easy to answer. Let's review the two products.

Upgrading Easily with Puppet Master

Puppet 4 includes the existing, well-known `puppet master` Rack application. If you are using any prior version of Puppet with a server (or "puppetmaster"), this is what you are using today.

 Puppet Enterprise 3.7 and above use the Puppet Server product described on the next page.

The Puppet master is a Rack application. It comes with a built-in application server known as WEBrick, which can accept only two concurrent connections. Any site larger than a few dozen nodes would easily hit the limitations of the built-in server.

The only scalable way to run a Puppet master was under a Rack application server such as Phusion Passenger. This allowed you to tune the platform to support a large number of nodes quickly and well. For most purposes, tuning a Puppet master was tuning the Passenger application server.

The following chapter will cover how to install, configure, and tune a Puppet master running under Phusion Passenger. Puppet 4's all-in-one installation has made this process easier than ever before.

If you already have Puppet master deployed and working well in your environment, you'll find it very easy to upgrade to Puppet 4's master. You already have the knowledge and experience to maintain and run it. The fairly minor changes you'll make to upgrade to Puppet 4 are covered in this chapter.

 Puppet master only supports Puppet 4 clients, so you will be forced to upgrade all clients to Puppet 4.

Embracing the Future with Puppet Server

The new, written-from-scratch Puppet Server is a self-standing product intended to extend and expand on the services previously provided by `puppet master`. Puppet Server is a drop-in replacement for a Puppet master, allowing you to use it in an existing environment with no changes to the Puppet agents.

Many of the changes with Puppet Server were a change in the technology stack. Puppet Server was written in Clojure and uses Java rather than Ruby as the underlying engine. This ties it more closely with PuppetDB and other Puppet Labs products, and will make it easier to leverage the technologies together. Puppet Labs intends to provide powerful extension points in the future based around this platform.

Puppet Server will continue to support Ruby module plugins using the JRuby interpreter. You can continue to develop facts, features, functions, and all other module plugins in Ruby.

Puppet Server was designed with speed in mind, and boasts some impressive benchmarks when compared to the Puppet master. In addition, the new service provides significantly more visibility into the server process. The new metrics can be made available through open standards like JMX to popular analytics tools like Graphite.

 Puppet Server is backward compatible with Puppet 3 clients. This can be essential if a Puppet agent cannot be upgraded for one reason or another.

Why There's Really No Choice

You'll notice that I didn't provide a side-by-side feature comparison of the two choices. This is due to one factor that makes your choice self-evident:

Puppet master has been deprecated, and will not exist in Puppet 5.

Puppet 4 is the final version with Puppet master. If you already have a Puppet environment, the next chapter will help you upgrade a Puppet master with few changes to an existing environment. The Puppet 4 master will snap right into the Rack application environment you already know how to support.

However, all development of Puppet master has ceased. You need to plan for migration to Puppet Server, where all new features will appear.

If you are brand new to Puppet and don't yet have a Puppet master server, ignore the Puppet master and start immediately with Puppet Server. Due to the complete change of technology stack, there is nothing about configuring or enabling the Puppet master Rack application that will help make you smarter or better with Puppet. Skip the next chapter entirely and go straight to Chapter 21.

Ensuring a High-Performance Server

Once you have finished testing and wish to deploy a Puppet server in production, there are two issues to consider for performance: available RAM and fast CPUs.

On a server with sufficient RAM for the Puppet server threads, the Puppet modules and Hiera data will be cached in file buffer memory. The only disk I/O will be to store

Puppet nodes reports (if enabled), and when module or data changes are written out. Disk usage will be write-heavy, generally doing 10:1 writes versus reads.

Memory utilization tends to be very stable. You will have more active threads when you have more concurrent nodes connecting at the same time. If your server is running low on memory, increase it until the file cache becomes stable and consistent. As I'm sure you know, any free memory not used by processes will be used for file cache. The Puppet modules and Hiera data should always reside in the file buffer cache.

The vast majority of the server's time will be spent compiling catalogs for the nodes, which is CPU-intensive. Other than ensuring enough memory is available, the most important things you need to consider for server performance are CPU cores, CPU cores, and more CPU cores.

If you exceed the capacity of a single Puppet server, you can scale Puppet servers horizontally. See "Deploying Puppet Servers at Scale" on page 364 near the end of Part III.

## CHAPTER 20

Creating a Puppet Master

This chapter will cover installing and tuning the well-known Puppet master Rack application.

At this point, we're going to spin up another virtual machine. You should open a new Terminal window, or add a new tab on your existing terminal for this virtual machine. This will allow you to switch back and forth between the machines, which is necessary in this chapter.

Starting the puppetmaster VM

In the new Terminal window, move into the directory where you checked out the learning-puppet4 Git repository (*https://github.com/jorhett/learning-puppet4*). Start up the puppetmaster instance just like we did the client instance at the beginning of the book:

```
~$ cd learning-puppet4
learning-puppet4$ vagrant up puppetmaster
Bringing machine 'puppetmaster' up with 'virtualbox' provider...
==> puppetmaster: Importing base box 'puppetlabs/centos-7.2-64-nocm'...
==> puppetmaster: Matching MAC address for NAT networking...
==> puppetmaster: Checking if box 'puppetlabs/centos-7.2-64-nocm' is up to date.
==> puppetmaster: Setting the name of the VM: learning-puppet4_puppetmaster_1437
...snip...
==> puppetmaster: Machine booted and ready!
```

Now that it is running, log in and get started:

```
learning-puppet4$ vagrant ssh puppetmaster
[vagrant@puppetmaster ~]$
```

Installing the Puppet Master

The Puppet master is included in the Puppet agent all-in-one (AIO) package. Install the `puppet-agent` package exactly as you did on the client instance. You can refer back to Part I for the installation instructions, or simply run the `fastsetup.sh` script shown here. This script installs all the dependencies and symlinks discussed earlier:

```
[vagrant@client ~]$ /vagrant/bin/fastsetup.sh
Installing utilities necessary for the lessons
warning: /var/cache/yum/x86_64/7/base/packages/gpm-libs-1.20.7-5.el7.x86_64.rpm:
   Header V3 RSA/SHA256 Signature, key ID f4a80eb5: NOKEY
Public key for gpm-libs-1.20.7-5.el7.x86_64.rpm is not installed
Importing GPG key 0xF4A80EB5:
 Userid     : "CentOS-7 Key (CentOS 7 Official Signing Key) <security@centos.org>"
 Fingerprint: 6341 ab27 53d7 8a78 a7c2 7bb1 24c6 a8a7 f4a8 0eb5
 Package    : centos-release-7-0.1406.el7.centos.2.3.x86_64 (@anaconda)
 From       : /etc/pki/rpm-gpg/RPM-GPG-KEY-CentOS-7

Installing Puppet
Public key for puppet-agent-1.4.0-1.el7.x86_64.rpm is not installed
Importing GPG key 0x4BD6EC30:
 Userid     : "Puppet Labs Release Key (Puppet Labs Release Key)"
 Fingerprint: 47b3 20eb 4c7c 375a a9da e1a0 1054 b7a2 4bd6 ec30
 Package    : puppetlabs-release-pc1-1.0.0-1.el7.noarch
 From       : /etc/pki/rpm-gpg/RPM-GPG-KEY-puppetlabs
warning: /etc/puppetlabs/puppet/puppet.conf created as
         /etc/puppetlabs/puppet/puppet.conf.rpmnew

Enabling convenience symlinks.
Changing owner of /etc/puppetlabs
```

This has installed Puppet and the tools you installed in Part I. It has also changed the owner of */etc/puppetlabs* to the `vagrant` user for your convenience:

```
[vagrant@puppetmaster ~]$ which puppet
/opt/puppetlabs/bin/puppet
[vagrant@puppetmaster ~]$ which git rsync vim nano emacs
/usr/bin/git
/usr/bin/rsync
/usr/bin/vim
/usr/bin/nano
/usr/bin/emacs
[vagrant@puppetmaster ~]$ ls -la /etc/puppetlabs
total 12
drwxr-xr-x    5 vagrant vagrant    48 Aug  2 21:50 .
drwxr-xr-x.  77 root    root     8192 Aug  2 21:53 ..
drwxr-xr-x    5 vagrant vagrant    96 Aug  2 21:50 code
drwxr-xr-x    2 vagrant vagrant   145 Aug  2 21:50 mcollective
drwxr-xr-x    3 vagrant vagrant   111 Aug  2 21:50 puppet
```

If you prefer an editor other than the three listed here, you'll need to install it as discussed in "Choosing a Text Editor" on page 23.

Configuring a Firewall for the Puppet Master

At this point, we'll need to adjust the firewall on the server. Puppet clients connect to servers on TCP port 8140 by default. Use the following commands to allow incoming TCP connections to this port:

```
[puppetmaster ~]$ sudo firewall-cmd --permanent --zone=public --add-port=8140/tcp
success
[puppetmaster ~]$ sudo firewall-cmd --reload
success
```

This change allows incoming connections to the Puppet master.

It is safe to run these commands in a virtual instance on your personal workstation. In a production setting, you'd want to limit access to specific IP networks. Don't make this change to a production system without reviewing your organization's existing security setup.

Guides for altering other firewalls can be found in Appendix B.

Running the WEBrick Server

In this section, we'll start up the Puppet master manually so that it can set up the directories and files it needs to run as a service. It is necessary to do this once, even if you plan to run it under Passenger or another Rack server.

At this point, we need to stop and create a user and group under which to run the Puppet master service. This service doesn't need any special permissions on the system that hosts it, as it is a typical application service that answers queries from nodes. It can and should run as a nonprivileged user.

This is different from the Puppet agent, which must run as a privileged account to make changes to the managed node.

It may surprise you that the installation package doesn't create the user and group for you. This is because the Puppet master has been deprecated. The Puppet Server package does create the puppet user and group during installation, but to run a Puppet master, we'll have to do it ourselves:

```
[vagrant@puppetmaster ~]$ sudo groupadd puppet
[vagrant@puppetmaster ~]$ sudo useradd -m -d /var/opt/puppetlabs -g puppet puppet
```

Now that everything has been prepared, let's start the service as a foreground process so that we can observe the initialization process. You will notice that it creates a certificate authority based on the configured `certname`, and then signs its own certificate:

```
[vagrant@puppetmaster ~]$ sudo /opt/puppetlabs/bin/puppet master -v --no-daemon
Notice: Signed certificate request for ca
Notice: puppet.example.com has a waiting certificate request
Notice: Signed certificate request for puppet.example.com
Notice: Removing file Puppet::SSL::CertificateRequest puppet.example.com at
 '/var/opt/puppetlabs/puppetserver/ssl/ca/requests/puppet.example.com.pem'
Notice: Removing file Puppet::SSL::CertificateRequest puppet.example.com at
 '/var/opt/puppetlabs/puppetserver/ssl/certificate_requests/puppet.example.com'
Warning: The WEBrick Puppet master server is deprecated and will be removed in a
future release. Please use Puppet Server instead.
See http://links.puppetlabs.com/deprecate-rack-webrick-servers for more...
Notice: Starting Puppet master version 4.4.0
```

By signing its own certificate, the Puppet master has become the root certificate authority for this Puppet installation. Only agents with certificates signed by this certificate authority will be able to access the service. We'll discuss ways to handle distributed or third-party certificate authorities in "Using an External Certificate Authority" on page 353.

I recommend at this point that you skip forward and complete all the steps in Chapter 22. Leave the Puppet master running on this screen. Use other windows to execute the commands in that chapter. As you finish each step, check back here and view the messages output by the Puppet master.

After you are comfortable with the Puppet master service, you can press Ctrl-C to stop this process. Then you can configure it to run as a limited test service, or configure it to support many nodes with Passenger.

Testing with the Puppet Master Service

Use the following process to enable a Puppet master service for your host. This service will only support a single connection at a time, but may be sufficient for testing Puppet 4 manifests.

As Puppet 4 has deprecated the Puppet master in favor of Puppet Server, the installation package does not include a service startup script. You can find one in the */vagrant* mount of the files from the Git repository used by this book:

```
[vagrant@puppetmaster ~]$ sudo cp /vagrant/systemd-puppet/puppetmaster.service \
        /usr/lib/systemd/system/puppetmaster.service
[vagrant@puppetmaster ~]$ sudo cp /vagrant/systemd-puppet/puppetmaster.sysconfig \
        /etc/sysconfig/puppetmaster
[vagrant@puppetmaster ~]$ sudo systemctl daemon-reload
```

```
[vagrant@puppetmaster ~]$ systemctl status puppetmaster
puppetmaster.service - Puppet master
   Loaded: loaded (/usr/lib/systemd/system/puppetmaster.service; disabled)
   Active: inactive (dead)
[vagrant@puppetmaster ~]$ sudo systemctl enable puppetmaster
ln -s '/usr/lib/systemd/system/puppetmaster.service'
      '/etc/systemd/system/multi-user.target.wants/puppetmaster.service'
```

After you have run the service manually as shown in the previous section, you can use the files we just installed to start it as a normal service. Use the standard `systemctl` commands to start and stop the service:

```
[vagrant@puppetmaster ~]$ sudo systemctl start puppetmaster
[vagrant@puppetmaster ~]$ sudo systemctl status puppetmaster
puppetmaster.service - Puppet master
   Loaded: loaded (/usr/lib/systemd/system/puppetmaster.service; enabled)
   Active: active (running) since Thu 2015-08-27 05:02:37 UTC; 10s ago
 Main PID: 4100 (puppet)
   CGroup: /system.slice/puppetmaster.service
           └─4100 /opt/puppetlabs/puppet/bin/ruby
               /opt/puppetlabs/puppet/bin/puppet master --no-daemonize

systemd[1]: Starting Puppet master...
systemd[1]: Started Puppet master.
puppet[4100]: Warning: The WEBrick Puppet master server is deprecated and
will be removed in a future release. Please use Puppet Server instead.
See http://links.puppetlabs.com/deprecat...more information.
puppet[4100]: Notice: Starting Puppet master version 4.4.0
Hint: Some lines were ellipsized, use -l to show in full.
```

As discussed previously, the `puppetmaster` service uses the Ruby WEBrick test server. This is only suitable for a few nodes. You should never use this for a production environment.

Scaling the Puppet Master with Passenger

This section covers the installation of Puppet to run as a service under Passenger Rack.

Before installing Passenger, you should first start up the Puppet master manually as documented on the previous page. This will create all of the required directories with the appropriate permissions for running Puppet under Passenger.

If you have enabled the `puppetmaster` service, you'll need to disable it, as it will conflict with the master service running under Passenger:

```
[vagrant@puppetmaster ~]$ sudo systemctl stop puppetmaster
[vagrant@puppetmaster ~]$ sudo systemctl disable puppetmaster
rm '/etc/systemd/system/multi-user.target.wants/puppetmaster.service'
```

Installing Apache

To run Puppet under Passenger, we'll use the Apache httpd to provide the base web service. Install Apache httpd, the Apache development tools, and the TLS module:

```
[vagrant@puppetmaster ~]$ sudo yum install -y httpd httpd-devel mod_ssl
Loaded plugins: fastestmirror
...snip...

Installed:
  httpd.x86_64 0:2.4.6-31.el7.centos      httpd-devel.x86_64 0:2.4.6-31.el7.centos
  mod_ssl.x86_64 1:2.4.6-31.el7.centos

Dependency Installed:
  apr.x86_64 0:1.4.8-3.el7               apr-devel.x86_64 0:1.4.8-3.el7
  apr-util.x86_64 0:1.5.2-6.el7          apr-util-devel.x86_64 0:1.5.2-6.el7
  cyrus-sasl.x86_64 0:2.1.26-17.el7      cyrus-sasl-devel.x86_64 0:2.1.26-17.el7
  expat-devel.x86_64 0:2.1.0-8.el7       httpd-tools.x86_64 0:2.4.6-31.el7.centos
  mailcap.noarch 0:2.1.41-2.el7          openldap-devel.x86_64 0:2.4.39-6.el7
  libdb-devel.x86_64 0:5.3.21-17.el7_0.1

Complete!
```

 You can also run Passenger under the nginx web server. This requires extensive manual configuration, and is thus not documented here. As Puppet Server provides its own web server, I recommend that you avoid this distraction and focus on upgrading instead.

Installing Phusion Passenger

We'll need to get some dependencies from the EPEL repository, so let's install that first:

```
[vagrant@puppetmaster ~]$ sudo yum install -y epel-release
Loaded plugins: fastestmirror
...snip...

Installed:
  epel-release.noarch 0:7-5

Complete!
```

Phusion provides a Yum repository with Passenger binaries. They don't provide a release RPM, just the repo configuration file. Download and install it with the following commands:

```
[vagrant@puppetmaster ~]$ curl -sSLo passenger.repo \
    https://oss-binaries.phusionpassenger.com/yum/definitions/el-passenger.repo
$ sudo mv passenger.repo /etc/yum.repos.d/passenger.repo
```

Now install Passenger. Yum will acquire necessary dependencies from the EPEL repository:

```
$ sudo yum install -y passenger mod_passenger
Loaded plugins: fastestmirror
...snip...

Installed:
  passenger.x86_64 0:5.0.16-8.el7          mod_passenger.x86_64 0:5.0.16-8.el7

Dependency Installed:
  rubygem-rack.noarch 1:1.5.2-4.el7

Complete!
```

Configuring the Puppet Master

Now we'll configure the system to start Apache with the Puppet master running as a Rack service under Phusion Passenger.

First, let's start up Apache and confirm that the Phusion Passenger configuration is correct:

```
$ sudo systemctl enable httpd
ln -s '/usr/lib/systemd/system/httpd.service'
     '/etc/systemd/system/multi-user.target.wants/httpd.service'
$ sudo systemctl start httpd
$ sudo passenger-config validate-install --validate-apache2 --auto
 * Checking whether this Passenger install is in PATH... ✓
 * Checking whether there are no other Passenger installations... ✓
 * Checking whether Apache is installed... ✓
 * Checking whether the Passenger module is correctly configured in Apache... ✓

Everything looks good. :-)
```

Apache comes with several configuration files useful for providing a friendly environment for setting up websites. We don't need and won't be using this configuration, so let's disable them. You can use either of the following commands:

```
[vagrant@puppetmaster ~]$ sudo rm /etc/httpd/conf.d/*.conf
```

Or perhaps less drastically, this will achieve the same effect:

```
[vagrant@puppetmaster ~]$ cd /etc/httpd/conf.d
[vagrant@puppetmaster conf.d]$ for cfg in *.conf; do sudo mv $cfg $cfg.dis; done
```

Instead, we'll install our own virtual configuration file that will include the specific Apache directives we require. This file contains a complete, self-standing service definition for the Puppet master service:

```
[vagrant@puppetmaster ~]$ cd /etc/httpd/conf.d/
[vagrant@puppetmaster conf.d]$ sudo cp /vagrant/etc-puppet/puppetmaster.conf ./
```

The next step is to configure the Puppet master application Rack service. Now we'll install a *config.ru* file with the Rack application configuration:

```
[vagrant@puppetmaster ~]$ mkdir -p /etc/puppetlabs/puppetmaster/public
[vagrant@puppetmaster ~]$ cd /etc/puppetlabs/puppetmaster
[vagrant@puppetmaster puppetmaster]$ sudo cp /vagrant/etc-puppet/config.ru ./
```

It is essential that the puppet user own all of the following files and directories. In particular, the Puppet master service will be started as the user who owns the *config.ru* file:

```
$ sudo chown puppet:puppet /etc/puppetlabs/puppetmaster/config.ru
$ sudo mkdir /var/run/puppetlabs/puppetmaster
$ sudo chown puppet:puppet /var/run/puppetlabs/puppetmaster
$ sudo mkdir /var/log/puppetlabs/puppetmaster
$ sudo chown puppet:puppet /var/log/puppetlabs/puppetmaster
```

Finally, restart Apache to pick up the changes. Check the status to ensure it is running successfully. Here's what it looks like when it is restarted successfully:

```
$ sudo systemctl restart httpd
$ sudo systemctl status httpd
httpd.service - The Apache HTTP Server
   Loaded: loaded (/usr/lib/systemd/system/httpd.service; enabled)
   Active: active (running) since Thu 2015-08-27 05:24:38 UTC; 5s ago
  Process: 14661 ExecStop=/bin/kill -WINCH ${MAINPID} (code=exited, status=0)
 Main PID: 14666 (httpd)
   Status: "Processing requests..."
   CGroup: /system.slice/httpd.service
           ├─14666 /usr/sbin/httpd -DFOREGROUND
           ├─14693 Passenger watchdog
           ├─14696 Passenger core
           ├─14703 Passenger ust-router
           ├─14714 /usr/sbin/httpd -DFOREGROUND
           ├─14715 /usr/sbin/httpd -DFOREGROUND
           ├─14716 /usr/sbin/httpd -DFOREGROUND
           ├─14717 /usr/sbin/httpd -DFOREGROUND
           └─14718 /usr/sbin/httpd -DFOREGROUND

Aug 27 05:24:38 puppetmaster systemd[1]: Starting The Apache HTTP Server...
Aug 27 05:24:38 puppetmaster systemd[1]: Started The Apache HTTP Server.
```

There are two logs that may contain errors from the Puppet master. Check the Apache error log for Passenger startup failures, and your syslog daemon log for messages from the Puppet master. The following command can be useful to view both of these logs when investigating problems:

```
[vagrant@puppetmaster ~]$ sudo tail -f /var/log/messages /var/log/httpd/error_log
```

IPv6 Dual-Stack Puppet Master

To enable IPv6 connections to a WEBrick Puppet master, add the `bindaddress` configuration setting to the `[master]` section of the Puppet configuration file, then restart the `puppetmaster` service:

```
[master]
  bindaddress = ::
```

This is completely unnecessary when the Puppet master runs under Apache/Passenger, and should be removed.

If you query for listening services using `netstat -an`, you'll see the Puppet master listening on a `tcp6` socket. This socket accepts both IPv4 and IPv6 connections:

```
[vagrant@puppetmaster ~]$ netstat -an |grep 8140
tcp6       0      0 :::8140                 :::*                    LISTEN
```

Clients will connect to the IPv6 or IPv4 port based on the configuration of the client node, and the addresses available from DNS or the hosts file. To force a node to connect using a specific protocol, only provide the address of the Puppet master in that format.

Debugging Puppet Master

You can find messages from the Puppet master in the syslog logfiles. To display the log output in a manner similar to the screen output provided by the `--no-daemonize` option, use this command:

```
[vagrant@puppetmaster ~]$ sudo tail -f /var/log/messages |grep puppet
```

## CHAPTER 21

Creating a Puppet Server

Puppet Server is a new product built from the ground up to provide higher performance and better integration with other Puppet Labs products.

Many of the changes with Puppet Server were a change in the technology stack. Puppet Server was written in Clojure and uses Java rather than Ruby as the underlying engine. This ties it more closely with PuppetDB and other Puppet Labs products. However, for most practical purposes you can use it without learning anything about the technology stack. We're going to skip over these details in favor of the practical concerns of installing and running.

At this point, we're going to spin up another virtual machine dedicated to hosting this product. You should open another terminal window, or add a new tab on your existing terminal for this virtual machine. This will allow you to switch back and forth between the machines, which is necessary in this chapter.

If you started up the puppetmaster VM in the last chapter, you may want to suspend it to save some memory:

```
learning-puppet4$ vagrant suspend puppetmaster
==> puppetmaster: Saving VM state and suspending execution...
```

Starting the puppetserver VM

In the new Terminal window, move into the directory where you checked out the learning-puppet4 Git repository (*https://github.com/jorhett/learning-puppet4*). Start up the puppetserver instance just like we did the client instance at the beginning of the book:

```
learning-puppet4$ vagrant up puppetserver
Bringing machine 'puppetserver' up with 'virtualbox' provider...
==> puppetserver: Importing base box 'puppetlabs/centos-7.2-64-nocm'...
```

```
==> puppetserver: Matching MAC address for NAT networking...
==> puppetserver: Checking if box 'puppetlabs/centos-7.2-64-nocm' is up to date...
==> puppetserver: Setting the name of the VM: learning-puppet4_puppetserver_1437612
...snip...
==> puppetserver: Machine booted and ready!

learning-puppet4$ vagrant ssh puppetserver
[vagrant@puppetserver ~]$
```

As this is a fresh new virtual machine, install the necessary utilities and a text editor of choice, as you did back in Chapter 2.

```
$ sudo yum install rsync git vim nano emacs-nox
```

Installing Puppet Server

Install the latest Puppet Labs Puppet Collection repository on the `puppetserver` instance. Starting in the home directory, take the following steps:

```
$ sudo yum install -y \
    http://yum.puppetlabs.com/puppetlabs-release-pc1-el-7.noarch.rpm
```

This command will install and enable the *puppetlabs-release-pc1* package repository, which contains the Puppet Server package. Now install the Puppet Server package:

```
$ sudo yum install -y puppetserver

Installed:
  puppetserver.noarch 0:2.3.0-1.el7

Dependency Installed:
  java-1.8.0-openjdk-headless.x86_64 1:1.8.0.51-1.b16.el7_1
  javapackages-tools.noarch 0:3.4.1-6.el7_0        lcms2.x86_64 0:2.5-4.el7
  libjpeg-turbo.x86_64 0:1.2.90-5.el7              libxslt.x86_64 0:1.1.28-5.el7
  puppet-agent.x86_64 0:1.4.0-1.el7                python-lxml.x86_64 0:3.2.1-4.el7
  python-javapackages.noarch 0:3.4.1-6.el7_0       tzdata-java.noarch 0:2015e-1.el7

Complete!
```

Configuring a Firewall for Puppet Server

At this point, we'll need to adjust the firewall on the server. Puppet clients connect to servers on TCP port 8140 by default. Use the following commands to allow incoming TCP connections to this port:

```
$ sudo firewall-cmd --permanent --zone=public --add-port=8140/tcp
success
$ sudo firewall-cmd --reload
success
```

This change allows incoming connections to the Puppet Server.

It is safe to run these commands in a virtual instance on your personal workstation. In a production setting, you'd want to limit access to specific IP networks. Don't make this change to a production system without reviewing your organization's existing security setup.

Guides for altering other firewalls can be found in Appendix B.

Configuring Puppet Server

Puppet Server takes its configuration values from two places:

- The primary configuration files at */etc/puppetlabs/puppetserver/conf.d/*
- Historic values it reads from the [master] and [main] blocks of */etc/puppetlabs/puppet/puppet.conf*

The settings from these files do not overlap. For any configuration option available in the Puppet Server configuration files, the setting in *puppet.conf* will be ignored.

A setting left undefined in the server configuration files will revert to the default value, instead of using the value from the Puppet configuration file.

The Puppet Server configuration files are as follows:

auth.conf
Authentication and authorization controls for Puppet Server and the Puppet Certificate Authority.

global.conf
Global configuration settings common to all components of Puppet Server. This contains only the location of the logback configuration file at this time.

puppetserver.conf
Configuration options for Puppet Server. Some of these options overlap with options in *puppet.conf*. Be careful to keep these matching, or Puppet Server and the puppet commands will use different directories.

webserver.conf
Web server configuration: authorization, TCP ports, and so on. If you were using the old Puppet master Rack application, this configuration file supersedes the Apache or nginx configuration files you were previously using.

web-routes.conf
> Service mount points for Puppet Server's web applications. Do not modify this file, as the Puppet agent depends on specific mount points being available. This file should be managed only by the Puppet Server package.

For a single server or testing setup, you don't need to change any of these values. We'll cover specific changes that may be necessary shortly.

> The Puppet Server configuration files do not use the INI file format used by *puppet.conf*. These files utilize a superset of JSON known as HOCON (*http://bit.ly/1XAAOvY*), which stands for Human-Optimized Config Object Notation. JSON doesn't support single quotes for strings, so you must avoid using single quotes in these config files.

Defining Server Paths

There are five variables that define the paths which the Puppet Server should use for its files. Unfortunately, these variables exist in two different files and must be kept in sync. See Table 21-1.

Table 21-1. Variables that define shared paths for Puppet applications

puppetserver.conf	puppet.conf	Default value
master-conf-dir	confdir	*/etc/puppetlabs/puppet*
master-code-dir	codedir	*/etc/puppetlabs/code*
master-var-dir	vardir	*/opt/puppetlabs/server/data/puppetserver*
master-run-dir	rundir	*/var/run/puppetlabs/puppetserver*
master-log-dir	logdir	*/var/log/puppetlabs/puppetserver*

Again, it is essential to keep these variables in sync between the two configuration files. If they differ, then Puppet Server will be looking in one place, and Puppet commands like `puppet certificate` will be looking in another.

Enabling use of /var filesystem

As recommended back in "Store Server Data Files Separately" on page 296, you should change the following values to conform to the Filesystem Hierarchy Standard (FHS) and most sysadmin expectations. The following change places all volatile and dynamic data within the */var/* filesystem.

Edit */etc/puppetlabs/puppet/puppet.conf*:

```
[user]
  vardir = /var/opt/puppetlabs/puppetserver
  ssldir = $vardir/ssl
```

```
[master]
  vardir = /var/opt/puppetlabs/puppetserver
  ssldir = $vardir/ssl
```

Double-check these values after installing the `puppetserver` package, as the package installation scripts will *change these values in an existing configuration file* during installation.

Make the corresponding change in */etc/puppetlabs/puppetserver/conf.d/puppet-server.conf*:

```
master-var-dir = /var/opt/puppetlabs/puppetserver
```

Then, create the directory we just named. Puppet Server will fail to run if the directory was not created prior to initialization:

```
[vagrant@puppetserver ~]$ mkdir -p /var/opt/puppetlabs/puppetserver
[vagrant@puppetserver ~]$ chown -R puppet:puppet /var/opt/puppetlabs/puppetserver
```

Limiting Memory Usage

By default, Puppet Server tries to allocate 2 gigabytes of RAM. This is not necessary for a test node, and won't work with Vagrant unless you add more memory to the node settings.

Tune down the memory reserved by changing the startup parameters. Edit */etc/sysconfig/puppetserver* and change the following line:

```
# Modify this if you'd like to change the memory allocation, enable JMX, etc.
JAVA_ARGS="-Xms512m -Xmx512m"
```

Note that the default file contains a `MaxPermSize` value in this field. It's OK to remove it, as the server would simply tell you:

```
Aug 03 00:55:02 puppetserver.example.com java[14652]:
  OpenJDK 64-Bit Server VM warning: ignoring option MaxPermSize=256m;
    support was removed in 8.0
```

 In large production environments, you will need to raise the memory limit rather than lower it.

Configuring TLS Certificates

Puppet Server accepts configuration of TLS keys and certificates in two different places. You can define the following override settings in */etc/puppetlabs/puppetserver/conf.d/webserver.conf*:

```
ssl-cert = /var/opt/puppetlabs/puppetserver/ssl/certs/puppet.example.com.pem
ssl-key = /var/opt/puppetlabs/puppetserver/ssl/private_keys/
  puppet.example.com.pem
ssl-ca-cert = /var/opt/puppetlabs/puppetserver/ssl/certs/ca.pem
ssl-crl-path = /var/opt/puppetlabs/puppetserver/ssl/crl.pem
```

 Paths are shown with the FHS-compliant directories recommended here. If you are using the default values, these files will reside in the */etc/puppetlabs/puppet/ssl/* directory.

If none of these variables are defined, Puppet Server will fall back to using the following defined or derived settings from */etc/puppetlabs/puppet/puppet.conf*, according to Table 21-2.

Table 21-2. Variables used for Puppet Server TLS file locations

puppetserver/conf.d/webserver.conf	puppet/puppet.conf
ssl-ca	localcacert
ssl-cert	hostcert
ssl-key	hostprivkey
ssl-crl-path	hostcrl

You can use either the settings in the first column or the second column. If you use the settings in *webserver.conf*, then you must use all four together. Otherwise, leave all four undefined and use the settings in *puppet.conf* (which is backward compatible with the Puppet master).

At this time, the Certificate Authority continues to use the following settings from *puppet.conf*. There isn't an equivalent in *puppetserver/conf.d/* files yet:

```
[master]
  cacert = /etc/puppetlabs/puppet/ssl/certs/ca.pem
  cacrl = /etc/puppetlabs/puppet/ssl/crl.pem
  hostcert = /etc/puppetlabs/puppet/ssl/certs/puppet.example.com.pem
  hostprivkey = /etc/puppetlabs/puppet/ssl/private_keys/puppet.example.com.pem
```

Due to the current mixture of settings in two files, I recommend that you consolidate settings in */etc/puppetlabs/puppet/puppet.conf*, and leave the settings blank in *webserver.conf*. This is the default, as-shipped configuration, so no changes are necessary.

The latest version of Puppet Server may have added new configuration options. Check the latest documentation at "Puppet Server: Differing Behavior in puppet.conf" (*http://bit.ly/21zpGjT*) on the Puppet docs site.

You can see the configuration values for the Puppet master and the Certificate Authority (defined or derived from defaults) with this command:

```
[vagrant@puppetserver ~]$ sudo puppet config print --section master
cfacter = false
confdir = /etc/puppetlabs/puppet
codedir = /etc/puppetlabs/code
vardir = /var/opt/puppetlabs/puppetserver
...etc
```

Avoiding Obsolete Settings

The following settings are valid for the Puppet master, but have been replaced by other configuration options in Puppet Server:

- autoflush—replaced by settings in *logback.xml*
- bindaddress—remove and configure ssl-host instead
- ca—uses CA information from *bootstrap.cfg* instead
- keylength—replaced by a fixed value of 4,096 bits
- logdir—replaced by settings in *logback.xml*
- masterhttplog—replaced by the access-log-config setting in *webserver.conf*
- masterlog—replaced by settings in *logback.xml*
- masterport—replaced by the ssl-port setting in *webserver.conf*
- ssl_client_header—ignored unless allow-header-cert-info is enabled in *auth.conf*
- ssl_client_verify_header—ignored unless allow-header-cert-info is enabled in *auth.conf*
- ssl_server_ca_auth—ignored in favor of ssl-ca-cert or cacert

The following settings used by the Puppet master are ignored by Puppet server, with no equivalent option:

- capass
- caprivatedir
- daemonize
- http_debug
- puppetdlog
- railslog
- syslogfacility
- user

The following three settings are valid for Puppet agents, but will be ignored by Puppet Server:

- configtimeout
- http_proxy_host
- http_proxy_port

Configuring Server Logs

Puppet Server uses the well-known JDK logback library. Logback is a successor to the log4j logging library provided with Java.

By default, the logback configuration file can be found at */etc/puppetlabs/puppet-server/logback.xml*. This is the standard XML configuration file format as documented in "Logback configuration" (*http://bit.ly/1R3wh4x*) on the Logback Project site.

By default, Puppet Server logs all messages at INFO level or higher to */var/log/puppet-labs/puppetserver/puppetserver.log*. Review the bolded sections of this *logback.xml* configuration snippet:

```
<appender name="F1" class="ch.qos.logback.core.FileAppender">
    <file>/var/log/puppetlabs/puppetserver/puppetserver.log</file>
    <append>true</append>
    <encoder>
        <pattern>%d %-5p [%t] [%c{2}] %m%n</pattern>
    </encoder>
</appender>

<root level="info">
    <appender-ref ref="F1"/>
</root>
```

If you are familiar with logback or log4j, you can modify this file far beyond the simple examples here.

> Do not change the ConsoleAppender definition that outputs console messages when running Puppet Server in the foreground debug mode.

If you want to send Puppet Server messages to the system logger syslog, then you may want to replace or supplement the FileAppender with the following:

```
<appender name="Syslog" class="ch.qos.logback.core.net.SyslogAppender">
    <syslogHost>loghost.example.com</file>
    <facility>DAEMON</facility>
</appender>

<root level="info">
```

```
        ...
        <appender-ref ref="Syslog"/>
    </root>
```

By default, logback scans for configuration files changes every minute. Restarting Puppet Server is not necessary. To disable this, change the `scan` attribute on the `configuration` element:

```
<configuration scan="true">
```

You can also adjust the scanning interval based on seconds, minutes, hours, or days:

```
<configuration scan="true" scanPeriod="30 minutes">
```

You will need to ensure the syslog server is configured to accept messages from the network. If logging to the local host, you will need to uncomment the following lines in */etc/rsyslog.conf*:

```
# Provides UDP syslog reception
$ModLoad imudp
$UDPServerRun 514
```

Configuring Server Authentication

Puppet Server authentication and authorization is defined in the */etc/puppetlabs/ puppetserver/conf.d/auth.conf* configuration file utilizing the *trapperkeeper-authorization* format.

This file contains an `authorization` block that contains the rules used to approve or deny requests.

 This section contains advanced settings for customized server environments. If you are new to Puppet, skip ahead to "Running Puppet Server" on page 321 and come back later.

Understanding authorization rules

Within the `authorization` block are a list of rules. Each rule contains a `name`, a `sort-order` parameter, a `match-request` definition, and `allow` or `deny` parameters that match the node's certificate name (`$trusted['certname']`).

The format of the rules is fairly self-evident, and the inline comments can help you understand why the existing rules are there. Multiple values for `allow` or `deny` should be written as an array.

The splat (*) value matches any validated node. The `allow-unauthenticated: true` setting is used to allow new nodes to submit certificate requests and retrieve the signed certificate.

Here is one of the more complex rules. This rule uses a regular expression capture group to match the node name requested. The `allow:` definition utilizes the captured node name to permit only that same node to request its catalog. See the bolded parts:

```
{
    # Allow nodes to retrieve only their own node definition
    match-request: {
        path: "^/puppet/v3/node/([^/]+)$"
        type: regex
        method: get
    }
    allow: "$1"
    sort-order: 500
    name: "puppetlabs node"
},
```

As shown, the validated node *client.example.com* can make a GET request for */puppet/v3/node/client.example.com*. Any other node requesting the catalog for *client.example.com* will be denied.

Controlling authorization for Puppet 3 agents

There are separate configuration options for Puppet 3 clients, which do not utilize the Puppet API.

In Puppet Server 2, the default behavior was to enable use of the older */etc/puppetlabs/puppet/auth.conf* configuration file originally used by `puppet master`. This behavior has been deprecated, and will likely be removed in Puppet Server 3.

Unless you have previously deployed a Puppet master with a customized *auth.conf* configuration file, you should disable the legacy configuration setting. If the following option can be found in */etc/puppetlabs/puppetserver/conf.d/puppetserver.conf*, set it to `false`:

```
# (optional) Authorize access to Puppet master endpoints via rules specified
# in the legacy Puppet auth.conf file (if true or not specified) or via rules
# specified in the Puppet Server HOCON-formatted auth.conf (if false).
use-legacy-auth-conf: false
```

> This parameter only affects Puppet 3.x agents that utilize the classic Puppet master endpoints. Puppet 4 agents utilize the Puppet API endpoints controlled by settings in */etc/puppetlabs/puppetserver/conf.d/auth.conf*.

To upgrade a Puppet master with a customized *auth.conf*, migrate the customizations to the new HOCON format auth file. A guide for converting old auth files is available at "Config File Auth: Deprecated Ruby Parameters" (*http://bit.ly/1UmVnhh*) on the Puppet docs site.

Running Puppet Server

Now it is time to start the server. While Puppet Server is a high-performance replacement for the old Puppet master, the Java service takes a bit longer to start. Start it like so:

```
[vagrant@puppetserver ~]$ sudo systemctl enable puppetserver
[vagrant@puppetserver ~]$ sudo systemctl start puppetserver
```

You can observe what it does during startup by looking at the logfiles:

```
$ sudo tail -f /var/log/puppetlabs/puppetserver/puppetserver.log
309 INFO [o.e.j.u.log] Logging initialized @12460ms
742 INFO [p.t.s.w.jetty9-service] Initializing web server(s).
874 INFO [p.s.j.jruby-puppet-service] Initializing the JRuby service
209 INFO [puppet-server] Puppet Puppet settings initialized; run mode: master
384 INFO [p.s.j.jruby-puppet-agents] Finished creating JRubyPuppet instance 1 of 1
410 INFO [p.s.c.puppet-server-config-core] Initializing webserver settings
603 INFO [p.s.c.certificate-authority-service] CA Service adding a ring handler
```

Observe the final line, which says that it started a CA Service with a ring handler. This obscure message is the only notification you'll receive that it has created a certificate authority based on its own `certname`, and then signed its own certificate.

By signing its own certificate, this Puppet Server has become the root certificate authority for this Puppet installation. Only agents with certificates signed by this certificate authority will be able to access the service. We'll discuss ways to handle third-party certificate authorities in "Using an External Certificate Authority" on page 353.

Adding Ruby Gems

Puppet Server has its own Ruby installation separate from your system Ruby, and even from the Puppet agent's Ruby. If you are using server-side plugins that require additional gems, use the `puppetserver gem` command to install them.

First, examine the gems that come preinstalled:

```
[vagrant@puppetserver ~]$ sudo puppetserver gem list

*** LOCAL GEMS ***

jar-dependencies (0.1.13)
jruby-openssl (0.9.7 java)
json (1.8.0 java)
rake (10.1.0)
rdoc (4.1.2)
```

The `puppetserver gem` command is identical to Ruby's `gem` command, but maintains the JRuby gem-store used by the Puppet Server. If you need other gems for a plugin running on the server, use `puppetserver gem` to install them exactly like you'd use Ruby's `gem` command:

```
$ sudo puppetserver gem install bundler --no-ri --no-rdoc
Fetching: bundler-1.10.6.gem (100%)
Successfully installed bundler-1.10.6
1 gem installed
```

Puppet Server uses JRuby, a high-performance, threaded Ruby interpreter. It is compatible with all native Ruby gems, but not with gems that use binary or compiled extensions. It is best to adjust the plugin to use a native Ruby gem whenever possible.

IPv6 Dual-Stack Puppet Server

Puppet Server uses IPv6 out of the box without any specific settings. If you are upgrading the Puppet configuration of a Puppet master, you'll need to remove or comment out the `bindaddress` configuration setting used to enable IPv6 on a Puppet master:

```
[master]
    # this setting isn't necessary for Puppet Server
    #bindaddress = ::
```

If you query for listening services using `netstat -an`, you'll see the Puppet master listening on a `tcp6` socket. This socket accepts both IPv4 and IPv6 connections:

```
[vagrant@puppetmaster ~]$ netstat -an |grep 8140
tcp6       0      0 :::8140                 :::*                    LISTEN
```

Clients will connect to the IPv6 or IPv4 port based on the configuration of the client node, and the addresses available from DNS or the hosts file. If you want nodes to connect using only one of these protocols, provide the address of the Puppet Server in that version's notation.

## CHAPTER 22

Connecting a Node

No matter if you are using the Puppet master or Puppet Server, at this point you are ready to connect a node to your server. Let's review this process one step at a time.

Creating a Key Pair

The easiest way to create a key pair for a node is to attempt to connect to a server. The Puppet agent will create the private and public TLS keys, and then submit a certificate signing request (CSR) to the server for authorization.

The default hosts file associates the name *puppet.example.com* with the puppetserver node. If you are using the deprecated Puppet master, you will need to edit */etc/hosts* to look like this:

```
192.168.250.5   puppetmaster.example.com puppet.example.com
192.168.250.6   puppetserver.example.com
```

If you are testing the Puppet Server, then you'll want that name associated with the puppetserver instance's IP address.

Once you have confirmed that this is correct, attempt a connection to the server using this command:

```
[vagrant@client ~]$ puppet agent --test --server=puppet.example.com
Info: Creating a new SSL key for client.example.com
Info: Caching certificate for ca
Info: csr_attributes file loading from /etc/puppetlabs/puppet/csr_attributes.yaml
Info: Creating a new SSL certificate request for client.example.com
Info: Certificate Request fingerprint (SHA256): C3:37:C8:76:CE:3A:D7:81:64:DF:80
Info: Caching certificate for ca
Exiting; no certificate found and waitforcert is disabled
```

There's a lot of information here, so let's review it. The client has done all of the following:

1. Created a private and public TLS key pair for itself.
2. Connected to the server, and retrieved a copy of the server's TLS certificate.
3. Created a CSR for itself and submitted it to the server.

 This CSR is identical to the CSR you create to get a TLS certificate for a website. In this case, the certificate authority who signs the request will be the Puppet server.

The client cannot proceed until it is authorized. You can run the command again and you'll see the same output. This is security for your environment—a node may not connect and download information that it has not been authorized for:

```
[vagrant@client ~]$ puppet agent --test --server=puppet.example.com
Exiting; no certificate found and waitforcert is disabled
```

Authorizing the Node

At this point, you'll need to return to the Puppet server and sign the client's CSR in order to authorize it. First, let's see what requests are waiting to be signed:

```
[vagrant@puppetserver ~]$ puppet cert --list
  "client.example.com" (SHA256) C3:37:C8:76:CE:3A:D7:81:64:DF:80
```

Compare the CSR's fingerprint with the request you made earlier to ensure that it is the request you created. Sign the request in order to authorize the client:

```
[vagrant@puppetserver ~]$ puppet cert --sign client.example.com
Notice: Signed certificate request for client.example.com
Notice: Removing file Puppet::SSL::CertificateRequest client.example.com
  at '/var/opt/puppetlabs/puppetserver/ssl/ca/requests/client.example.com.pem'
```

The next time the client connects, it will be given the signed certificate and a Puppet catalog will be built for it.

Downloading the First Catalog

Now that the request has been signed, you can return to the client node and retry the connection attempt:

```
[vagrant@client ~]$ puppet agent --test --server=puppet.example.com
Info: Caching certificate for client.example.com
Info: Caching certificate_revocation_list for ca
Info: Caching certificate for client.example.com
```

```
Info: Retrieving pluginfacts
Info: Retrieving plugin
Info: Caching catalog for client.example.com
Info: Applying configuration version '1438539603'
Notice: Applied catalog in 0.01 seconds
```

The Puppet agent has received the signed certificate for the node and stored it. Then it performed all the steps listed in "Understanding the Catalog Builder" on page 291:

1. The agent submitted the node name, environment, and facts to the Puppet server.
2. The Puppet master built a Puppet catalog for the node in 0.28 seconds.
3. The agent evaluates the catalog on the node in 0.01 seconds.

How did we know that the catalog was built in 0.28 seconds? You can find this in the syslog logfile:

```
[vagrant@puppetmaster ~]$ grep client.example.com /var/log/messages
Aug  2 18:20:03 puppetmaster puppet: Notice: Compiled catalog for
  client.example.com in environment production in 0.28 seconds
```

You'll probably be thinking two things right now:

- Wow, evaluating a policy in 0.01 seconds is fast!
- But this didn't do anything…

You are absolutely correct. At this moment in time, the catalog given back to the node was completely empty. Let's go on to configure the server with your Hiera data and modules.

Installing Hiera Data and Modules

If you are building a new Puppet environment, install the Hiera data, environments, and modules you built in Part II. You can simply copy these from the client instance used earlier in the book.

On the client instance, give the vagrant user a password:

```
[vagrant@client ~]$ sudo passwd vagrant
Changing password for user vagrant.
New password: a good password
Retype new password: a good password
passwd: all authentication tokens updated successfully.
```

On the puppetserver instance, recursively copy over the entire code-dir path:

```
[vagrant@puppetserver ~]$ rsync -aH client:/etc/puppetlabs/code /etc/puppetlabs/
vagrant@client.example.com's password:
```

With this simple process you have installed the Hiera data and modules built and tested earlier with puppet apply for use on the Puppet server.

Testing with a Client Node

At this time, you can now test your manifests, exactly as you did in Part II. The only difference is that this time the Puppet server will evaluate the manifest and build the catalog, instead of the local Puppet agent. On the client node, run this command:

```
$ sudo puppet agent --test --server=puppet.example.com --environment=test
Info: Retrieving pluginfacts
Info: Retrieving plugin
Info: Loading facts
Info: Caching catalog for client.example.com
Info: Applying configuration version '1438557124'
Notice: Client is using catalog from the Test environment.
Notice: /Stage[main]/Main/Notify[UsingTest]/message: defined 'message' as
  'Client is using catalog from the Test environment.'
Notice: /Stage[main]/Puppet::Agent/Service[puppet]/ensure:
  ensure changed 'stopped' to 'running'
Info: /Stage[main]/Puppet::Agent/Service[puppet]:
  Unscheduling refresh on Service[puppet]
Notice: Applied catalog in 0.65 seconds

$ ps auwx |grep puppet
root    13615  0.0  7.4 256776 37340 ?      Ssl  22:52   0:00
  ruby /bin/puppet agent --server=puppet.example.com --environment=test
```

As you can see, the agent has configured the node exactly the same as when Puppet was run with the local manifests.

 If the outcome is not exactly the same, double-check all the paths and files to ensure that the Hiera data and modules are installed in the expected places.

Learning More About Puppet Server

The absolute best way to expand on what you have learned in this chapter is to build out a Puppet server. Configure the client to use it, and test the process. Once you have this working, do all of the following:

1. Start Puppet agent on the client instance to connect to the server.
2. Review the certificate request and compare the fingerprint on the puppetserver instance.
3. Sign the agent's certificate request.
4. Observe the Puppet agent implement the empty catalog on the client instance.
5. Review the node report stored in the $vardir/reports directory.

6. Copy the module and Hiera data from the `client` instance to the `puppetserver` instance.
7. Run the Puppet agent on the `client` instance again to observe the module convergence.

For extra credit, go on to perform advanced configuration changes:

1. Alter the list of classes assigned to the node in Hiera.
2. `vagrant up web1`, install Puppet, and connect it to the Puppet server.

## CHAPTER 23

Migrating an Existing Puppet Master

This chapter will cover how to install Hiera data and modules from an existing Puppet environment. This will allow you to test an existing Puppet installation with Puppet Server (or Puppet master 4).

The first step is to copy the Puppet master configuration, Hiera configuration, and environment data from your existing Puppet environment to this Puppet server. There are three steps to this.

Migrating the Puppet Master Config

This is very straightforward. Copy the entire block named [master] from */etc/puppet/puppet.conf* on an existing Puppet master. Add this to */etc/puppetlabs/puppet/puppet.conf* on the new Puppet server you have created.

After you have done that, you'll need to perform the following changes:

Check the previous master's puppet.conf for settings in [main]
> Check the master's [main] section for any variables that affect the server configuration. Refer to "Configuring Puppet Server" on page 313 if necessary. Some master settings could be placed in the wrong section of the config. If in doubt, copy the entire section.

Remove file paths found in the file
> As every directory has changed with the migration to Puppet 4, it is best to comment out or remove every path you find in the configuration file. Embrace the new, more consistent path structure.

(Testing) Adjust the `certname` *parameter in the* [`master`] *block*

If you are building a separate and distinct server intended only to test your modules for compatibility with Puppet 4, adjust the `certname` parameter to indicate the new server name. If you are building a drop-in replacement for the previous Puppet master, leave the name the same.

(Production) Copy the entire TLS file hierarchy

If you are creating a drop-in replacement for an existing Puppet master, copy the entire file hierarchy to the new */var/opt/puppetlabs/puppetserver/ssl/* directory:

```
$ sudo rsync -aHv oldmaster:/var/lib/puppet/ssl \
    /var/opt/puppetlabs/puppetserver/
```

Synchronizing All Environments

Sync the entire environment directory structure from the previous Puppet master to the new server. If you were already using environments, this could be as simple as the following command (adjust the server names and the source path as necessary):

```
$ rsync -aHP oldmaster:/etc/puppet/environments /etc/puppetlabs/code/
```

If you were not using environments previously, then I recommend the following approach:

```
$ cd /etc/puppetlabs/code
$ rsync -aHP oldmaster:/etc/puppet/modules environments/production/
```

You could also copy the modules into `basemodulepath` or */etc/puppetlabs/code/ modules*. This directory is sourced as a backup for modules shared across all environments. It is simpler, but it has limitations (which we'll discuss in Part IV).

```
$ rsync -aHP oldmaster:/etc/puppet/modules /etc/puppetlabs/code/
```

After you have copied these files, you'll need to update any files that have Puppet config paths to reflect Puppet 4 standards. These are most likely to be environment configuration files: */etc/puppetlabs/code/environments/*/environments.conf*, but if you have a Puppet module that configures Puppet for your nodes (like the `puppet` module created in Chapter 13), then you'll need to update the paths in that as well.

I have found the following commands very helpful for finding paths that may need to be updated (you may want to check other paths depending on your old Puppet file paths):

```
$ grep -rH etc/puppet /etc/puppet /etc/puppetlabs
$ grep -rH var/lib/puppet /etc/puppet /etc/puppetlabs
```

Best Practice

Avoid using the older paths with Puppet 4. Invest in the new standardized paths to ensure maximum consistency and compatibility going forward.

Copying Hiera Data

Copy the previous Hiera configuration file from the previous master to the new Puppet server. This is usually installed in */etc/puppet/hiera.yaml* on previous Puppet versions. You'll want to copy this file to */etc/puppetlabs/code/hiera.yaml*:

```
$ scp -aHv oldmaster:/etc/puppet/hiera.yaml /etc/puppetlabs/code/
$ rsync -aHP oldmaster:/etc/puppet/hieradata /etc/puppetlabs/code/
```

After you have copied the file, you'll need to update the paths in the file to reflect Puppet 4 standards. If you were not using environments before, your Hiera configuration file may have had paths like this:

```
:yaml:
  :datadir: /etc/puppet/hieradata
```

If you want all environments to share the same Hiera data like the preceding example, you can adjust it as follows:

```
:yaml:
  :datadir: /etc/puppetlabs/code/hieradata
```

If you had separate copies of data for each environment, it may have had paths that utilized the environment variable in the path:

```
:yaml:
  :datadir: /etc/puppet/environments/%{::environment}/hieradata
```

Adjust it to use the $environmentpath standard for Puppet 4 utilizing the $::environment variable:

```
:yaml:
  :datadir: /etc/puppetlabs/code/environments/%{::environment}/hieradata
```

Ensure that you utilize the :: top-level prefix on this variable.

Finally, copy over the Hiera data to the location referenced in the configuration you just adjusted:

```
$ rsync -aHP oldmaster:/etc/puppet/hieradata /etc/puppetlabs/code/
```

Or:

```
$ cd /etc/puppetlabs/code
$ rsync -aHP oldmaster:/etc/puppet/hieradata environments/production/
```

Moving the MCollective Config Directory

If you were using MCollective previously, copy its configuration files from the previous Puppet master to the new server. These were installed in */etc/mcollective* previously. Copy the entire hierarchy to */etc/puppetlabs/mcollective/*:

```
$ sudo rsync -aHv oldmaster:/etc/mcollective /etc/puppetlabs/
```

After you have copied the files, you will need to update paths in the configuration files to reflect the new Puppet file paths. Adjust any paths that reference */etc/mcollective* with */etc/puppetlabs/mcollective*.

Add the following line to both the *server.cfg* and *client.cfg* files:

```
libdir = /opt/puppetlabs/mcollective/plugins
```

This adds the new AIO installer paths to the library load path. Leave the old `libdir` lines in the file as many plugins still install in the OS standard directories.

Removing Node Inheritance

If you were using node inheritance to apply common classes to groups of systems in *manifests/site.pp/* or another file imported there, you'll need to break this up into Hiera class assignments. Node assignment remains possible in Puppet 4, but node inheritance has been completely removed.

For example, this assignment style:

```
node 'puppetserver' inherits default {
  class { 'puppet::server': }
}
node 'webserver' inherits default {
  class { 'apache': }
}
node default {
  class { 'ntp': }
  class { 'puppet::agent': }
}
```

will yield this result:

```
ERROR [puppet-server] Puppet Node inheritance is not supported in Puppet >= 4.0.0
See http://links.puppetlabs.com/puppet-node-inheritance-deprecation
```

The ability to look up classes in Hiera data has significantly improved this situation. You can now assign classes to nodes based on Hiera's flexible hierarchy of information sources.

The alternative is much cleaner and easier to read when many systems are involved. Start by adding the following lookup to the *manifests/site.pp*, which does nothing more than look up classes to declare from Hiera and other data sources:

```
# Lookup all classes defined in Hiera and other data sources
lookup('classes', Array[String], 'unique').include
```

Then create a default YAML definition for classes in *hieradata/common.yaml* with the list of classes that every node applies:

```
classes:
  - ntp
  - puppet::agent
```

Finally, remove every `inherits` from the node definitions in the manifest. This won't get you all the way to proper Hiera-assigned classes as described in "Assigning Modules to Nodes" on page 153, but it will get you past the loss of node inheritance in Puppet 4.

Take the time and make the investment in using the Hiera hierarchy for class assignment. It may seem like a difficult change, but once you've gained the advantages you'll be pleased with the outcome.

Testing a Client Node

At this time, you can now test your manifests, exactly as you would with an older Puppet master:

```
[vagrant@client ~]$ sudo puppet agent --test --server=puppet.example.com
Info: Retrieving pluginfacts
Info: Retrieving plugin
Info: Loading facts
Info: Caching catalog for client.example.com
Info: Applying configuration version '1438557124'
```

It is hard to predict what you will see at this point, as it depends on how your modules and data are configured. If your modules were written according to Puppet 3 best practices, you may have very little that is necessary to fix. Many of my own modules worked with zero or just a few changes with Puppet 4.

Don't assume that no visible errors means no problems were found. Check the client logfile (*/var/log/messages*) and the server logfile (*/var/log/puppetlabs/puppetserver/puppetserver.log*) for warnings and deprecation messages.

If you see any problems in the client or server logfiles, go through the modules and adjust them to work properly in a Puppet 4 environment. You may want to refer back to these parts of the book for information specific to upgrades:

- "Reviewing Puppet 4 Changes" on page 30
- Chapter 8

Upgrading Clients

Puppet Server contains backward-compatible functions to support Puppet 3 clients, albeit with some limitations. In contrast, the Puppet 4 master will not support Puppet 3 clients. Try connecting one when running it in foreground mode, and you'll get a clear warning about this:

```
[vagrant@puppetmaster ~]$ sudo puppet master --verbose --no-daemonize
Info: Not Found: Error: Invalid URL -
  Puppet expects requests that conform to the /puppet and /puppet-ca APIs.

Note that Puppet 3 agents aren't compatible with this version;
 if you're running Puppet 3, you must either upgrade your agents to match the
 server or point them to a server running Puppet 3.
```

There are two ways to handle this:

- Put an upgrade module on the Puppet 3 master that installs Puppet 4 on client nodes.
- Replace the Puppet 3 master with Puppet Server.

No matter which option you choose, you'll need a module that removes the old Puppet configuration and replaces it with Puppet 4. You learned how to build one in Part II.

## CHAPTER 24

Utilizing Advantages of a Puppet Server

A Puppet server provides several features above and beyond what's possible in a `puppet apply` environment. Let's review each of these server-based features.

Using Server Data in Your Manifests

When using a Puppet server you gain several data sources not available to you with `puppet apply`.

Trusted Facts

When a node connects to the server it transmits a list of facts about the node. Unfortunately, there is no way to validate that these facts are correct. If you have conditions in your code based on node information that provide access to security-related data, the data could be accessed by a compromised node that forged its facts.

There is a new hash available named `$trusted[]`. It contains facts that have been validated by the server, and can be trusted to be correct.

`$trusted['authenticated']`
> The possible values are:

> `remote`
>> Confirms a successful validation of the remote client's certificate

> `local`
>> Indicates that `puppet apply` is being used and validation is unavailable

> `false`
>> Warns that the *auth.conf* file is misconfigured to allow unauthenticated requests

`$trusted['certname']`
> This contains the certificate name validated by the Puppet server if remote, or the value of $certname in the Puppet configuration if local.

`$trusted['hostname']` *and* `$trusted['domain']`
> hostname will contain the part before the first period of the certificate name, and domain will contain the remainder. This is useful when you're using FQDN cert names, and confusing in other situations.

`$trusted['extensions']`
> The value of this will be a hash containing all certificate extensions present in the certificate. You can find out how to create certificate extensions in "Policy-Based Autosigning" on page 349.

You can significantly improve security by altering the Hiera hierarchy to use the `trusted[]` facts provided by the server instead of the `facts[]` supplied by the client:

```
:hierarchy:
  - "nodes/%{trusted.certname}"
  - "os/%{facts.osfamily}"
  - common
```

More values could be added to Trusted Facts by later releases of Puppet. You can see the current list at "Facts and Built-in Variables: Trusted Facts" (*http://bit.ly/21zpz82*) on the Puppet docs site.

Server Facts

The server sets certain variables for use in manifests. Unfortunately, if the node provides facts of the same name, these values will be overridden. If you enable the following setting, the Puppet server will define a new hash of server facts that a client cannot override:

```
[master]
    trusted_server_facts = true
```

When this value is enabled (and the Puppet server reloaded), there will be a new hash available named `$server_facts[]` that provides the following values:

`$server_facts['serverversion']`
> Version of Puppet used by the server. *Not the version of Puppet Server!*

`$server_facts['servername']`
> The certificate name (certname) of the server. The name used to sign all certificates if the server provides the CA function.

`$server_facts['serverip']`
> The IP address it was contacted on. This can vary on multihomed servers.

`$server_facts['environment']`

The environment selected by the server for the node. It is possible for the node to request one environment from its configuration files, or command-line arguments, but provide a fact that sets the top-level variable to another value. It won't be the value used when building the catalog, which could be confusing. This entry in the `server_facts[]` hash will always contain the environment used for processing the node's catalog.

 Best Practice

Always enable `trusted_server_facts`. Always refer to `facts[`*fact name*`]` for client-provided facts, and `server_facts[`*factname*`]` for server-validated facts. Avoid using top-scope variables due to the possibility of the node-level override.

More server facts could be added by later releases of Puppet. You can see the current list at "Language: Facts and Build-in Variables" (*http://bit.ly/1R3w1Tc*) on the Puppet docs site.

Server Configuration Settings

As shown in the following example, Puppet servers make every configuration setting available as `$::setting::`*setting_name*:

```
notice("Trusted server facts are enabled: ${::settings::trusted_server_facts}")
```

Note that this is not a hash but a namespace, so you cannot iterate over it to output each value.

There is no equivalent access to node configuration settings by default, other than the following:

- `trusted['certname']`
- `facts['clientnoop']`
- `facts['agent_specified_environment']`

To gain access to a node's configuration values, add a custom fact or external fact to a Puppet module, as documented in "Adding Custom Facts" on page 217.

Backing Up Files Changed on Nodes

As discussed in "Managing Files" on page 43, every file changed by a Puppet `file` resource, or reviewed by the `audit` resource, is backed up to the directory specified in the `clientbucketdir` configuration setting. You can view these local file backups using the `puppet filebucket --local list` command.

The default configuration is a single filebucket named *puppet* that points to the value of $clientbucketdir:

```
filebucket { 'puppet':
  path => $clientbucketdir,
}
File {
  backup => 'puppet',
}
```

When using a Puppet server, you can move backups of file changes to the Puppet server instead. This is enabled by defining a `filebucket` resource with the `path` attribute set to `false`:

```
filebucket { 'puppet.example.com':
  path   => false,                 # This is required for remote filebuckets.
  server => 'puppet.example.com', # defaults to the current puppet server
  port   => '8140'                 # defaults to the current server port
}
```

As the defaults are always the current server, if you want to back up every file to that server the simplest declaration could be:

```
filebucket { 'local_server':
  path => false,
}
File {
  backup => 'local_server',
}
```

This resource should generally be defined in a top-scope manifest in the environment's *manifests/* directory. You can define multiple filebucket resources, and declare within the resource or in a resource default which bucket to use:

```
file { '/etc/sudoers':
  ...
  backup => 'security-files',
}
```

 Backing up files to the Puppet server is required for Puppet Dashboard to display the file changes.

Processing Puppet Node Reports

As you have seen in previous examples, the Puppet agent will send all log messages generated by the agent (according to the log level configured) to the node's syslog facility, or a configured logfile. Agents that connect to a Puppet server will also deliver a report to the same server by default. These reports can be stored and processed in a wide variety of ways.

Some people mistakenly attempt to use log surfing programs to observe problems with Puppet configuration. This is an attempt at deducing failure based on problems seen before. I have never found this practice to satisfactorily meet the client needs. They lose hundreds of hours trying to tune every resource with a custom log level.

It is faster and easier to access the entire Puppet node report, and select the details that interest you from that report.

Best Practice

Don't waste time super-tuning the log levels of every resource. Node reports provide direct access to every detail of the Puppet convergence process.

Enabling Transmission of Reports

Agents communicating with a Puppet server send a node convergence report to the same server from which they received the catalog. You can change this configuration with the following parameters in */etc/puppetlabs/puppet/puppet.conf*:

```
[agent]
  report = true
  report_server = $server
  report_port = $masterport
```

The preceding settings are enabled by default, and you could leave them out to achieve the normal submission behavior. You should only add them to the Puppet configuration file if you are changing them, such as to disable the sending of reports or to specify an alternate report processor.

Running Audit Inspections

If you have resources defined with the `audit` attribute, you can run the `puppet inspect` command on the node to generate a node report containing the detailed status of all audited resources. The node report will be submitted to the default Puppet server, or to the server passed on the command line:f

```
[vagrant@client ~]$ sudo puppet inspect
Notice: Finished inspection in 1.40 seconds
```

If you are using Puppet Dashboard, you can find the inspection report under the Node details page, as shown in "Reviewing a node's history" on page 391.

If you have enabled a server-backed file bucket, you can add the `--archive_files` option to back up copies of audited file resources during the inspection:

```
$ sudo puppet inspect --archive_files --archive_file_server=puppet.example.com
```

The `--archive_file_server` argument is optional and defaults to the configured Puppet server.

If you make use of `audit`, you may want to run this from cron on all client nodes:

```
cron { 'audit-file-changes':
  command   => 'puppet inspect --archive_files',
  user      => 'root',
  hour      => '0',
  minute    => '0',
}
```

You can use Puppet Dashboard to review the report, or write a custom processor to analyze and compare reports. You'll learn how to write a custom report processor in "Creating a Custom Report Processor" on page 344.

 `puppet inspect` was broken from Puppet 3.0 until Puppet 4.4.1; see Puppet bug PUP-5233 (*https://tickets.puppetlabs.com/browse/ PUP-5233*) for the patch if you have a version before 4.4.1 and get the `Could not find catalog` error.

Storing Node Reports

The default behavior of a Puppet server is to store the reports in YAML format in the directory specified by the `reportdir` configuration parameter. With the settings we recommend in this book, this would default to the following settings in */etc/puppet-labs/puppet/puppet.conf*:

```
[master]
  reports = store
  reportdir = /var/opt/puppetlabs/puppetserver/reports
```

 If you aren't using the */var* filesystem settings as recommended, the report directory will be */opt/puppetlabs/puppet/cache/reports*.

You can examine this directory now and see the report from the `client` instance. As the report directories are owned and readable only by the Puppet server, you will have to either `chown()` the directories or become the `puppet` user to read the files:

```
[vagrant@puppetserver ~]$ sudo -u puppet bash
bash-4.2$ cd /var/opt/puppetlabs/puppetserver/reports/
bash-4.2$ ls -la
total 0
drwxr-x--- 3 puppet puppet 31 Aug 16 21:23 .
```

```
drwxrwxr-x 12 puppet puppet 139 Aug  7 06:33 ..
drwxr-x---  2 puppet puppet  30 Aug 16 21:23 client.example.com

bash-4.2$ ls -la client.example.com
total 8
drwxr-x--- 2 puppet puppet   30 Aug 16 21:23 .
drwxr-x--- 3 puppet puppet   31 Aug 16 21:23 ..
-rw-r----- 1 puppet puppet 6706 Aug 16 21:23 201508162123.yaml

bash-4.2$ head -10 client.example.com/201508162123.yaml
--- !ruby/object:Puppet::Transaction::Report
metrics:
  resources: !ruby/object:Puppet::Util::Metric
    label: Resources
    name: resources
    values:
    - - total
      - Total
      - 7
    - - skipped
```

The report contains a log message for every action taken by the node, in addition to metrics about the number of resources processed, skipped, applied, or failed and the elapsed time Puppet spent evaluating and applying resources.

On the client node, you can find the same report file at */opt/puppetlabs/puppet/cache/state/last_run_report.yaml*.

Logging Node Reports

If you are happy with log messages on the agent nodes, or their ability to send the logs to a centralized log server using the local logger, then you don't need the log report handler. The Puppet agent will send each message at or above the configured log level to the configured log target (the default is syslog).

If your Puppet server has access to a centralized log server unavailable to the agent nodes, or the server is functioning as a log aggregator, then it can be helpful to have the server send all agent messages to its own logs. You can enable this by adding the log action to the list of report processors in */etc/puppetlabs/puppet/puppet.conf*:

```
[master]
  reports = log,store
```

Breaking Change

A Puppet master will send logs to syslog by default, or the log target defined in */etc/puppetlabs/puppet/puppet.conf*. Puppet Server will send logs to the targets defined in */etc/puppetlabs/puppetserver/logback.xml*.

Transmitting Node Reports via HTTP

A Puppet server can be configured to submit node reports to another system. This facility is used by Puppet Dashboard and some alternative web dashboards for Puppet.

Enable transmission of node reports to a URL by adding the `http` action to the list of report processors, and specifying a target with with the `reporturl` setting in /etc/puppetlabs/puppet/puppet.conf:

```
[master]
  reports = http,store
  reporturl = https://puppet-dashboard.example.com/
```

We'll cover installing and using Puppet Dashboard in Part IV.

You can create your own service to process reports delivered via HTTP. The data will arrive by POST method with a `Content-Type` of *application/x-yaml*. The YAML content will be the same as the contents of the file stored on disk on both the node and the master, as described earlier.

Transmitting Node Reports to PuppetDB

PuppetDB provides a report processor that can be used to submit node reports to the PuppetDB server. Enable transmission of node reports to PuppetDB by adding the `puppetdb` action to the list of report processors in /etc/puppetlabs/puppet/puppet.conf. The normal configuration for PuppetDB would look something like this:

```
[master]
  storeconfigs = true
  storeconfigs_backend = puppetdb
  reports = puppetdb, store
```

This will transmit the reports to the PuppetDB server specified in the /etc/puppetlabs/puppet/puppetdb.conf. This is covered briefly in Part IV.

Emailing Node Reports

Previous versions of Puppet included a report processor called *tagmail*, which would send email messages containing log messages that matched defined tags. This was removed from the Puppet core, and is now a separate Puppet module. To use this report processor, you'll need to do the following on the Puppet server:

```
[vagrant@client ~]$ puppet module install puppetlabs-tagmail
Notice: Preparing to install into
  /etc/puppetlabs/code/environments/production/modules ...
Notice: Downloading from https://forgeapi.puppetlabs.com ...
Notice: Installing -- do not interrupt ...
/etc/puppetlabs/code/environments/production/modules
└── puppetlabs-tagmail (v2.1.0)
```

After installing it on the Puppet server, create a */etc/puppetlabs/puppet/tagmail.conf* file containing a map of Puppet tags and recipients.

 How to tag resources was covered in "Filtering with Tags" on page 84. The `tagmail` report handler allows tags to be used for filtering changes to specific resources as well.

Each line of the [`tagmap`] section should contain one of the following formats:

- A list of tags or negated tags, followed by a colon and a comma-separated list of email addresses
- A list of log levels or negated log levels, followed by a colon and a comma-separated list of email addresses

Each log entry for a resource tagged with one of these tags, or matching the log level specified, will be added to an email sent to listed recipients. Here's an example file showing you the ideas:

```
[tagmap]
# Log levels
all: log-archive@example.com
emerg: puppet-admins@example.com

# Tags
frontend, java: fe-dev-team@example.com, java-platform@example.com
database, mysql: dba@example.com
mongodb, !database: nosql-admins@example.com

[transport]
reportfrom = puppetserver@example.com
sendmail = /usr/sbin/sendmail

# Alternative direct SMTP delivery
#smtpserver = smtp-relay.example.com
#smtphelo = puppet.example.com
#smtpport = 25
```

The settings in the [`transport`] section of the file should be obvious to any experienced system admin. You can enable SMTP auth settings in your mailer of choice, or utilize basic SMTP delivery by enabling the `smtpserver` option.

Tag reports by email are useful when you limit them to watch for specific, noteworthy conditions. For example, we notify the DBAs any time a database server configuration change takes place. That's a few dozen nodes, and it happens roughly twice a month. When a watched event happens that affects every node in an environment, you will get buried in email.

Enable transmission of email reports by adding the `tagmail` action to the list of report processors in */etc/puppetlabs/puppet/puppet.conf*:

```
[master]
    reports = store, tagmail
```

More documentation for `tagmail` can be found at *puppetlabs/tagmail* (*http://bit.ly/22oQXew*) on the Puppet Forge.

Creating a Custom Report Processor

Custom report processors must be written in the Ruby language and follow the rules listed here. You can write a wrapper in Ruby that calls another program, as long as it works in the following manner:

- The Ruby script must be named according to the rules for Ruby symbols (alphanumeric only) with a trailing *.rb* suffix.
- It must have `require 'puppet'` at the top of the script.
- It must call `Puppet::Reports.register_report()` with a block of code, passing in its own name as a symbol as the only parameter.
- The block of code must contain:
  — A call to `desc` with a text or Markdown-formatted string that describes the report processor.
  — A defined method named `process` that does whatever you want it to do.

The process method will be an object of type Puppet::Transaction::Report. It can retrieve details of the report by querying the attributes shown at "Formats: Reports" (*http://bit.ly/21zpCAA*) on the Puppet docs site, or get YAML data by calling the `self.to_yaml()` method.

Here is an example report processor that creates a different log message for each Puppet agent run. It's not unique or helpful as it stands, but it can be used as a starting point:

```
require 'puppet'
require 'syslog/logger'
log = Syslog::Logger.new 'logActionTime'

Puppet::Reports.register_report( :logActionTime ) do
  desc "Sends one log message containing agent action times."
```

```
  def process
    source = "#{self.time} #{self.host} "
    action = "did #{self.kind} with result #{self.status} "
    version = "for config #{self.configuration_version} "
    environment = "in environment #{self.environment}"
    log.info source + action + version + environment
  end
end
```

For a real report processor, you'd want to explore the `self.resource_statuses` and `self.metrics` hashes, or the `self.logs` array.

Add this report processor to the *lib/puppet/reports* directory of a Puppet module. If you don't have a more appropriate module in mind, add it to the Puppet module you created in Part II.

Enable the report processor by adding its name to the list of report processors in */etc/puppetlabs/puppet/puppet.conf*:

```
[master]
  reports = store, puppetdb, logActionTime
```

## CHAPTER 25

Managing TLS Certificates

You've learned how to connect a Puppet agent to a Puppet server, and how to sign the client's certificate using the `puppet cert` command. In this chapter, we'll go into more detail on how the authentication works, and methods to automate the signing process. We'll also cover how to utilize an external certificate authority for all certificate creation and authorization.

Reviewing Node Authentication

The topic of TLS authentication has been mentioned repeatedly, but you may be a bit confused by the details at this point. So let's review how Puppet agents and servers use TLS public key authentication and encryption to communicate securely.

Bidirectional validation, where both the Puppet server and agent validate the other's certificate as shown in Figure 25-1, prevents *man-in-the-middle attacks*. Once both sides have validated each other, they use the certificates (which are signed cryptographic keys) to negotiate an encrypted communication session secure from eavesdropping.

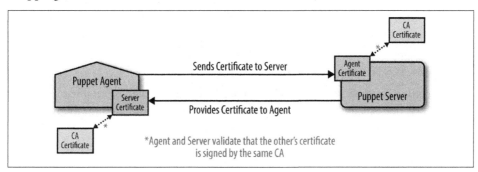

Figure 25-1. Bidirectional TLS validation

While this may sound complex, Puppet makes it trivially easy to implement and maintain. In fact, Puppet TLS keys are easier to create and utilize than any other private crypto system—so much so that Puppet certs are often used as the central authority for key management by other applications and security frameworks.

When Puppet provides the certificate authority (CA), the process for how this occurs is easy to understand:

1. A CA server is configured to sign Puppet agent CSRs.
2. Each Puppet server has a certificate signed by the Puppet CA.
3. Each agent submits a CSR to the CA before attempting to contact a server.
4. The CSR is signed manually via the `puppet cert` command, or by matching criteria for automatic signing.
5. The agent retrieves the signed certificate, and only then connects to the Puppet server.
6. The Puppet server verifies the agent's certificate was signed by the same CA.
7. The agent verifies that the Puppet server's certificate was signed by the same CA.

Autosigning Agent Certificates

As you can imagine, manual authorization and signing of each agent to be connected is not appropriate for every environment. It definitely provides a higher level of control and security, but may not be sustainable in highly volatile or dynamically scaled environments.

This section covers how to enable several different types of automatic certificate signing. Each of these techniques solves different problems, and each has certain security risks. We'll discuss all of them in detail.

Name-Based Autosigning

Name-based autosigning is used to automatically sign certificates based on the name given by the requestor. To enable name-based autosigning, set the value of `autosign` in the [`master`] section of the Puppet configuration file to the name of a configuration file containing certificate names that should be signed automatically:

```
[master]
    autosign = $confdir/autosign.conf
```

The preceding is the default value. Name-based autosigning will be enabled if that file exists and is not executable by the Puppet user. The file should contain the full name or glob(*)-style wildcards that match the certificates to be signed.

In short, this means that the following would enable autosigning for any node in *example.com*:

```
$ echo "*.example.com" > /etc/puppetlabs/puppet/autosign.conf
```

The glob-style wildcard character * will only match a single name at the front of the certificate name. It will not match periods (.) in the name or work in a trailing position. A certificate request by *web.server.example.com* will match either of the following:

- `web.server.example.com`
- `*.server.example.com`

...but will not match either of these:

- `*.example.com`
- `web.server.*`

 Name-based autosigning does not provide security. Any user with or without root access can create a Puppet certificate request using any name. They only need to guess what names you have selected for autosigning.

Name-based autosigning should be used only where access to the Puppet server is controlled by firewalls and other security mechanisms. In this mode, any Puppet agent that can connect to the server and guess the appropriate name (based on the hostnames around it) will have its certificate signed. It will then gain access to any information that the Puppet server provides.

Policy-Based Autosigning

Policy-based autosigning will automatically sign certificates based on the response provided by an external program. To enable policy-based autosigning, set the value of autosign in the [master] section of the Puppet configuration file to the name of an executable program:

```
[master]
  autosign = /path/to/decision-maker
```

The program can be written in any compiled or scripting language, so long as it is executable by the puppet user. It will receive the certname requested as the only command-line argument, and the contents of the certificate signing request (CSR) in PEM format on standard input (STDIN). The program needs to return an exit code of 0 for success, or nonzero to reject the certificate request.

If the program will make the decision based entirely on the name of the requestor, then it can ignore the CSR and evaluate the name. However, this provides no more security than name-based autosigning. The program should parse the PEM data for information to validate the nature of the request.

There are numerous data sources that could be queried to validate a request, including the following:

- Internal databases containing lists of provisioned nodes
- APIs used to provision virtual nodes, such as OpenStack, VMWare, or AWS
- Unique identifying information such as an encryption key added to the CSR

 The security of policy-based signing will depend on the security of the data sources queried. If an attacker can easily acquire or manipulate data from this source, it will not improve security.

Adding Custom Data to CSRs

To provide custom data in a CSR, you must perform the following steps on the node:

1. Create a YAML format file containing the custom data.
2. Specify the YAML file with the `csr_attributes` Puppet configuration setting.
3. Generate a new certificate for the node.

The default location for the CSR attributes file is *$confdir/csr_attributes.yaml*. This file must contain two keys, the value of which should be a hash containing the attributes to be provided. Here is an example file:

```
---
# Custom attributes will be discarded when the certificate is signed
custom_attributes:
  2.999.5.1.3: "Custom value 513 in the documentation OID"
  pp_uuid: "A unique instance identifier to be validated"

# Extension requests will be added to the final certificate,
# and available to the Puppet server during catalog build
extension_requests:
  pp_cost_center: "Custom value used in catalog build"
```

For convenience and readability, I recommend using the following short names for the Puppet-specific regular certificate extension OIDs as the keys in your hash:

- `pp_application`
- `pp_cluster`
- `pp_cost_center`

- pp_created_by
- pp_department
- pp_employee
- pp_environment
- pp_image_name
- pp_instance_id
- pp_preshared_key
- pp_product
- pp_provisioner
- pp_role
- pp_service
- pp_software_version
- pp_uuid

If you are experienced and comfortable with OIDs and want to build your own OID structure, you can use the Puppet Labs private certificate extension OID 1.3.6.1.4.1.34380.1.2 as documented at "SSL Configuration: CSR Attributes and Certificate Extensions" (*http://bit.ly/1RTDNvo*) on the Puppet docs site.

Populate this file with data from whatever mechanism you use to configure new nodes, such as:

- Launch tools like Linux Kickstart, Solaris Jumpstart, or HashiCorp Terraform
- Virtualization platform config tools like AWS or OpenStack cloud-init
- Launch infrastructure like Terraform, Cobbler, or Foreman
- Manually creating the file by hand

Only after the *csr_attributes.yaml* file is populated should you attempt to connect to the Puppet server, which will create your certificate request. If you have mistakenly created a certificate request without the right attributes, you can purge the TLS keys and start over like so:

```
[vagrant@client ~]$ rm -rf /etc/puppetlabs/puppet/ssl
[vagrant@client ~]$ puppet agent --test --server=puppet.example.com
```

Inspecting CSRs

The custom data provided in the CSR can be found in the Attributes or Requested Extensions block of the CSR. Your program will have to parse the PEM-format CSR data to retrieve these values. Libraries to parse PEM format files are available in every programming language. Refer to the documentation of the language used for your policy-based validator.

You can manually examine an unsigned certificate request using the standard openssl tool:

```
[vagrant@puppetserver ~]$ sudo bash
[root@puppetserver vagrant]# cd /var/opt/puppetlabs/puppetserver/ssl/ca/requests
[root@puppetserver requests]# openssl req -noout -text -in certname.pem
Certificate Request:
    Data:
        Version: 0 (0x0)
        Subject: CN=client.example.com
        Subject Public Key Info:
...base64-encoded bits...
        Attributes:
            1.3.6.1.4.1.34380.1.1.1  :
                A unique instance identifier to be validated
            2.999.5.1.3              :
                Custom value 513 in the documentation OID
        Requested Extensions:
            1.3.6.1.4.1.34380.1.1.5:
                ..Custom value used in catalog build
```

As you can tell, the openssl command does not know the short names for the Puppet-specific OIDs.

After the certificate has been signed, you can view the certificate with a much simpler puppet cert print command, which is aware of the Puppet-specific OIDs:

```
[vagrant@puppetserver ~]$ sudo puppet cert print client.example.com
Certificate:
    Data:
        Version: 3 (0x2)
        Serial Number: 2 (0x2)
        Signature Algorithm: sha256WithRSAEncryption
        Issuer: CN=Puppet CA: puppet.example.com
        Validity
            Not Before: Aug  6 06:33:41 2015 GMT
            Not After : Aug  5 06:33:41 2020 GMT
        Subject: CN=client.example.com
        Subject Public Key Info:
...base64-encoded bits...
            X509v3 extensions:
                Netscape Comment:
                    .(Puppet Ruby/OpenSSL Internal Certificate
                Puppet Node Cost Center Name:
                    ..Custom value used in catalog build
```

As previously discussed, the custom_attributes have been discarded and only the extension_requests are available in the final certificate.

More details about TLS certificate extensions can be found at "CSR Attributes and Certificate Extensions" (*http://bit.ly/22s5AdF*) on the Puppet docs site.

Using Extension Requests in Puppet

The data stored in the client's certificate extension requests is available to the Puppet server when building the catalog, which makes it available for use in Puppet manifests. The data can be referenced by the `extensions` hash key of the trusted node facts:

```
notify { 'cost-center':
  message => "Cost center is ${trusted['extensions']['pp_cost_center']}",
}
```

If you used site-specific private OID space, you'll need to use the OID as a key, or create a YAML file mapping OIDs to names. I'm not going to cover OID mapping here, as people who enjoy playing with OIDs are rare creatures, and for them it is well documented at "Config Files: custom_trusted_oid_mapping.yaml" (*http://bit.ly/ 1UaPDI0*) on the Puppet docs site.

Naive Autosigning

Naive autosigning is to believe or trust any agent that connects to the Puppet server. In this mode, every CSR is immediately signed, giving the agent instant access to data the Puppet server provides. Anyone who can open a connection to the server, directly or indirectly through a compromised access point, can retrieve any information the Puppet server is configured to provide.

Best Practice

Do not use naive autosigning outside of a test lab.

If you want to provide your configuration data to anyone, set the value of `autosign` in the [`master`] section of the Puppet configuration file to `true`:

```
[master]
  autosign = true
```

Using an External Certificate Authority

As discussed in the previous chapters, by default the Puppet server will create its own TLS key and self-signed certificate when you install it. In doing so, it becomes its own certificate root authority. It will sign any agent's automatic or manually approved CSR with its own certificate. In effect, it creates a new certification tree in which it is the root authority.

This works well for small environments, or situations where the Puppet certificates are used within their own framework only.

In large enterprises, it is often necessary or desirable to have all keys issued from a centralized certificate authority outside of Puppet. You can enable this by following the steps in this chapter.

Puppet servers support three configurations:

- A Puppet server is the sole certificate authority, and signs all certificates.
- A single external certificate authority signs certificates for both Puppet servers and Puppet agents.
- Two different external certificate authorities sign certificates, one for Puppet servers and another for Puppet agents.

Distributing Certificates Manually

Perhaps the biggest reason to avoid using an external certificate authority (CA) is that Puppet has no way to help you distribute those files. Puppet is a fantastic tool for distributing web server TLS certificates, Java keystores, and licenses. However, the Puppet agent must have a key signed by the CA in order to receive a catalog from a Puppet server, so you cannot use Puppet to distribute the necessary Puppet agent key and certificate to the node. It's a classic catch-22 situation.

You'll have to use some other mechanism, depending on your own CA solution and its resources, to create and distribute the private keys and signed certificates each Puppet agent requires. The following are some technology solutions that are good for bootstrapping nodes up to the point where Puppet can be run to finish configuration of the node:

- Node provisioning tools like HashiCorp Terraform, Cobbler, and Foreman
- Virtualization platform config tools like AWS or OpenStack cloud-init
- Key automation software like CertNanny

When you have the certificates available, install them in the configured locations on each node. You can verify those locations with this command:

```
$ sudo puppet config --section agent print hostcert hostprivkey localcacert
hostcert = /etc/puppetlabs/puppet/ssl/certs/puppet.example.com.pem
hostprivkey = /etc/puppetlabs/puppet/ssl/private_keys/puppet.example.com.pem
localcacert = /etc/puppetlabs/puppet/ssl/certs/ca.pem
```

If the certificates are issued by an intermediate CA instead of a root CA, you'll also need to set a configuration value for the location of the intermediate CA's certificate in */etc/puppetlabs/puppet/puppet.conf*:

```
[agent]
  ssl_client_ca_auth = /etc/puppetlabs/puppet/ssl/certs/intermediate.pem
```

Installing Certificates on the Server

When you use an external certificate authority, you are required to create a certificate request for the server and get it signed by the external authority on your own. There is no automation to do this for you.

When you have the certificates available, install them in the configured locations. You can query those locations with these commands:

```
$ sudo puppet config --section master print hostcert hostprivkey localcacert
hostcert = /var/opt/puppetlabs/puppetserver/ssl/certs/puppet.example.com.pem
hostprivkey = /var/opt/…/puppetserver/ssl/private_keys/puppet.example.com.pem
localcacert = /var/opt/puppetlabs/puppetserver/ssl/certs/ca.pem
```

Copy the Puppet server's key to the hostprivkey location, the certificate signed by the external CA to the host location, and a copy of the CA's certificate to the localca cert location. If the Puppet server's certificate was signed by an intermediate certificate authority, you'll need to concatenate the root CA and the intermediate CA's certificate in the localcacert file.

Disabling CA on a Puppet Server

To prevent Puppet Server from trying to sign certificates, as it doesn't have the CA's key to do this, comment out the following line in */etc/puppetlabs/puppetserver/bootstrap.cfg*:

```
#puppetlabs.services.ca.certificate-authority-service/
    #certificate-authority-service
```

and uncomment or add the following line in its place:

```
puppetlabs.services.ca.certificate-authority-disabled-service/
    certificate-authority-disabled-service
```

Ensure that */etc/puppetlabs/puppetserver/conf.d/webserver.conf* contains the following settings:

```
webserver: {
  ssl-key      : /var/opt/…/puppetserver/ssl/private_keys/puppet.example.com.pem
  ssl-cert     : /var/opt/…/puppetserver/ssl/certs/puppet.example.com.pem
  ssl-ca-cert  : /var/opt/puppetlabs/puppetserver/ssl/ca/ca_crt.pem
  ssl-cert-chain: /var/opt/puppetlabs/puppetserver/ssl/ca/ca_crt.pem
  ssl-crl-path : /var/opt/puppetlabs/puppetserver/ssl/crl.pem
}
```

Disabling CA on a Puppet Master

To prevent a Puppet master from trying to sign certificates, as it doesn't have the CA's key to do this, disable the ca configuration option in */etc/puppetlabs/puppet/puppet.conf*:

```
[master]
    ca = false
```

Externally signed certificates can only be validated if you are using the Rack-enabled master running under Fusion Passenger, with all of the `RequestHeader` configuration lines from the example configuration file used by this book: */vagrant/etc-puppet/ puppetmaster.conf.* These configuration parameters tell Apache to validate the client certificate, and pass the validation data to the Puppet server in the named headers.

 The test WEBrick instance cannot provide certificate validation.

If the Puppet agent certificates are signed by an intermediate CA, you'll need to modify the configuration to disable this line:

```
SSLVerifyDepth 1
```

…and enable the following lines with the name of the intermediate CA:

```
# Allow clients with a TLS certificate issued by the intermediate CA
<Location />
    SSLRequire %{SSL_CLIENT_I_DN_CN} eq "Intermediate CA Common Name"
</Location>
SSLVerifyDepth 2
```

Place the full `Common Name` (CN) of the intermediate CA that will sign Puppet agent certificates in the quotes as shown.

Using Different CAs for Servers and Agents

It is possible to have the certificate authority tree set up such that two different intermediate certificate authorities are used. One will sign certificates issued to Puppet servers, while the other signs certificates issued to Puppet agents.

This is configured exactly as described on the previous pages, with two simple changes:

Puppet servers
> The Puppet servers have the root CA certificate and the intermediate CA certificate that signs Puppet agent keys in the file referenced by `localcacert`. This allows them to validate any agent certificate, but will fail to validate the certificate of another Puppet server.

Puppet agents
> Puppet agents will need the certificate of the intermediate CA that signs keys for Puppet servers installed in the location specified by the `ssl_client_ca_auth` setting.

This provides enhanced security, as Puppet agent certificates successfully validate on other Puppet agents, nor will Puppet servers accept keys from other Puppet servers. The enhanced security provides a necessary wall that's useful when different teams control different Puppet servers yet share the same root certificate authority.

Distributing the CA Revocation List

You can enable certificate revocation list (CRL) checking on both Puppet servers and Puppet agents. It must be distributed to the nodes through the same mechanism that was used to get the certs there. Install the CRL in the configured locations. You can query that location with these commands:

```
$ sudo puppet config --section agent print hostcrl
/etc/puppetlabs/puppet/ssl/crl.pem
```

 Puppet CAs provide a CRL to all agents. The agent retrieves it when acquiring its certificate back from the CA.

If a revocation list is not provided by the external CA, you must disable CRL checking on the agent. Disable the following parameters in */etc/puppetlabs/puppet/puppet.conf*:

```
[agent]
  certificate_revocation = false
```

If this parameter is not disabled, the agent will attempt to download the file from the Puppet server. As the Puppet server has its CA service disabled, the request will fail.

Learning More About TLS Authentication

The absolute best way to expand on what you have learned in this chapter is to try these processes out:

1. Configure the server to autosign certificates for `*.example.com`.
2. Run `vagrant up web2` and install Puppet.
3. Start Puppet agent on the instance to connect to the server.
4. Observe the Puppet agent immediately receive back a signed certificate.
5. Observe the module convergence without having to run Puppet again.
6. Review the node report stored in the *$vardir/reports* directory.

7. Log out and run `vagrant destroy web2` to recover the memory used.

For extra credit, implement an `autosign` program to validate certificate requests:

1. Create a script to inspect CSR Attributes and exit with a nonzero exit code if a certain value isn't in one.
2. Specify this program as the value of the `autosign` configuration variable on the Puppet server.
3. Run `vagrant up web3`, and install Puppet.
4. Attempt to connect it to the Puppet server. Observe the rejection.
5. Regenerate the CSR with the custom attribute you are looking for.
6. Attempt to connect it to the Puppet server.

## CHAPTER 26

Growing Your Puppet Deployment

This chapter introduces and advises you on topics and considerations necessary for large Puppet deployments.

Using a Node Terminus

A *node terminus* is a node data provider for the Puppet server. A node terminus can do the following:

- Override the `environment` supplied by the node
- Declare classes and parameters to apply to the node
- Define top-scope variables

You can use one of the following two types of node terminus, each of which is described shortly:

- External node classifier (ENC)
- LDAP terminus

Best Practice

ENCs are rarely necessary, as the global and environment data providers have completely eclipsed the more limited data that ENCs can provide. Use an ENC only when you cannot retrieve the data through Puppet Lookup.

You can use a node terminus when using `puppet apply` (without a Puppet server). It is configured in a similar way, shown in the next section.

Running an External Node Classifier

An external node classifier is a program that provides environment, class, and variable assignments for nodes. The ENC is executed by the exec node terminus of the Puppet server prior to selecting the node's environment.

The ENC is called by the Puppet instance which builds the catalog. This would be the Puppet server in server/agent configurations, and the node itself in a `puppet apply` implementation.

The node classifier can be any type of program. Use the following configuration settings in the [master] section of */etc/puppetlabs/puppet/puppet.conf*:

```
[master]
    node_terminus = exec
    external_nodes = /path/to/node_classifier
```

If you want to use an ENC with `puppet apply`, then you need to place these configuration options in the [user] section of the configuration file.

The program will receive a single command-line argument: the `certname` of the node (which defaults to the fully qualified domain name). The program should output YAML format with `parameters` and `classes` hashes, and an optional `environment` string:

`environment`: *(optional)*
The environment to be used while building the node's catalog. If supplied, this value overrides the `environment` configuration value of the agent.

`parameters`: *(optional if `classes` hash is defined)*
Node variables declared in the top scope (e.g., `::parameter`)

`classes`: *(optional if `parameters` hash is defined)*
A hash of classes to be declared, much like what you can provide with the Hiera hash of the same name. Unlike Hiera, you can indent input parameters below each class name.

The output should be in the same YAML format as used by Hiera. Following is example output showing both single-level and multilevel parameter and class names:

```
$ /path/to/node_classifier client.example.com
---
environment: test
parameters:
  selinux: disabled
  time:
    timezone: PDT
    summertime: true
classes:
  ntp:
  dns:
    search : example.com
    timeout: 2
    options: rotate
  puppet::agent:
    status : running
    enabled: true
```

The hash of values indented beneath each class name is supplied as parameter input for the class. In the preceding example, we have passed `status = true` as an input parameter to the `puppet::agent` class.

 Notice that ENC output uses the term *parameters* differently than it does in the Puppet language. Puppet variables are declared with the ENC hash named `parameters`. Puppet class parameters are declared underneath the class name.

The node classifier must exit with a success status (0) and must provide either a `parameters` or `classes` hash in the output. If it fails to deliver a successful response, the catalog build process will be aborted.

If no parameters or classes should be assigned, then return an empty hash as the result for one or both of the parameters:

```
$ /path/to/node_classifier client.example.com
---
classes: {}
parameters: {}
```

Querying LDAP

An LDAP server can be queried as a node terminus to provide the same node data as provided by an ENC. You can only store Puppet attributes in LDAP if you are competent with LDAP configuration, and have the rights to modify the LDAP schemas available on the server.

LDAP management is too complex to cover in a book about Puppet. I highly recommend Gerald Carter's book *LDAP System Administration* (O'Reilly) if you need to learn more about LDAP.

To enable LDAP as a node terminus, add the following configuration settings to */etc/puppetlabs/puppet/puppet.conf*:

```
[master]
  node_terminus = ldap
  ldapserver = ldapserver.example.com
  ldapport = 389
  ldaptls = true
  ldapssl = false
  ldapuser = readuser
  ldappassword = readonly
  ldapbase = ou=Hosts,dc=example,dc=com
```

To add the schema to your server, download the Puppet LDAP schema from Puppet-Labs LDAP Schema on GitHub (*http://bit.ly/1SYAMPl*) and install it on your LDAP server according to the documentation for your specific LDAP server.

Then you need to add LDAP entries for each Puppet node, which again will be specific to your LDAP implementation and the tools available to you. A Puppet node entry in LDAP similar to the one specified for the ENC would look like this:

```
dn: cn=client,ou=Hosts,dc=example,dc=com
objectClass: device
objectClass: puppetClient
objectClass: top
cn: client
environment: test
puppetClass: dns
puppetClass: puppet::agent
puppetVar: selinux=disabled
```

LDAP does not provide the flexibility to provide multilevel variables or parameters for classes. However, if you have additional attributes associated with the host, such as the IP address from the `ipHost objectClass`, these will be available as top-scope variables for the node.

You can create a `default` entry to be used when an exact match is not found in LDAP:

```
dn: cn=default,ou=Hosts,dc=example,dc=com
objectClass: device
objectClass: puppetClient
objectClass: top
environment: production
```

For this to work you must also add the following line to the named environment's *manifests/site.pp* file:

```
[vagrant@puppetserver ~]$ echo "node default {}" \
  >> /etc/puppetlabs/code/environments/production/manifests/site.pp
```

You can find more details at "The LDAP Node Classifier" (*http://bit.ly/1XAAsFt*) on the Puppet docs site.

Starting with Community Examples

You don't need to build your own node classifier from scratch. There are many community-provided examples you can utilize, or use as a starting point for development. Here are just a few examples, chosen mostly for diversity of their approach:

ilikejam/hiera-enc on GitHub (https://github.com/ilikejam/hiera-enc)
A simple ENC to read the value of environment from a Hiera lookup and output it. This is useful because Hiera cannot override the environment supplied by a node, but an ENC can. This allows you to store everything in Hiera. You'll need to modify this ENC to use environment-based pathnames.

hsavolai/spacewalk-puppet-enc on GitHub (https://github.com/hsavolai/spacewalk-puppet-enc)
This ENC integrates two great systems, Spacewalk Server (or Red Hat Network Satellite) and Puppet. The sync tool retrieves class information from Spacewalk Server. The ENC tool reads the classification information and outputs YAML for the node terminus.

georgecodes/fencing on GitHub (https://github.com/georgecodes/fencing)
Fencing is an ENC that will hold back node definitions until a different node's facts meet the required conditions. This is useful to configure nodes with a service dependency. Use this ENC to release node definitions only when certain conditions are met on other nodes.

jantman/nodemeister on GitHub (https://github.com/jantman/nodemeister)
NodeMeister is an ENC written in Python using the Django framework. It supports hierarchical groups, exclusions, and overrides, and aims to provide a fully functional ENC for those more comfortable with Python.

awesomescot/mysql-enc on GitHub (https://github.com/awesomescot/mysql-enc)
mysql-enc is an ENC that queries a MySQL backend data source.

There are a lot of ENCs on GitHub that read their data from a YAML file, or even call Hiera directly. It's really not clear to me that these provide any value, as classes and parameters could be more easily specified in Hiera directly. To me the value of an ENC is when you need to query a data source outside of Hiera. The one and only advantage that an ENC has over Hiera is the ability to override the environment requested by the node. Perhaps there is value in Hiera-backed ENC lookups that never applied to the sites at which I've worked.

It could make sense if there are different teams or authority levels managing separate Hiera data sources, although this may be better served by environment-specific data sources, as described in "Binding Data Providers in Environments" on page 436.

Deploying Puppet Servers at Scale

The good news about Puppet is that replicating servers is easy—in fact, trivially easy. Given the same module code, the same Hiera data, and access to the same resources used by ENCs or data lookups in modules, two different Puppet servers will render the same catalog for the same node every time.

The only problems managing multiple Puppet servers are deciding how to synchronize the files, and whether or not to centralize the signing of TLS certificates.

There are several ways to implement server redundancy with Puppet. Let's review each of them.

Keeping Distinct Domains

One deployment strategy implements a Puppet server for each group of nodes. This can be simple and efficient when different teams manage different servers and nodes. Each Puppet server acts as its own certificate authority—which is by far the easiest way to bring up new Puppet agents. Each team validates and authorizes the nodes that connect to its server.

In this configuration, the Puppet servers can host the same Puppet modules, a distinct set of Puppet modules and configurations, or a combination thereof. This provides ultimate freedom to the team managing each group of nodes.

You can achieve redundancy by using a hybrid config with other techniques described next, or by simply restoring the Puppet server vardir to another node and pointing the server's name at it.

Sharing a Single Puppet CA

Another solid deployment strategy implements a single Puppet CA server for the entire organization. Configure the Puppet agent to submit all CSRs to this one CA server, using the following parameters in the [agent] section of */etc/puppetlabs/ puppet/puppet.conf*:

```
[agent]
  ca_server = puppet-ca.example.com
  server = puppetserver01.example.com
```

With this configuration, every server and agent will get certificates from the single Puppet CA. Nodes point at different servers for all normal Puppet transactions.

This works much easier than using an external CA, because the Puppet agent will request and install the certificates for you. The only complication is that you'll need to sync all approved agent certificates from the CA server down to the normal Puppet servers.

You can utilize a Network File System (NFS) to share the server's TLS directory (*/var/opt/puppetlabs/puppetserver/ssl*), or you can use something like `rsync` to keep the directories in sync.

If you are utilizing NFS, you may want to also share the */var/opt/puppetlabs/puppetserver/reports* directory so that all client reports are centrally stored.

Using a Load Balancer

If you have many nodes in a single site, it may be necessary to put multiple Puppet servers behind a load balancer. Configure Puppet much as you would configure any other TCP load-balanced service and it will work fine.

I would not enable TLS offloading on the load balancer. It can be done successfully, but has never in my experience provided sufficient performance benefit to be worth the custom reconfiguration necessary on the Puppet servers.

The servers themselves must each have the same Puppet modules and Hiera data stored on them, or they must mount the data from the same place. I have found that NFS works well for this purpose, as there is generally not a high number of reads, and the files end up in the server's file cache. You would want to share the following directories between servers:

/etc/puppetlabs/code
Puppet modules and Hiera data

/var/opt/puppetlabs/puppetserver/bucket
File backups from agent nodes

/var/opt/puppetlabs/puppetserver/jruby-gems
Ruby gems used by the server

/var/opt/puppetlabs/puppetserver/reports
Node reports

/var/opt/puppetlabs/puppetserver/tls
TLS keys and certs

/var/opt/puppetlabs/puppetserver/yaml
> Node facts

The list of directories may change over time.

Managing Geographically Dispersed Servers

There are three different ways to synchronize data on globally disparate Puppet servers (naturally, each option has its own benefits and trade-offs):

Manually
> While this may work for a short period of time, it will quickly become painful. It is only a workable solution when different teams share only a small fraction of Puppet code and data.

Every server pulls the Puppet code and data from a central source
> A very common deployment model has each Puppet server check out the modules and data from a source code respository (which we'll cover in "Managing Environments with r10k" on page 441). This can be done by schedule, triggered by a post-commit handler, or manual authorization or automated triggers of orchestration tools like as MCollective.
>
> This technique has the advantage of fairly quick synchronization of changes to all servers.

Rolling push of Puppet code and data
> In some environments, it is desirable to progressively deploy changes through staging and *canary* ("in a coal mine") environments. In these situations, automation schedulers like Jenkins are used to progressively roll the changes from one environment to the other.
>
> This technique enables a cautious, slow-roll deployment strategy.

Which one is best for your needs? Well, it depends on your needs and your testing model.

The single source pull model is simple to configure, requires very few components, and promotes change quickly. It can also promote a breaking change quickly, which will create large-scale outages in a very short period of time.

The rolling push of change through stages requires a nontrivial investment in services, systems, and custom automation to deploy. Once built, these systems can help identify problems long before they reach production. Depending on the automation created, the deployment automation can identify the breaking committer, open trouble tickets, roll back the changes, and even bake and butter your bread.

In reality, very few organizations use only one approach or the other. Most situations have a hybrid solution that meets their most important needs. For example:

Simple pull with distinct zones

Multiple zones of Puppet servers, each of which utilizes the simple pull approach. Change is manually elevated from testing to canary, and then from canary to production zones.

Rolling push through testing environments

All servers use a simple pull approach from a single central source. Change is automatically pushed through different Puppet environments for test, canary, and production. Each node can opt in for the stable or canary data by changing the environment configuration variable.

 Every team should alter the deployment strategy to best meet its own needs. It is not necessary for teams that utilize the same Puppet server to roll out deployments the same way.

Managing Geographically Dispersed Nodes

There are two different ways to distribute Puppet nodes globally (each option has its own benefits and trade-offs):

Servers close to the client nodes

With Puppet servers in each local network, you must synchronize code and data out to each server. This can result in lag and inconsistency between nodes in different regions for a period of time. It depends on your needs whether or not this is a problem.

Centralized servers

With central Puppet servers, synchronization is not a problem. A large cluster in a single location can mount the same directories. However, connectivity between the clients and the server can be inconsistent, and network latency can slow down the transaction—tying up a server thread for a longer period of time. You'll have to monitor the servers to determine if this is a problem or not.

Which one is best for your needs? Well, it depends. There is no silver bullet and no single answer, as the problems one group will have won't match others. If you are distributing many or large files using Puppet, latency will be very important. I've worked in environments where it was absolutely necessary to keep all nodes in sync within 20 seconds of a release. File synchronization latency created problems.

I've worked in other environments where the Puppet configuration was small without any significant file transfer. It also wasn't essential that a node picked up changes more than once or twice a day, so a single cluster of Puppet servers handled 2,000 small remote sites. This was very easy to manage and maintain, and met the needs and expectations for that client.

Global deployments with fast node convergence requirements are usually best served with the hybrid of the choices previously shown. The process for building the hybrid solution requires two steps:

1. Break up the worldwide deployment into zones based on reachability and access stability.
2. Create a redundant set of load-balanced servers in each zone.

This improves access and latency for nodes by placing a well-connected Puppet server in their region. It limits the problems around synchronization time by pushing the files to a limited set of well-connected centers.

Falling Back to Cached Catalogs

When managing that which may lose connectivity to a remote Puppet server, you can decide whether or not the client should run Puppet with the last cached catalog. There are two parameters to control this. The defaults are shown here:

```
# these are the default values
[agent]
  usecacheonfailure = true
  use_cached_catalog = false
```

usecacheonfailure
: This allows the Puppet agent to use the last good catalog if the Puppet server doesn't respond with a new catalog. This will ensure that it fixes anything that has changed from expected policy, including restarting stopped services and logging changes to audited files. You almost always want this.

use_cached_catalog
: This tells the Puppet agent to always use the last good catalog, and not to check for a new one from the Puppet server. This is only useful when you deploy changes by orchestrating Puppet runs with this option disabled.

With the default configuration, the agent will ask the Puppet server for a new catalog but fall back to the last cached catalog if the Puppet server cannot be contacted.

Making the Right Choice

Which of these choices best meets your needs? Only you can tell. Each of them works to solve one set of problems. If you're not sure which selection is best, simply make a choice. If you build the servers as suggested in this book, it won't be difficult to migrate the servers to a different deployment strategy later. Changing from one configuration to another isn't usually that difficult either.

However, the best thing about these choices is that none of them is exclusive. You can combine each and any of these techniques to solve more requirements.

Perhaps you've come up with a better choice, or you've seen a problem I didn't mention here? I'd love to hear about it.

Best Practices for Puppet Servers

Before you move on to the next chapter, I'd like to remind you of best practices for managing Puppet servers:

- The server is not the node. Name the server with an alias—for example, *puppet.example.com*—that points to the node hosting it.
- The node is not the Puppet server. Configure the node as a normal Puppet agent using its own unique hostname. This will make it easier to migrate or replicate the server service later.
- Store the Puppet server's volatile data files in the */var* filesystem.
- Don't use naive or unvalidated autosigning outside of a test lab.
- Puppet Lookup is significantly more flexible than an external node classifier. Don't use an ENC unless it provides some content you cannot retrieve using Puppet Lookup.
- Don't waste time super-tuning the log levels of every resource. Node reports provide direct access to every detail of the agent's covergence report.

And finally, remember that Puppet master is at the end of the road. It is only useful to help test your modules with Puppet 4, or to utilize an existing Rack infrastructure. Prepare to migrate to Puppet Server in the future.

Reviewing Puppet Servers

In this chapter, you've created a small learning environment with Puppet Server (or a Puppet master), that you can use for testing Puppet manifests. You've learned the following about Puppet servers:

- How the catalog build process is offloaded to the Puppet server.
- How to install and configure Puppet Server and the (deprecated) Puppet master.
- How a node's Puppet agent connects to the server.
- How to manually and automatically authorize Puppet agents.
- How to use an external node classifier to provide node configuration data.
- How to collect, store, and process Puppet agent convergence reports.
- What to consider when growing Puppet deployments to thousands of nodes.

## PART IV

Integrating Puppet

In this part, we'll discuss advanced tools and configurations that support, enhance, and extend your Puppet implementation. As you work your way through the chapters in this part, you will find out how to:

- View node status using Puppet Dashboard
- Install and configure Puppet on Windows
- Use environments to support module testing and diverse teams
- Manipulate nodes using the MCollective Puppet agent
- Deploy and administer network infrastructure with Puppet
- Compare and contrast server-based versus server-less Puppet implementations
- Plan and prepare for the challenges of large-scale deployments

In this part of the book, the answers become less firm, and best practices may vary depending on your individual needs. This part of the book attempts to cover a wide variety of concerns. It will explain and outline the possibilities rather than define a single philosophy.

## CHAPTER 27

Tracking Puppet Status with Dashboards

Puppet provides fantastic tools for managing your nodes. In a stable, well-tuned environment, Puppet is omnipresent but completely invisible. Nodes build themselves. Applications configure themselves. Everything "just works."

Unfortunately, most of us never get all the way to that perfectly stable state. There's always a new deployment going on, a refactoring of an older project. There's always something that happened you want to find details for.

And let's be honest. Everyone likes big green lights and flashing red alarms. You just can't get away from them. So let's cover some ways to provide a dashboard for your Puppet nodes. We'll start by one created by Puppet Labs themselves.

Using Puppet Dashboard

Puppet Dashboard provides a web interface to browse the results of Puppet runs on your client nodes. It stores node reports in a database and provides a web UI to review those changes.

In addition, the dashboard can be used as an ENC. It provides a web interface to group nodes and associate them with classes and parameters. This can be a user-friendly interface for node classification.

Puppet Dashboard was originally a Puppet Labs product, but it has since become a community-maintained project. Within Puppet Labs the dashboard evolved to become the commercial Puppet Enterprise Console, discussed in the next section.

Some people question why anyone would use Puppet Dashboard now that PuppetDB is available. I agree that PuppetDB provides more comprehensive storage for Puppet report data. PuppetDB is a full-featured data storage solution that requires some knowledge and know-how to extract useful data. Puppet Dashboard provides a drop-in, immediately available overview in a format that is easy for service desks to see happy green and problematic red. It's quite easy to install and get useful data from the dashboard in 30 minutes.

I know many sites that continue to use Puppet Dashboard long after deploying PuppetDB.

Installing Dashboard Dependencies

In this section, we will build a node and install the dependencies necessary for hosting Puppet Dashboard.

As with a Puppet server, you should not name the node that hosts the dashboard with the same name as the service. Puppet Dashboard is a web service that likely will end up being moved to another node at some point. Furthermore, the dashboard gets it own certificate signed by the Puppet server—separate and distinct from the key and certificate issued to the Puppet agent running on the node.

In a production installation, you would create a CNAME for the service name pointing at the node that hosts the service.

For our testing setup, the node is named dashserver while the dashboard itself will be viewable at the common service name of *https://dashboard.example.com/*. Both of these names are on the same line in the hosts file provided.

Starting the dashboard VM

Start up the dashboard virtual instance. This boots a machine which is named dash server as just noted:

```
learning-puppet4$ vagrant up dashboard
Bringing machine 'dashboard' up with 'virtualbox' provider...
==> puppetserver: Importing base box 'puppetlabs/centos-7.2-64-nocm'...
==> puppetserver: Matching MAC address for NAT networking...
==> puppetserver: Checking if box 'puppetlabs/centos-7.2-64-nocm' is up to date...
==> puppetserver: Setting the name of the VM: learning-puppet4_dashboard_144075009
...snip...

learning-puppet4$ vagrant ssh dashboard
[vagrant@dashserver ~]$
```

As this is a new virtual instance, install the necessary utilities and a text editor of choice, as you did back in Chapter 2:

```
$ sudo yum install rsync git vim nano emacs-nox
```

Preparing the database

First, we'll install a database in which dashboard will store node reports and node classification.

 I have chosen to cover the MySQL installation as more people use Puppet Dashboard with MySQL today, and thus it has been better tested. It is also possible to use PostgreSQL with the dashboard.

CentOS 7 uses the MariaDB fork of MySQL by MySQL's original creator, rather than the version maintained by Oracle. If you are using a different OS, the package used in the next command might be `mysql-server`:

```
[vagrant@dashserver ~]$ sudo yum install -y mariadb-server
Loaded plugins: fastestmirror
...snip...

Installed:
  mariadb-server.x86_64 1:5.5.44-1.el7_1

Dependency Installed:
  mariadb.x86_64 1:5.5.44-1.el7_1          mariadb-libs.x86_64 1:5.5.44-1.el7_1
  libaio.x86_64 0:0.3.109-12.el7
  perl-Compress-Raw-Bzip2.x86_64 0:2.061-3.el7
  perl-Compress-Raw-Zlib.x86_64 1:2.061-4.el7
  perl-DBD-MySQL.x86_64 0:4.023-5.el7      perl-DBI.x86_64 0:1.627-4.el7
  perl-Data-Dumper.x86_64 0:2.145-3.el7    perl-IO-Compress.noarch 0:2.061-2.el7
  perl-Net-Daemon.noarch 0:0.48-5.el7      perl-PlRPC.noarch 0:0.2020-14.el7

Complete!
```

The very first thing to do is to enable security for the database. Start the database and run the script shown here to secure your installation. The following output is shortened for brevity, but shows all of the prompts that you need to answer:

```
[vagrant@dashserver ~]$ sudo systemctl start mariadb
[vagrant@dashserver ~]$ /usr/bin/mysql_secure_installation

Enter current password for root (enter for none): [HIT ENTER]
OK, successfully used password, moving on...

Set root password? [Y/n] y
New password: something secret
Re-enter new password: something secret
Password updated successfully!
Reloading privilege tables..
 ... Success!
```

```
Remove anonymous users? [Y/n] y
 ... Success!

Disallow root login remotely? [Y/n] y
 ... Success!

Remove test database and access to it? [Y/n] y
 - Dropping test database...
 ... Success!
 - Removing privileges on test database...
 ... Success!

Reload privilege tables now? [Y/n] y
 ... Success!
```

Now we need to create a database and user for Puppet Dashboard to use. We'll log in as the root user to create the new database and user. During login, provide the same password you used in the previous step, where it said *something secret*. Provide a different password for the dashboard user you are creating here:

```
[vagrant@dashserver ~]$ mysql -u root -p
Enter password: password you entered above
Welcome to the MariaDB monitor.  Commands end with ; or \g.
Type 'help;' or '\h' for help. Type '\c' to clear the current input statement.

MariaDB [(none)]> CREATE DATABASE dashboard_production CHARACTER SET utf8;
Query OK, 1 row affected (0.01 sec)

MariaDB [(none)]> GRANT all ON dashboard_production.*
     TO dashboard@localhost IDENTIFIED BY 'PickYourOwnPassword';
Query OK, 0 rows affected (0.00 sec)

MariaDB [(none)]> quit
Bye
```

We need to expand max_allowed_packet to 32 megabytes. We do so with the following command (typed exactly as printed):

```
[vagrant@dashserver ~]$ sudo sed -i.bak /etc/my.cnf.d/server.cnf \
  -e 's/\[mysqld\]/[mysqld]\nmax_allowed_packet = 32M/'
```

Or you can edit the file by hand if you prefer. Ensure it contains this:

```
[mysqld]
max_allowed_packet = 32M
```

Finally, restart mariadb to pick up the changes:

```
[vagrant@dashserver ~]$ sudo systemctl restart mariadb
[vagrant@dashserver ~]$ sudo systemctl status mariadb
mariadb.service - MariaDB database server
   Loaded: loaded (/usr/lib/systemd/system/mariadb.service; disabled)
   Active: active (running) since Fri 2015-08-28 09:06:29 UTC; 6s ago
```

```
   Process: 4222 ExecStartPost=/usr/libexec/mariadb-wait-ready $MAINPID
   Process: 4193 ExecStartPre=/usr/libexec/mariadb-prepare-db-dir %n
  Main PID: 4221 (mysqld_safe)
    CGroup: /system.slice/mariadb.service
            ├─4221 /bin/sh /usr/bin/mysqld_safe --basedir=/usr
            └─4391 /usr/libexec/mysqld --basedir=/usr --datadir=/var/lib/mysql
    --plugin-dir=/usr/lib64/mysql/plugin --log-error=/var/log/mariadb/mariadb
    --pid-file=/var/run/mariadb/mariadb.pid --socket=/var/lib/mysql/mysql.sock

systemd[1]: Starting MariaDB database server...
mysqld_safe[4221]: Logging to '/var/log/mariadb/mariadb.log'.
mysqld_safe[4221]: Starting mysqld daemon with databases from /var/lib/mysql
systemd[1]: Started MariaDB database server.
```

At this point we have installed, secured, and configured MySQL appropriately for Puppet Dashboard.

Ensuring dependencies

One of the reasons I recommend putting Puppet Dashboard on a separate server is because it has a tremendous amount of dependencies. We're going to install many of them now.

Our first step is to install the EPEL package repository:

```
[vagrant@puppetmaster ~]$ sudo yum install -y epel-release
```

Puppet Dashboard is a Rails application, so we need to install Ruby, RubyGems, Rake, and Bundler:

```
[vagrant@dashserver ~]$ sudo yum -y install ruby ruby-devel rake rubygem-bundler
Loaded plugins: fastestmirror
…snip…

Installed:
 ruby.x86_64 0:2.0.0.598-25.el7_1      ruby-devel.x86_64 0:2.0.0.598-25.el7_1
 rubygem-bundler.noarch 0:1.3.1-3.el7  rubygem-rake.noarch 0:0.9.6-25.el7_1

Dependency Installed:
 libyaml.x86_64 0:0.1.4-11.el7_0       ruby-irb.noarch 0:2.0.0.598-25.el7_1
 ruby-libs.x86_64 0:2.0.0.598-25.el7_1 rubygem-bigdecimal.x86_64 0:1.2.0-25.el7_1
 rubygem-json.x86_64 0:1.7.7-25.el7_1  rubygem-io-console.x86_64 0:0.4.2-25.el7_1
 rubygem-psych.x86_64 0:2.0.0-25.el7_1 rubygems.noarch 0:2.0.14-25.el7_1
 rubygem-rdoc.noarch 0:4.0.0-25.el7_1  rubygem-thor.noarch 0:0.17.0-3.el7
 rubygem-net-http-persistent.noarch 0:2.8-5.el7

Complete!
```

We'll need compilers and a JavaScript runtime installed to build native binaries for some extensions. Install the gcc-c++ and nodejs packages to get the necessary tools:

```
[vagrant@dashserver ~]$ sudo yum -y install gcc-c++ nodejs
Loaded plugins: fastestmirror
...snip...

Installed:
  gcc-c++.x86_64 0:4.8.3-9.el7              nodejs.x86_64 0:0.10.36-3.el7

Dependency Installed:
  c-ares.x86_64 0:1.10.0-3.el7              libstdc++-devel.x86_64 0:4.8.3-9.el7
  libuv.x86_64 1:0.10.34-1.el7              v8.x86_64 1:3.14.5.10-17.el7
  http-parser.x86_64 0:2.0-4.20121128gitcd01361.el7

Dependency Updated:
  cpp.x86_64 0:4.8.3-9.el7                  gcc.x86_64 0:4.8.3-9.el7
  libgcc.x86_64 0:4.8.3-9.el7               libgomp.x86_64 0:4.8.3-9.el7
  libstdc++.x86_64 0:4.8.3-9.el7

Complete!
```

It also depends on having the MySQL, PostgreSQL, SQLite, and XML development libraries available. You can install them like so:

```
[vagrant@dashserver ~]$ sudo yum -y install mariadb-devel \
                        libxml2-devel libxslt-devel sqlite-devel
Loaded plugins: fastestmirror
...snip...

Installed:
  libxslt-devel.x86_64 0:1.1.28-5.el7       libxml2-devel.x86_64 0:2.9.1-5.el7_1.2
  mariadb-devel.x86_64 1:5.5.44-1.el7_1     sqlite-devel.x86_64 0:3.7.17-6.el7_1.1

Dependency Installed:
  zlib-devel.x86_64 0:1.2.7-13.el7          libgcrypt-devel.x86_64 0:1.5.3-12.el7_1
  krb5-devel.x86_64 0:1.12.2-14.el7         libcom_err-devel.x86_64 0:1.42.9-7.el7
  libselinux-devel.x86_64 0:2.2.2-6.el7 libgpg-error-devel.x86_64 0:1.12-3.el7
  libsepol-devel.x86_64 0:2.1.9-3.el7       libverto-devel.x86_64 0:0.2.5-4.el7
  libxslt.x86_64 0:1.1.28-5.el7             openssl-devel.x86_64 1:1.0.1e-42.el7.9
  pcre-devel.x86_64 0:8.32-14.el7           xz-devel.x86_64 0:5.1.2-9alpha.el7
  keyutils-libs-devel.x86_64 0:1.5.8-3.el7

Dependency Updated:
  e2fsprogs.x86_64 0:1.42.9-7.el7           e2fsprogs-libs.x86_64 0:1.42.9-7.el7
  krb5-libs.x86_64 0:1.12.2-14.el7          libcom_err.x86_64 0:1.42.9-7.el7
  libgcrypt.x86_64 0:1.5.3-12.el7_1.1       libxml2.x86_64 0:2.9.1-5.el7_1.2
  libss.x86_64 0:1.42.9-7.el7               openssl.x86_64 1:1.0.1e-42.el7.9
  openssl-libs.x86_64 1:1.0.1e-42.el7.9     pcre.x86_64 0:8.32-14.el7
  sqlite.x86_64 0:3.7.17-6.el7_1.1          xz.x86_64 0:5.1.2-9alpha.el7
  xz-libs.x86_64 0:5.1.2-9alpha.el7

Complete!
```

Installing Apache for Puppet Dashboard

To run the dashboard under Passenger, we'll use Apache httpd to provide the base web service. Install Apache httpd, the Apache development tools, and the TLS module as follows:

```
[vagrant@dashserver ~]$ sudo yum install -y httpd httpd-devel mod_ssl
Loaded plugins: fastestmirror
...snip...

Installed:
  httpd.x86_64 0:2.4.6-31.el7.centos      httpd-devel.x86_64 0:2.4.6-31.el7.centos
  mod_ssl.x86_64 1:2.4.6-31.el7.centos

Dependency Installed:
  apr.x86_64 0:1.4.8-3.el7               apr-devel.x86_64 0:1.4.8-3.el7
  apr-util.x86_64 0:1.5.2-6.el7          apr-util-devel.x86_64 0:1.5.2-6.el7
  cyrus-sasl.x86_64 0:2.1.26-17.el7      cyrus-sasl-devel.x86_64 0:2.1.26-17.el7
  expat-devel.x86_64 0:2.1.0-8.el7       httpd-tools.x86_64 0:2.4.6-31.el7.centos
  mailcap.noarch 0:2.1.41-2.el7          openldap-devel.x86_64 0:2.4.39-6.el7
  libdb-devel.x86_64 0:5.3.21-17.el7_0.1

Complete!
```

 You can also run Passenger under the nginx web server. However, it requires significantly more manual configuration, and is thus left as an exercise for the reader.

Installing Passenger for Puppet Dashboard

Phusion provides a Yum repo with Passenger binaries. They don't provide a release RPM, just the repo configuration file. Download and install it with the following commands:

```
[vagrant@dashserver ~]$ curl -sSLo passenger.repo \
    https://oss-binaries.phusionpassenger.com/yum/definitions/el-passenger.repo
[vagrant@dashserver ~]$ sudo mv passenger.repo /etc/yum.repos.d/passenger.repo
```

Now install Passenger and the Passenger module for Apache:

```
$ sudo yum install -y passenger mod_passenger
Loaded plugins: fastestmirror
...snip...

Installed:
  passenger.x86_64 0:5.0.16-8.el7          mod_passenger.x86_64 0:5.0.16-8.el7

Dependency Installed:
  rubygem-rack.noarch 1:1.5.2-4.el7
```

Start up Apache and confirm that the Phusion Passenger configuration is correct:

```
$ sudo systemctl enable httpd
ln -s '/usr/lib/systemd/system/httpd.service'
        '/etc/systemd/system/multi-user.target.wants/httpd.service'
$ sudo systemctl start httpd
$ sudo passenger-config validate-install --validate-apache2 --auto
  * Checking whether this Passenger install is in PATH... ✓
  * Checking whether there are no other Passenger installations... ✓
  * Checking whether Apache is installed... ✓
  * Checking whether the Passenger module is correctly configured in Apache... ✓

Everything looks good. :-)
```

At this point, the system is prepared for the dashboard to be installed.

Configuring Firewall for Puppet Dashboard

Next, we need to adjust the firewall on the server. Puppet servers will connect to the dashboard to deliver reports. System administrators and DevOps engineers will also browse the results using a web browser:

```
[dashboard ~]$ sudo firewall-cmd --permanent --zone=public --add-port=80/tcp
success
[dashboard ~]$ sudo firewall-cmd --permanent --zone=public --add-port=443/tcp
success
[dashboard ~]$ sudo firewall-cmd --permanent --zone=public --add-port=3000/tcp
success
[dashboard ~]$ sudo firewall-cmd --reload
success
```

 It is safe for you to run these commands on a virtual host running on your personal workstation. In a production setting, you'd want to limit access to specific IP networks.

Enabling the Puppet agent on Puppet Dashboard

At this point, we should add the dashserver node to the Puppet server, to take advantage of the configuration management available. Connect to the server using this command:

```
[vagrant@dashserver ~]$ puppet agent --test --server=puppet.example.com
Info: Creating a new SSL key for dashserver.example.com
Info: Caching certificate for ca
Info: csr_attributes file loading from /etc/puppetlabs/puppet/csr_attributes.yaml
Info: Creating a new SSL certificate request for dashserver.example.com
Info: Certificate Request fingerprint (SHA256): 4A:25:F1:3A:B5:DC:0F:64:CC...
Info: Caching certificate for ca
Exiting; no certificate found and waitforcert is disabled
```

When the command succeeds, you'll need to log in to the Puppet server and sign the certificate, as done in Part III and shown here:

```
[vagrant@puppetserver ~]$ puppet cert --sign dashserver.example.com
Notice: Signed certificate request for dashserver.example.com
Notice: Removing file Puppet::SSL::CertificateRequest dashserver.example.com
  at '/var/opt/puppetlabs/puppetserver/ssl/ca/requests/dashserver.example.com.pem'
```

Rerun the `puppet agent` command on the dashboard server, and your node will receive the Puppet configuration you built in Part II.

Enabling Puppet Dashboard

At this point, we will download and configure the Puppet Dashboard Rails application.

Puppet Dashboard requires no special permissions on the node. Therefore we will create a `puppet-dashboard` user, and complete the setup using that user account.

Installing Puppet Dashboard

Create a `puppet-dashboard` user account. You can place the home directory anywhere you want, but *usr/share/puppet-dashboard* and *opt/puppet-dashboard* are the most common places. For the following example, I have chosen the home directory in *opt/puppet-dashboard*. Give `useradd` the `-m` option to create the home directory, for reasons I'll explain shortly:

```
[vagrant@dashserver ~]$ sudo useradd -d /opt/puppet-dashboard -m puppet-dashboard
```

At this point, we want to become the dashboard user. All further installation steps will be done as the dashboard user. We want all the files installed to be owned by the dashboard user, and operating as that user guarantees that.

The first thing we'll need to do is fix the permissions and remove all files from the application root. Run the following commands:

```
[vagrant@dashserver ~]$ sudo su - puppet-dashboard
[puppet-dashboard@dashserver ~]$ chmod 755 /opt/puppet-dashboard
[puppet-dashboard@dashserver ~]$ rm .[a-z]*
[puppet-dashboard@dashserver ~]$ ls -la
total 0
drwx------  2 puppet-dashboard puppet-dashboard  6 Aug 29 06:38 .
drwxr-xr-x. 4 root             root             61 Aug 29 06:38 ..
```

The directory must be empty or the following `git clone` operation will fail. As the dashboard user we're going to clone the *puppet-dashboard* Git repository into this directory:

```
$ git clone https://github.com/sodabrew/puppet-dashboard.git ./
Cloning into '.'...
remote: Counting objects: 24226, done.
```

```
remote: Total 24226 (delta 0), reused 0 (delta 0), pack-reused 24226
Receiving objects: 100% (24226/24226), 13.54 MiB | 5.41 MiB/s, done.
Resolving deltas: 100% (12058/12058), done.
```

At this point, we have a complete installation of Puppet Dashboard in an appropriate installation directory. Now run `bundler` to install the Ruby gems upon which the Dashboard depends. As you'll see, it installs many, many gems. Bundler will install the dependencies within the dashboard user's home directory, and not pollute the system paths:

```
[puppet-dashboard@dashserver ~]$ bundle install --deployment --without postgresql
Fetching gem metadata from https://rubygems.org/...........
Using rake (0.9.6)
Installing i18n (0.6.11)
Installing multi_json (1.10.1)
Installing activesupport (3.2.21)
 …snip…
Installing uglifier (1.3.0)
Installing will_paginate (3.0.7)
Your bundle is complete! It was installed into ./vendor/bundle
```

We have installed Puppet Dashboard and its dependencies into the */opt/puppet-dashboard* directory. Next, we'll configure the dashboard and initialize the database.

Configuring Puppet Dashboard

To configure Puppet Dashboard, you'll need to modify two configuration files. The first file is */opt/puppet-dashboard/config/database.yml*. You can copy this from the example and then edit it, or simply create it in the format shown here:

```
[puppet-dashboard@dashserver ~]$ cd config/
[puppet-dashboard@dashserver config]$ cp database.yml.example database.yml
[puppet-dashboard@dashserver config]$ $EDITOR database.yml
[puppet-dashboard@dashserver config]$ cat database.yml
production:
  adapter: mysql2
  database: dashboard_production
  username: dashboard
  password: the password you specified for the dashboard user
  encoding: utf8
[puppet-dashboard@dashserver config]$ chmod 0440 database.yml
```

As you can see, the database config file contains the database type, username, and password. The `chmod` command ensures that it is only readable by the dashboard user.

The second file is */opt/puppet-dashboard/config/settings.yml*. You should copy this much more extensive file from the example and then edit it:

```
[puppet-dashboard@dashserver config]$ cp settings.yml.example settings.yml
[puppet-dashboard@dashserver config]$ $EDITOR settings.yml
```

There are only five settings you must change, which I've shown here (obviously you should change the names to match your own domain if you aren't using *example.com* to learn):

```
# CN that is used in Dashboard's certificate.
cn_name: 'dashboard.example.com'

# Hostname of the certificate authority.
ca_server: 'puppet.example.com'

# Hostname of the inventory server.
inventory_server: 'puppet.example.com'

# Hostname of the file bucket server.
file_bucket_server: 'puppet.example.com'

disable_legacy_report_upload_url: true
```

If you want the dashboard to show times in a specific time zone, uncomment this line and set the appropriate environment:

```
# Uncomment the following line to set a local time zone.  Run
# "rake time:zones:local" for the name of your local time zone.
#time_zone: 'Pacific Time (US & Canada)'
```

You can add custom links to the top bar of the dashboard by uncommenting and editing the following lines (this can be useful to direct people to other useful services):

```
# Adds optional custom links in the top bar of puppet dashboard.
# Example that will add two links:
#custom_links:
# -
#   href: /link/href
#   title: The title that will be displayed
# -
#   href: /node_groups/1
#   title: Special group
```

Puppet Dashboard can be used as an ENC. This allows you to assign configuration classes (modules) to hosts from the dashboard web interface. If you only intend to use the dashboard to review node status and reports, you should enable the read_only_mode setting. If you intend to use the dashboard as an ENC, this setting must be set to false:

```
# Disables the UI and controller actions for editing nodes, classes,
# groups and reports.  Report submission is still allowed
enable_read_only_mode: true
```

Puppet Dashboard doesn't provide a history of changes to the node configuration. Most people feel this makes it unsuitable for tracking change in production environments. Best practice is to enable the `enable_read_only_mode` setting, and use a different ENC that provides an audit trail.

Finally, delete this next-to-last line with the secret token, as you'll be generating a unique one to use:

```
# Generate a new secret_token for production use!
secret_token: 'b1bbd28f6f9ebfc25f09da9bff4....
```

Generate a new secret key and add it to the configuration file:

```
[puppet-dashboard@dashserver config]$ cd ../
[puppet-dashboard@dashserver ~]$ export RAILS_ENV=production
[puppet-dashboard@dashserver ~]$ echo "secret_token: \
   '$(bundle exec rake secret)'" > config/settings.yml
```

Defining the Puppet Dashboard schema

There is a Rake task that populates the MySQL database with the appropriate schema (database tables and columns) for Puppet Dashboard. This task produces a lot of output that may not make a lot of sense. However, it will complain loudly if it fails for any reason:

```
[puppet-dashboard@dashserver ~]$ bundle exec rake db:setup
dashboard_production already exists
-- create_table("delayed_job_failures", {:force=>true})
   -> 0.0104s
-- create_table("delayed_jobs", {:force=>true})
   -> 0.0019s
-- add_index("delayed_jobs", ["failed_at", "run_at", "locked_at",
...snip...
-- initialize_schema_migrations_table()
   -> 0.0153s
-- assume_migrated_upto_version(20141217071943,
   ["/home/vagrant/puppet-dashboard/db/migrate"])
   -> 0.0215s
```

 The only errors I've seen at this point were if the MySQL server was not running, or if the passwords in the configuration file were not correct.

Now that the database has been defined, you can precompile all static assets for higher performance:

```
[puppet-dashboard@dashserver ~]$ bundle exec rake assets:precompile
/usr/bin/ruby /opt/puppet-dashboard/vendor/bundle/ruby/bin/rake
  assets:precompile:all RAILS_ENV=production RAILS_GROUPS=assets
```

Connecting Puppet Dashboard to Puppet Server

Generate a unique TLS key and certificate request using the following commands. The cert:request command will submit the CSR to the Puppet CA:

```
[puppet-dashboard@dashserver ~]$ bundle exec rake cert:create_key_pair
[puppet-dashboard@dashserver ~]$ bundle exec rake cert:request
```

You may get the following error at this point:

```
[puppet-dashboard@dashserver ~]$ bundle exec rake cert:request
rake aborted!
404 "Not Found"
/opt/puppet-dashboard/lib/puppet_https.rb:34:in 'put'
/opt/puppet-dashboard/lib/tasks/install.rake:50:in 'block (2 levels) in <top>'
Tasks: TOP => cert:request
(See full trace by running task with --trace)
```

When the command succeeds, you'll need to log in to the Puppet server and sign the certificate, as done in Part III and shown here:

```
[vagrant@puppetserver ~]$ puppet cert --sign dashboard.example.com
Notice: Signed certificate request for dashboard.example.com
Notice: Removing file Puppet::SSL::CertificateRequest dashboard.example.com
  at '/var/opt/puppetlabs/puppetserver/ssl/ca/requests/dashboard.example.com.pem'
```

Return to the dashboard server and execute the following request to download and store the signed certificate. The dashboard will also retrieve the CA's certificate and the CA revocation list:

```
[puppet-dashboard@dashserver ~]$ bundle exec rake cert:retrieve
[puppet-dashboard@dashserver ~]$ ls -1 certs/
dashboard.ca_cert.pem
dashboard.ca_crl.pem
dashboard.cert.pem
dashboard.private_key.pem
dashboard.public_key.pem
```

At this point, Puppet Dashboard is an authorized client of the Puppet server and can submit requests to it.

We are done taking action as the dashboard user, so exit back to our normal vagrant user login. As you won't need to log in as this user again, we can disable the shell for it at this time:

```
[puppet-dashboard@dashserver ~]$ exit
[vagrant@dashserver ~]$ sudo usermod -s /bin/nologin puppet-dashboard
```

Enabling the Dashboard Rails service

Now we'll configure Apache to start up Puppet Dashboard running as a Rails application under Phusion Passenger. First, Apache comes with several configuration files that provide a helpful defaults for setting up Rails applications. We don't need and won't be using this configuration, so let's remove them:

```
[vagrant@dashserver ~]$ cd /etc/httpd/conf.d
[vagrant@dashserver conf.d]$ sudo rm ssl.conf welcome.conf userdir.conf
```

Best Practice

Puppet Dashboard works best configured as a single-purpose server.

Install an Apache configuration file from the *learning-puppet4* repo. This file contains a complete, self-standing service definition for the Puppet Dashboard service:

```
[vagrant@dashserver conf.d]$ sudo cp /vagrant/etc-puppet/dashboard.conf ./
```

Restart Apache to pick up the changes. Here's what it looks like when it restarted successfully:

```
$ sudo systemctl restart httpd
$ sudo systemctl status httpd
httpd.service - The Apache HTTP Server
   Loaded: loaded (/usr/lib/systemd/system/httpd.service; enabled)
   Active: active (running) since Thu 2015-08-27 05:24:38 UTC; 5s ago
  Process: 14661 ExecStop=/bin/kill -WINCH ${MAINPID} (status=0/SUCCESS)
 Main PID: 14666 (httpd)
   Status: "Processing requests..."
   CGroup: /system.slice/httpd.service
           ├─14666 /usr/sbin/httpd -DFOREGROUND
           ├─14693 Passenger watchdog
           ├─14696 Passenger core
           ├─14703 Passenger ust-router
           ├─14714 /usr/sbin/httpd -DFOREGROUND
           ├─14715 /usr/sbin/httpd -DFOREGROUND
           ├─14716 /usr/sbin/httpd -DFOREGROUND
           ├─14717 /usr/sbin/httpd -DFOREGROUND
           └─14718 /usr/sbin/httpd -DFOREGROUND

dashboard.example.com systemd[1]: Starting The Apache HTTP Server...
dashboard.example.com systemd[1]: Started The Apache HTTP Server.
```

There are two logs that may contain errors from the dashboard initialization. Check the Apache error log for Passenger startup failures, and your syslog daemon log for messages from the running Puppet Dashboard service. The following command can be useful to view both logs when you are debugging problems:

```
[vagrant@dashserver ~]$ sudo tail -f /var/log/messages /var/log/httpd/error_log
```

Viewing the dashboard

At this point, you should open a browser and connect to the dashboard. If you are running the Dashboard on a Vagrant node, you will need to add the node's IP address to the hosts file on your personal computer.

On a Mac or Linux system, add the following line to */etc/hosts*. On a Windows machine, add the same line to *C:\Windows\System32\drivers\etc\hosts*:

```
192.168.250.7  dashboard.example.com
```

Now open up a browser and connect to *http://dashboard.example.com/*.

 At this point, you will get a TLS certificate error. You can safely ignore this when running Vagrant on your personal machine. We have documented how to resolve this problem in "Eliminating certificate errors" on page 401.

You should see a screen that looks exactly like Figure 27-1.

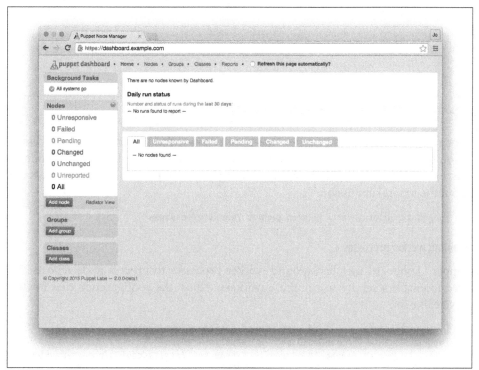

Figure 27-1. Puppet Dashboard with no node reports

There's no information here, as no nodes are reporting here yet. Let's configure the Puppet server to send node reports to the Dashboard.

Sending node reports to the dashboard

Enable the dashboard as a target for node reports on your Puppet server. Do so by adding http to the report processors, and a reporturl setting pointing to the dashboard in */etc/puppetlabs/puppet/puppet.conf*:

```
[master]
  reports = store, http
  reporturl = https://dashboard.example.com:3000/reports/upload
```

Restart the Puppet server, and it will start forwarding node reports to the dashboard. For Puppet Server the command would be:

```
[vagrant@puppetserver ~]$ sudo systemctl restart puppetserver
```

For the deprecated Puppet master, you would restart Apache:

```
[vagrant@puppetmaster ~]$ sudo systemctl reload httpd
```

Now you should run Puppet on a client node. After the run has finished, check back and you should see the message shown in Figure 27-2 on the top left of the console.

Figure 27-2. One node report has been received

A pending task means that a report has been received and is waiting to be processed. If you see this message, node report forwarding is working properly. If you do not see this on the dashboard, check the system log on your Puppet server for messages about the report submission:

```
[vagrant@puppetserver ~]$ grep puppet /var/log/messages
```

Enabling worker processes

Puppet Dashboard uses background worker processes to process node reports. We need to enable a service to run these workers. Adjust the configuration files for this service like so:

```
[vagrant@dashserver ~]$ cd /opt/puppet-dashboard/ext/redhat
[vagrant@dashserver redhat]$ sed -e 's#usr/share#opt#' \
        puppet-dashboard.sysconfig | sudo tee /etc/sysconfig/puppet-dashboard
[vagrant@dashserver redhat]$ echo "WORKERS=$(grep cores /proc/cpuinfo \
        | cut -d' ' -f3)" | sudo tee /etc/sysconfig/puppet-dashboard-workers
```

This has adjusted the system configuration files for the dashboard installation path, and selected the correct number of workers. Now enable and start the `puppet-dashboard-workers` service like so:

```
[vagrant@dashserver ~]$ sudo systemctl enable puppet-dashboard-workers
ln -s '/etc/systemd/system/puppet-dashboard-workers.service'
  '/etc/systemd/system/multi-user.target.wants/puppet-dashboard-workers.service'
[vagrant@dashserver ~]$ sudo systemctl start puppet-dashboard-workers
```

Now that the worker processors are enabled, the pending tasks should reduce to zero. You should also see some information in the node reports.

If Background Tasks says 1 new failed task, click it. Do you see a message about an attribute that was supposed to be an array, like the one shown in Figure 27-3?

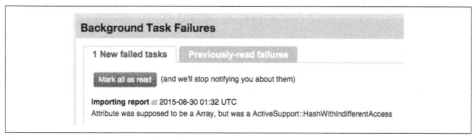

Figure 27-3. Background task failure

If so, then you should download and apply the patch from Puppet Dashboard Pull Request 329 (*http://github.com/sodabrew/puppet-dashboard/pull/329*), which contains a fix for processing reports from Puppet 4 nodes. Then restart the workers service:

```
[vagrant@dashserver ~]$ sudo -u puppet-dashboard bash -l
[puppet-dashboard@dashserver vagrant]$ cd
[puppet-dashboard@dashserver ~]$ curl -sL \
    http://github.com/sodabrew/puppet-dashboard/pull/329.diff | patch -u -p1
patching file app/models/report.rb
[puppet-dashboard@dashserver ~]$ exit
[vagrant@dashserver ~]$ sudo systemctl restart puppet-dashboard-workers
```

Viewing node status

Now that you have enabled the worker processes, you can see the results of each node's Puppet agent convergence in the web interface. Puppet Dashboard provides an extensive amount of information for your review. Let's review each of the pages now.

 Puppet Dashboard refers to the *Puppet run*, while this book uses the more accurate term *catalog evaluation* or *convergence*. In this chapter, we utilize the same terms you'll see on the display for Puppet dashboard.

Viewing nodes by status

The home page of Puppet Dashboard provides an overview of the convergence history of Puppet nodes that connect to the Puppet server.

In the toolbar on the left, the *Nodes* widget contains a count of all nodes with reports, and another count of the number of nodes that last reported each status, as shown in Figure 27-4.

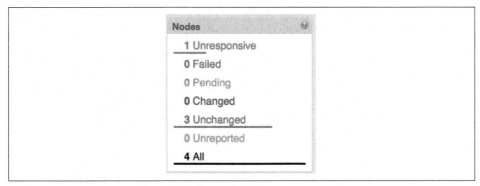

Figure 27-4. Puppet Dashboard: Nodes widget

In the main display, you'll find a graphic display of run status over the last 30 days, as shown in Figure 27-5.

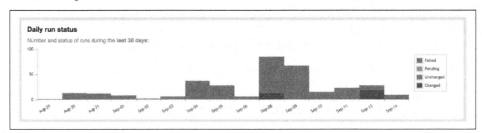

Figure 27-5. Puppet Dashboard: Run status graph

Beneath it you'll find a list of nodes and the last time they reported (Figure 27-6).

Node	↓ Latest report	Total	Failed	Pending	Changed	Unchanged
Total		102	0	0	0	102
✔ puppetmaster.example.com	2015-09-14 02:17 PDT	41	0	0	0	41
✔ dashserver.example.com	2015-09-14 02:16 PDT	27	0	0	0	27
✔ client.example.com	2015-09-14 01:42 PDT	27	0	0	0	27

Figure 27-6. Puppet Dashboard: Node list

Just above the list of nodes is a tab bar of node statuses. Selecting one of these tabs will limit the list to show you only nodes that last reported the selected status (Figure 27-7).

Figure 27-7. Puppet Dashboard: Node status tabs

Reviewing a node's history

If you click on a node name, you'll be taken to the node's overview page (Figure 27-8). This contains a graph of the node's Puppet run (catalog evaluation) status over 30 days, a graph of the run time, and a table showing the status from every stored run report for that node.

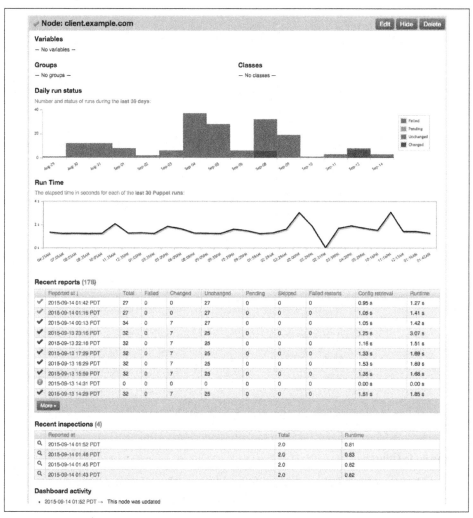

Figure 27-8. Node overview

In the preceding figure, you'll notice that four inspections were reported, which contain the current status of all resource attributes for which auditing was enabled. The report was created by running `puppet inspect` on the node. The dashboard provides an interface to browse through both run reports and audit inspections.

Analyzing a node's run report

If you click on the datestamp next to a node name, you'll see an overview of that node's Puppet catalog evaluation (Figure 27-9). This report includes detailed statistics about the number of resources, the changes made during the run, and the time intervals of each stage of the Puppet run.

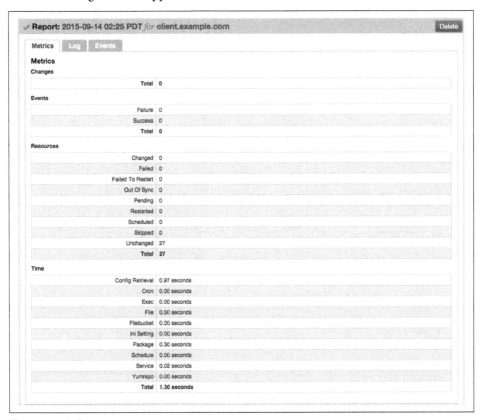

Figure 27-9. Puppet run report

Finding node failures

Puppet Dashboard can help you identify problems with nodes. If a Puppet agent convergence fails on a node, the node will show up in the red Failed count on the left.

You can see a list of all nodes whose most recent Puppet run failed by clicking Failed in the widget bar on the left, or by clicking Failed on the Status tab bar in the main display (Figure 27-10).

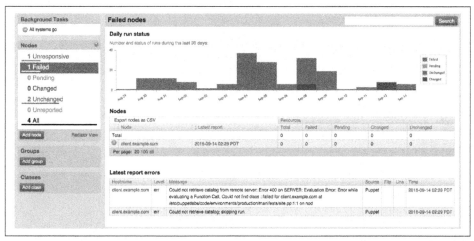

Figure 27-10. Node status: Failed

You can see a list of all failed Puppet runs, current and previous, by clicking on Reports at the top right, and then Failed in the tab bar shown on that page (Figure 27-11).

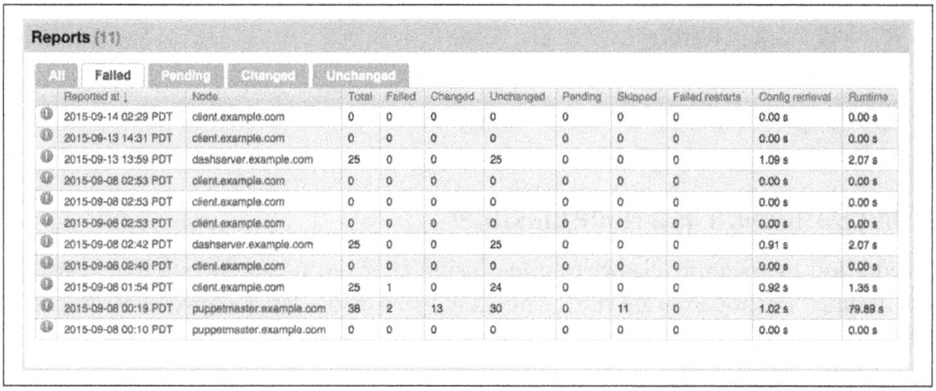

Figure 27-11. Run reports: Failed

Identifying out-of-sync nodes

The Puppet Dashboard can help you identify nodes that are out of sync with policy. If a node has not sent a Puppet report in a few hours, the node will show up in the grey Unreported count on the left.

If you click on Unresponsive in the node status widget, you'll find a report of nodes that have not reported recently (Figure 27-12).

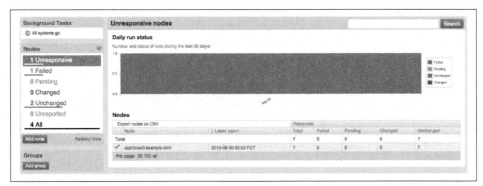

Figure 27-12. Node status: Unresponsive

There are a number of reasons why nodes may not be reporting:

- The node has a networking problem.
- The node has been shut down.
- Puppet has been prevented from running on the node.

Unfortunately, Puppet Dashboard can't identify why the node hasn't sent a report to the Puppet server recently. Someone will need to investigate this situation.

Best Practice

Create a tool that opens an incident to investigate when a node transitions to Unresponsive status.

Using Dashboard as a Node Classifier

In addition to assigning classes to nodes using Hiera, you can do assignment within the Puppet Dashboard interface. The dashboard provides a convenient graphical interface to assign classes and input parameters to nodes.

Puppet Dashboard doesn't provide a history of changes to the node configuration. Sites with auditing requirements may find this unsuitable for tracking change in production environments.

Let's walk through this process so you can see how it works.

To enable the ENC functionality, ensure that the `enable_ready_only_mode` setting is disabled in */opt/puppet-dashboard/config/settings.yml*:

```
# Disables the UI and controller actions for editing nodes, classes,
# groups and reports.  Report submission is still allowed
enable_read_only_mode: false
```

If you have changed the value, restart the httpd process to pick up the change with `systemctl reload httpd`.

Setting the environment for a node

Click on the *client.example.com* node name in the main screen. Then click the Edit button near the top right of the title bar for the node, shown in Figure 27-13.

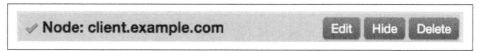

Figure 27-13. Puppet Dashboard: Node title bar

On the following screen (Figure 27-14), you have the option to set the node's environment, to assign classes to the node, or to define parameters (top-level variables) for the node.

Edit node

Node
client.example.com

Environment
testing

Description
Enter a description for this node here...

Variables

Key	Value
key	value

Add variable

Classes

Groups
Clients ×

Update or Cancel

Figure 27-14. Puppet Dashboard: Edit node

While it can be useful to assign classes or parameters to individual nodes, you will generally want to do this with a node group, as described shortly. At this time, write a description for the node and select the test environment for it.

Click Update to save your changes.

Repeat this process for each node you wish to add a description for, or assign to the test environment.

Adding classes to the dashboard

Under Classes in the left sidebar, click the "Add class" button. On the following page, enter the name of a class available on the Puppet server. Add a description for the dashboard display, then click Create (Figure 27-15).

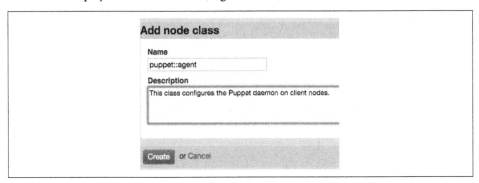

Figure 27-15. Puppet Dashboard: Add node class

To make use of the module created in Part II, enter **puppet::agent** as the class name.

Repeat this process for each class you wish to assign to nodes. You may wish to add **mcollective::server** to the class list, for example.

Creating node groups

Under Groups in the left sidebar, click the "Add group" button. On the following page enter a name you'd like to use for a group of nodes (Figure 27-16).

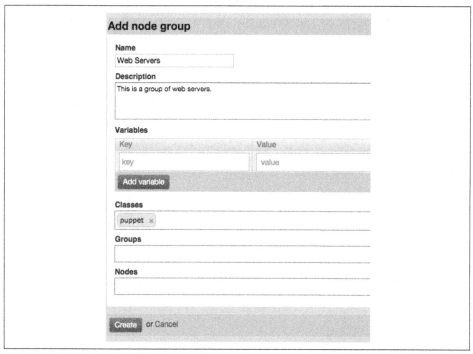

Figure 27-16. Puppet Dashboard: Add node group

Enter a description for dashboard users to understand the meaning of the group. As you can see from this screen, a group can contain:

- Nodes that are included in the group
- Other groups that are included in the group
- Classes that apply to all nodes in the group
- Parameter keys and values provided with the group

For practice, you can create a group named Clients, with a node of `client.exam ple.com` and classes `puppet::agent` and `mcollective::server`. For testing purposes, add a parameter named `findme` with any value you like.

You'll notice that the dashboard autocompletes entries based on node and class information in its database.

When you are done, click Create. You will see a filtered status view that contains only the results from nodes within the group (Figure 27-17).

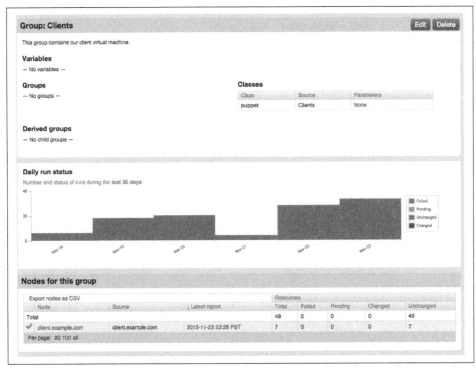

Figure 27-17. Puppet Dashboard: View Clients group

Installing the node classifier

To enable ENC lookups from the dashboard's nodes and classes, install the exter
nal_node query script on the Puppet server. You can copy this file from the dash
board instance, or download it directly from the GitHub repository:

```
[vagrant@puppetserver ~]$ sudo mkdir -p /opt/puppet-dashboard/bin
[vagrant@puppetserver ~]$ sudo chown vagrant /opt/puppet-dashboard/bin
[vagrant@puppetserver ~]$ cd /opt/puppet-dashboard/bin
[vagrant@puppetserver bin]$ curl -sL -o external_node \
    https://github.com/sodabrew/puppet-dashboard/raw/master/bin/external_node
[vagrant@puppetserver bin]$ chmod 755 external_node
```

There are two ways to make the node classifier work correctly:

- Edit the script to contain the correct dashboard URL and filenames.
- Provide the Dashboard URL and the server's TLS key and certificate filenames with environment variables.

I have found that editing the script (or installing it with a customized template using Puppet) is easiest. You can edit it as follows:

```
[vagrant@puppetserver ~]$ $EDITOR /opt/puppet-dashboard/bin/external_node
```

Adjust the following settings near the top of the script:

```
DASHBOARD_URL = "https://dashboard.example.com:3000"

# These settings are only used when connecting to dashboard over https (TLS)
CERT_PATH = "/etc/puppetlabs/puppet/ssl/certs/puppetserver.example.com.pem"
PKEY_PATH = "/etc/puppetlabs/puppet/ssl/private_keys/puppetserver.example.com.pem"
CA_PATH   = "/etc/puppetlabs/puppet/ssl/certs/ca.pem"
```

Why Specify the Server's Key?

The server's key and certificate are necessary to authenticate to the Dashboard.

When installing the dashboard, we had it connect and be authorized by the Puppet server for access to node information. At that time, the dashboard stored the CA certificate for later use.

When a Puppet server connects to the dashboard to retrieve node information, Puppet Dashboard will validate that the Puppet server is using credentials signed by the same CA. If the key and certificate provided to the external_node script are not signed by the CA configured in the dashboard's Apache service configuration, the connection attempt will be refused.

Testing class and parameter assignment

Before enabling the ENC for the Puppet server, test that ENC node lookup is working properly with the dashboard. The following test query should retrieve the data configured in the Dashboard for the client node:

```
$ sudo /opt/puppet-dashboard/bin/external_node client.example.com
---
name: client.example.com
environment: test
classes:
  mcollective::server: {}
  puppet::agent: {}
parameters:
  findme: It works!
```

As you can see, the output contains the environment configured with the node, plus the classes and parameters assigned to the Clients group. The group name itself does not appear in the output, as this is a user interface feature internal to the dashboard.

If you are using an unmodified external_node script, then you may need to set environment variables when performing the query:

```
[vagrant@puppetserver ~]$ cd /var/opt/puppetlabs/puppetserver
[vagrant@puppetserver puppetserver]$ sudo /usr/bin/env \
  CA_PATH=ssl/certs/ca.pem \
```

```
    CERT_PATH=ssl/certs/puppetserver.example.com.pem \
    PKEY_PATH=ssl/private_keys/puppetserver.example.com.pem \
    PUPPET_DASHBOARD_URL=https://dashboard.example.com:3000 \
    /opt/puppet-dashboard/bin/external_node client.example.com
```

Test out the results with different hostnames. When the output is what you expect, enable the node classifier, as described next.

Querying the dashboard's ENC

Enable the Puppet Dashboard as an ENC using the following settings in the [master] section of */etc/puppetlabs/puppet/puppet.conf* on the Puppet server:

```
[master]
  node_terminus = exec
  external_nodes = /opt/puppet-dashboard/bin/external_node
```

Alternatively, pass the Puppet server's key and certificate to the script using environment variables as follows:

```
[master]
  node_terminus = exec
  external_nodes = /usr/bin/env CA_PATH=$ssldir/certs/ca.pem
    CERT_PATH=$ssldir/certs/puppetserver.example.com.pem
    PKEY_PATH=$ssldir/private_keys/puppetserver.example.com.pem
    PUPPET_DASHBOARD_URL=https://dashboard.example.com:3000
    /opt/puppet-dashboard/bin/external_node
```

After making these changes, you'll need to restart the Puppet server:

```
[vagrant@puppetserver ~]$ sudo systemctl restart puppetserver
```

Fast Reload of Configuration Files

Puppet Server v2.3.0 allows a fast reload of the Puppet Server configuration without restarting the entire JVM. Send the running process a HUP signal:

```
[vagrant@puppetserver ~]$ sudo pkill -HUP -f puppet-server-release.jar
```

Hopefully Puppet Server v2.3.1 will add a systemctl reload action.

Sending a HUP signal to the puppetserver process with Puppet Server 2.2 or earlier will kill the server. A complete restart is necessary.

From this point forward, the dashboard will be queried for the environment, classes, and parameters (node variables) of each node. The response from the dashboard will be used along with the results of Puppet Lookup to configure the node.

Implementing Dashboard in Production

This section contains important processes you should follow when building a production Puppet Dashboard instance. None of these are necessary for a test instance running on Vagrant. Skip over this section for now if you'd like, and come back to it when implementing a production server.

Eliminating certificate errors

If you are familiar with Apache configuration, you may have observed that the Puppet Dashboard service has been configured to answer on both TCP port 3000 and port 443. This configuration enhances security and improves the user experience.

The Puppet Dashboard service on port 3000 has special rules to allow only connections that utilize TLS certificates signed by the Puppet certificate authority. The Puppet server must provide its own TLS certificate when communicating with the dashboard.

When users connect to view node status, they will connect to the standard TLS port of 443. If their browser is given a certificate signed by the Puppet certificate authority (which is not authorized as a trusted CA in any browser), they will receive a certificate error from their browser.

Best Practice

Never ask users to click through certificate warnings. One day they'll click through a fraudulent intercept, and give their credentials (or worse) to an imposter.

You can provide a better experience by obtaining a TLS certificate from a certificate authority trusted by web browsers, the same as you would do for any public website. Generate an TLS key and CSR, and install the key and signed certificate on the dashboard server.

Starting at line 23 in */etc/httpd/conf.d/dashboard.conf* are the keys and certificate settings for the `VirtualHost` handling users on port 443. Comment out or remove the lines referencing the Puppet keys and uncomment the lines referencing the new key and certificate. Following is an example that shows a key and certificate installed in the RedHat standard TLS directories:

```
# This cert was signed by the Puppet CA and will produce a browser warning
#SSLCertificateFile     /opt/puppet-dashboard/certs/dashboard.cert.pem
#SSLCertificateKeyFile  /opt/puppet-dashboard/certs/dashboard.private_key.pem
# Change to keys and certificates issued by a trusted certificate authority
# to avoid browser errors
SSLCertificateFile     /etc/pki/tls/certs/dashboard.crt
SSLCertificateKeyFile  /etc/pki/tls/private/dashboard.key
```

Optimizing the database

The dashboard database is a normal MySQL database. You can back it up, restore it, and optimize it using standard tools and processes.

There is a special job that optimizes the dashboard's database schema. You should configure this to run from the dashboard user's cron once a month. Edit the dashboard user's cron like so:

```
[vagrant@puppetserver ~]$ sudo crontab -u puppet-dashboard -e
```

The contents of the crontab should contain something like this:

```
MAILTO=you@example.com
RAILS_ENV=production

* 3 1 * * /bin/bundle exec rake db:raw:optimize
```

This is the bog-standard Unix crontab format you can find documented everywhere. The operational line here will run the optimize job on the first day of the month at 3 a.m., and email the results to you. You should adjust the email address and timing of the optimization to whatever you desire.

Pruning old reports

Reports will remain in the database forever unless they are pruned. To keep the database size from outgrowing the space available, you should run the following job to prune old reports after they are no longer useful.

As in the previous example, configure this to run from the dashboard user's cron once a month. Add the following line to the dashboard user's crontab:

```
MAILTO=you@example.com
RAILS_ENV=production

* 4 * 0 * /bin/bundle exec rake reports:prune upto=3 unit=mon
```

This runs the prune job every Sunday at 4 a.m., and emails any output to you. As written, it will expire any report older than three months. You should adjust this parameter based on the disk storage available, and your organization's data retention requirements.

Rotating logs

While most messages go to the system logger, some low-level log messages are stored in the *log/* subdirectory of the installation directory. To keep these files from growing too large, install the dashboard's *logrotate* file, which tells the nightly logrotate process how to trim these files.

The only necessary change to this file is to alter the installation path to match where Puppet Dashboard was installed:

```
$ cd /opt/puppet-dashboard/ext/redhat
$ sed -e 's#usr/share#opt#' puppet-dashboard.logrotate \
    | sudo tee /etc/logrotate.d/puppet-dashboard
```

This will keep the dashboard's logfiles from getting out of control.

Ensuring a high-performance dashboard

Once you have finished testing and wish to deploy Puppet Dashboard in production, there are two issues to consider for performance: available RAM and fast storage. The dashboard tends to be write-heavy, generally doing 5:1 writes versus reads at most sites.

The dashboard server only needs sufficient RAM and for the database to be stored on the fastest disks available. Some of the best ways to meet these requirements are as follows:

Physical server
  Mirror the root and operating system volumes for redundancy on small, stable disks. Put the MySQL database on a RAID 0+1 or RAID-6 high-speed disk array.

Virtual server
  Put the operating system on the regular shared storage volumes used by other virtualized systems. Place the MySQL database on direct attached storage using VMWare's Raw Device Mapping or OpenStack Block Storage.

Cloud server
  Put the operating system on the regular instance volumes (such as AWS GP2 EBS volume). Place the MySQL database on direct attached SSD if possible (e.g., AWS R3 instance), or a remote drive with dedicated bandwidth and high IOPS commitment (e.g., AWS C4 instance with an EBS Provisioned IOPS volume).

Keep in mind this is all relative. If you have fewer than 100 nodes, almost any server will suffice. If you have thousands of nodes and an information radiator querying the dashboard every minute, you'll want to spend significant effort tuning the server appropriately.

Sizing the dashboard database

The data store size is one of the most important considerations when building a production Puppet Dashboard service. Running out of disk space can cripple the dashboard, and rebuilding a MySQL database on a new volume is nobody's idea of a fun Friday night.

Thankfully, there is a formula you can use to size your dashboard pretty much exactly as required.

On your Puppet server, you will find node reports in the *$vardir/reports* directory. These reports contain messages for each resource processed during the Puppet run. The more resources that are applied to a client node, the larger the report file will be.

The dashboard server will be storing every node report for as long as you tune the report database to retain the information. In practice, the MySQL data store uses slightly more space than the compact YAML file in the reports directory.

Using this information, calculate the disk space for the MySQL database by multiplying all of the following pieces of information and rounding up:

- Number of nodes
- Size of the reports
- Puppet runs per day (48 by default)
- Number of days before data is purged
- Average increase in MySQL data versus YAML file = 1.2

In a very stable environment where all nodes apply similar amount of Puppet resources, and very few ad hoc Puppet runs are done out of schedule, it is possible to target the disk space very closely:

Nodes	Report size	Puppet runs	Purge time	DB size adj	Expected disk space
50	128 KB	48	30	1.2	**12 GB**
100	128 KB	48	90	1.2	**67 GB**
2,000	256 KB	48	90	1.2	**2.5 TB**

In reality, it's not usually so simple, for a variety of reasons:

- Ongoing work adds new nodes on a regular basis.
- Autoscaled environments have a dynamic number of nodes.
- Different node types have vastly different numbers of resources applied to them, creating a large discrepancy in report sizes.

To give you a concrete example, at one customer we had these node types:

- More than 10,000 globally distributed nodes running Puppet four times a day, and managing only 120 resources.
- A little more than 200 servers in the core data center running Puppet the standard 48 times a day, each with more than 5,000 managed resources.
- An on-demand testing platform that built and tore down complete cluster sets. Nodes in the cluster ran Puppet exactly twice, with more than 14,000 resources applied between the two runs before being destroyed at the end of the test.

To scale the dashboard appropriately in this environment, we did three separate calculations, including a reasonable estimate for the maximum on-demand runs in a single day, and expected growth for servers and remote sites. That estimate was accurate enough that it is still running with average 80% space utilization on the same size disk cluster two years later.

Not every situation is so easy to predict. Last year I worked with a company that has two very large peak periods within the year, during which time the production deployment tripled in size. The saving grace is that during these rush periods the number of ad hoc convergence runs drops to nearly zero, as nonemergency deployments are limited during these periods. All of the reporting systems were scaled to handle peak load, and thus ran with extra capacity outside of the rush periods.

Evaluating Alternative Dashboards

There are several alternatives to the dashboards created by Puppet Labs. Depending on your needs or requirements, these may suit you better.

Some of these dashboards make use of PuppetDB's data, which can provide more detailed introspection of node status than available in the Puppet Dashboard. Any dashboard that gets node information from PuppetDB requires you to install PuppetDB before it will be useful.

Puppetboard

Puppetboard is a web interface to PuppetDB aiming to replace the reporting functionality of Puppet Dashboard (see Figures 27-18 and 27-19).

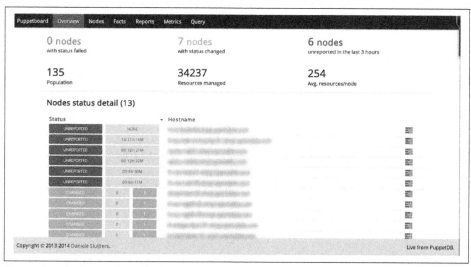

Figure 27-18. Puppetboard: Overview

At the time this book was written, the website still had an old disclaimer about how young the project was. Puppetboard is now over two years old with constant and progressive development during that time period.

> Puppetboard is supposed to be a tool, not a solution. So it's always gonna be less polished and more utilitarian than something like Puppet Enterprise.

—Spencer Krum / nibalizer

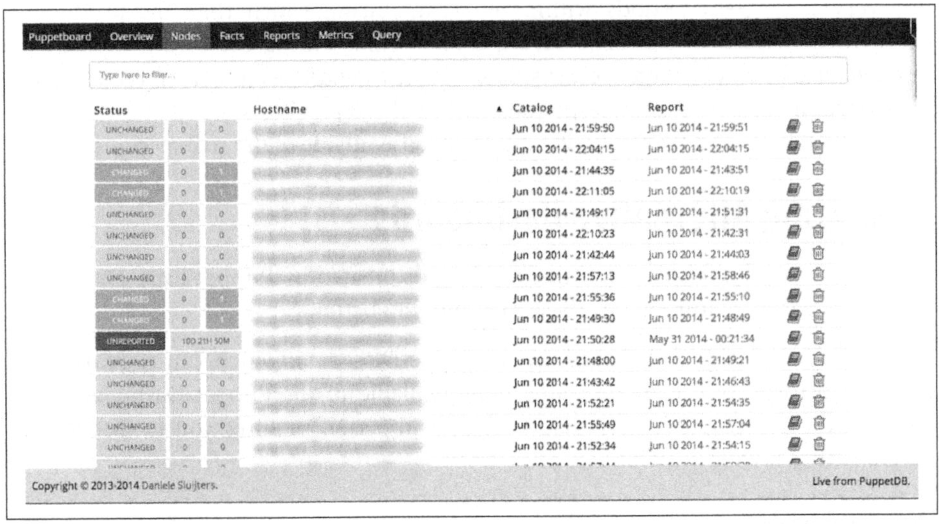

Figure 27-19. Puppetboard: Nodes

You can find more information about Puppetboard at *https://github.com/voxpupuli/puppetboard*. There is a Puppet module to install Puppetboard available at *puppet/puppetboard* (*http://bit.ly/1pQO8S4*) on the Puppet Forge.

Puppet Explorer

Puppet Explorer is a web application to explore PuppetDB data (see Figures 27-20 and 27-21). It is made using AngularJS and CoffeeScript and runs in the client browser. A small web server providing the static resources, and one or more PuppetDB servers, are the only backend systems required.

You can find more information about Puppet Explorer at *https://github.com/spotify/puppetexplorer*. There is a Puppet module maintained by the project available at *spotify/puppetexplorer* (*http://bit.ly/1Z9VsEB*) on the Puppet Forge.

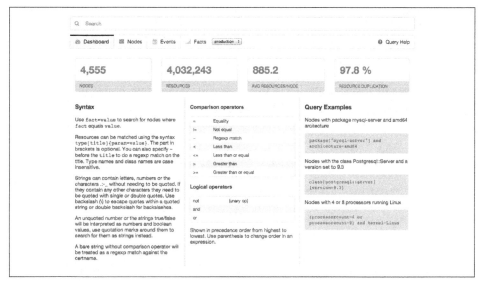

Figure 27-20. Puppet Explorer: Dashboard

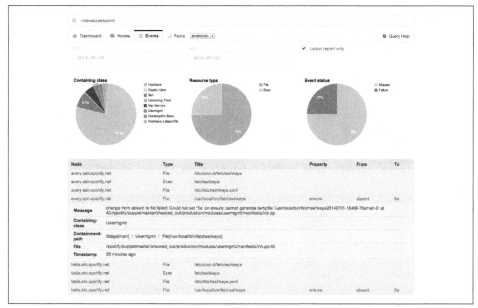

Figure 27-21. Puppet Explorer: Events

Spotify uses this dashboard in its operations, and provides regular updates.

PanoPuppet

Panorama Puppet, or PanoPuppet for short, is a web frontend that interfaces with PuppetDB and gives you a panorama view over your Puppet environments (see Figures 27-22 and 27-23). It's coded in Python 3 using the Django framework for the web interface and requests library to interface with PuppetDB. It also uses Bootstrap for the CSS and JQuery for some table sorting.

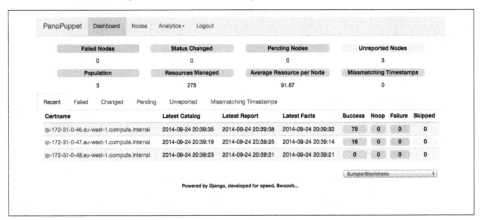

Figure 27-22. PanoPuppet: Dashboard

Figure 27-23. PanoPuppet: Nodes

The screenshots shown on the project are impressive and look powerful. As the author, *propyless*, says on the website:

The interface was written originally as an idea from work, we have tried to use different types of web interfaces that show the status of the Puppet environment. Most of them were too slow, too bloated to give us the information we wanted quickly. Why should PuppetDB which has an amazing response time suffer from a slow frontend? When you reach a point where the environment could have over 20,000 puppetized nodes you need something fast.

You can find more information about PanoPuppet at *https://github.com/propyless/ panopuppet*.

ENC Dashboard

ENC Dashboard is a project that replicated the functionality of Puppet Dashboard in a new Rails 3 design (see Figures 27-24 and 27-25). This project looks very familiar if you have used Puppet Dashboard before, but provides a faster interface and some additional new features.

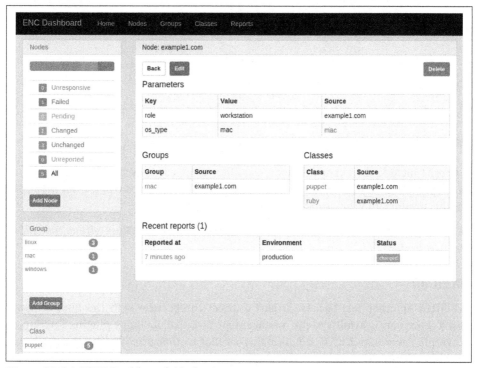

Figure 27-24. ENC Dashboard: Node view

This dashboard provides the ability to disable, enable, or trigger a Puppet run on a node, if you have installed the Puppet agent for MCollective (we'll cover this in Chapter 30).

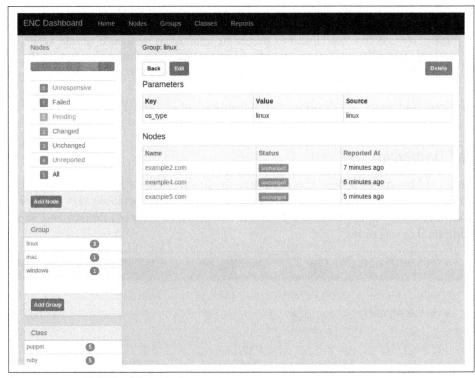

Figure 27-25. ENC Dashboard: Group view

It doesn't include the `external_node` classifier script used on the server for submission, so you'd need to copy that from the Puppet Dashboard project. I haven't tested out this product, but the developer was responsive to inquiries.

You can find more information about ENC Dashboard at *https://github.com/jbuss-dieker/ruby-enc*.

Foreman

I've listed Foreman last because it isn't a direct comparison with the Puppet Dashboard. Foreman is a full system management tool that includes plugins for Puppet providing reports and ENC functionality similar to that provided by Puppet Dashboard (see Figure 27-26).

From the Foreman website (*http://theforeman.org/introduction.html*):

> Foreman is a complete lifecycle management tool for physical and virtual servers. We give system administrators the power to easily automate repetitive tasks, quickly deploy applications, and proactively manage servers, on-premise or in the cloud.

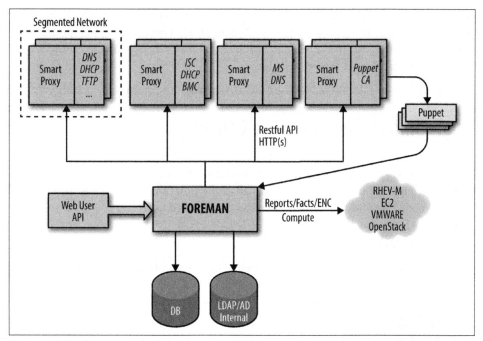

Figure 27-26. Foreman: Architecture

Foreman provides both a dashboard overview of Puppet nodes, and an interface for defining and customizing class and variable assignments for use as an ENC (see Figure 27-27).

Figure 27-27. Foreman: Puppet classes

You can find more information about Foreman at *https://www.theforeman.org/intro-duction.html (http://theforeman.org/introduction.html)*. There is a Puppet module officially maintained by the Foreman project at *theforeman/foreman (http://bit.ly/1UaPtAr)* on the Puppet Forge.

Foreman is actively developed by RedHat and supporting community members.

Upgrading to the Enterprise Console

Puppet Enterprise provides a full-featured dashboard within the Enterprise Console. The Enterprise Console is a completely rewritten replacement for the Puppet Dashboard that utilizes PuppetDB. It includes all of the functionality provided by the original dashboard, and adds enterprise features and functionality.

Viewing Status

The Enterprise Console provides a clean overview of node and server status (Figure 27-28).

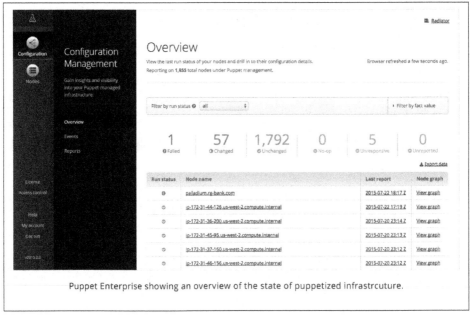

Puppet Enterprise showing an overview of the state of puppetized infrastrcuture.

Figure 27-28. Puppet Enterprise: Configuration management overview

From here you can quickly drill down to review details of any event.

Classifying Nodes

The Enterprise Console provides a rules-based classification engine far more capable than the basic grouping functionality provided by Puppet Dashboard (Figure 27-29).

Figure 27-29. Puppet Enterprise: Node management and classification

In addition to grouping nodes and assigning classes and parameters (as done in Puppet Dashboard), rules can use facts and metadata provided by the node to dynamically assign nodes to groups, and override the environment used by the node. This significantly reduces the monotony of setting up many similar nodes.

Inspecting Events

The Enterprise Console provides an interface to view every resource in the node's catalog to determine the precise reason for the failure (Figure 27-30).

You can click through to find specific details from the attempt to apply the resource on the node. The console provides a visualization of the DAG-model dependency graph of the Puppet catalog, making it possible to visually trace resource relationships.

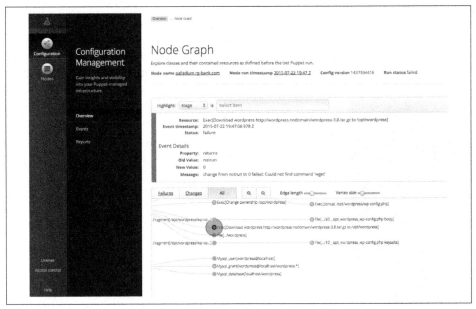

Figure 27-30. Puppet Enterprise: Node graph

Tracking Changes

The Enterprise Console tracks changes on a per-node basis as well as a per-class basis. This makes it easy to determine what changes were applied, and exactly when (Figure 27-31).

Figure 27-31. Puppet Enterprise: Change management

This allows you to quickly see and react to problems that occur when changes are applied to the nodes.

The Reports interface provides detailed insight into Puppet run reports and statistics, as shown in Figure 27-32.

Figure 27-32. Puppet Enterprise: Reports

You can click on a node to see the resources managed on it and their last reported state. Or you can click on the report time and see the history of changes in that report.

Controlling Access

The Enterprise Console provides for granular role-based access control (RBAC). This makes it possible to delegate control over specific resources to individuals and groups within your organization. Users and groups can be defined within the Enterprise Console, or imported from an external authentication mechanism such as LDAP or Microsoft Active Directory.

Evaluating Puppet Enterprise

You can find a comparison of Puppet Open Source and Puppet Enterprise at "What Puppet Enterprise Brings to Puppet" (*http://bit.ly/1UHmNgx*) on the Puppet Labs website.

A detailed list of the Puppet Enterprise features that focuses on the Enterprise Console can be found at "Enterprise Features" (*https://puppetlabs.com/puppet/commercial*) on the Puppet Labs website.

Puppet Enterprise can be downloaded from the Puppet Labs website and evaluated for free at "Puppet Enterprise Download" (*https://puppetlabs.com/puppet-enterprise-download*).

Finding Plugins and Tools

Following is a short list of tools and plugins that you may find useful. Each of the following descriptions came from the README of the project. I've added comments in italics for clarification purposes where necessary:

https://github.com/manuq/puppet-dashboard-nodefiles-plugin
Plugin for Puppet Dashboard to add arbitrary files from nodes.

https://github.com/garethr/puppet-shelf
A Puppet report processor and a web service that consumes a report and *colorfully* displays the current state of your Puppet agents. This focuses on two things I think are important: Puppet run time and number of failures during a run.

https://github.com/xaque208/puppetdashboardmonitor
A tool for monitoring the highlights of Puppet Dashboard. *For example, you can use this to create alarms in a monitoring system for failed Puppet runs.*

https://github.com/simonswine/zabbix-puppetdashboard
This template allows *you* to monitor *and graph* Puppet reports via Puppet Dashboard *in Zabbix.*

https://github.com/homeaway/puppetlinker
A Chrome extension that finds all references to a Puppet file (*.pp*) from Puppet Dashboard and links them back to a source control repo (e.g., GitHub) where that file *originated.*

https://github.com/skylost/puppetdash-rundeck
A simple Ruby application to integrate Puppet Dashboard with Rundeck. *This gets a node list from Puppet Dashboard in the XML format used by Rundeck APIs for building lists.*

To find other projects, query GitHub for "puppet dashboard" (*https://github.com/ search?q=puppet+dashboard*). Keep in mind that many things on GitHub sound like good ideas but appear to have been abandoned or never started.

## CHAPTER 28

Running the Puppet Agent on Windows

The fastest-growing segment of Puppet users is companies who utilize Puppet agent to manage their Windows nodes. Puppet brings a configuration management toolset (and mindset) to Windows administration far beyond the tools provided by Microsoft. The Windows admins I have met who have become Puppet users cannot imagine how they would do without it now.

Puppet on Windows with the Puppet Labs Supported modules provides the ability to:

- Create, modify, and remove users and groups
- Install and configure applications
- Manage registry keys and values
- Download and execute PowerShell and cmd scripts
- Control icons on the user's desktop
- Build IIS sites and applications
- Install and manage SQL Server

Everything you've already learned about Puppet applies to Puppet on Windows. For the remainder of this chapter, we'll review the differences between Windows and Linux nodes.

Creating a Windows Virtual Machine

If you want to build a Windows virtual machine for testing against the Puppet Server virtual machine used in this book, follow the steps outlined in the following sections.

If you aren't using the Vagrant virtual machines as your learning environment, skip ahead to "Installing Puppet on Windows" on page 423.

Creating a VirtualBox Windows VM

To create a Windows virtual machine, start the VirtualBox Manager program as follows (see Figure 28-1):

- Mac: Applications → VirtualBox
- Windows: Start Menu → Programs|Apps → VirtualBox → VirtualBox Manager

Create a new virtual machine as follows:

1. Click New in the top menu.
2. Give the machine a name.
3. Selected a version of Windows—for example, Windows 10 (64-bit).
4. Click Continue.
5. Select 4096 MB memory size if the arrow remains in the green range.
6. Click through, selecting the defaults for all other options.

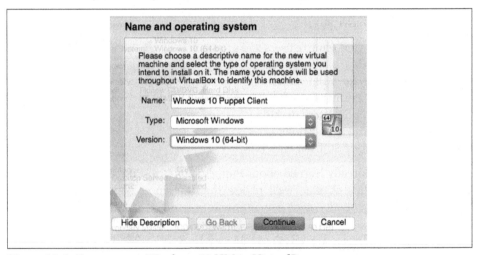

Figure 28-1. Create a new Windows 10 VM in VirtualBox

Adding an Internal Network Adapter

Now attach an internal network interface used to communicate with the Puppet server as follows (see Figure 28-2):

1. Return to the VirtualBox Manager program.
2. Select the Windows VM in the left sidebar, then click Settings.
3. Click Network in the top menu bar.
4. Select Adapter 2 in the tab bar.
5. Check Enable Network Adapter.
6. Attached to: Internal Network.
7. Click OK.

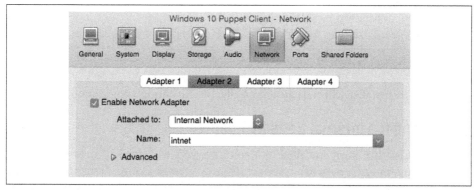

Figure 28-2. Attach Adapter 2 to the Internal Network

Connecting the Windows Installation Media

Acquire an ISO image of the Windows version you would like to install. Windows 10 ISOs can be found on Microsoft's site at "Download Windows 10 Disc Image" (*http://bit.ly/22s4E9o*).

Now make the Windows installation media ISO image available as a mounted drive as follows (see Figure 28-3):

1. Return to the VirtualBox Manager program.
2. Select the Windows VM in the left sidebar, then click Settings.
3. Click Storage in the top menu bar.
4. Select the small DVD icon that says Empty.
5. Click the small DVD icon on the far right.
6. Find the Windows installation media ISO file—for example, *Win10_English_x64.iso*
7. Click OK.
8. Click Start → in the top menu

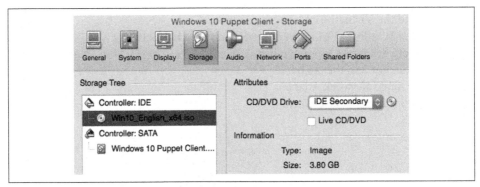

Figure 28-3. Select the Win10 English x64 ISO

The Windows Installer will start automatically. Install Windows as you normally do.

Configuring the Internal Network Adapter

After Windows has been installed and running, you will need to configure the IP address of the internal network interface. Open Network Connections in one of the many ways that Windows provides. In Windows 10, you would do as follows (see Figure 28-4):

1. Click the Windows start menu button on the bottom left.
2. Click Settings.
3. Click the Network & Internet box.
4. Select Ethernet on the left sidebar.
5. Under "Related settings," click "Change adapter options."

The internal network interface will likely be named Ethernet 2. You may want to rename this for convenience.

Figure 28-4. Windows 10: Network connections

Now configure this interface to have an IP on the same network as the Puppet server by performing the following steps (see Figure 28-5):

1. Double-click or right-click on the internal connection and choose Properties.
2. Select Internet Protocol Version 4 (TCP/IPv4) and click Properties.
3. IP address: 192.168.250.21.
4. Subnet mask: 255.255.255.0.
5. Leave all other fields blank and click OK.

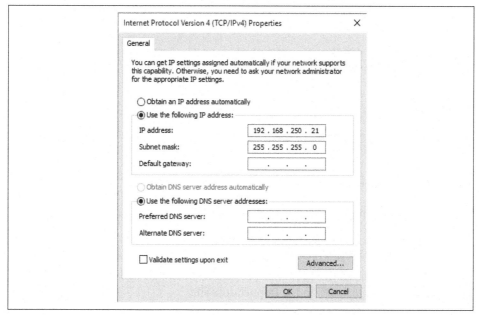

Figure 28-5. Windows IPv4 configuration

On this interface, we configure only a unique IP on the same network as the Puppet server. All other fields are blank as DNS and routing will happen on the primary interface.

Installing Puppet on Windows

Download the Puppet agent for Windows from "Open Source Puppet" (*https://puppet labs.com/puppet/puppet-open-source*) on the Puppet Labs site:

1. Click the options for Open Source until you reach the Installation Instructions screen.
2. Under Download & Install, select Microsoft Windows.
3. From the package list, select *puppet-agent-x64-latest.msi.*
4. Run this installer, accepting the defaults, as shown in Figure 28-6.
5. When prompted for a Puppet server, enter **puppet.example.com** when using the Vagrant instances (or the name of your server if you called it something else).

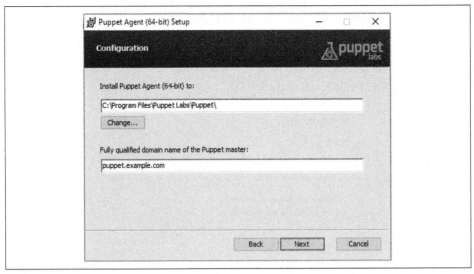

Figure 28-6. Puppet Windows setup

You can also install Puppet noninteractively with the same installer:

```
C:\> msiexec /qn /norestart /i puppet-latest.msi \
     PUPPET_MASTER_SERVER=puppet.example.com
```

You can find a list of all the MSI exec properties at "Installing Puppet: MSI Proper-ties" (*http://bit.ly/1UmSJrM*) on the Puppet docs site.

Configuring Puppet on Windows

On Windows the Puppet configuration file can be found at *C:\ProgramData\Puppet-Labs\puppet\etc\puppet.conf*. This file contains the same configuration settings in the same format as on Linux, but paths with spaces in them must be quoted.

 Do not be confused by the file *C:\Program Files\Puppet Labs \Puppet\puppet\conf\puppet.conf*. This is the same file, but it is not used by the Puppet agent.

Check the *puppet.conf* file to ensure it contains the following:

```
[agent]
    server = puppet.example.com
```

The file as installed by default should work as well. Just ensure that the server name is correct:

```
[main]
  server=puppet.example.com
  pluginsync=true
  autoflush=true
  environment=production
```

Then edit the hosts file at *C:\Windows\System32\drivers\etc\hosts* to add an entry for the Puppet server. You can do this from an administrator Command Prompt with the following commands:

```
C:\> set hostspath=%windir%\System32\drivers\etc\hosts
C:\> echo 192.168.250.6 puppet.example.com >> %hostspath%
```

Running Puppet Interactively

The Puppet installer creates a folder in the Start menu with shortcuts to Puppet documentation, and direct invocation of many Puppet commands, including `Facter` and `Puppet Agent` (see Figure 28-7). Each of these will request elevated privileges in order to run.

Figure 28-7. Puppet Start menu items

After installation, when you start Command Prompt or PowerShell, you'll find the Puppet command in your `PATH` by default. Running Puppet commands with or without elevated privileges behaves exactly the same as running Puppet commands on Linux with or without sudo.

The menu option "Start Command Prompt with Puppet" initializes a command prompt with many Puppet installation directories in the PATH. Furthermore, the environment will contain the necessary settings for using Ruby gem and related commands. Start this command prompt and run set by itself to see the values for:

- FACTER_DIR
- FACTER_env_windows_installdir
- HIERA_DIR
- MCOLLECTIVE_DIR
- PL_BASEDIR
- PUPPET_DIR
- RUBYLIB
- SSL_CERT_DIR
- SSL_CERT_FILE

Every command shown in this chapter will need to be run with administrator privileges. The best way to execute these commands is to right-click on "Start Command Prompt with Puppet" and select "Run as administrator," as shown in Figure 28-8.

Figure 28-8. Start Command Prompt with Puppet -> Run as administrator

The alternative is to preface each command with the following: runas /noprofile/ user:Administrator, which is the Windows equivalent of sudo.

Starting the Puppet Service

The Puppet agent must run with elevated privileges. You can select one of two Start menu items:

- Command Prompt
- Start Command Prompt with Puppet

Either one needs to be started by right-clicking and choosing "Run as administrator."

Use the following commands to stop, start, and query the Puppet service on Windows:

```
C:\> sc stop puppet
C:\> sc start puppet
C:\> sc query puppet
```

You can configure the service to start at boot or run only on demand. Choose the appropriate command:

```
C:\> sc config puppet start= disabled
C:\> sc config puppet start= auto
C:\> sc config puppet start= demand
```

 The space after the equals sign is necessary!

Debugging Puppet Problems

To run the Puppet service with debug output, use the following command arguments:

```
C:\> sc stop puppet
C:\> sc start puppet --debug --logdest eventlog
```

You'll find detailed Puppet debugging in the Windows Event Viewer.

You can find more suggestions for debugging at "Troubleshooting Puppet on Windows" (*http://bit.ly/1Wwcueo*) on the Puppet docs site.

Writing Manifests for Windows

For most things, writing Puppet manifests for Windows hosts is identical to writing them for Linux hosts, with some fairly straightforward exceptions:

Semicolon path separator
Windows uses a semicolon for path separation instead of a colon.

Case-insensitive
Files, users, groups, and random other attributes are case-insensitive on Windows but case-sensitive within Puppet. Windows users need to be aware of case when writing manifests.

Windows service name
> Always use the Windows short name for the service, not the display name.

Filesystem paths
> Puppet uses forward slashes for filesystem paths even on Windows. This works most of the time in my experience, but you'll need to use backslashes in a limited set of cases, documented at "Handling File Paths on Windows" (*http://bit.ly/1RrbUu9*) on the Puppet docs site.

Double backslash in double quotes
> As the backslash is an escape character used to prevent interpolation, backslashes inside double quotes need to have an additional backslash to indicate that it was the intended character. Alternatively, place the entire path inside single quotes.

Line endings
> Everyone loves line feeds versus carriage-return/line-feed differences, don't they? Unfortunately, this means you'll need to edit file sources or templates for Windows hosts to contain the CR/LF line-ending combination. (If you make your own resource providers, the `flat` filetype can handle this translation for you.)

You can find the latest tips for writing manifests for Windows hosts on the Puppet docs site at "Puppet on Windows: Writing Manifests" (*http://bit.ly/1XAzOb9*).

Finding Windows-Specific Modules

There is a combined package of the Puppet Forge's best Windows modules available in the *puppetlabs/windows* (*https://forge.puppetlabs.com/puppetlabs/windows*) collection on the Puppet Forge.

A few of my personal favorites on the Puppet Forge above and beyond this collection are:

opentable/windowsfeature (http://bit.ly/1Lv9yy5)
> Disable or enable Windows Server features.

puppetlabs/inifile (http://bit.ly/1pyMqVM)
> Manage settings in INI files.

You can find other modules that support Windows by performing a Puppet Forge search filtered with Operating System = Windows (*http://bit.ly/1PgM4aR*).

When you attempt to use Puppet to upgrade a package on Windows, you'll get an unexpected result:

```
Failed to apply catalog: Parameter ensure failed on Package[thing]:
  Provider must have features 'upgradeable' to set 'ensure' to 'latest'
```

That's right—the built-in package management in Windows doesn't allow for upgrades of packages.

You might be wishing you had the Yum or Apt package managers on Windows right about now. The good news that something similar exists, and has been used successfully at thousands of sites. The Chocolatey (*https://chocolatey.org/about*) package manager provides an API for automated installation and removal of packages:

> [Chocolatey] was designed to be a decentralized framework for quickly installing applications and tools that you need. It is built on the NuGet infrastructure currently using PowerShell as its focus for delivering packages from the distros to your door, err computer.

The Puppet module to use Chocolatey can be found at *chocolatey/chocolatey* (*https:// forge.puppetlabs.com/chocolatey/chocolatey*) on the Puppet Forge.

 Even Microsoft has added support for the Chocolatey package repositories, as explained in the Windows Management Framework V5 Preview (*http://bit.ly/1RpnlbK*).

Concluding Thoughts on Puppet Windows

Adding your Windows servers to Puppet will give you consistent management of Windows resources in a way that you'd never believe if I tried to describe it to you.

In many organizations, this creates social dynamic changes that were hard to imagine a decade ago. It will break down the door between your Linux and Windows support teams, allowing each to benefit from the knowledge and experience of the other. Be prepared to embrace this opportunity.

## CHAPTER 29

Customizing Environments

Way back at the beginning of Part II, you set up testing and production environments. Now that you've learned more about Puppet, Puppet servers, and deployment methodologies, it's time to talk about how to use environments effectively.

Environments provide isolation for modules and data. They provide useful ways to organize and separate modules and configuration data for different requirements. There are numerous reasons that people divide systems into different environments, but here are just a few:

- Support multiple team environments with different needs but some shared code
- Distinguish evolutions of product development (stable, beta, staging, test, dev)
- Avoid conflicts for dependency modules that share names
- Isolate security-sensitive data
- Stage tests for bug fixes or feature changes

In this chapter, we'll discuss how to use environments for all of these purposes.

Even if you don't think you need separate environments, I encourage you to read through this chapter so that you can consider what environments have to offer you. Even the smallest Puppet sites use environments, and there are good reasons for that.

Understanding Environment Isolation

An environment is not a namespace—it's a hard wall where a module or data either exists in the environment or not. Two Puppet nodes requesting data from two environments might as well be talking to two different Puppet servers. You can have the same data or the same modules in multiple environments, but neither is shared by default.

To make it really clear:

- A module that doesn't appear in the `modulepath` of an environment doesn't exist for that environment. This means that two modules with the same name can exist without collision in two different environments.
- Data that is not loaded for an environment does not exist, and cannot be referenced within the environment (barring someone writing a module that peeks into another environment path on the filesystem to read their data).

This isolation enables many ways of working across teams, business units, and diverse requirements. We'll show you how to utilize all of these features here.

Enabling Directory Environments

Unlike previous versions of Puppet, environments are enabled "out of the box" with Puppet 4. No configuration changes are necessary.

Puppet 4 expects to find a directory for each environment in the location specified by the `$environmentpath` configuration setting, which defaults to */etc/puppetlabs/code/ environments*. Each directory within this path is an environment. Within each environment should exist the following:

environment.conf file
An optional file to customize the environment.

hieradata directory
Configuration data for the environment.

manifests
Location for manifest files outside of any modules. In modern practice, this is only used for setting resource defaults for the environment.

modules
Location for modules, whether downloaded from the Puppet Forge or created on your own.

The default environment for Puppet nodes is *production*. With a default configuration file, Puppet 4 expects your modules to be installed at */etc/puppetlabs/code/environments/production/modules*. The default Hiera configuration expects data for your environment to be at */etc/puppetlabs/code/environments/production/hieradata*.

There is one additional place that Puppet will look for modules: the directories specified by `$basemodulepath`. This defaults to */etc/puppetlabs/code/modules*. Any modules you place inside this directory will be shared among all modules.

Assigning Environments to Nodes

By default, a client informs the Puppet server which environment to use based on the configuration file setting, command-line input, or the default of *production*. This makes it easy for you to test module or data changes using a test environment by running `puppet agent` with a different environment on the command line.

A node terminus or ENC can assign a different environment to the client than the one it requested.

> This can be particularly useful when environment separations are done for security reasons—can't let nodes change environments just by asking...

For this reason, there are no per-environment settings for ENCs, as the ENC must be queried before the environment is chosen.

Configuring an Environment

Within each environment directory can exist an optional *environment.conf* file. This has the same configuration format as other Puppet configuration files, but does not support sections.

> It's perfectly fine, and quite common, to leave out this file and accept the defaults. Many organizations never need to change these values.

Environment configuration files are parsed after the main configuration file, so configuration options defined in the Puppet configuration file can be used within the environment configuration. The following settings are allowed in this file:

config_version
> A script that can be run to provide a configuration version number. If this is not specified, the current *epoch time* will be used as a configuration version.

manifest
> The manifest file or directory that will be read before catalogs are built for this environment. It defaults to the value of the global setting `default_manifest`, which defaults to the *manifests/* directory within the environment directory.

modulepath

> A list of directories to load modules from. Defaults to the *modules/* directory of this environment, followed by basemodulepath. The module path will be searched until the first location is found that contains a directory with that module name. Modules that exist in multiple directories are never merged.

environment_data_provider

> The name of a data provider class, or function to indicate that a function will be used to provide the environment data. By default, no environment data provider is configured.

environment_timeout

> This sets a per-environment cache timeout. You may want to set a value of 0 for environments undergoing active development, such as a temporary bugfix environment. Stable environments should use a value of unlimited.

Best Practice

Set the environment timeout at unlimited and use a trigger to refresh the Puppet environment cache whenever new code is deployed. Using a value other than 0 will cause inconsistent cache states between server threads. More details can be found in "Invalidating the Environment Cache" on page 447.

Here is an example environment configuration file. This file shows the default values, as if the configuration file did not exist. Any relative paths within the environment configuration file are interpreted relative to the environment directory:

```
# Defaults to $environmentpath/$environment/manifests
manifest = manifests

# Defaults to $environmentpath/$environment/modules:$basemodulepath
modulepath = modules:$basemodulepath

# Environment data provider
#environment_data_provider = 'function'  # If a 'data' function is provided
#environment_data_provider = 'hiera'     # If a hiera.yaml exists
                                         # in the environment

# Cache until API call to clear cache is received
environment_timeout = unlimited

# A script to supply a configuration version
#config_version = (a script)
```

You can review a specific environment's settings using the following command:

```
$ puppet config print --environment environment
```

It is entirely possible (albeit unintuitive) for you to use a different environment path for puppet apply versus puppet agent when using a server. You do so by changing environmentpath in the [agent] section of the Puppet configuration file. You can check the agent's settings like so:

```
$ puppet config print --section agent --environment environment
```

Choosing a Manifest Path

The manifest path can point to a specific file or a directory. If the target is a directory, every manifest *.pp* file in the directory will be read in alphabetical order. It can also point to a specific file, in which case only that single file will be read.

In older versions of Puppet it was common or necessary to assign classes to nodes in a *manifests/site.pp* file. That is no longer necessary or common practice. Assign classes to nodes using Hiera data or with a node terminus (ENC).

Best Practice

All code should reside in modules. You should assign classes using Hiera hierarchies. Independent manifests should contain only resource defaults for the environment.

There is a global configuration setting, disable_per_environment_manifest, that overrides the environment setting for manifest. If it's set to true, then the target of default_manifest is used regardless of which environment the client is associated with. This can be used to centralize resource defaults across all environments.

Utilizing Hiera Hierarchies

Another global constant across all environments is the Hiera configuration file. At this time, there is only one Hiera configuration file common to all environments.

The Hiera configuration we recommended for testing in this book sources all data from the same directory, regardless of which environment the node is using. This works well for single-purpose servers, where the nonproduction environments are only for testing changes:

```
:yaml:
  :datadir: /etc/puppetlabs/code/hieradata
```

If you have multiple teams using environments for delegation of control, then you very likely want to separate the data as well. This is easy, as the environment of the client is known before the Hiera configuration is parsed, which allows you to use the environment path within the Hiera hierarchy. Simply alter the data directory to include the $::environment variable:

```
  :yaml:
    :datadir: /etc/puppetlabs/code/environments/%{::environment}/hieradata
  :json:
    :datadir: /etc/puppetlabs/code/environments/%{::environment}/hieradata
```

A frequently asked question is how to have a separate Hiera hierarchy per environment. You can do this by creating an Hiera data source specific to the environment. We'll cover how to manage environment data sources next.

Binding Data Providers in Environments

As discussed in "Binding Data Providers in Modules" on page 242, in Puppet 3 and earlier, data for manifests and classes had to be provided within the module, or sourced from the sole global data provider: Hiera.

Puppet 4.3 introduced a tiered, pluggable approach to data access called *Puppet Lookup*. As discussed in "Accepting Input" on page 166, parameter values are automatically sourced from the following locations in order:

1. The global data provider (Hiera v3)
2. The environment data provider specified in *environment.conf*
3. The module data provider specified in *metadata.json*

There are only two steps to provide a data source specific to an environment:

1. Define environment_data_provider in the *environment.conf* file.
2. Create a function or a Hiera configuration file as the data source.

 Data providers in environments can replace the use of ::environ ment in the global Hiera :datadir:.

The net effect of this change is that each environment can select a custom data hierarchy while continuing to utilize shared global data. This can be especially useful when environments are used by distinct teams with their own data management practices.

Querying Data from a Function

Create a function named environment::data(), as described in "Defining Functions" on page 225.

The function can be a Puppet language function defined in *${environmentpath}/${environment}/functions/data.pp*, or it can be a Ruby function defined in *${environmentpath}/${environment}/lib/puppet/functions/environment/data.rb*.

A Ruby function would look much like this:

```
Puppet::Functions.create_function(:'environment::data') do
  def data()
    # the following is just example code to be replaced
    # Return a hash with parameter name to value mapping for the user class
    return {
      'specialapp::user::id'   => 'Default for parameter $id',
      'specialapp::user::name' => 'Default for parameter $name',
    }
  end
end
```

Replace this simple example function with your own. The `data()` function must return a hash with keys containing the entire class name, exactly the same as how keys must be defined in Hiera.

 This is very similar but not exactly the same as creating a module data source. The function name does not change based on the environment name, which allows the same function to be used in different environments.

To enable this function as an environment data source, modify the *environment.conf* file to set `environment_data_provider = function`:

```
# Environment data provider
environment_data_provider = 'function'
```

The environment data function will be queried after the Hiera global source, and before the module's data source.

Querying Data from Hiera

To enable the Hiera data source for your module, modify the *environment.conf* in the environment directory to set `environment_data_provider = hiera`.

Create a *hiera.yaml* in the same directory that defines a Hiera hierarchy for the environment. The file is named the same, but uses a v4 configuration format different from, the global Hiera configuration file.

The *hiera.yaml* file defines where to find the Hiera data, and how to merge results (if applicable). The file must contain a `version` key with value 4, and a `datadir` that identifies a path relative to, and contained within, the environment directory. The `hierarchy` in the file must be an array of hashes. An example file is shown here:

```
---
version: 4
datadir: hieradata
hierarchy:
  - name: "Hostname"
    backend: json
    path: "hostname/%{trusted.hostname}

  - name: "common"
    backend: yaml
```

Create the *hieradata/* directory specified in the file, and populate Hiera data files with data specific to this environment.

 This environment data provider will be called after the global Hiera data provider, and before the module's data provider, for all catalogs built in this environment.

Strategizing How to Use Environments

In this section, we're going to document some well-known patterns for development, and how to structure the environments to support those patterns.

Promoting Change Through Layers

The most common development strategy is to develop changes to a module on a feature branch. Merge that module's changes to *master* for testing. Then tag a new branch or merge to an existing release branch to push the changes into production.

It is easy to support this development workflow with a fixed set of environments. The environments would be structured and used as shown in Table 29-1.

Table 29-1. Simple trio of environments for development, testing, and production

Environment	Branch name	Description
dev	dev	Develop and test changes here.
test	master	Merge to master and test on production-like nodes.
production	master	Push master to production nodes and/or Puppet servers.

While the branch names and the steps involved differ slightly from team to team, this is a well-known strategy that many development teams use, and every code management tool is capable of implementing. In a small environment, or with a small DevOps team, this might be sufficient.

A small variation, outlined in Table 29-2, can support many more engineers, including feature and hotfix branches working on the same module at the same time. A new environment is created for each feature branch. After testing is complete, the change is merged to *test* for testing against a production-like environment. The feature branch environment is destroyed when the change is merged to master and pushed to production.

Table 29-2. Per-feature environments with stable test and production instances

Environment	Branch name	Description
feature_name	feature_name	A new branch for a single feature or bugfix
test	test	Merge to test for review, Q/A, automated tests, etc.
production	master	Merge to master and push to production. Destroy feature branch.

You can utilize any method that supports your workflow. Tables 29-1 and 29-2 show two basic and common structures.

Whichever strategy you use, with a small set of environments that track a single common master branch, you can use Puppet with "out of the box" defaults.

Solving One-Off Problems Using Environments

It is very common to have a test environment where changes to modules are tried out. That's exactly what we created in Chapter 10. This might serve your needs for testing new modules if you're part of a small team.

It is often necessary to test changes in isolation, avoiding other modules in a different stage of development, when you're fixing a production problem. In this scenario, it's a good practice to use a one-off test environment.

Simply go into the *$codedir/environments/* directory and create a new environment named for the problem. I tend to use the ticket number of the problem I'm working on, but any valid environment name, such as your login name or even *annoying_bug/*, will work.

There are two strategies for doing this. One is to check out everything from the production environment into this environment's diretory. Another is to set modulepath to include the production environment's modules directory (*$environmentpath/production/modules/*), and then check out only the problematic module into this environment's *modules/* directory. Here is an *environment.conf* file that implements that strategy:

```
environment_timeout = 0
manifest = $environmentpath/production/manifests
modulepath = ./modules:$environmentpath/production/modules:$basemodulepath
```

Check out only the modules related to this bug in the testing environment's module directory. When looking for modules, the server will find the module you are working on first. All other modules will be found in the production module directory. This allows you to work on a quick fix without pulling in dozens or hundreds of unrelated modules.

 This is suitable for small fixes, but the copy-of-everything approach provides more isolation and may be necessary in some situations, depending on how your integration testing is performed.

When the problem is solved and merged back to the production code base, rm -r the one-off environment and go grab a cup of your favorite poison.

 Don't forget to copy or symlink *hiera.yaml* and your Hiera data directory if you are using an environment data provider.

Supporting Diverse Teams with Environments

Environments allow diverse teams to segregate their code and data according to their own standards. This allows for the freedom of self-direction, while also letting both teams share common code and organization data.

To give each team freedom with its own modules and data, start with the following configuration and adjust as necessary for your teams:

1. Put shared modules in a directory specified in basemodulepath, usually */etc/ puppetlabs/code/modules/*.
2. Put global Hiera data in the */etc/puppetlabs/code/hieradata* directory.
3. Put team modules in the */etc/puppetlabs/code/environments/team/modules* directory.
4. Enable hiera as the environment data provider in */etc/puppetlabs/code/environments/<team>/environment.conf*.
5. Define a team-specific Hiera hierarchy in */etc/puppetlabs/code/environments/ <team>/hiera.yaml*.
6. Put team data in the */etc/puppetlabs/code/environments/<team>/hieradata/* directory.

The per-environment Hiera hierarchy should contain only data specific to this team's nodes. There's no performance impact because even if Puppet doesn't cache the environment data, this data is used for every catalog build so these files always reside in the filesystem cache.

Managing Environments with r10k

Environments provide a useful separation that allows independent development of new features and bug fixes. However, it does enable a diverse structure of many modules in multiple states of development. Tracking dependencies would be a nightmare without a tool to manage this. *r10k* provides a way to track and manage dependencies that snaps right into a branch-oriented workflow.

 Puppet Enterprise includes r10k in the Code Manager (*http://bit.ly/1PgKhCq*) installation, which makes the following step unnecessary.

Create a cache directory for r10k and make it writable by the vagrant user before installing the r10k gem:

```
sudo mkdir /var/cache/r10k
sudo chown vagrant /var/cache/r10k
$ sudo gem install r10k
Fetching: r10k-2.2.0.gem (100%)
Successfully installed r10k-2.2.0
Parsing documentation for r10k-2.2.0
Installing ri documentation for r10k-2.2.0
1 gem installed
```

Listing Modules in the Puppetfile

Within each environment directory, create a file named *Puppetfile*. Following is an example that should be pretty easy to understand:

```
# Puppet forge
forge "http://forge.puppetlabs.com"
moduledir = 'modules'   # relative path to environment (default)

# Puppet Forge modules
mod "puppetlabs/inifile", "1.4.1"   # get a specific version
mod "puppetlabs/stdlib"             # get latest, don't update thereafter
mod "jorhett/mcollective", :latest  # update to latest version every time

# track master from GitHub
mod 'puppet-systemstd',
  :git => 'https://github.com/jorhett/puppet-systemstd.git'
```

```
# Get a specific release from GitHub
mod 'puppetlabs-strings',
    :git     => 'https://github.com/puppetlabs/puppetlabs-strings.git',
    #:branch => 'yard-dev'          # an alternate branch

    # Define which version to install using one of the following
    :ref     => '0.2.0'            # a specific version
    #:tag     => '0.1.1'           # or specific tag
    #:commit => '346832a5f88a0ec43d' # or specific commit
```

As you can see, this format lets you control the source and the version on a module-by-module basis. Development environments might track the `master` branch to get the latest module updates, whereas production environments can lock in to release versions. This allows each environment individual levels of specification and control.

You can validate the *Puppetfile* syntax using the `puppetfile check` command. This only works when you are in the environment directory containing the *Puppetfile* and *modules/* subdirectory:

```
[vagrant@client ~]$ cd /etc/puppetlabs/code/environments/test
[vagrant@client test]$ r10k puppetfile check
Syntax OK
```

r10k can remove any module not specified in the *Puppetfile*. This can be especially useful after a major update has been merged, where some modules are no longer necessary:

```
[vagrant@client ~]$ cd /etc/puppetlabs/code/environments/test
[vagrant@client test]$ r10k puppetfile purge -v
INFO -> Removing unmanaged path
  /etc/puppetlabs/code/environments/test/modules/now-obsolete
```

 The purge command will silently wipe out any module that you forgot to add to the *Puppetfile*. Always use -v or --verbose when performing a purge.

To prevent r10k from wiping out a module you are building, you can add an entry to the *Puppetfile* that tells r10k to ignore it:

```
# still hacking on this
mod 'my-test', :local => true
```

Creating a Control Repository

Create a new repository to contain a map of environments in use. This is called a *control repository*.

If you are unsure of how or where to place a control repository, follow the instructions in "Publishing a Module on GitHub" on page 285 to create a new GitHub repository.

Add the following files from your production environment:

- *environment.conf*
- A *Puppetfile*
- The *manifests/* directory and everything in it
- The *hieradata/* directory (optional)

If you want to import from your existing setup, the process could look something like this:

```
[vagrant@client ~]$ cd /etc/puppetlabs/code/environments/production
[vagrant@client production]$ git init
[vagrant@client production]$ git checkout -b production
Switched to a new branch 'production'
[vagrant@client production]$ git add environment.conf
[vagrant@client production]$ git add Puppetfile
[vagrant@client production]$ git add manifests
[vagrant@client production]$ git commit -m "production environment"
[production (root-commit) 7204191] production environment
 3 files changed, 71 insertions(+)
 create mode 100644 environment.conf
[vagrant@client production]$ git remote add origin \
    https://github.com/example/control-repo.git
[vagrant@client production]$ git push --set-upstream origin production
Counting objects: 3, done.
Compressing objects: 100% (2/2), done.
Writing objects: 100% (3/3), 657 bytes | 0 bytes/s, done.
Total 3 (delta 0), reused 0 (delta 0)
To https://github.com/jorhett/control-repo-test.git
 * [new branch]      production -> production
Branch production set up to track remote branch production from origin.
```

 Don't forget to change the branch name as the first step. This will avoid creating a master branch that you need to remove.

If you want to start from an existing example, clone the Puppet Labs control repository template (*https://github.com/puppetlabs/control-repo*).

Configuring r10k Sources

You'll need to create an r10k configuration file at */etc/puppetlabs/r10k/r10.yaml*. You can install one from the learning repository we've been using with this command:

```
$ mkdir /etc/puppetlabs/r10k
$ cp /vagrant/etc-puppet/r10k.yaml /etc/puppetlabs/r10k/
```

Edit the file to list your control repository as a source. The file should look like this:

```
# The location to use for storing cached Git repos
cachedir: '/var/cache/r10k'

# A list of repositories to create
sources:
  # Clone the Git repository and instantiate an environment per branch
  example:
    basedir: '/etc/puppetlabs/code/environments'
    remote: 'git@github.com:jorhett/learning-mcollective'
    prefix: false

# An optional command to be run after deployment
#postrun: ['/path/to/command','--opt1','arg1','arg2']
```

You can list multiple sources for teams with their own control repositories. Enable the `prefix` option if the same branch name exists in multiple sources. As almost every control repo has the *production* branch, this will almost always be necessary:

```
sources:
  storefront:
    basedir: '/etc/puppetlabs/code/environments'
    remote: 'git@github.com:example/storefront-control'
    prefix: true

  warehouse:
    basedir: '/etc/puppetlabs/code/environments'
    remote: 'git@github.com:example/warehouse-control'
    prefix: true
```

Adding New Environments

Create a branch of this repository for each environment in the *$codedir/environments* directory, as shown here:

```
[vagrant@client ~]$ cd /etc/puppetlabs/code/environments
[vagrant@client environments]$ git clone production test
[vagrant@client production]$ cd test
[vagrant@client test]$ git checkout -b test
```

If the environment directory already exists inside the specified `basedir`, the `clone` command will fail. You may want to rename the existing environment directory, then move the files to the newly created repository:

```
[vagrant@client production]$ mv test test.backup
[vagrant@client environments]$ git clone production test
[vagrant@client production]$ cd test
[vagrant@client test]$ git checkout -b test
[vagrant@client test]$ mv ../test.backup/* ./
```

Make any changes that are specific to the test environment, then commit the repository back to the control repo with the following commands:

```
[vagrant@client production]$ git add changed files
[vagrant@client production]$ git commit -m "adding test environment"
[vagrant@client production]$ git push --set-upstream origin test
```

Follow this process any time you wish to create a new environment. No changes to
the r10k configuration are necessary, as each branch is automatically checked out into
an environment path of the same name.

Populating a New Installation

Now that you have configured everything, use the display command to see what
r10k would do for you:

```
[vagrant@puppetmaster environments]$ r10k deploy display -v
example (/etc/puppetlabs/code/environments)
    - test
        modules:
            - inifile
            - stdlib
            - mcollective
            - systemstd
            - strings
    - production
        modules:
            - inifile
            - stdlib
            - mcollective
            - systemstd
            - strings
```

That looks exactly like what we have configured. Now you can either move to another
server that doesn't have this environment data, or you can move it aside:

```
[vagrant@client ~]$ cd /etc/puppetlabs/code
[vagrant@client code]$ mv environments environments.backup
```

Now redeploy your environments using r10k, as shown here:

```
[vagrant@client ~]$ r10k deploy environment -p -v
Deploying environment /etc/puppetlabs/code/environments/test
Deploying module /etc/puppetlabs/code/environments/test/modules/inifile
Deploying module /etc/puppetlabs/code/environments/test/modules/stdlib
Deploying module /etc/puppetlabs/code/environments/test/modules/mcollective
Deploying module /etc/puppetlabs/code/environments/test/modules/systemstd
```

```
Deploying module /etc/puppetlabs/code/environments/test/modules/strings
Deploying environment /etc/puppetlabs/code/environments/production
Deploying module /etc/puppetlabs/code/environments/production/modules/inifile
Deploying module /etc/puppetlabs/code/environments/production/modules/stdlib
Deploying module /etc/puppetlabs/code/environments/production/modules/mcollective
Deploying module /etc/puppetlabs/code/environments/production/modules/systemstd
Deploying module /etc/puppetlabs/code/environments/production/modules/strings
```

It's that easy to deploy your environments on a Puppet server or on a Vagrant instance for testing purposes. Anyone with access to the control repo can re-create the known state of every environment in a minute. You can use this approach for building new Puppet servers, staging infrastructure, or development setups on your laptop. Seriously, it doesn't get easier than this.

When a module is added or upgraded, the changes can be tested in one environment and then merged from the development branch to production.

Updating a Single Environment

To check out or update the files in an environment (*environment.conf*, *Puppetfile*, modules, etc.), use this command:

```
[vagrant@puppetmaster ~]$ r10k deploy environment test -v
```

To update the modules specified by an environment's *Puppetfile*, use this command:

```
[vagrant@puppetmaster ~]$ r10k deploy environment test --puppetfile -v
```

You can update a specific module in all environments, or just one environment:

```
[vagrant@puppetmaster ~]$ r10k deploy module stdlib -v
[vagrant@puppetmaster ~]$ r10k deploy module -e test mcollective -v
```

 r10k operates silently unless you supply the -v verbose option. The purge command will silently remove modules that aren't listed in the *Puppetfile*. Always use -v or --verbose when performing destructive operations.

When you are comfortable using r10k, you may wish to utilize r10k commands within Git post-commit hooks, in Jenkins jobs, or through MCollective to automatically push out changes to environments.

Replicating Hiera Data

When using environment-specific Hiera data, you'll want to deploy the Hiera data along with the modules. In that situation, add the *hiera.yaml* and *hieradata/* directory to the control repo. This is a common strategy when the same people edit the code and the data.

When the data in every environment is similar, an alternative strategy is to place all Hiera data within its own repo, and utilize r10k to install the data separately from the code. This is useful when you have different permissions or deployment processes for data changes and code changes.

To enable automatic data checkout, add the hiera Hepo as a source to the r10k configuration file */etc/puppetlabs/r10k/r10.yaml*:

```
sources:
  control:
    basedir: '/etc/puppetlabs/code/environments'
    remote: 'git@github.com:example/control'
    prefix: false

  hiera:
    basedir: '/etc/puppetlabs/code/hieradata'
    remote: 'git@github.com:example/hieradata'
    prefix: false
```

Then add `data_provider = hiera` to *environment.conf*, or add the environment directory to the global data provider by using the `$::environment` variable in */etc/puppetlabs/code/hiera.yaml*:

```
:yaml:
  :datadir: /etc/puppetlabs/code/environments/%{::environment}/hieradata
```

This setup requires that the branch names in both the code and data repositories are identical, as the branch name determines the environment directory in which the data will be installed.

Invalidating the Environment Cache

As mentioned in "Configuring an Environment" on page 433, it is best practice to configure stable environments with `environment_timeout` set to `infinite`. This provides the highest performance for remote clients.

After pushing a change to the environment, you will need to ask the server to invalidate the environment cache. A trigger like this can be easily created in Jenkins, Travis CI, or any other code deployment tool.

Environment cache invalidation is a new API on Puppet Server. This is not possible with a Puppet master.

Create a client key for this purpose. Do not use a node key, as this key will be assigned special privileges. Create a unique key with a name that makes the purpose obvious:

```
[jenkins@client ~]$ puppet config set server puppet.example.com
[jenkins@client ~]$ puppet agent --certname code-deployment --test --noop
Info: Creating a new SSL key for code-deployment
Info: csr_attributes file loading from /etc/puppetlabs/puppet/csr_attributes.yaml
Info: Creating a new SSL certificate request for code-deployment
Info: Certificate Request fingerprint (SHA256):
    96:27:9B:FE:EB:48:1B:7B:28:BC:CD:FB:01:C8:37:B8:5B:29:02:59:D7:31:F8:80:8A:53
Exiting; no certificate found and waitforcert is disabled
```

Authorize the key on the Puppet server with `puppet cert sign` if autosign is not enabled. Then rerun with the following command:

```
[jenkins@client ~]$ puppet config set server puppet.example.com
[jenkins@client ~]$ puppet agent --certname code-deployment --no-daemonize --noop
```

At this point, you have a key and certificate signed by the Puppet CA. Next, add rules to permit this certificate access to delete the environment cache in */etc/puppetlabs/ puppetserver/conf.d/auth.conf* file. The bolded section shown here should be added prior to the default deny rule:

```
# Allow code deployment certificate to invalidate the environment cache
{
    match-request: {
        path: "/puppet-admin-api/v1/environment-cache"
        type: path
        method: delete
    }
    allow: [ code-deployment ]
    sort-order: 200
    name: "environment-cache"
},
{
  # Deny everything else. This ACL is not strictly
```

 These configuration files are HOCON format (a superset of JSON), which does not use single quotes around strings. Double-quote the certificate names or leave them unquoted.

Restart the Puppet Server service in order to activate the change.

```
[vagrant@puppetserver ~]$ sudo systemctl restart puppetserver
```

At this point, you should be able to invalidate the cache by supplying the code deployment key and certificate with your request. Here's an example using the `curl` command:

```
[jenkins@client ~]$ ln -s .puppetlabs/etc/puppet/ssl ssl
[jenkins@client ~]$ curl -i --cert ssl/certs/code-deployment.pem \
    --key ss/private_keys/code-deployment.pem \
    --cacert ssl/certs/ca.pem -X DELETE \
    https://puppet.example.com:8140/puppet-admin-api/v1/environment-cache
HTTP/1.1 204 No Content
```

Build this request into your code deployment mechanism, and you'll get the updated manuscripts immediately after the code push is complete.

204 No Content is the expected response. An error will return a 5xx code.

Restarting JRuby When Updating Plugins

As discussed earlier, Puppet modules can add plugins to be utilized by a Puppet server, such as resource types, functions, providers, and report handlers.

After deploying changes to module plugins, inform Puppet Server of the changes so that it can restart the JRuby instances. This should be added to the deployment process immediately after invalidating the environment cache.

As part of the same deployment automation, utilize the client key created in the previous section for this purpose. Permit this certificate access to restart the JRuby instances in the */etc/puppetlabs/puppetserver/conf.d/auth.conf* file. The bolded section shown here should be added prior to the default deny rule:

```
# Allow code deployment certificate to restart the JRuby instances
{
    match-request: {
        path: "/puppet-admin-api/v1/jruby-pool"
        type: path
        method: delete
    }
    allow: [ code-deployment ]
    sort-order: 200
    name: "jruby-pool"
},
{
    # Deny everything else. This ACL is not strictly
```

These configuration files are HOCON format (a superset of JSON), which does not accept single quotes around strings.

Restart the Puppet Server service in order to activate the change:

```
[vagrant@puppetserver ~]$ sudo systemctl restart puppetserver
```

At this point, you should be able to restart the JRuby pool by supplying the code deployment key and certificate with your request. Here's an example using the curl command:

```
[jenkins@client ~]$ ln -s .puppetlabs/etc/puppet/ssl ssl
[jenkins@client ~]$ curl -i --cert ssl/certs/code-deployment.pem \
    --key ss/private_keys/code-deployment.pem
    --cacert ssl/certs/ca.pem -X DELETE \
    https://puppet.example.com:8140/puppet-admin-api/v1/jruby-pool
HTTP/1.1 204 No Content
```

Build this request into your code deployment mechanism to ensure that changes to functions, report handlers, and other plugins are visible immediately.

Reviewing Environments

In this chapter, you've learned how to:

- Use environments to limit access to data of another team.
- Separate environments to provide independence for teams with different needs.
- Assign environments to nodes in configuration and using ENCs.
- Change the module or manifest path for an environment.
- Customize the paths that Hiera looks in for data files based on the environment name.
- Create a data provider or function and bind it as the environment's data source.
- Set up environments to support feature branches, and test/release strategies.
- Automatically deploy environment code and data.

Don't limit yourself to just the strategies mentioned here. I've covered a few common patterns to provide you with a basic understanding of the choices available, and how to use them. Keep reading, learning, and trying new things.

## CHAPTER 30

Controlling Puppet with MCollective

In this chapter, we will configure and enable the orchestration tool that shipped as part of Puppet 4: the Marionette Collective, or MCollective. You'll learn how to use MCollective to control the Puppet agent on your nodes.

MCollective can:

- Query, start, stop, and restart the Puppet agent.
- Run the Puppet agent with special command-line options.
- Query and make changes to the node using Puppet resources.
- Choose nodes to act on based on the Puppet classes or facts on the node.
- Control concurrency of Puppet runs across a group of nodes.

 If you have used `puppet kick` in the past, you are likely aware that Puppet Labs has obsoleted and has removed support for it in Puppet 4. The MCollective Puppet agent replaces Puppet kick in both the community and Puppet Enterprise product lines, and provides significantly more features and functionality.

Configuring MCollective

In this section, you will:

- Install ActiveMQ to provide middleware on the Puppet server.
- Install the MCollective server on every node.
- Install the MCollective clients on a system of your choice.
- Enable TLS encryption for all connections.
- Install the Puppet agent plugin for ad hoc control of Puppet.

Enabling the Puppet Labs Repository

Puppet Labs provides Yum and Apt repositories containing packages for the MCollective server, clients, and some officially supported plugins. This community repository supplements the OS vendor repositories for the more popular Linux distributions.

Install that repository as follows:

```
$ sudo yum install http://yum.puppetlabs.com/puppetlabs-release-el-7.noarch.rpm

Installed:
  puppetlabs-release.noarch 0:7-11
```

Installing the MCollective Module

Install the MCollective Puppet module from the Puppet Forge like so:

```
$ cd /etc/puppetlabs/code/environments/production
production$ puppet module install jorhett-mcollective --modulepath=modules/
Notice: Preparing to install into environments/production/modules ...
Notice: Downloading from https://forgeapi.puppetlabs.com ...
Notice: Installing -- do not interrupt ...
/etc/puppetlabs/code/environments/production/modules
└── jorhett-mcollective (v1.2.1)
└── puppetlabs-stdlib (v4.3.0)
```

As shown here, the Puppet module installer will pull in the puppetlabs/stdlib module if you don't have it already.

Generating Passwords

Setting up MCollective is quick and easy. For this installation you will create four unique strings for authentication:

Client password
    Used by the MCollective client to authenticate with the middleware.

Server password
    Used by nodes to authentication with the middleware.

Preshared salt
    Used by clients and servers to validate that requests have arrived intact.

Java keystore password
    Used to protect a Java keystore.

The server credentials installed on nodes will allow them to subscribe to command channels, but not to send commands on them. If you use the same credentials for clients and servers, anyone with access to a server's configuration file will have command control of the entire collective. Keep these credentials separate.

You won't type these strings at a prompt—they'll be stored in a configuration file. So we'll generate long and complex random passwords. Run the following command four times:

```
$ openssl rand -base64 32
```

Copy these random strings into your Sticky app or text editor, or write them down somewhere temporarily. We'll use them in the next few sections to configure the service.

 Many online guides and Puppet modules for MCollective instruct you to configure it with unencrypted command channels and plain-text validation of commands. The process here will secure MCollective with encrypted channels and cryptographic validation of requests.

The TLS security plugins can encrypt the transport and provide complete cryptographic authentication. However, the simplicity of the preshared key model is useful to help get you up and running quickly and provides a reasonable level of security for a small installation.

Configuring Hiera for MCollective

We already did this earlier in the book, but take a moment and verify that you've enabled class assignment from Hiera in your environment's manifest (*${environment-path}/${environment}/manifests/site.pp*):

```
# Look up classes defined in Hiera
lookup('classes', Array[String], 'unique').include
```

Put the following Hiera configuration data in the *common.yaml* file. Note that you'll be using the random passwords you generated earlier:

```
# every node installs the server
classes:
  - mcollective::server

# The Puppet Server will host the middleware
mcollective::hosts:
  - 'puppet.example.com'
mcollective::collectives:
  - 'mcollective'
```

```
mcollective::connector: 'activemq'
mcollective::connector_ssl: true
mcollective::connector_ssl_type: 'anonymous'

# Access passwords
mcollective::server_password: 'Server Password'
mcollective::psk_key: 'Pre-shared Salt'

mcollective::facts::cronjob::run_every: 10
mcollective::server::package_ensure: 'latest'
mcollective::plugin::agents:
  puppet:
    version: 'latest'

mcollective::client::unix_group: vagrant
mcollective::client::package_ensure: 'latest'
mcollective::plugin::clients:
  puppet:
    version: 'latest'
```

Every node will install and enable the mcollective::server. The remaining values identify the type of connection.

Enabling the Middleware

I had considered using another Vagrant instance to provide the middleware instance for MCollective, but we're already burning lots of memory, and honestly the middleware doesn't require much memory or CPU until you have hundreds of nodes.

Therefore, I recommend that you install the middleware on the puppetserver VM. Its resource needs are very minimal.

At this point, we'll need to adjust the firewall on the middleware node. MCollective clients and servers connect to the middleware on TCP port 61614. Let's allow incoming TCP connections to this port on the Puppet server node:

```
$ sudo firewall-cmd --permanent --zone=public --add-port=61614/tcp
success
$ sudo firewall-cmd --reload
success
```

Now adjust the Hiera data file for this node to enable the extra features. Create a per-host YAML file for the Puppet server named *hostname/puppetserver.yaml*:

```
# hostname/puppetserver.yaml
classes:
  - mcollective::middleware
  - mcollective::client

# Middleware configuration
mcollective::client_password: 'Client Password'
```

```
mcollective::middleware::keystore_password: 'Keystore Password'
mcollective::middleware::truststore_password: 'Keystore Password'
```

This class assignment enables installation of ActiveMQ middleware on the Puppet server by adding the mcollective::middleware class. It also installs the MCollective client software with the mcollective::client class.

Finally, run Puppet to configure this node:

```
[vagrant@puppetserver ~]$ sudo puppet agent --test
```

This should configure your middleware node without any problems if the data was entered correctly.

Connecting MCollective Servers

Go to each server in your network and run puppet agent to configure MCollective. In the virtualized test setup, this would be the client and dashboard nodes. Their configuration will be simpler than what you observed on the middleware node:

```
[vagrant@dashserver ~]$ sudo puppet agent --verbose
Info: Caching catalog for dashserver.example.com
Info: Applying configuration version '1441698110'
Notice: /Mcollective/Package[rubygem-stomp]/ensure: created
Info: Computing checksum on file /etc/puppetlabs/mcollective/server.cfg
Notice: /Mcollective::Server/File[/etc/puppetlabs/mcollective/server.cfg]/content:
  content changed '{md5}73e68cfd79153a49de6f' to '{md5}bb46f5c1345d62b8a62bb'
Notice: /Mcollective::Server/File[/etc/puppetlabs/mcollective/server.cfg]/owner:
  owner changed 'vagrant' to 'root'
Notice: /Mcollective::Server/File[/etc/puppetlabs/mcollective/server.cfg]/group:
  group changed 'vagrant' to 'root'
Notice: /Mcollective::Server/File[/etc/puppetlabs/mcollective/server.cfg]/mode:
  mode changed '0644' to '0400'
Info: /Mcollective::Server/File[/etc/puppetlabs/mcollective/server.cfg]:
  Scheduling refresh of Service[mcollective]
Notice: /Mcollective::Server/Mcollective::Plugin::Agent[puppet]/
  Package[mcollective-puppet-agent]/ensure: created
Info: /Mcollective::Server/Mcollective::Plugin::Agent[puppet]/
  Package[mcollective-puppet-agent]: Scheduling refresh of Service[mcollective]
Notice: /Mcollective::Server/Service[mcollective]/ensure:
  ensure changed 'stopped' to 'running'
Notice: /Mcollective::Facts::Cronjob/Cron[mcollective-facts]/ensure) created
Notice: Applied catalog in 17.02 seconds
```

At this time, the MCollective service should be up and running, and attempting to connect to the middleware. You should see the node connected to the middleware node on port 61614:

```
$ netstat -an | grep 61614
tcp   0   0 192.168.200.10:51026      192.168.200.6:61614      ESTABLISHED
```

If you are using IPv6, the response may look like this:

```
$ netstat -an -A inet6 | grep 61614
tcp    0    0 2001:DB8:6A:C0::200:10:45743 2001:DB8:6A:C0::200:6:61614  ESTABLISHED
```

 You may find that you are using IPv6 when you didn't expect it. This isn't a problem in most sites, so don't rush to turn it off. If you need to only use IPv4, set the `mcollective::hosts` array values to DNS hostnames that only provide an IPv4 address.

If you don't see an established connection, ensure that you've made the firewall change documented in the previous section.

Validating the Installation

At this point, all of your nodes should be online and connected to the middleware. You can verify that each of them is reachable using the low-level `ping` command:

```
[vagrant@puppetserver ~]$ mco ping
dashserver.example.com                  time=182.17 ms
client.example.com                      time=221.34 ms
puppetmaster.example.com                time=221.93 ms

---- ping statistics ----
3 replies max: 221.93 min: 182.17 avg: 208.48
```

If you get back a list of each server connected to your middleware and its response time, then congratulations! You have successfully created a collective using Puppet.

If this does not work, there are only three things that can be wrong. They are listed here in the order of likelihood:

The middleware host isn't allowing connections to port 61614
    If this is the case, you won't see any connections to port 61614 on the `puppet server` VM. Follow the firewall configuration steps in "Enabling the Middleware" on page 454 to resolve this issue.

The middleware host doesn't have the same server password as the nodes
    You can verify this by checking */var/log/messages* on the servers for errors about authentication. This can only happen if the Hiera data for the middleware node (puppetserver) is overriding the `server_password` value to something different. It is easiest and best to only define that value in the *common.yaml* file so that all nodes share the same value.

The middleware host doesn't have the same client password as your client

This will be very obvious because you'll get an immediate error response when you try to run any mco command. Ensure that the same value for client_pass word is used on both the client and the middleware host. You can also place this in the common file to ensure consistency.

In the virtualized environment we've created for learning, this will "just work." In a mixed-vendor environment, you may have more problems, but you can identify and resolve all of them by reading the logfiles. If necessary, change the log level to debug in *common.yaml*, as shown here:

```
mcollective::client::loglevel: 'debug'
mcollective::server::loglevel: 'debug'
```

You'll find that debug logs contain details of the inner workings of each layer of MCollective.

Creating Another Client

You only need to install the client software on systems from which you will be sending requests. In a production environment, this may be your management hosts, or a bastion host, or it could be your laptop or desktop systems in the office. In the virtualized test environment, we have enabled the MCollective client on the puppet server node.

If you would like to enable the client commands on the client node, then create a per-host Hiera data file for it, such as */etc/puppetlabs/code/hieradata/hostname/client.yaml*:

```
# Client configuration
classes:
  - mcollective::client

mcollective::client_password: 'Client Password'
```

These two settings are all you need to enable the MCollective clients on the node you selected. Run Puppet agent in test mode to see the changes made:

```
$ sudo puppet agent --test
Info: Retrieving pluginfacts
Info: Retrieving plugin
Info: Loading facts
Info: Caching catalog for client.example.com
Info: Applying configuration version '1441700470'
Info: Computing checksum on file /etc/puppetlabs/mcollective/client.cfg
Notice: /Mcollective::Client/File[/etc/puppetlabs/mcollective/client.cfg]/content:
    content changed '{md5}af1fa871fed944e3ea' to '{md5}2846de8aa829715f394c49f04'
Notice: /Mcollective::Client/File[/etc/puppetlabs/mcollective/client.cfg]/owner:
    owner changed 'vagrant' to 'root'
```

```
Notice: /Mcollective::Client/File[/etc/puppetlabs/mcollective/client.cfg]/mode:
  mode changed '0644' to '0440'
Notice: /Mcollective::Client/Mcollective::Plugin::Client[puppet]/
  Package[mcollective-puppet-client]/ensure: created
Notice: Applied catalog in 7.41 seconds
```

 With the preshared key security model, anyone who can read the *client.cfg* file can find the salt used to validate requests to the hosts.

Tune which group has read access to this file using the following Hiera configuration option:

```
mcollective::client::unix_group: 'vagrant'
```

Obviously you won't use this group on productions systems. I recommend that you choose a limited group of people who you trust to execute commands on every system.

Installing MCollective Agents and Clients

The important thing we want to install is the MCollective Puppet agent. This is automatically installed through the following Hiera values (which we already applied):

```
mcollective::plugin::agents:
  puppet:
    version: latest
    dependencies:
      - Package['puppet-agent']

mcollective::plugin::clients:
  puppet:
    version: latest
```

These configuration values in Hiera will ensure that the Puppet agent plugin is installed on all servers, and the Puppet client plugin is installed on all client machines.

You can install other MCollective agents by adding them to the `mcollective::plugin::agents` hash. For each plugin, you can specify the agent version and any dependencies that must be installed first. Many plugins won't work until the software they provide extensions for is installed. The preceding example declares that the Puppet agent plugin requires the `puppet-agent` package to be installed before the plugin.

Dependencies should be expressed in the capitalized resource names used by the Puppet ordering metaparameters, for reasons I believe you can grasp. This example is a bit redundant, as Puppet is enforcing this policy, and we therefore know that it is already installed.

You can install MCollective client plugins by adding them to the `mcollective::plugin::clients` hash. For each plugin, you can specify the client version and any dependencies that must be installed first.

Sharing Facts with Puppet

The facts that Puppet gathers from the node can be made available to MCollective. Facts are a hash of key/value strings with details about the node, as covered in "Finding Facts" on page 57.

Facts provide a powerful information source, and are useful to filter the list of nodes that should act upon a request.

You populate the */etc/puppetlabs/mcollective/facts.yaml* file by giving the `mcollective::facts::cronjob::run_every` parameter a value. This enables a cron job schedule that creates the *facts.yaml* file with all Facter- and Puppet-provided facts:

```
mcollective::facts::cronjob::run_every: '10'
```

The value should be a quoted `String` value containing the number of minutes between updates to the file. The Hiera data you added to the *hieradata/common.yaml* file a few pages back set this to `10` for all nodes.

Take a look at the generated file, and you'll find all the facts stored in YAML format for MCollective to use. You can also use an `inventory` request and read through the output to see all facts available on a node:

```
$ mco inventory client.example.com | awk '/Facts:/','/^$/'
   Facts:
      architecture => x86_64
      augeasversion => 1.0.0
      bios_release_date => 01/01/2007
      bios_vendor => Seabios
      ...etc...
```

You can query for how many nodes share the same value for facts. For example, every node shown here (from a different testlab) has the `hostname` fact, but only three nodes have the `kernel` fact:

```
$ mco facts operatingsystem
Report for fact: kernel

        Linux                                   found 2 times
        FreeBSD                                 found 1 times

Finished processing 3 / 3 hosts in 61.45 ms

$ mco facts hostname
Report for fact: hostname

        fireagate                               found 1 times
        geode                                   found 1 times
        tanzanite                               found 1 times
        sunstone                                found 1 times

Finished processing 5 / 5 hosts in 68.38 ms
```

Tanzanite is a Windows operating system that doesn't have the kernel fact.

Pulling the Puppet Strings

Now that MCollective is installed, the fun begins. In this section, you will:

- Get an inventory of facts and classes from each node.
- Run the Puppet agent on demand for specific nodes.
- Use filters and limits to control request targets.
- Manipulate and control Puppet resources on nodes.

You will be amazed at the level of control and immediacy that MCollective gives you over nodes. MCollective enables new ways of using Puppet that simply aren't possible from agent, cron-run, or even command-line usage of Puppet.

Viewing Node Inventory

One of the commands built into the MCollective client is an inventory query. This command allows you to see how a given server is configured: what collectives it is part of, what facts it has, what Puppet classes are applied to it, and the server's running statistics.

Run this command against one of your nodes and examine the output:

```
$ mco inventory client.example.com
Inventory for client.example.com:

   Server Statistics:
                   Version: 2.8.2
                Start Time: 2015-09-08 10:44:09 +0000
                Config File: /etc/puppetlabs/mcollective/server.cfg
                Collectives: mcollective
```

```
                 Main Collective: mcollective
                      Process ID: 20896
                  Total Messages: 4
          Messages Passed Filters: 4
               Messages Filtered: 0
                Expired Messages: 0
                    Replies Sent: 3
            Total Processor Time: 1.43 seconds
                     System Time: 0.61 seconds

     Agents:
        discovery        puppet           rpcutil

     Data Plugins:
        agent            collective       fact
        fstat            puppet           resource

     Configuration Management Classes:
        mcollective              mcollective::facts::cronjob    mcollective::params
        mcollective::server      puppet4                        puppet4::agent
        puppet4::params          puppet4::user                  settings

     Facts:
        augeas => {"version"=>"1.4.0"}
        disks => {"size"=>"20 GiB", "size_bytes"=>"21474836480", "vendor"=>"ATA"}
        dmi => {"bios"=>{"vendor"=>"innotek GmbH", "version"=>"VirtualBox"}
        …snip…
```

You can create reports from the inventory service as well. Write a short Ruby script to
output the values, such as this one:

```
$ cat inventory.mc
# Format: hostname: architecture, operating system, OS release.
inventory do
  format "%20s: %8s %10s %-20s"
  fields {[
    identity,
    facts["os.architecture"],
    facts["operatingsystem"],
    facts["operatingsystemrelease"]
  ]}
end
```

Now call the inventory command with the --script option and the name of the
Ruby script, as shown here:

```
$ mco inventory --script inventory.mc
              geode:   x86_64      CentOS 6.4
           sunstone:    amd64      Ubuntu 13.10
         heliotrope:   x86_64      CentOS 6.5
          tanzanite:   x86_64     Windows 7 Ultimate SP1
          fireagate:    amd64     FreeBSD 9.2-RELEASE
```

This can be very useful for creating reports of your managed nodes.

 I took this output from a different test lab, as the virtual machines we created in this book are sadly uniform in nature.

Checking Puppet Status

You can now query the Puppet agent status of any node using the MCollective client. First, let's get a list of nodes that have the MCollective Puppet agent installed. The example shown here uses the find command to identify nodes that have the agent:

```
$ mco find --with-agent puppet
client.example.com
dashserver.example.com
puppetserver.example.com
```

Now ask the Puppet agents what they are doing:

```
$ mco puppet count
Total Puppet nodes: 3

          Nodes currently enabled: 3
         Nodes currently disabled: 0

   Nodes currently doing puppet runs: 0
          Nodes currently stopped: 3

      Nodes with daemons started: 3
   Nodes without daemons started: 0
       Daemons started but idling: 3
```

Finally, let's get a graphical summary of all nodes:

```
$ mco puppet summary
Summary statistics for 3 nodes:

              Total resources: ██     ▄        min: 25.0   max: 39.0
         Out Of Sync resources: _____     min: 0.0    max: 0.0
            Failed resources: _____      min: 0.0    max: 0.0
           Changed resources: _____      min: 0.0    max: 0.0
 Config Retrieval time (seconds): █           min: 0.9    max: 1.2
      Total run-time (seconds): █  ▄         min: 1.3    max: 9.4
  Time since last run (seconds): ████  █ █   min: 244.0  max: 1.6k
```

You'll notice that Puppet runs very quickly on these nodes, as they have few resources involved. The two modules you enabled have only a few dozen resources. A production deployment will usually have much longer runtimes and thousands of resources applied.

Disabling the Puppet Agent

During maintenance you may want to disable the Puppet agent on certain nodes. When you disable the agent, you can add a message letting others know why you did so:

```
$ mco puppet disable --with-identity client.example.com message="Disk failed"

 * [ ============================================> ] 1 / 1

Summary of Enabled:
   disabled = 1

Finished processing 1 / 1 hosts in 85.28 ms
```

If someone tries to run Puppet on the node, they'll get a message back telling them why Puppet was disabled on the node:

```
$ mco puppet runonce --with-identity client.example.com

 * [ ============================================> ] 1 / 1

heliotrope                          Request Aborted
   Puppet is disabled: 'Disk failed'
   Summary: Puppet is disabled: 'Disk failed'

Finished processing 1 / 1 hosts in 84.22 ms
```

Re-enabling the Puppet agent is just as easy:

```
$ mco puppet enable --with-identity client.example.com

 * [ ============================================> ] 1 / 1

Summary of Enabled:
   enabled = 1

Finished processing 1 / 1 hosts in 84.36 ms
```

You can easily apply these commands to enable or disable the Puppet agent on multiple nodes matching a filter criteria, as discussed in "Limiting Targets with Filters" on page 466.

Invoking Ad Hoc Puppet Runs

The MCollective Puppet agent provides powerful control over the Puppet agent. The simplest invocation is naturally to tell Puppet agent to evaluate the catalog immediately on one node:

```
$ mco puppet runonce --with-identity client.example.com

 * [ ==================================================> ] 1 / 1

Finished processing 1 / 1 hosts in 193.99 ms

$ mco puppet status --with-identity client.example.com

 * [ ==================================================> ] 1 / 1

   client.example.com: Currently idling; last completed run 02 seconds ago

Summary of Applying:
   false = 1

Summary of Daemon Running:
   running = 1

Summary of Enabled:
   enabled = 1

Summary of Idling:
   true = 1

Summary of Status:
   idling = 1

Finished processing 1 / 1 hosts in 86.43 ms
```

If you examine the help text for mco puppet, you'll find the same options for controlling Puppet as you have for puppet agent or puppet apply:

```
$ mco puppet --help
...snip...
Application Options
   --force                Bypass splay options when running
   --server SERVER        Connect to a specific server or port
   --tags, --tag TAG      Restrict the run to specific tags
   --noop                 Do a noop run
   --no-noop              Do a run with noop disabled
   --environment ENV      Place the node in a specific environment for this run
   --splay                Splay the run by up to splaylimit seconds
   --no-splay             Do a run with splay disabled
   --splaylimit SECONDS   Maximum splay time for this run if splay is set
   --ignoreschedules      Disable schedule processing
   --rerun SECONDS        When performing runall do so repeatedly
                          with a minimum run time of SECONDS
```

What if you had an emergency patch for Puppet to fix a security problem with the */etc/sudoers* file? If you simply updated Puppet data, the change would be applied gradually over 30 minutes, as you can see from the results of this command:

```
$ mco puppet status --wf operatingsystem=CentOS

  * [ ================================================> ] 3 / 3

        client.example.com: Currently idling; last completed run 2 minutes ago
  puppetserver.example.com: Currently idling; last completed run 16 minutes ago
    dashserver.example.com: Currently idling; last completed run 25 minutes ago
```

To make this emergency change get applied ASAP on all CentOS nodes, you could use the following MCollective command:

```
$ mco puppet runonce --tags=sudo --with-fact operatingsystem=CentOS

  * [ ================================================> ] 3 / 3

  Finished processing 3 / 3 hosts in 988.26 ms
```

So, how's .98 seconds for fast?

Cannot Specify Custom Options When the Agent Service Is Running

It is only possible to pass runtime options like - -tags and - -noop if the Puppet daemon is not running as a service on the host:[1]

```
$ mco puppet runonce --tags packages --wi client.example.com

  * [ ============================================================> ] 1 / 1

  client                            Request Aborted
     Cannot specify any custom puppet options when the daemon is running
```

To enable configurable options with the agent, run puppet agent - -onetime periodically from cron, or an orchestration system like MCollective.

What risks do you run commanding every node to run Puppet at the same time? In server-based environments, the Puppet servers could be overloaded by simultaneous Puppet agent catalog requests.

You may need to limit the number of hosts that provide a service from evaluating their policies at the same time, to prevent too many of them being out of service simultaneously.

Here is any example where we slow-roll Puppet convergence, processing only two at a time:

---

1 This is being tracked in Feature Request MCOP-268 (*https://tickets.puppetlabs.com/browse/MCOP-268*).

```
$ mco puppet runall 2
2014-02-10 23:14:00: Running all nodes with a concurrency of 2
2014-02-10 23:14:00: Discovering enabled Puppet nodes to manage
2014-02-10 23:14:03: Found 39 enabled nodes
2014-02-10 23:14:06: geode schedule status: Signaled the running Puppet
2014-02-10 23:14:06: sunstone schedule status: Signaled the running Puppet
2014-02-10 23:14:06: 37 out of 39 hosts left to run in this iteration
2014-02-10 23:14:09: Currently 2 nodes applying the catalog; waiting for less
2014-02-10 23:14:17: heliotrope schedule status: Signaled the running Puppet
2014-02-10 23:14:18: 36 out of 39 hosts left to run in this iteration
 ...etc...
```

Run Puppet on all web servers, up to five at at time:

```
$ mco puppet runall 5 --with-identity /^web\d/
```

Note that runall is like batch except that instead of waiting for a sleep time, it waits for one of the Puppet daemons to complete its run before it starts another. If you didn't mind some potential overlap, you could always use the batch options instead:

```
$ mco puppet --batch 10 --batch-sleep 60 --tags ntp
```

Limiting Targets with Filters

Filters are used by the *discovery* plugin to limit which servers are sent a request. Filters can be applied to any MCollective command.

The syntax for filters are documented in the online help, as shown here:

```
$ mco help

Host Filters
    -W, --with FILTER               Combined classes and facts filter
    -S, --select FILTER             Compound filter combining facts and classes
    -F, --wf, --with-fact fact=val  Match hosts with a certain fact
    -C, --wc, --with-class CLASS    Match hosts with a certain Puppet class
    -A, --wa, --with-agent AGENT    Match hosts with a certain agent
    -I, --wi, --with-identity IDENT Match hosts with a certain configured identity
```

There are long and short versions of every filter option. We're going to use the long versions throughout the documentation because they are easier to read on the page, and easier to remember.

 In the following examples, you will see commands I haven't introduced yet. Don't worry about understanding every command feature or option now. Instead, focus on how flexible and powerful the filtering language is for selecting target nodes.

Here are some examples of using host filters. Each one outputs a list of hosts that match the criteria. These are good to run before executing a command, to ensure that you are matching the list of hosts you expect to match. In our first example, we'll find all hosts whose `identity` (FQDN) matches a regular expression:

```
$ mco find --with-identity /serv/
dashserver.example.com
puppetserver.example.com
```

List all hosts that apply the Puppet class *mcollective::client*:

```
$ mco find --with-class mcollective::client
puppetserver.example.com
```

Show all hosts whose facts report that they are using the *Ubuntu* `operatingsystem`:

```
$ mco find --with-fact operatingsystem=Ubuntu
```

Whoops, no results. There are no Ubuntu hosts in this test environment. Show all hosts that have the *puppet* agent installed on them:

```
$ mco find --with-agent puppet
client.example.com
dashserver.example.com
puppetserver.example.com
```

There are two types of combination filters. The first type combines Puppet classes and Facter facts. Following is an example where we find all *CentOS* hosts with the Puppet class *nameserver* applied to them:

```
$ mco find --with "/nameserver/ operatingsystem=CentOS"
```

The second type is called a `select` filter and is the most powerful filter available. This filter allows you to create searches against facts and Puppet classes with complex Boolean logic. This is the only filter where you can use the operands and and or. You can likewise negate terms using not or !.

For example, find all *CentOS* hosts that are not in the *test* environment:

```
$ mco find --select "operatingsystem=CentOS and not environment=test"
```

The final example matches virtualized hosts with either the `httpd` or `nginx` Puppet class applied to them. This combination search is only possible with the `select` filter type:

```
$ mco find --select "( /httpd/ or /nginx/ ) and is_virtual=true"
```

A `select` filter will always use the `mc` discovery plugin, even if a different plugin is requested or configured.

Providing a List of Targets

MCollective supports multiple discovery plugins, including lookup from MongoDB, MySQL, and other big data solutions. Not all filters are supported by every discovery method. Consult the documentation for a discovery method to determine which filters are available.

In addition to mc's dynamic discovery filters, you can specify which nodes to make requests of using a file with one identity (FQDN) per line:

```
$ mco puppet runonce --disc-method flatfile --disc-option /tmp/list-of-hosts.txt
```

You can also pipe the list of nodes to the command:

```
$ cat list-of-hosts.txt | mco puppet runonce --disc-method stdin
```

If you use the flatfile or stdin discovery methods, only the *identity* filter can be used.

These can be very useful when you have a list of nodes generated from a database, or collected from another query, which need to be processed in order. In most other situations, manually building a list of targets is a waste of time. You will find it much easier to use MCollective filters to target nodes dynamically.

Limiting Concurrency

By default, every node that matches the filter will respond to the request immediately. You may want to limit how many servers receive the request, or how many process it concurrently.

While it is impressive to see every node in your network instantly jump to perform your request, there are times it isn't appropriate. For example, you probably don't want every node in a load-balanced pool to upgrade itself at the same moment.

Following are command options to control how many servers receive the request in a batch, and how much time to wait between each batch.

The --one argument requests a response from a single (effectively random) node:

```
$ mco puppet status --one
dashserver.example.com: Currently idling; last completed run 12 minutes ago
```

The --limit argument can specify either a fixed number of servers or a percentage of the servers matching a filter:

```
$ mco puppet status --limit 2
        client.example.com: Currently idling; last completed run 20 minutes ago
   puppetserver.example.com: Currently idling; last completed run 4 minutes ago
```

Here's an example asking for one-third of the nodes with the `mcollective` Puppet class applied to them to run a command to return their FQDN:

```
$ mco shell run "hostname --fqdn" --limit 33% --with-class webserver
```

 This is only possible if you add the shell agent and client to the list of plugins installed, as documented in "Installing MCollective Agents and Clients" on page 458.

It's also possible to process systems in batches. Specify both a batch size and a time period before initiating the next batch. In the example shown here, we run the Puppet agent on five German servers every 30 seconds:

```
$ mco puppet runonce --batch 5 --batch-sleep 30 --with-fact country=de
```

In this example, we upgrade the `sudo` package in batches of 10 nodes spaced two minutes apart:

```
$ mco package upgrade sudo --batch 10 --batch-sleep 120
```

Manipulating Puppet Resource Types

The MCollective Puppet agent enables you to interact instantly with a node's resources using Puppet's Resource Abstraction Layer (RAL). You express a declarative state to be ensured on the node, with the same resource names and attributes as you would use in a Puppet manifest.

For example, if you wanted to stop the `httpd` service on a node, you could do the following:

```
$ mco puppet resource service httpd ensure=stopped --with-identity /dashserver/

 * [ ===========================================> ] 1 / 1

dashserver.example.com
   Changed: true
    Result: ensure changed 'running' to 'stopped'

Summary of Changed:
   Changed = 1

Finished processing 1 / 1 hosts in 630.99 ms
```

You could also fix the `root` alias on every host at once:

```
$ mco puppet resource mailalias root recipient=me@example.com
```

You should obviously limit actions in all the ways specified in "Limiting Targets with Filters" on page 466. For example, you probably only want to stop Apache on hosts where it is not being managed by Puppet:

```
$ mco puppet resource service httpd ensure=stopped --wc !apache
```

 This section documents extremely powerful controls. Enabling the Puppet RAL allows direct, instantaneous, and arbitrary access to any Puppet resource type it knows how to affect.

Restricting which resources can be controlled

By default, no resources can be controlled from MCollective. The feature is enabled in the MCollective configuration, but it has an empty whitelist by default.

 Consider this feature a really powerful shotgun. The whitelist protects you and everyone who depends upon that foot you are aiming at.

These are the default configuration options:

```
mcollective::server::resource_type_whitelist: 'none'
mcollective::server::resource_type_blacklist: null
```

To allow resource control, define the preceding configuration values in your Hiera data. Add a list of resources to be controlled to the whitelist, as follows:

```
mcollective::server::resource_type_whitelist: 'package,service'
```

You can also define a blacklist of resources that should be immune to MCollective tampering:

```
mcollective::server::resource_type_blacklist: 'user,group,exec'
```

MCollective does not allow you to mix whitelists and blacklists. One of the preceding values must be undefined, or null.

Block MCollective from Puppet resources

A resource declared in the Puppet catalog should not be controlled from MCollective, so as to prevent MCollective from making a change against the Puppet policy. Alternate values specified for a resource in the Puppet catalog are most likely to be overwritten the next time Puppet agent converges the run. In a worse case, well... sorry about the foot.

To allow MCollective to alter resources defined in the node's Puppet catalog, enable the `allow_managed_resources` configuration option:

```
mcollective::server::allow_managed_resources: true
```

If you are (rightly) scared of breaking a resource that Puppet controls, and the damage to your foot that this tool is capable of, the best protection would be the following change:

```
mcollective::server::allow_managed_resources: false
```

Comparing to Puppet Application Orchestration

Right before this book went to press, Puppet Labs released Puppet Enterprise 2015.3, which contains the first implementation of Puppet Application Orchestration. Application Orchestration handles the deployment and management of applications that span multiple nodes in a Puppet environment.

Without Puppet Application Orchestration, an organization must write Puppet modules that export shared data to PuppetDB, and then use MCollective to kick off Puppet runs on dependent nodes to use the data. This works quite well, and can be finely tuned to operate seamlessly, but requires the organization to develop this automation itself.

Puppet Application Orchestration extends the Puppet configuration language to allow declaration of environment-wide application resources that span multiple nodes. The application instance declares which nodes provide the service, and the order in which they should be evaluated. The `puppet job` command is used to kick off the multinode convergence of an application.

You can find more information at "Application Orchestration" (*http://bit.ly/1TUejUL*) on the Puppet Labs site. An example workflow can also be found on the Puppet docs site, at "Application Orchestration Workflow" (*http://bit.ly/1RpkUpF*).

Without making use of Application Orchestration, you could use the `puppet job` tool to run Puppet on all nodes in an environment. It does not provide the powerful filters available in MCollective, but can be useful regardless:

```
$ puppet job run --concurrency 1
New job id created: 7
Started puppet run on client.example.com ...
Finished puppet run on client.example.com - Success!
        Applied configuration version 1451776604
        Resource events: 0 failed 3 changed 27 unchanged 0 skipped 0 noop
Started puppet run on puppetserver.example.com ...
```

This book does not cover Application Orchestration, as it is exclusive to Puppet Enterprise at this time, and likely to evolve very quickly. Later updates to this book will include more details if this functionality is released for Puppet Open Source.

In my opinion, Puppet Application Orchestration is a welcome and useful addition to Puppet, but does not replace all of the orchestration features provided by MCollective. I suspect most sites will use both together to leverage the strengths of each.

Learning More About MCollective

MCollective is capable of far more than just managing Puppet agents. It provides an orchestration framework that complements your Puppet installation. Puppet takes many steps to ensure that thousands of details are correct on each node. MCollective makes small things happen instantly or according to schedule on hundreds or thousands of nodes at exactly the same time.

Don't limit MCollective in your mind to only *puppets dancing on your strings*. You can build MCollective agents and plugins that act on events or triggers specific to your needs. Consider a fishing model where the marionette holds the strings cautiously, waiting for the strings to go taut. I've built autohealing components that listen passively to server inputs. When the event trigger occurs, the MCollective agent sends a message. Other agents respond to that message by taking action to correct the problem without any human involvement.

Every team I've talked to who has implemented MCollective has found it useful beyond their original expectations. Administrators find themselves wondering how they ever got along without it before.

The MCollective Puppet module has dozens of parameters available to customize the MCollective deployment. The module can create and manage a large distributed network of brokers. After doing the simplified installation used in this book, take some time to read the documentation for the module.

You can learn more about how to use, scale, and tune MCollective with *Learning MCollective (http://bit.ly/learn-mcollective)*, shown in Figure 30-1.

Figure 30-1. Learning MCollective

You might even recognize the author.

## CHAPTER 31

Managing Network Infrastructure with Puppet

While DevOps teams have been building dynamic, push-button node and application deployments, the infrastructure in which they operate has not benefited from the same agility. In many organizations, the DevOps team has to toss a request over the wall to a slow, hand-built infrastructure team. Many other organizations avoid that discrepancy by placing all nodes on a flat network, forsaking the security benefits of functional isolation in order to retain the ability to repurpose nodes dynamically.

Speaking as someone who identified as a network engineer most of my early career, I believe network engineering would be vastly improved by declarative and idempotent implementation. There are hundreds of network planning and management tools—most of which end up being little more than frustrating and limited model makers—to create designs that end up being implemented by hand on the network devices. Infrastructure teams can be slow and inflexible for the same reasons outlined in "Is Puppet DevOps?" on page xxxiv—a slower process is necessary to manage and track change, and work around the limitations of the tools available.

Few things are as exciting, and as valuable, as the cultural changes that are achievable when the network infrastructure and security teams can participate in a swift-moving, Agile-based workflow made possible by dynamically declared infrastructure.

Puppet's ability to configure and audit network devices creates an exciting growth opportunity. Puppet has had limited, albeit powerful, support for configuring network devices for many years. In the last 12 months, we have witnessed many vendors releasing officially supported Puppet agents on a large number of network devices.

This chapter will review the options available today. As this specific area is experiencing significant growth right now, I expect this chapter will contain the largest amount of changes in the next revision.

Managing Network Devices with Puppet Device

The first support for managing networking devices was provided by a Puppet agent acting as a proxy for the network device.

A node running puppet device would log in to the network device to gather facts, then connect to a Puppet server and request a catalog for the device. The device agent would then apply the catalog resources to the network device. This proxy implementation allows for management of network devices incapable of running a Puppet agent on their own.

This works surprisingly well, and provides power and flexibility to manage Cisco routers and switches without an embedded Puppet agent. Let's configure one now.

Enabling SSH on the Switch

Let's enable SSH on the switch or router, and configure a Puppet user with enough rights to configure the switch. This will be a short review, as all of these commands should be self-evident to an experienced network administrator.

 You could also use telnet, but you're smarter than that, aren't you?

Note that we are doing nothing more than configuring the exact minimum necessary to enable SSH and provide enough configuration (Base IP setup, DNS, and NTP) for Puppet to do all remaining configuration. Be certain to assign a unique hostname and the correct domain name to the unit. The hostname and domain name will be concatenated together by Puppet to create a certname for the unit:

```
Switch#conf t
Enter configuration commands, one per line.  End with CNTL/Z.
Switch(config)#hostname switch01
switch01(config)#ip domain-name example.com
switch01(config)#ip name-server 192.168.1.10
switch01(config)#ip name-server 192.168.1.11
switch01(config)#ntp server 192.168.1.10
switch01(config)#ntp server 192.168.1.11
switch01(config)#crypto key generate rsa general-keys modulus 2048
The name for the keys will be: switch01.example.com
```

```
% The key modulus size is 2048 bits
% Generating 2048 bit RSA keys ...[OK]

switch01(config)#
03:25:35: %SSH-5-ENABLED: SSH 1.99 has been enabled
switch01(config)#ip ssh version 2
switch01(config)#line vty 0 4
switch01(config-line)#transport input ssh
switch01(config-line)#line vty 5 15
switch01(config-line)#transport input ssh
switch01(config-line)#int vlan1
switch01(config-if)#ip address 192.168.1.253 255.255.255.0
switch01(config-if)#exit
```

Now you should create a privileged user account for the Puppet user. I recommend using an intuitive username like puppet, which would clearly identify the automated process in access logs. Do not share or reuse the login identity of a human.

If you have already customized authentication in your environment, use an authentication setup appropriate for your environment. If you do not have centralized authentication for your network devices, the following can provide a reasonable starting point. Choose appropriate passwords for the following secrets:

```
switch01(config)#enable secret enable-password
switch01(config)#aaa new-model
switch01(config)#aaa authentication login default local
switch01(config)#aaa authorization exec default local
switch01(config)#username admin priv 15 secret admin-password
switch01(config)#username puppet priv 15 secret puppet-password
switch01(config)#end
switch01#copy run start
Building configuration...
[OK]
```

The previous example was written using a Cisco 3560 switch. A few of these commands may require different options on newer or older OS versions, but this should provide you with enough information to work out the right commands for your specific unit.

 All standard practices for security hardening should be implemented as described in the vendor documentation, such as using an access control list to limit where SSH logins can originate from. Puppet requires only SSH access to the unit from the node running puppet device.

Configuring the Puppet Proxy Agent

Select a node that can complete both of the following network connections:

- SSH to the Cisco switch or router (destination TCP port 22)
- Connect to the Puppet server (destination TCP port 8140)

On this node, create a non-privileged user account to use for device management. There is no reason to use the root account. You can use a single shared account for all devices, or a different user account for each device if you prefer. The process shown here will create a non-privileged user and an appropriate Puppet configuration file:

```
[vagrant@client ~]$ sudo useradd -U -m -c "Puppet Device Manager" devicemgr
[vagrant@client ~]$ sudo -u devicemgr -i
[devicemgr@client ~]$ mkdir -p .puppetlabs/etc/puppet
[devicemgr@client ~]$ ln -s .puppetlabs/etc/puppet
[devicemgr@client ~]$ $EDITOR .puppetlabs/etc/puppet/puppet.conf
```

Create *~/.puppetlabs/etc/puppet/puppet.conf* with the following settings:

```
[agent]
    server = puppet.example.com
```

Create *~/.puppetlabs/etc/puppet/device.conf* with a list of devices, their type, and a URL to access them. The URL must contain both the username and password to access the device, and the enable password if required:

```
[switch01.example.com]
type cisco
url ssh://puppet:password@switch01.example.com/?enable=admin
```

Secure the file containing passwords, for obvious reasons:

```
[devicemgr@client ~]$ chmod 0600 .puppetlabs/etc/puppet/device.conf
```

Now we will connect this network device to the Puppet server, using a process very similar to how new nodes are connected. Initialize the proxy agent for this device with the command puppet device followed by the node name:

```
$ puppet device switch01.example.com --verbose
applying configuration to switch01.example.com at ssh://switch01.example.com/
Info: Creating a new SSL key for switch01.example.com
Info: Caching certificate for ca
Info: Creating a new SSL certificate request for switch01.example.com
Info: Certificate Request fingerprint (SHA256): 65:FC:AA:E3:F5:E5:5D:05:D0:D9:…
Info: Caching certificate for ca
```

You may need to run puppet cert sign *switch01.example.com* on the Puppet server to authorize the network device, and then run the command again.

This process has created a new Puppet agent dedicated to managing this network device. All of the configuration files, TLS certificates, logs, and state files for this device can be found in the *~/.puppetlabs/* directory structure. They never mix or interfere with the Puppet agent running as root on this node.

This network device can now be configured through idempotent declarations in Puppet manifests. Let's get started making changes.

Installing the Device_Hiera Module

One of the less-than-ideal circumstances around device configuration with Puppet was that each configuration entry on a device required a resource definition in the manifest. This often meant that Puppet device manifests were nearly as long as the device configurations that they generated.

The `device_hiera` module makes use of Hiera hierarchies and hash merging to utilize default port configurations, and enable *DRY* network configuration. Instead of specifying each interface specifically, we'll make use of defaults and then add minimal overrides when necessary.

Don't Repeat Yourself (DRY)

DRY is a principle of software development aimed at reducing repetition of information. When the DRY principle is applied successfully, a modification of any single element of a system does not require a change in other logically unrelated elements. Additionally, elements that are logically related all change predictably and uniformly, and are thus kept in sync.

(Source: *http://bit.ly/1RTzKPv*)

Let's install this module on the Puppet server to make switch configuration easier, as shown here:

```
[vagrant@puppetserver ~]$ puppet module install jorhett/device_hiera
Notice: Preparing to install into
  /etc/puppetlabs/code/environments/production/modules
Notice: Downloading from https://forgeapi.puppetlabs.com ...
Info: Resolving dependencies ...
Info: Preparing to install ...
Notice: Installing -- do not interrupt ...
/etc/puppetlabs/code/environments/production/modules
└─┬ jorhett-device_hiera (v0.3.0)
  └── puppetlabs-stdlib (v4.9.0)
```

Defining Resource Defaults in Hiera

In your Hiera data, let's assign the `device_hiera` class to this device. Do so by creating a file for this specific device in the Hiera data hierarchy, such as *hostname/switch01.yaml*:

```
# node-specific overrides for switch01
classes:
  - device_hiera
```

Next, list the resource types to be configured on devices. As these types take no action without explicit configuration, we should add this definition to the global *common.yaml* file for a DRY implementation. In the example shown here, we've enabled configuration of VLANs and network interfaces:

```
# global lookup defaults in common.yaml
device_hiera::resources:
  - vlan
  - interfaces
```

For each device resource type, define the default parameters to be used. For a DRY implementation, place default values in the global *common.yaml* file. The following example configures interfaces in dynamic negotiation mode, with an access VLAN ID of 20, if a more specific configuration is not provided:

```
# global lookup defaults in common.yaml
device_hiera::defaults::vlan:
  ensure: present

device_hiera::defaults::interface:
  description  : 'Default interface configuration'
  mode         : 'dynamic auto'
  encapsulation: 'negotiate'
  access_vlan  : '20'
```

 Observe that it defines the default for the interface resource, even though we add interfaces in the resources list in the preceding example. I will explain that discrepancy soon.

These definitions don't do anything by themselves, but instead provide defaults for VLANs or interfaces declared for the device that do not have a custom definition. Keep in mind that these are Puppet resources, so you can use ordering metaparameters to ensure that things happen in a specific order:

```
# global defaults in common.yaml
device_hiera::defaults::interface:
  access_vlan: '20'
  require     : 'Vlan[20]'
```

In this case it won't matter, as the VLAN will be created automatically because it was declared as the access VLAN to use by an automatic dependency. This can be useful in less obvious cases—for example, where a BGP peer resource depends on an access list used by the BGP peer configuration to be added first.

Take a moment to consider the power of this ability to declaratively map infrastructure dependencies using the ordering attributes you learned about in Chapter 7.

Centralizing VLAN Configuration

To configure VLANs on your switches, create a definition like the following example. As VLANs tend to be common across an entire site, you may want to place the VLAN configuration in the global *common.yaml* file. However, you can also place local VLAN definitions within a more specific file in your Hiera hierarchy, such as *hostname/switch01.yaml*:

```
# global lookup defaults in common.yaml
device_hiera::resources:
  - vlan

device_hiera::defaults::vlan:
  ensure: present

device_hiera::vlan:
  '20':
    description: 'Servers'
  '30':
    description: 'Middleware'
```

This definition would create the common VLANs 20 and 30 on every switch.

Documentation for the vlan resource and parameters can be found at "Type Reference: vlan" (*http://bit.ly/1UaMqrT*) on the Puppet docs site.

Applying Default Configs to Interfaces

Interfaces are special because there are so many of them, and you usually have to provide mostly redundant configuration details for each one. To make this easier to handle, the device_hiera module allows you to list slots in the chassis along with a range of ports that should be configured.

Define the device_hiera::interfaces::ports array. Each array value should be a hash with a single key and value pair. The key must be a quoted String value containing the slot name, and the value must also be a quoted String value containing a single range of ports, in the format: *MIN-MAX*. A slot can be listed multiple times to include multiple port ranges.

This example shows port definitions for a typical Cisco Catalyst 48-port switch with 10G uplinks:

```
device_hiera::interfaces::ports:
  - 'GigabitEthernet1/0'  : '1-48'
  - 'TenGigabitEthernet1/1': '1-2'
```

Place the list of slots and ports inside the Hiera data file for each individual device, such as *hostname/switch01.yaml*. Each of these interfaces will be configured with the default values provided in the device_hiera::defaults::interface configuration, unless the interface is specified in the device_hiera::interfaces::custom hash.

 If you have a dozen of these switches on site, the interface defaults plus this port array would configure 600 ports with just 8 lines of text.

If you have many devices of the same type, take advantage of your Hiera hierarchy and put the slot and port ranges in a Hiera file shared by the same devices. Don't repeat yourself.

Customizing Interface Configurations

It's possible to customize the configuration of any interface on the device. Define a device_hiera::interfaces::custom hash inside the Hiera data file for the device, such as *hostname/switch01.yaml*.

Each entry should be a quoted String hash key of the entire interface name. The value should be a hash with the parameters for the interface resource. Anything not specified will use the default values provided in the device_hiera::defaults::interface hash. The value absent can be used to clear a default value. The interface names can overlap with, or be outside the slots and port ranges supplied in device_hiera::interfaces::ports.

The following example will configure two 10G ports as VLAN-trunking uplink ports:

```
device_hiera::interfaces::custom:
  'TenGigabitEthernet1/1/3':
    description  : 'Uplink to core 1'
    mode         : 'trunking'
    encapsulation: 'dot1q'

  'TenGigabitEthernet1/1/4':
    description  : 'Uplink to core 2'
    mode         : 'trunking'
    encapsulation: 'dot1q'
```

One of the advantages of Hiera is that if every switch uses the same ports for uplink to the core, you could place this data in a shared Hiera file, and then override it just once in the definition of the core switch. Take advantage of Hiera's hash merging to stay DRY.

Testing Out the Switch Configuration

Shown here is the output when I ran puppet device against the 48-port Cisco switch we created the puppet device proxy for, using the preceding example's Hiera data:

```
$ puppet device --verbose
Info: starting applying configuration to switch01.example.com
Info: Retrieving pluginfacts
Info: Retrieving plugin
Info: Caching catalog for switch01.example.com
Info: Applying configuration version '1447670000'
Notice: /Stage[main]/Device_hiera::Vlans/Vlan[20]/ensure: created
Notice: /Stage[main]/Device_hiera::Vlans/Vlan[30]/ensure: created
Notice: /Stage[main]/Device_hiera::Interfaces/Interface[GigabitEthernet1/0/1]/
  access_vlan: access_vlan changed '1' to '20'
Notice: /Stage[main]/Device_hiera::Interfaces/Interface[GigabitEthernet1/0/1]/
  description: defined 'description' as 'Default configuration'
Notice: /Stage[main]/Device_hiera::Interfaces/Interface[GigabitEthernet1/0/2]/
  access_vlan: access_vlan changed '1' to '20'
Notice: /Stage[main]/Device_hiera::Interfaces/Interface[GigabitEthernet1/0/2]/
  description: defined 'description' as 'Default configuration'
...repeated for ports 3 through 48...
Notice: /Stage[main]/Device_hiera::Interfaces/Interface[TenGigabitEthernet1/1/3]/
    description: defined 'description' as 'uplink to core 1'
Notice: /Stage[main]/Device_hiera::Interfaces/Interface[TenGigabitEthernet1/1/3]/
    mode: mode changed 'dynamic auto' to 'trunk'
Notice: /Stage[main]/Device_hiera::Interfaces/Interface[TenGigabitEthernet1/1/3]/
    encapsulation: encapsulation changed 'negotiate' to 'dot1q'
Notice: /Stage[main]/Device_hiera::Interfaces/Interface[TenGigabitEthernet1/1/4]/
    description: defined 'description' as 'uplink to core 2'
Notice: /Stage[main]/Device_hiera::Interfaces/Interface[TenGigabitEthernet1/1/4]/
    mode: mode changed 'dynamic auto' to 'trunk'
Notice: /Stage[main]/Device_hiera::Interfaces/Interface[TenGigabitEthernet1/1/4]/
    encapsulation: encapsulation changed 'negotiate' to 'dot1q'
Notice: Applied catalog in 63.93 seconds
```

As you can see, we have configured a VLAN and 50 interfaces on this switch in 63 seconds. That's a lot faster than doing it by hand, isn't it?

Adding Resource Types and Providers

Puppet only includes the two resources we've just shown for puppet device to use: interface and vlan.

There are modules in the Puppet Forge that provide additional resource types and providers, as well as support for other vendors' devices. Resources designed for Net-Dev (described next) only work with an embedded Puppet agent on the device. The following modules from the Puppet Forge are designed to be used with puppet device:

puppetlabs/f5 *(http://bit.ly/22oPdC2)*
    Manages F5 BIG-IP Application Delivery Controllers

puppetlabs/netapp *(http://bit.ly/1Rr8N5h)*
    Manages resources on NetApp Cluster Data ONTAP devices

puppetlabs/netscalar *(http://bit.ly/1Z9OSOj)*
    Enables Puppet configuration of Citrix NetScaler devices through types and
    REST-based providers

mburger/networkdevice *(http://bit.ly/1Rr8LKJ)*
    Network Device Extensions for Cisco

Note that you will need to install these modules on both the Puppet server and your
local Puppet environment, as the manifests are used when the server builds the catalog, but the device providers are used locally by the puppet device agent. So install
the module in the device manager account:

```
[devicemgr@client ~]$ puppet module install mburger/networkdevice
```

…and also on the Puppet server:

```
[vagrant@puppetserver ~]$ puppet module install mburger/networkdevice
```

Merging Defaults with Other Resources

Any other resource type can also be created with parameters supplied in a hash under
their title. They can likewise fall back to default values for the type. Values for the
resource types and parameters should be taken from the module that provides the
resource type in question.

For example, if you have installed the puppetlabs/ciscopuppet module, you could
use the following for OSPF configuration:

```
device_hiera::resources:
  - cisco_interface_ospf

device_hiera::defaults::cisco_interface_ospf:
  ensure: present
  cost  : 200
  ospf  : default

device_hiera::cisco_interface_ospf:
  'Ethernet1/2 default':
    area: '172.16.0.0'
```

Wait, isn't that type only used by the Puppet agent onboard a Cisco NX-OS device? Yep, the `device_hiera` module can be used with both proxy and embedded agents!

There's nothing in the `device_hiera` module that is specific or tied to `puppet device`. You can utilize this module just as easily with the embedded Puppet agents we're going to talk about next.

Using the NetDev Standard Library

Puppet Labs has released a standard library of resources and providers that serves as a starting point for vendors looking to add a Puppet agent to their devices. Documentation on how to use this library and create vendor-specific providers is available at "Type definitions for Networking Device (NetDev) Standard Library" (*http://bit.ly/ 1R8GhGp*) on the Puppet Forge.

The vast majority of vendors build Puppet providers to implement the standard NetDev types, before adding their own vendor-specific resources as appropriate for their product.

Finding NetDev Vendor Extensions

There are a growing number of devices with complete NetDev support, including the following:

`juniper/netdev_stdlib_junos` *(http://bit.ly/1pt1aER)*
   Junos Provider code for Networking Device

`puppetlabs/ciscopuppet` *(http://bit.ly/1Lv62Uu)*
   Cisco Puppet providers and types for NX-OS devices

`aristanetworks/netdev_stdlib_eos` *(http://bit.ly/1MeMzYh)*
   NetDev Providers for Arista EOS

`mellanox/netdev_stdlib_mlnxos` *(http://bit.ly/1TUdc7g)*
   Provider definition for implementing Networking Device (netdev) Library for Mellanox OS (mlnx-os)

In theory, you can utilize NetDev standard resources across any device. Obviously this works best with things like DNS and less well with custom vendor extensions. Most vendors add their own specific resources in the same or a different Puppet module.

For example, Arista Networks types and providers for configuring EOS devices are available at aristanetworks/eos (*https://forge.puppetlabs.com/aristanetworks/eos*) on the Puppet Forge. Cumulus Linux and Mellanox also have networking components separated into different modules.

Creating a NetDev Device Object

Each device must declare a single `netdev_device` resource. The NetDev provider creates automatic dependencies between this resource and the other NetDev resources. If this resource fails to be applied, no other NetDev resource will be evaluated.

As this resource takes only a name, the `device_hiera` module implements the `net dev_device` type for a simple, one-shot definition. The following two lines of Hiera data will create a unique `netdev_device` resource for every NetDev vendor:

```
device_hiera::resources:
  - netdev_device
```

You can optionally override the name for a given node by defining `device_hiera::netdev_device::node_name` but this is not necessary. The value of the device's unique `certname` is used to avoid duplication.

 On some platforms, the `netdev_device` resource will fail to apply if the `puppet` user doesn't have permissions to configure the device, or if the configuration is locked by a different user.

Reducing Duplication with Device_Hiera

The `device_hiera` module can also be used with any NetDev extensions module to minimize repetition. The following example creates NetDev resource defaults that can safely be placed in the global *common.yaml* file:

```
device_hiera::resources:
  - network_dns
  - network_interface
  - netdev_device

device_hiera::defaults::network_interface:
  duplex: 'full'
  enable: 'true'
  mtu   : '1500'

device_hiera::defaults::network_dns:
  ensure : present
  domain : 'example.com'
  search : ['example.com','example.net']
  servers: ['192.168.51.10','192.168.51.11']
```

To utilize these defaults, assign the device_hiera class and override parameters as necessary within a specific host's Hiera configuration data, such as *hostname/switch01.yaml*:

```
classes:
  - device_hiera

device_hiera::network_dns:
  settings:
    # this host is outside the firewall, use Google DNS
    servers: ['8.8.8.8','8.8.4.4']

device_hiera::network_interface:
  'Ethernet1':
    description: 'Engineering'
```

Use this configuration style for DRY configuration of devices with NetDev provider modules.

Puppetizing Cisco Nexus Switches

Just before this book went to print, Puppet Labs and Cisco announced full support of Cisco Nexus switches provided by Puppet Labs. Nexus switches running NX-OS 7.0(3)12 and higher can install a Puppet 4 agent running on the device.

Install the Puppet Labs Supported module puppetlabs/ciscopuppet (*https://forge.puppetlabs.com/puppetlabs/ciscopuppet*). This module provides the Puppet resource types and Cisco-specific providers to configure:

- Interfaces
- VLANs and VLAN Trunking Protocol (VTP)
- OSPF interfaces and virtual routers
- Cisco TACACS+ servers
- SNMP users and servers
- Any Cisco IOS command

The NX-OS devices are officially supported by Puppet Labs using this module with Puppet Server or Puppet Enterprise 2015. This module will not work with an older version of Puppet.

Configuring the Puppet Server

Before configuring the Cisco NX-OS device, install the puppetlabs/ciscopuppet module (*https://forge.puppetlabs.com/puppetlabs/ciscopuppet*) on a Puppet Server:

```
[vagrant@puppetserver ~]$ puppet module install puppetlabs/ciscopuppet
Notice: Install into /etc/puppetlabs/code/environments/production/modules ...
Notice: Downloading from https://forgeapi.puppetlabs.com ...
```

```
Notice: Installing -- do not interrupt ...
/etc/puppetlabs/code/environments/production/modules
└─ puppetlabs-ciscopuppet (v1.0.0)
```

Preparing the NX-OS Device

The Puppet agent runs best in the *Guest Shell* environment. By default, the Guest Shell doesn't have enough resources. Therefore, preparation requires that we resize the Guest Shell on each switch:

```
n3k# guestshell disable

n3k# guestshell resize rootfs 400
Note: Please disable/enable or reboot the Guest shell for rootfs to be resized

n3k# guestshell resize memory 300
Note: Please disable/enable or reboot the Guest shell for memory to be resized

n3k# guestshell enable
n3k# show guestshell detail
Virtual service guestshell+ detail
 State                 : Activated

     Resource reservation
     Disk           : 400 MB
     Memory         : 300 MB
```

The next step is to configure an IP address for the management interface, then the DNS resolver, and finally the NTP time service:

```
[root@guestshell]# config term
  interface mgmt0
    vrf member management
    ip address 192.168.1.21/24

  vrf context management
    ip domain-name example.com
    ip name-server 192.168.1.10
    ip name-server 192.168.1.11
    end

  ntp server 192.168.1.10 use-vrf management
end
```

The GuestShell environment is a secure Linux container running CentOS 7. This container has its own networking, which must be configured separately:

```
n3k# guestshell

[root@guestshell]# sudo su -
[root@guestshell]# chvrf management
[root@guestshell]# hostname nxswitch01
[root@guestshell]# echo 'nxswitch01' > /etc/hostname
```

```
[root@guestshell]# echo 'domain example.com' > /etc/resolv.conf
[root@guestshell]# echo 'search example.com' >> /etc/resolv.conf
[root@guestshell]# echo 'nameserver 192.168.1.10' >> /etc/resolv.conf
[root@guestshell]# echo 'nameserver 192.168.1.11' >> /etc/resolv.conf
```

Installing the NX-OS Puppet Agent

Install Puppet using a process eerily similar to what we've used throughout this book (that is correct—the Guest Shell uses the Enterprise Linux repository):

1. yum install http://yum.puppetlabs.com/puppetlabs-release-pc1-el-7.noarch.rpm
2. yum install puppet-agent

After installing Puppet on the NX-OS device, you'll need to install some Ruby gems:

```
[root@guestshell]# gem install cisco_node_utils
[root@guestshell]# gem list | egrep 'cisco|net_http'
cisco_node_utils (1.0.0)
cisco_nxapi (1.0.0)
net_http_unix (0.2.1)
```

If you are running on a Highly Available (HA) platform, exit the Guest Shell and sync these changes to the backup processor:

```
n3k# guestshell sync
```

Enabling the NX-OS Puppet Agent

At this point, you have a complete Puppet v4 client installed on the NX-OS device. You configure it and authorize it exactly like any other Puppet agent on CentOS 7, as follows:

1. Run export PATH=/opt/puppetlabs/puppet/bin:\ /opt/puppetlabs/puppet/lib:$PATH.
2. Configure */etc/puppetlabs/puppet/puppet.conf* with the server name.
3. Run puppet agent --test to connect to the server.
4. Sign the certificate request on the Puppet server if not using autosign.
5. Run the Puppet agent again to download and apply the catalog.
6. Run systemctl enable puppet.

It is necessary to edit the startup process prior to starting the agent. The following change ensures that Puppet runs in the NX-OS management namespace:

```
[root@guestshell]# sed -i.bak \
  -e 's#^ExecStart=#ExecStart=/bin/nsenter --net=/var/run/netns/management #' \
  /usr/lib/systemd/system/puppet.service
```

Finally, you can start the Puppet agent service:

```
[root@guestshell]# systemctl start puppet
```

If you are running on a Highly Available (HA) platform, exit the guestshell and sync these changes to the backup processor:

```
n3k# guestshell sync
```

Managing Configuration

Documentation for the NX-OS resources can be found on the Puppet Forge at "Cisco Puppet NX-OS devices: Resource Reference" (*http://bit.ly/1XAwkFC*).

I highly recommend that you make use of the `device_hiera` module documented in "Managing Network Devices with Puppet Device" on page 474. This module works equally well with devices that have an embedded Puppet agent, and will allow the configuration to be DRY.

For example, you may want to configure all the default OSPF instance name and cost. In the global *common.yaml* file, define these defaults:

```
device_hiera::resources:
  - cisco_interface_ospf

device_hiera::defaults::cisco_interface_ospf:
  ensure: present
  cost  : 200
  ospf  : default
```

Assign the `device_hiera` class and override these parameters as necessary within a specific device's Hiera configuration data, such as *hostname/switch01.yaml*.

```
classes:
  - device_hiera

device_hiera::cisco_interface_ospf:
  'Ethernet1/2 default':
    area: '172.16.0.0'
```

Puppetizing Juniper Devices

Many recent Juniper devices including QFX, EX, and MX switches and routers can support a complete Puppet agent running on the device. This allows you to provision the device without using a proxy node.

The Juniper-provided `juniper/netdev_stdlib_junos` module (*http://bit.ly/1pt1aER*) contains the Junos-specific Puppet provider code that implements all standard Net-Dev resources. Support is provided by Juniper through the Juniper GitHub project (*http://bit.ly/1nULNE9*).

This module provides Junos providers for all NetDev standard resources, and the following Junos features:

- Physical interfaces configuration
- Switch or router port network settings
- IP address assignment
- VLANs
- Link aggregation groups (port trunking)
- BGP Peering
- System services (ssh, netconf, telnet…)
- Syslog message facility and level assignments
- Event policies and scripts

There is a video demonstrating the module's capabilities on the Juniper Learning Portal at Automating VLAN Provisioning on Multiple Junos Devices Using Puppet (*http://juni.pr/1MrMUSh*). The presenter configures two QFX5100 devices to communicate with each other on the same VLAN.

The video shows the older Puppet resource-style declarations. We're going to show you how to configure Junos devices using the `device_hiera` module described earlier in this chapter.

At the time this book was written, the latest version of Puppet provided with a Junos device was version 3.61. This works with Puppet Server, but Puppet master is not backward compatible.

We hope to see an upgraded *jpuppet-4* package made available in the near future.

Supported Devices

Puppet is supported on modern EX, MX, and QFX switches and routers with Enterprise features enabled. The updated list of supported devices is documented on the Puppet Forge at *juniper/netdev_stdlib_junos* (*http://bit.ly/1pt1aER*).

`jpuppet-1.0` was based on Puppet 2.7.19, while `jpuppet-3.6.1` is Puppet 3.6. I'd be very surprised if JPuppet v1 works with Puppet Server.

The Juniper device runs the Puppet agent. The agent utilizes the `netdev` library to translate Puppet configuration into `netconf` instructions the device can understand (see Figure 31-1).

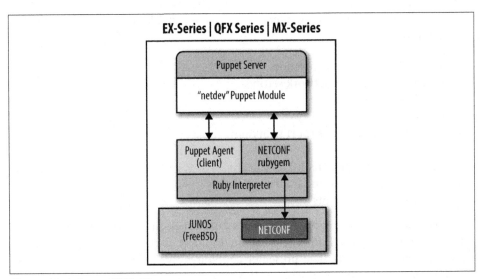

Figure 31-1. Junos SDK: JPuppet overview

It would appear from the documentation that you could download the virtualized MX Series Universal Edge Router (vMX) free trial (*http://www.juniper.net/us/en/dm/ free-vmx-trial/*) to set up a virtualized test lab. Documentation for the vMX platform and installation images can be downloaded from "vMX - Download Software" (*http:// www.juniper.net/support/downloads/?p=vmx*) on the Juniper Support site.

Installing Modules on the Puppet Server

On the Puppet server, you will need to install the `netconf` RubyGem:

```
[vagrant@puppetserver ~]$ sudo puppetserver gem install netconf
Fetching: nokogiri-1.6.6.2-java.gem (100%)
Successfully installed nokogiri-1.6.6.2-java
Fetching: net-ssh-2.9.2.gem (100%)
Successfully installed net-ssh-2.9.2
Fetching: net-scp-1.2.1.gem (100%)
Successfully installed net-scp-1.2.1
Fetching: netconf-0.3.1.gem (100%)
Successfully installed netconf-0.3.1
4 gems installed
```

Then install the Junos Puppet module:

```
[vagrant@puppetserver ~]$ sudo puppet module install juniper-netdev_stdlib_junos
Notice: Preparing to install into environments/production/modules ...
Notice: Downloading from https://forgeapi.puppetlabs.com ...
Notice: Installing -- do not interrupt ...
/etc/puppetlabs/code/environments/production/modules
└─┬ juniper-netdev_stdlib_junos (v2.0.0)
  └── netdevops-netdev_stdlib (v1.0.0)
```

Preparing the Junos Device

Configure the management interface, DNS domain name, and NTP servers if that hasn't been done already. All of these are necessary in order to communicate with Puppet Server:

```
root@junos> configure
[edit]
root@junos# set interfaces fxp0.0 family inet address 192.168.1.21/24
root@junos# set system host-name device-name
root@junos# set system domain-name example.com
root@junos# set system domain-search [ example.com example.net ]
root@junos# set system name-server 192.168.1.10
root@junos# set system name-server 192.168.1.11
root@junos# set system ntp time-zone America/Los_Angeles
root@junos# set system ntp server 192.168.1.10
root@junos# set system ntp server 192.168.1.11
root@junos# edit system extensions
[edit system extensions]
root@junos# set providers juniper license-type juniper deployment-scope commer
root@junos# commit and-quit
commit complete
root@junos>
```

This example is presented without explanation because we expect that you know the Junos configuration commands already.

Installing the Junos Puppet Agent

Download Puppet for Junos from *https://downloads.puppetlabs.com/junos/*. Select the version known to work with your platform, listed at *juniper/netdev_stdlib_junos* (*http://bit.ly/1R8HjCf*) on the Puppet Forge. Copy this file to the */var/tmp* directory on the device.

> Some devices running Junos with enhanced automation have the Puppet agent integrated into the software. If you see the word *puppet* in the output of show version, then you can skip this step.

In this example, we'll configure an EX4300 switch, which utilizes the PowerPC architecture. AFter downloading the appropriate Puppet version from the Juniper site, run this:

```
$ scp jpuppet-3.6.1_1.junos.powerpc.tgz junos-device:/var/tmp/
```

Log in to the device and install the software like any other Junos software package:

```
root@junos>request system software add /var/tmp/jpuppet-3.6.1_1.junos.powerpc.tgz
```

Creating the Puppet User

Create a puppet user on the device. This user account will be used by Puppet when configuring the device. Do not share this account with a real human being, or any other automation:

```
root@junos> configure
[edit]
root@junos# set system login user puppet class superuser
root@junos# set system login user puppet authentication plain-text-password'
New password: type a secure password
Retype new password: retype the password
root@junos# set system login user puppet password plain-text-password
root@junos# set system login user puppet shell csh
root@junos# commit and-quit
commit complete
root@junos>
```

Now log in to the device as the puppet user and create the following files and directories:

```
$ ssh puppet@junos-device
Password: password

puppet@junos> start shell csh
puppet@junos% echo "setenv PATH ${PATH}:/opt/jet/juniper/bin" >> $HOME/.cshrc
puppet@junos% echo "limit data 128M" >> $HOME/.cshrc
puppet@junos% mkdir -p $HOME/.puppet/var/run
puppet@junos% mkdir -p $HOME/.puppet/var/log
puppet@junos% vi $HOME/.puppet/puppet.conf
```

Create a Puppet configuration file like so:

```
[main]
    pluginsync = true
    libdir = $vardir/lib
    logdir = $vardir/log/puppet
    rundir = $vardir/run/puppet
    ssldir = $vardir/ssl

[agent]
    server = puppet.example.com
```

Save the file, then exit the shell and log out. Log in to the unit again in order to validate the environment:

```
puppet@junos% exit
puppet@junos> exit

$ ssh puppet@junos-device
Password: password
```

Start the shell and run the `facter` command to confirm that Puppet executables are in the PATH now:

```
puppet@junos> start shell csh
puppet@junos% facter
architecture => i386
domain => example.com
fqdn => junos-device.example.com
...snip...
```

Now connect to the server, just like any other Puppet agent:

1. Run `puppet agent --test` to connect to the server.
2. Sign the certificate request on the Puppet server if not using `autosign`.
3. Run the Puppet agent again to download and apply the catalog.

Adjusting Physical Interface Settings

The following example uses `device_hiera` with NetDev resources to configure physical interfaces on a Junos device.

The `netdev_interface` resource declares the attributes for a physical interface, such as speed, MTU, or duplex. As these tend to be consistent throughout a deployment, you may not need the custom configuration.

In the global *common.yaml* file, define defaults for physical interfaces:

```
device_hiera::resources:
  - netdev_device
  - netdev_interfaces

device_hiera::defaults::netdev_interface:
  # many are resource defaults we could leave out
  ensure: present
  active: 'true'
  admin : 'up'
  duplex: 'auto'
  speed : 'auto'
  mtu   : '1500'
```

Assign the `device_hiera` class and override these parameters as necessary within a specific host's Hiera configuration data, such as *hostname/switch01.yaml*:

```
classes:
  - device_hiera

device_hiera::netdev_interfaces::ports:
  - 'ge-1/0/': '1-8'
  - 'ge-2/1/': '1-48'
```

```
device_hiera::netdev_interfaces::custom:
  'ge-1/0/13':
    description: 'bad port'
    enable     : 'false'
  'ge-4/0/1':
    description: 'External firewall interface'
    speed      : '100m'
```

This Hiera data will configure `device_hiera` to ensure that interface physical attributes are consistent on 56 ports, with a custom interface configuration on port `ge-4/0/1`. Port `ge-1/0/13` is disabled with a comment explaining why.

Simplifying Layer-2 VLANs

The `netdev_l2_interface` resource declares the attributes for layer-2 switching services. It can reference VLANs created using `netdev_vlan` resources, or it can reference VLANs statically defined on the device.

In the global *common.yaml* file, define common defaults for VLANs, physical interfaces, and layer-2 interfaces. As VLANs are shared in this example deployment, we'll place those in this common data:

```
device_hiera::resources:
  - netdev_device
  - netdev_l2_interfaces
  - netdev_vlan

device_hiera::defaults::netdev_vlan:
  active: 'true'
  ensure: 'present'

device_hiera::defaults::netdev_l2_interface:
  ensure        : present
  active        : true
  vlan_tagging  : 'disable'
  untagged_vlan : 'corporate'

device_hiera::netdev_vlan:
  'corporate':
    vlan_id    : '100'
    description: 'Corporate Network'
  'hardware':
    vlan_id    : '101'
    description: 'Hardware Development'
  'testing':
    vlan_id    : '102'
    description: 'Test Network'
```

Assign the `device_hiera` class and override these parameters as necessary within a specific host's Hiera configuration data, such as *hostname/switch01.yaml*:

```
classes:
  - device_hiera

device_hiera::netdev_l2_interfaces::ports:
  - 'ge-1/0/': '1-8'
  - 'ge-2/1/': '1-48'

device_hiera::netdev_l2_interfaces::custom:
  'ge-4/0/2':
    description: 'Uplink to core'
    vlan_tagging : 'enable'
    untagged_vlan: 'absent'
    tagged_vlans : ['corporate','hardware','testing']
```

This Hiera data will configure device_hiera to ensure the following:

- Default access port configuration on 56 ports on the first two slots
- A custom layer-2 trunking configuration on port ge-4/0/2

That's 57 detailed port configurations in a dozen lines of text. It doesn't get easier than this.

Enabling Link Aggregation

The netdev_lag resource declares the attributes for a *link aggregation group* (*LAG*), sometimes referred to as a *port channel* or *bonded interface*. The LAG can optionally enable the use of link aggregation control protocol (LACP) to maintain a peer relationship with the remote side.

In the global *common.yaml* file, define common defaults for VLANs, physical interfaces, and layer 2 interfaces. As VLANs are shared in this example deployment, we'll place those in this common data:

```
device_hiera::resources:
  - netdev_device
  - netdev_lag
  - netdev_l2_interface

device_hiera::defaults::netdev_lag:
  lacp  : 'passive'
```

Assign the device_hiera class and override these parameters as necessary within a specific host's Hiera configuration data, such as *hostname/switch01.yaml*:

```
classes:
  - device_hiera

device_hiera::netdev_lag:
  'ae0':
    links: ['ge-4/0/1', 'ge-4/0/2', 'ge-5/0/1', 'ge-5/0/2']
```

```
device_hiera::netdev_l2_interfaces::custom:
  'ae0:
    vlan_tagging : 'enable'
    tagged_vlans : ['corporate','hardware','testing']
```

This Hiera data will configure `device_hiera` to ensure the following:

- Bind four ports on two slots together as a bonded LACP port group.
- Configure three tagged VLANs on the newly created port group.

Short, simple, and easy to read.

Defining Ad Hoc Configuration Parameters

It is possible to apply Junos configuration statements for which there is no Puppet resource. For this purpose, you'll need to create a Puppet module containing templates for the configuration:

```
[vagrant@puppetserver ~]$ puppet module generate myorg/junos_config
...snip...
[vagrant@puppetserver ~]$ cd junos_config/
[vagrant@puppetserver ~]$ mkdir templates
```

Create ERB templates as documented in "Using Ruby ERB Templates" on page 175. These templates should resolve to a list of Junos configuration commands after parsing, like so:

```
set system domain-name example.com
set system domain-search [ example.com example.net ]
set system name-server 192.168.1.10
set system name-server 192.168.1.11
set system ntp time-zone America/Los_Angeles
set system ntp server 192.168.1.10
set system ntp server 192.168.1.11
```

Finally, create a manifest that makes use of the template:

```
netdev_stdlib_junos::apply_group { 'dns-ntp-servers':
  ensure        => present,
  active        => true,
  template_path => 'junos_config/dns-ntp-servers.erb',
}
```

Obviously, it would be smarter to pass in Puppet variables and iterate over arrays for maximum flexibility. We'll leave this as an exercise for the reader. Some useful examples of configuring BGP can be found at Puppet + ERB Templates + Junos = Increased automation agility and flexibility (*http://juni.pr/21zn19S*).

The juniper/netdev_stdlib_junos module contains a few templates built in, with examples of how to use them in a manifest on the Puppet Forge at *juniper/netdev_stdlib_junos* (*http://bit.ly/ 1R8HjCf*) on the Puppet Forge.

Here's an example manifest that uses of one of these templates. This template looks for a variable named $service to be defined with an array of system services to enable:

```
# only enable SSH and NetConf configuration
$services = [ [ 'netconf', 'ssh' ] ]

netdev_stdlib_junos::apply_group{ "services_group":
  ensure        => present,
  active        => 'true',
  template_path => 'netdev_stdlib_junos/services.set.erb',
}
```

Distributing Junos Event Scripts

It is possible to copy Junos SLAX scripts to devices and assign them as event handlers:

```
[vagrant@puppetserver production]$ cd modules/junos_config
[vagrant@puppetserver junos_config]$ mkdir files
```

Place the event script file in the *files/* directory. Then declare a file resource to copy the file to the device:

```
file { '/var/db/scripts/event/checklogs.slax':
  ensure => file,
  owner  => 'puppet',
  group  => 'wheel',
  mode   => '0644',
  source => 'puppet:///files/junos_config/checklogs.slax'
}
```

After running Puppet, you should see the files installed on your Junos device, as shown here:

```
$ ssh puppet@junos-device
Password: password

puppet@junos> file list /var/db/scripts/event/
```

To make the Junos script run automatically based on event trigger, create a manifest that declares $policy and $event_script variables before making use of the *event-options.xml.erb* template:

```
# Files to copy
$event_script = ['checklogs.slax']

# Configure event policy
$policy = {
  'check_logs' => {
    'events'        => [ 'sshd_login_failed' ],
    'action'        => 'then',
    'event-script' => 'checklogs.slax',
  }
}

# Now apply the commands using the 'event-options' template
netdev_stdlib_junos::apply_group{ 'event_options_group':
  ensure        => present,
  active        => true,
  template_path => 'netdev_stdlib_junos/event-options.xml.erb',
}
```

You can declare multiple policies in the $policy hash, and multiple files in the $event_script array. You can find a list of events to match with set event-options policy check_logs events.

Documentation for event scripts can be found at Junos Event Automation: Event Scripts and Event Policy (*http://juni.pr/1R4J1H7*)

Running Puppet Automatically

To enable Puppet to update the device automatically, enable a cron schedule for Puppet to run. Add the following cron resource to your Juniper configuration module:

```
cron { 'puppet_agent':
  user        => 'puppet',
  environment => 'PATH=/bin:/usr/bin:/sbin:/usr/sbin:/opt/sbin:\
                   /opt/bin:/opt/jet/juniper/bin:/opt/sdk/juniper/bin'
  command     => 'puppet agent --onetime --no-daemonize',
  minute      => '*/30',
}
```

Troubleshooting

The Junos Puppet agent logs its actions extensively, making it easy to audit Puppet changes:

- The agent logs all commit operations with the provided Puppet catalog version.
- Puppet logs include a Junos source indicator.
- The Puppet agent makes configuration changes under exclusive lock, preventing multiple agents or users from overlapping commits.

These features enable report extraction and problem isolation in production environments.

On some platforms, the `netdev_device` resource (and all other Junos resources) will fail to apply if the Puppet user account doesn't have permission to configure the device, or if another user is interactively working in configuration mode. When this occurs, you'll see an error like this:

```
err: JUNOS: configuration database locked by:
  jorhett terminal p0 (pid 6129) on since 2015-12-19 15:57:29 UTC
      exclusive {master:0}[edit]
```

To verify that the Puppet agent has downloaded and committed a specific catalog, use the `show system commit` operational mode command to view the commit history and catalog versions:

```
root@junos.example.com> show system commit
0   2015-12-19 10:50:17 PST by puppet via netconf
    Puppet agent catalog: 1359474609
1   2015-12-19 10:49:54 PST by jorhett via cli
2   2015-12-19 10:48:00 PST by puppet via netconf
    Puppet agent catalog: 1359474408
3   2015-12-19 06:47:37 PST by root via cli
4   2015-12-19 04:16:57 PST by puppet via netconf
    Puppet agent catalog: 1359474408
```

Best Practices for Network Devices

Let's review some of the best practices for managing network devices with Puppet:

- Use SSH or NetConf rather than plain-text protocols like telnet.
- Passwords are stored in files, so use long and complex passwords.
- Use the `device_hiera` module and a DRY style to minimize cruft.
- Run `puppet device` in a non-privileged user account to keep config and data separate.

Keep checking the Puppet Forge, as more NetDev-compatible vendor modules are added every month.

Reviewing Network Devices

Using Puppet to configure and audit network devices can be an exciting project. Puppet has powerful support for configuring network devices. The last year has seen the emergence of Puppet providers maintained and supported by a large number of network device vendors.

In this chapter, we have covered how to:

- Use `puppet device` to manage network devices without embedded Puppet agents.
- Install and configure a Puppet agent on Cisco NX-OS network switches.
- Install and enable Puppet agent on Junos devices.
- Use standardized NetDev resources to manage any vendor with NetDev support.
- Use `jorhett/device_hiera` for DRY configuration, managing hundreds of ports with just a few lines of Hiera data.

Network device management with Puppet is a fast-growing part of the Puppet community. I expect this chapter will be updated and revised significantly over the next year.

## CHAPTER 32

Assimilating Puppet Best Practices

- This chapter of the book is not about Puppet.
- This chapter covers the most important use of Puppet that I have ever written.

Both of these statements are true.

This part of the book doesn't provide you with any new technology from Puppet Labs. Instead, it discusses successful ways of using Puppet within different types of organizations. It outlines the advantages and disadvantages of different implementation choices. It proposes questions you should be considering as you first deploy Puppet, or grow the deployment within your organization.

This part of the book is devoted to providing you with a window into the experiences and successes of the DevOps community as it has evolved.

Managing Change

Puppet and DevOps practices can bring incredibly beneficial change. There are many types of change, and we're going to cover a few of them here.

Expecting Change

There is one universal truth about DevOps. When you first embrace DevOps—when you can declare the manifestation, when you embrace constant iteration and improvement, when you can encourage change rather than react to the consequences —your job will become bigger and greater than ever before. You can do more than ever before. Your environment will change.

You will change.

In many cases, a new Puppet implementation will enable months of rapid and exhilarating change. In some cases, it will be slow and progressive, and you won't notice the depth of change until you look back and realize how far you've come. But no matter how wide and diverse the experience, no matter what your industry or background, everyone who walks down these roads experiences dramatic change.

Go out and talk to people who are using Puppet. Ask them to compare their job before and after Puppet. Ask them if they want their old job back. Watch the look on their faces.

It's easy to say, "You'll get so many benefits," and "You'll be able to accomplish more than ever before." Those statements are absolutely true. Puppet will give you powerful tools. Your success with Puppet will change the way your job is viewed, and the scope of decisions you are involved in. Fast change can be good, but even slow and progressive change will redefine the landscape eventually. The questions asked of you will change.

Change will come to you, to your processes, and to your expectations. Expect change.

Controlling Rate of Change

Puppet provides powerful tools for managing changes on systems. However, only in really small environments do all servers apply at the same time. Most environments run the Puppet agent every 30 minutes. Nodes receive their configuration changes spread out over time. This means that at any point in time, there are two different configurations running.

In large-scale environments with multiple teams, the rate of change can be such that one set of changes is not yet done rolling out while another is starting to hit the first nodes. At any moment at my current job, there are between 3 and 7 module changes getting pushed to live nodes every second of the day. I've seen as many as 20 different active configurations in globally diverse Puppet environments, although 2 or 3 was by far the most common.

This can be good, as problems with a change can be spotted and reverted before it breaks all nodes. This can be bad when consistency is crucial.

Orchestration tools like MCollective are necessary to accelerate change and limit the inconsistent period to a few seconds. MCollective provides a framework to apply immediate changes that bring your nodes into sync. If you skipped over Chapter 30, listen to my advice that this is a crucial tool for managing change.

Tracking Change

Absolutely everyone should implement tracking of Puppet convergence results. This can be done in several ways:

- Parsing log messages provided by Puppet
- Tracking status from a dashboard that evaluates Puppet reports
- Processing Puppet node reports with a custom report handler

Parsing log messages with analysis tools like Splunk, Graylog, or Logstash is easy for basic uses (to capture failures) but difficult, time-consuming, and subject to evolving requirements to gather new statistics. It is considerably better to provide a standard data storage mechanism like PuppetDB, and enable users to store and retrieve their own data.

Dashboards provide a drop-in, immediately available overview of node results reported by nodes. Any of the dashboards reviewed here can provide a wall display useful for service desks to see happy green and problematic red immediately. Detailed analysis of the Puppet node reports depends on the features available in the dashboard selected.

PuppetDB stores and aggregates data about changes to nodes. All dashboards provide a web interface to review the data from PuppetDB. Futhermore, multiple reporting tools can utilize the same PuppetDB as a data source. PuppetDB's independent data source provides a clear advantage for tracking change.

If your organization uses a different tool for tracking change, you may be able to leverage it for tracking change on your Puppet nodes. Create a custom report processor that extracts data from node reports and feeds it to the existing tool's input mechanism. I have done this dozens of times with only a few hours effort required to make the Puppet data available in the organization's existing toolset.

Choosing Puppet Apply Versus Puppet Server

Perhaps the most hotly debated decision among Puppet users concerns using `puppet agent` with centralized Puppet servers, versus running `puppet apply` on each node. As mentioned at the start of Part IV, this is not something for which there is a single answer that fits every purpose. There are a lot of advantages with either choice, and there are some conditions required to support either method of working.

The changes in Puppet 4 have provided a much more balanced set of features between the two methods. They are now closer than ever before, each mode now providing features previously available only with the other working method.

This section will be devoted to discussing the advantages and requirements of both methods. We will highlight changes that Puppet 4 has brought to each, and identify the well-known scenarios for which one mode is more likely to work than the other.

Benefits of Puppet Apply

In Part I, you interacted with Puppet only through `puppet apply`. You saw how to invoke it on demand to immediately evaluate the declared state, and apply the requested state.

There are numerous advantages to using `puppet apply`:

- Allows use by detached nodes without access to a shared server.
- Does not require TLS certificate signing before the node can apply changes.
- Can enforce policy in containerized microservices with short lifespans.
- Uses only local resources without depending on infrastructure for a shared service.
- Access to local system state and data sources unavailable to a remote server.
- Executes function calls on local system during the catalog build.
- Converges many nodes in parallel without "storming" a shared server.
- Enables simple code pushes without learning Puppet environments and architecture.
- NTP time synchronization is not essential unless you are also using MCollective.

The independent, local source for information works very well for some organizations. This implementation is very common among some of the largest Puppet customers with the highest total node counts.

Some of the advantages for `puppet apply` create requirements that must be satisfied outside of Puppet. Depending on your needs, these requirements can actually nullify the advantages:

- You'll have to create a service to synchronize Puppet modules and data down to each node.
- It requires a constant development effort to push only the necessary modules and data to each node. In most organizations, all Puppet modules and data are pushed to every node for simplicity, which can make unrelated security-sensitive data available for anyone with (authorized or not) privileged access on the managed node.
- Making changes to the Puppet code—even a one-line attribute change—would require recycling all containers with static copies of the Puppet data.
- Every node requires access to every data source. This could require complex firewall or VPN infrastructure if remote or public nodes access private data sources.
- Security credentials required for data access will have to be synchronized out to every node that needs to query the data source to build a Puppet catalog.
- Having each node connect independently to data sources will consume significantly more resources on the central service than having the server connect and

cache the response. Nodes remote from the resource will have significantly longer catalog build times due to latency of data access.

I've probably forgotten an advantage or disadvantage here, but I think this gives you an idea of the concerns.

Benefits of Puppet Server

In a server-centered configuration, the code and data only needs to reside on the Puppet server. The Puppet agent on each node submits its locally evaluated facts to the Puppet server, and receives back a catalog containing only the resources that should be applied locally.

There are numerous advantages to using a Puppet server, including the following:

- Requires no configuration of client nodes beyond the TLS certificate signing.
- Requires no presynchronization of data sources to utilize.
- Provides file synchronization services for applications.
- Receives only the resources and data applicable to that node. No manual work separating files is necessary to avoid placing unrelated data on the wrong nodes.
- Outsources the resource-intensive catalog build process to the servers, allowing the use of low-power, low-memory Puppet agents on network devices and embedded systems.
- Deploy code only to Puppet servers, rather than to every individual node.
- Evaluating change in a short-lived Canary environment can be done without a code deployment framework.
- The server caches the modules and data in short-term memory, whereas a node with other priorities will reload from disk on every run.
- Centralize storage of modified files and change reports.
- Puppet servers scale horizontally very easily.
- Puppet servers can be collocated near every node, or centralized globally depending on the need.
- Puppet servers run functions when building the catalog, which can request data from sources unavailable to every node.
- The Puppet service utilizes a single encrypted TCP connection from each node, making it easier to pass through a firewall and more secure than many other data access protocols (DB queries, LDAP, etc.).
- The server could utilize security credentials for data access that do not need to be synchronized to every node.
- Servers can be collocated near the data sources for fast catalog builds. The latency of one request from an Puppet agent to the server is much lower than having the node use independent queries that each have different connection setup and latency costs.

That's quite a long list of advantages. It is easy to see why the use of a Puppet server is the easiest to implement, and is by far the most common solution (when you're counting organizations, rather than nodes).

As with the other mode, the use of TLS authentication and the nature of centralized servers create some requirements that must be satisfied. Some of the disadvantages of using a Puppet server include:

- Requires either a manual key authorization, a pre-creation and synchronization of the node's keys using a build system, or an automatic signing policy to add nodes to the server.
- TLS validation requires working DNS or synchronization of IP to name mappings.
- NTP time synchronization is required for successful TLS authentication.
- A badly performing Puppet server can slow down application of new resources, if nodes are unable to get a revised catalog for several connection attempts.
- It is not possible for every node to receive its catalog at the same moment in time unless the ratio of clients to servers is quite low.
- The Puppet server cannot access data sources that are only available to the node.
- A Puppet server caches custom functions, requiring an API call for it to reload a changed function.

There is one significant difference in the requirements of each method. The Puppet server can provide code to resolve any dependency other than network access from the node to the server. You can write a Puppet module that spreads out client connections to avoid storming the servers, for example. You can write custom facts that contain information only accessible by the client node.

Benefits Shared

Quite often a person will state that they use either a Puppet server or `puppet apply` because only that method provides certain functionality. This is typically followed by a dozen people pointing out that they use the other method to do the same thing. Both methods share a lot of advantages, especially in Puppet 4.

Let's list the shared advantages so that you know what either can do, and what you can use no matter which method you select:

Puppet servers can be autoscaled too
> If your environment is scaled on demand, you can also scale your Puppet servers on demand. In fact, as Puppet servers are always bound by CPU limitations, and response time degrades linearly according to the usage, I have found it easier to successfully build the auto-scaling rules than with almost any other service.

ENCs can be used by both a Puppet server and `puppet apply`
> You can enable an exec terminus in either the [`master`] or the [`user`] section, depending on which way you invoke Puppet. This can be very useful if the node invokes an application to provide necessary data.
>
> If you call back to a central service to gather node information, it's very unlikely that it provides any advantage in speed and resilience over using a Puppet server.

You can always use `puppet apply` to evaluate local manifests as necessary
> Many sites have the Puppet server synchronize out a directory of manifests to be used by `puppet apply` on demand by other deployment mechanisms (including MCollective). Some sites use the Puppet server as a file synchronization source, and `puppet apply` to build the catalogs on the node.

MCollective works perfectly fine with either solution
> There is absolutely nothing about MCollective that is benefited by either solution, other than the synchronization of data issues already discussed.

Puppet agents can continue to apply cached catalogs
> If the Puppet server is unavailable, the node can fall back and apply the last catalog it received. This is no different from using apply mode and having a file synchronization problem.

Summarizing the Differences

After having read five long lists, you're probably wishing it was easier to understand. Unless you were able to spot concerns that are especially important, you might be looking for advice on which way to go.

There is no golden rule, but the most obvious use cases can be summarized as follows:

- A Puppet server makes it trivially easy to synchronize data to nodes. You need only run one command to submit a certificate request. All other required files can be supplied by the server to the node going forward.
- Local catalog build and evaluation can be used with distributed nodes lacking centralized servers, so long as another file distribution mechanism is available.
- It is more efficient and secure to authorize a few Puppet servers to a secured data set than to provide access for every remote node.
- `puppet apply` can make use of data sources accessible only by the node. This situation is rare, and confined almost exclusively to managed service providers with off-net equipment.
- If client nodes are underpowered or lack storage, you can outsource the compute and storage requirements to a Puppet server.

- For static container images with short lifespans, `puppet apply` avoids the need for TLS certificate authorization.

I think this clearly outlines the most common situations that make one method stand out over the other.

Creating a Private Puppet Forge

If you wish to create an internal repository, there are several software projects to help you provide and maintain the repository. Next, we will cover some of these projects as described on their websites.

I have deliberately avoided including forge software that doesn't support the Forge API v3 used by Puppet 3.6 and up, or that appears not to have received updates in a few years. Please bring to my attention any forges that I have overlooked, so I can include them in updates to this book.

Pulp

Pulp: Juicy Software Repository Management (*http://www.pulpproject.org/*) provides the ability to inventory Puppet modules and serve them from the Pulp server. This includes both uploading modules to the Pulp server, as well as selectively downloading and keeping up-to-date modules served at Puppet Forge.

Instructions for installing and using Pulp can be found at *http://www.pulpproject.org/*.

Puppet Forge Server

The Puppet Forge Server serves modules from local module files and proxies to other Puppet forges.

Puppet Forge Server includes a web UI that looks very similar to the official Puppet Forge web page and provides a simple module search feature.

Instructions for installing and using the Puppet Forge Server can be found at *https://github.com/unibet/puppet-forge-server*.

Django Forge

Django Forge provides a Forge service using a Django implementation of third version (v3) of the JSON web services necessary to house (or mirror) a private, standalone version of the Forge.

Instructions for installing and using Django Forge can be found at *https://github.com/jbronn/django-forge*.

Good Practices

The following are good practices that you should employ to take care of your Puppet servers.

Indenting Heredoc

Heredoc format can suppress leading spaces, allowing you to maintain indentation in the code without this showing up to the user:

```
else {
  if( $keeping_up_with_jones ) {
    $message_text = @(END)
      This is a bit of a rat race, don't you think $username?
      All this running about, for $effort and $gain,
      the results of which we can't see at all.
      |- END
  }
}
```

Furthermore, you can tell Heredoc the syntax inside the block and it can validate the syntax for you. Geppetto will display it according to the appropriate syntax scheme:

```
$certificates = @(END:json)
  {
    "private_key": "-----RSA PRIVATE KEY----...",
    "public_key": "-----BEGIN PUBLIC KEY-----...",
    "certificate": "-----BEGIN CERTIFICATE-----..."
  }
  | END
```

Splaying Puppet Agent Cron Jobs

If you run Puppet from cron and use Puppet or any shared data sources, you can't run them all at the same time or you will overload the data source. In situations with only a few hundred nodes, you can simply use the `splay` feature and the random distribution will be random enough:

```
cron { 'puppet-agent':
  ensure      => present,
  environment => 'PATH=/usr/bin:/opt/puppetlabs/bin'
  command     => 'puppet agent --onetime --no-daemonize --splay --splaylimit 30m',
  user        => 'root',
  minute      => 0,
}
```

In my experience, after a few hundred nodes you'll find that a quarter of them end up in the same three minutes and you'll experience the "thundering herd" phenomenon. At that point, you'll want a mechanism to guarantee a more consistent spread of hosts.

The way to do this is to have the server calculate a different minute number for each node, and add the cron resource to its catalog with that minute. The number selection must be consistent, as random numbers will change on each connection.

The easiest way with zero development on your part is to use the `fqdn_rand(minutes,string)` function, which will always produce the same value between 0 and the minutes provided. If you don't provide a string, it will use the current node name as salt. It is possible to supply any value (which doesn't change on a node) as salt. Here are some of my favorite sources for the string:

- Any unique identifier for each node, such as a serial number.
- The node's IP address. The unique `fe80::` address is always good.
- Node certificate name or fully qualified domain name.
- A unique identifier for each node from an internal datastore.

It really doesn't matter how you generate the source number for the node, so long as it is evenly distributed and does not change often. However you generate the number, add 30 for the second run. Place both of these numbers in a resource like so:

```
$minute = fqdn_rand( 30, $facts['certname'] )
cron { 'puppet-agent':
  ensure  => present,
  command => '/opt/puppetlabs/bin/puppet agent --onetime --no-daemonize',
  user    => 'root',
  minute  => [ $minute, $minute+30 ]
}
```

Cleaning Puppet Reports

The reports created by Puppet nodes are never removed by the server. You'll have to add jobs to clean them up. Shown here is a resource for your server to clean up reports after 90 days:

```
cron { 'clean-puppetserver-reports':
  command => 'find /var/opt/puppetlabs/puppetserver/reports -ctime +90 -delete',
  user    => 'root',
  minute  => '2',
  hour    => '3',
}
```

While it's not likely to fill up quite so fast, the same problem does exist for the node itself. Here's a resource to apply to every node to clean up the reports once a month:

```
cron { 'clean-puppet-agent-reports':
  command => 'find /opt/puppetlabs/puppet/cache/reports -ctime +90 -delete',
  user    => 'root',
  day     => '1',
  minute  => '2',
  hour    => '3',
}
```

Adjust the timing of the runs and the retention length to meet your own needs. In many environments we centrally archive the reports on long-term storage, and delete reports older than two days on the node every night.

Trimming the File Bucket

The file backups made by Puppet on the node can be really useful. If Puppet only manages text files, you can likely leave the backups around for as long as your security policy permits.

If you are using Puppet to manage large files, you may need to trim back the archive periodically. Here's a resource to remove files older than 3 days from the backup bucket. This example should be added to your `puppet::agent` class:

```
cron { 'clean-puppet-client-filebucket':
  command => 'find /opt/puppetlabs/puppet/cache/clientbucket -mtime +30 -delete',
  user    => 'root',
  day     => '1',
  minute  => '2',
  hour    => '3',
}
```

If you have enabled a `filebucket` on a Puppet server, you may need to trim back that bucket as well. Here's a resource you could use in a `puppet::server` class to purge backups after 365 days:

```
cron { 'clean-puppetserver-filebucket':
  command => 'find /var/opt/puppetlabs/puppetserver/bucket -mtime +365 -delete',
  user    => 'root',
  day     => '1',
  minute  => '2',
  hour    => '3',
}
```

Adjust the timing and retention length to meet your own needs.

Drinking the Magic Monkey Juice

The *Magic Monkey Juice* is a grab bag of tips and tricks that seemed distracting or a bit too advanced for the early chapters of the book.

A few of the following are best practices. Some are offensive violations of common sense. There are a few neat tricks, side by side with stunts you'd only consider six hours into an all-night bender. They've all been useful for me at one time or another, although some of them are for reasons I won't admit to.

Hating on Params.pp

The Puppet Style Guide recommends placing all parameter default values inside *params.pp*. I completely agree with this logic for operating system defaults and values that must be derived through lengthy selectors and case logic.

Doing this for static values violates the idea of favoring readability. For example, a subclass that declares a single service should not use this design:

```
class apache_httpd::service (
  String $status = $apache_httpd::service_status,
) inherits apache_httpd::params {
  service 'httpd' {
    ensure => $status,
  }
}
```

That's a tiny little module that fits on half of a page. To be forced to look in the *params.pp* class to find the value is annoying.

In larger modules, *params.pp* ends up crammed with many variables that satisfy the needs of a wide variety of subclasses. This can be a management nightmare all its own, especially as these variables are divorced from the classes that depend on them. Someone refactors one module and breaks another because they weren't aware that the modules shared a data source.

I have found that patterns like the following can be significantly more readable in large modules with many declared resources. Static default values are there to read, and the source of the default value is likewise clear.

Define the `params` class as a wrapper class that includes multiple other classes named for the type of data provided:

```
# static wrapper for value parameters that includes multiple data sources
class mcollective::params() {
  include mcollective::os_defaults
  include mcollective::puppet_defaults
}
```

Then inherit from `params` in the class definition, but set the default value to the specific source class so that it's self-documenting, as shown here:

```
class mcollective::client(
  # Derived these values from the OS
  $package      = $mcollective::os_defaults::client_package_name,
  $group_owner  = $mcollective::os_defaults::admin_group,

  # Derive these from the Puppet version
  $etcdir       = $mcollective::puppet_defaults::etcdir,
```

```
    # Common values used below
    $logger_type  = 'console',
    $log_level    = 'warn',
    $keeplogs     = '5',
    $max_log_size = '2097152',
)
inherits mcollective::params {
```

Your mileage may vary.

Disabling Environments

If you are truly hardcore about not wanting environment directories, then create the following file and place it at */etc/puppetlabs/code/environments/production/environment.conf*:

```
# Remove environment directory from path
manifest = /etc/puppetlabs/code/manifests

# Just use /etc/puppetlabs/code/modules
modulepath = $basemodulepath
```

 You can always add a test environment in its normal directory if you change your mind.

Tracking Providers

Something that I have really found useful is the definition of *provides* variables. The simplest example is when you support multiple types of web servers. Is it nginx or Apache? In that situation, you may want to build your application configurations to not be aware of which web server is used.

Who Provides That?

There's a running joke at $DAYJOB that we support every type of everything. Between acquisitions and differing technology choices by teams, we seem to have deployed every relevant alternative of any given technology. Please don't mention one we're not supporting today where a developer can hear you...

I've implemented this using `Provides::Webserver` hashes that can be dereferenced by other classes:

```
# poor innocent class with no knowledge of web server setup
file 'config-file-for-other-service' {
  ...
  path    => "${provides::webserver::sites_directory}/other_service.conf",
  require => Class[ $provides::webserver::class ],
  notify  => Service[ $provides::webserver::service ],
}
```

You can set these variables in Hiera using the hierarchy based around operating system, or cluster name, or anything your hierarchy makes available to you. Or you can create a `provides` module that has a `webserver` class that a module could declare to instantiate itself as the provider.

Breaking the Rules

Sometimes better judgment needs to take priority over following the rules. For example, the Puppet Style Guide says that every parameter should receive a default value such that the class can be successfully declared with no input values, and it should implement the most common use case.

That's a great practice, and certainly applicable to installing most software packages where default configurations work fairly well.

However, some systems cannot be, or should never be, configured with default values. For instance, modules that create security key stores should never use default passwords. If the user fails to set an appropriate value, the key store can be opened by anyone who can read the default password from your code. Modules that configure routers or firewalls should likewise demand customized values before instantiating security-related infrastructure.

In these situations, it may be better to force a failure to ensure that the user reads the module documentation completely before using it. Announcing "I'm using a default value for this"—even with all caps and dozens of exclamation points—will get overlooked far more often than you can imagine.

 I was criticized for making this choice in my MCollective module. I felt that default passwords were too risky—enough to justify breaking the rule—as MCollective runs as `root` on nodes. I've simply seen too many sites get cracked by someone who read the passwords from the code.

Sometimes the right thing to do requires breaking the rules.

Working Good, Fast, Cheap

Puppet is a fantastic tool for ensuring that things are exactly as you declared them. MCollective provides a mechanism to make change happen fast, everywhere.

- Write quick, small manifests to achieve exactly one thing well with Puppet.
- Use best practices. Declare final state. Log useful information.
- Invoke puppet apply using MCollective for immediate response.

Cheap. Good. Fast. You can do it.

Choosing Fight or Flight

If the resource being evaluated is noncritical, it may be better to log an error but return successfully, to allow the remainder of the dependent Puppet resources to be applied. Can this resource wait until someone fixes the problem before this bit of functionality is enabled? Sometimes, this answer might be more acceptable than you think.

Likewise, if your site doesn't have a good logging or alerting infrastructure, or the nodes are being built autonomically, perhaps a big explosion is the better path. Define your module as a dependency for a bunch of other modules. When your module fails to converge, the dependency structure will cause Puppet to skip over the other poor, innocent modules you're holding hostage. It may be better to ensure that nothing works, than to allow the application to start half of the necessary services, and start causing errors visible to the customer.

Your mileage will vary, tremendously. Make it work for you.

Letting the Strings Pull You

> If the puppets are alive, the marionette can learn from the strings.

During the convergence process, Puppet analyzes the state of resources to determine if change should be applied. Therefore, Puppet agents can provide a high amount of analytic data with a minimal effort for collection. PuppetDB provides one method of collecting this data.

Alarms (triggers) and state transitions (events) can flow upward from the managed nodes using queues or frameworks like MCollective to event management systems that respond to the input in an appropriate manner.

Leveraging Puppet for Small Changes

Do you have event handlers that log in to a node and take corrective action—say restarting a Tomcat service when it locks up? What happens when those simple commands fail? How do you know if it succeeded? Are the logs of these events available where you track other system changes?

How about leveraging the Puppet infrastructure to track these changes for you?

1. Write a small Puppet manifest that declares how the state should be. Yes, you can declare that the service should be stopped before the service is restarted.
2. Synchronize this manifest down to the related nodes.
3. Adjust the event handler to invoke `puppet apply` *EventResponse*.pp
4. Observe the response handler actions in the log entries added by Puppet.
5. Review the number of occurrences and other statistics in your Puppet dashboard.

 If this declaration is a subset of the normal Puppet run, you could tag the related resources with a special tag and invoke `puppet agent --tags` *TagEventResponse*, instead of using `puppet apply` on the node.

Tossing Declarative to the Wind

Some days, sometimes, you just end up tossing declarative to the wind and implementing something imperative in Puppet.

You end up with a product for which you are paying for support, and the only supported method to install it is to run five commands in a row. You could totally wrap this up with your own installation with templates and such, but it could break on the next update and business or legal constraints limit your choices.

Because sometimes (as illustrated by the quote from Rob Nelson presented earlier), you have no choice but to get Stone Age about it:

> If you try hard enough, you can make [Puppet] act like an imperative language. That would be akin to ripping the bottom out of your car, dressing in a leopard-print toga and a ratty blue tie, and driving to work with your feet.

When that day comes, you put on the leopard-print toga and you punch out something that violates every bit of common sense.

Don't Make Me Go Flintstones on You

At one company I worked with the DevOps team had put Rob's quote up on top of the Sprint whiteboard. After I had committed something really atrocious for reasons I can't share, someone found a Flintstones plush Dino doll and put it above my desk. After that point, it became a running joke to move this to whomever committed something exec-heavy. Nobody wanted to be the last person...

If you absolutely must implement something in a bunch of sequential `exec` statements, make heavy use of `timeout` to prevent hangs, and `creates` and `returns` to verify that the operation succeeded. Abuse `require` and `refreshonly` to ensure commands aren't run if the previous command failed. If you can't find appropriate information written out by the previous step, write state somewhere that can be referenced by `onlyif`, `unless`, and `creates` attributes for the following statements.

I've inherited that Dino doll a few too many times. I've also written some extremely long imperative sequences that were stateful, and could handle being killed off at any step and then complete properly in the next run. If you have to run to work with bare feet, ensure you don't have to answer your mobile phone en route.

Allowing Anyone to sudo puppet

It can be tempting to allow people to run Puppet any time they want using `sudo`. I mean why not—Puppet just talks to its server, and does what you tell it, right?

Well, look at these commands that a user could run:

`sudo puppet apply pinky.pp`
> Because you've always wanted to be 0wned by Brain.

`sudo puppet agent --server thebrain.local`
> Because burlap chafes me so?

`sudo puppet cert clean --all`
> If you can find a chicken, 20 yards of spandex, and smelling salts at this hour...

You really want to do this using a small wrapper script that accepts very limited input.

## CHAPTER 33

Finding Support Resources

There is a wide variety of ways to find help with using and developing for Puppet.

Accessing Community Support

Puppet users mailing list
> Sign up for or browse the archives of the Puppet users mailing lists (*http://bit.ly/ 1UmKoUW*).

Freenode IRC channels
> Many Puppet users and Puppet Labs employees provide ad hoc assistance on the community IRC channels. See the Community Guidelines (*http://bit.ly/ 1XAvBUK*) for details on how to use them.

Nobody on IRC Is Paid to Help You

It is amazingly common to see someone drop into the IRC channel and post a question without providing many details. Even if I am staring at the IRC channel (which isn't that often), I spend a few minutes pulling together a list of all the questions I need to ask. And try to phrase it such that I don't insult the person's intelligence.

Right about the time I start typing back the list of things we need to know, the person disappears from the mailing list because they didn't get an answer in 60 seconds.

Very seriously, there are many wicked smart people who can help you puppetize the 2100 space program, and can automate your 1950s TV set too if you'll give them some time to respond. Sometimes we toss something out, then get the desk interrupt or pulled into incident response. Even the people who work for Puppet Labs that help out on IRC are rarely able to focus on IRC response. You just aren't gonna find working DevOps engineers who aren't overemployed these days.

Phrase the question with as many specifics as you can. Provide a `pastebin` or `gist` with both your code and the output you are seeing. You are asking for free support: make it easy for people to help you.

Then wait for a response. If you presented your question well, you'll likely get an answer (or many) in a fairly short (but rarely immediate) time frame.

If you must have an answer sooner, then your needs can only be satisfied by our next topic.

Engaging Puppet Labs Support

If you find a bug in Puppet, you can submit it to Puppet Labs without a support contract by following the instructions on the Puppet docs site at "Puppet Projects Workflow" (*http://bit.ly/1pyHWhL*).

Puppet Labs provides Enterprise Support Plans for both Puppet Enterprise and Puppet Open Source installations. These plans vary from inexpensive packages of priority incidents, to 24/7 support and Puppet Labs professional services engineers working onsite at your location.

Reach out to them for a custom quote at *https://puppetlabs.com/services/support-plans*.

Contacting the Author

For any questions or concerns about the book, feel free to contact me at any of the following locations:

- The Feedback and Errata submission page for this book (*http://oreil.ly/1Ww80Et*)
- Comments in the Safari Books Online copy of this book (*http://bit.ly/1TVabDL*)
- *www.netconsonance.com* has my technical blog
- On Twitter: *twitter.com/jorhett*

I am happy to assist as best I can with ad hoc responses to any issues found in the book or my code examples. Unfortunately, I can only answer when time permits—which varies unpredictably from day to day. But I will respond.

I am rarely able to provide lengthy assistance with a problem unique to your deployment. You should utilize the community or enterprise support offerings previously mentioned.

I have been known to take on short-term consulting projects, but that is rare.

I would be happy to give a talk at your technical conference. Feel free to propose a subject, or ask me what I've got ready. I often have DevOps topics I'm prepared to discuss and promote.

Afterword

I hope you have learned what you wanted when reading this book. Moreover, I hope you find it incredibly useful in your journey. It was a lot of fun to write this book, and I hope I made you laugh at least once. I have two final thoughts I'd like to share with you.

Some Best Practices May Not Work for You

There are very few golden rules, and they aren't what you might expect. Every organization I've worked with tunes its environments and data sources to meet its own needs. One team might find a certain strategy implausible, while another team found that the same strategy solved all of their problems.

Learning to Fail is the Secret to Success

The most important lesson you can learn from DevOps is how to fail. Break the rules when you need to. But don't hold course when it's not working. Fail fast—recognize the failure and adjust course. Be agile.

Trying and learning from the experience is the DevOps way. Walking this path means having sometimes uncomfortable experiences, and adding to the conversation in our community as DevOps practices mature, mutate, and evolve.

I look forward to seeing what you bring to our community.

Installing Puppet on Other Platforms

In this appendix, we will cover how to install Puppet on platforms other than CentOS/RHEL 7.

Debian and Ubuntu

To install the Puppet Package Collection repositories on Debian or Ubuntu, perform the following steps:

1. Go with a browser to *https://apt.puppetlabs.com/* and identify the appropriate *.deb* repository file for the operating system release.
2. Download and install the repository file.
3. Update the Apt repository cache.

The process looks like this for Ubuntu 15.04, the latest version of Ubuntu:

```
$ wget https://apt.puppetlabs.com/puppetlabs-release-pc1-vivid.deb
...
$ sudo dpkg -i puppetlabs-release-pc1-vivid.deb
...
$ sudo apt-get update
...
$ sudo apt-get install puppet-agent
```

Some gems used in the book require the following development libraries to compile binary extensions:

```
[vagrant@client ~]$ sudo apt-get install build-essential ruby ruby-dev \
        libxml2-dev libxslt1-dev zlib1g-dev
```

Fedora

To install the Puppet Package Collection repositories on Fedora, perform the following steps:

1. Install the repository package file for your version of Fedora.
2. Install the Puppet agent.

The process looks like this for Fedora 22:

```
$ yum install --assumeyes \
    http://yum.puppetlabs.com/puppetlabs-release-pc1-fedora-22.noarch.rpm
...
$ yum install --assumeyes puppet-agent
```

Other Platforms

Puppet Labs provides binary packages for Mac (*http://bit.ly/22oP41q*) and Windows (*http://bit.ly/1pyHFvv*) at Open Source Puppet Downloads (*http://bit.ly/21zltgc*). Installation of the Windows package is covered in Chapter 28.

For any other system, Puppet and its dependencies will need to be installed from gems or compiled from source, as documented on the Puppet docs site at "Platforms Without Packages" (*http://bit.ly/1R4GRah*).

Puppet Enterprise supports has a broader set of operating systems, listed on the Puppet docs site at "Puppet Enterprise: Supported Operating Systems" (*http://bit.ly/1UaM5Wa*).

Configuring Firewalls on Other Platforms

This appendix covers how to enable incoming TCP connections to services provided by Puppet on platforms other than CentOS/RHEL 7.

IP Tables

If you are using an older operating system that comes with the IP tables firewall (such as CentOS 6 or Debian), you may need to invoke the `iptables` command directly. For example, the command shown here must be run on a Puppet server to allow incoming connections from clients:

```
[vagrant@puppetserver ~]$ sudo iptables -A INPUT -p tcp --dport 8140 -j ACCEPT
[vagrant@puppetserver ~]$ sudo /sbin/service iptables save
iptables: Saving firewall rules to /etc/sysconfig/iptables:[  OK  ]
```

For the Puppet Dashboard, you'll need to enable two ports:

```
[vagrant@dashserver ~]$ sudo iptables -A INPUT -p tcp --dport 443,3000 -j ACCEPT
```

Uncomplicated Firewall

Ubuntu comes standard with the Uncomplicated Firewall (UFW). You can uninstall this, and install `firewalld` to use the commands shown in this book:

```
$ sudo apt-get remove ufw
$ sudo apt-get install firewalld
```

Or you can utilize the following commands with UFW on a Puppet server:

```
[vagrant@puppetserver ~]$ sudo ufw allow 8140/tcp
[vagrant@puppetserver ~]$ sudo ufw status numbered
```

For Puppet Dashboard, you'll need to enable three ports:

```
[vagrant@puppetserver ~]$ sudo ufw allow 443/tcp
[vagrant@puppetserver ~]$ sudo ufw allow 3000/tcp
[vagrant@puppetserver ~]$ sudo ufw status numbered
```

Installing Ruby

In this appendix, we will cover how to install Ruby on your personal system. To install the exact same version of Ruby utilized by Puppet, run the following command on one of the test hosts:

```
[vagrant@client ~]$ /opt/puppetlabs/puppet/bin/ruby --version
ruby 2.1.8p440 (2015-12-16 revision 53160) [x86_64-linux]
```

As of the last update of this book, Puppet uses Ruby 2.1.8.

Ruby for Mac

Macintosh systems come with a modern version of Ruby installed. You can utilize the system Ruby successfully for every purpose in this book. The only thing necessary is to install the Bundler gem:

```
$ sudo gem install bundler --no-ri --no-rdoc
Fetching: bundler-1.11.2.gem (100%)
Successfully installed bundler-1.11.2
1 gem installed
```

If you'd prefer to install the exact version of Ruby that Puppet uses, install HomeBrew (*http://brew.sh/*) and then use the following commands:

```
$ brew install rbenv ruby-build
...
$ eval "$(rbenv init -)"
$ rbenv install 2.1.8
...
$ rbenv shell 2.1.8
```

Any time you wish to utilize this version of Ruby, just run these commands again:

```
$ eval "$(rbenv init -)"
$ rbenv shell 2.1.8
```

Ruby for Windows

Install the latest Ruby 2.1 (or whatever version Puppet uses today) from RubyInstaller for Windows (*http://rubyinstaller.org/downloads/*). You should also install the 64-bit DevKit for Ruby.

After these are installed, use the gem command to install Bundler:

```
C:\> gem install bundler --no-ri --no-rdoc
Fetching: bundler-1.11.2.gem (100%)
Successfully installed bundler-1.11.2
1 gem installed
```

Ruby for Linux

You can use the Ruby version that comes with your operating system. If you are using CentOS 7 as recommended in this book, it is easy to install Ruby into the system packages:

```
[vagrant@client ~]$ sudo yum install -y ruby-devel rubygems rake libxml2-devel
```

For any other operating system, use the system Ruby, rbenv (*https://github.com/rbenv/rbenv*), or RVM (*https://rvm.io/*) to install the Ruby version matching what Puppet uses (the latest version of Ruby 2.1).

Here is a quick installation of Ruby and Bundler using rbenv that should work on any Unix/Linux environment:

```
$ git clone https://github.com/rbenv/rbenv.git ~/.rbenv
...
$ git clone https://github.com/rbenv/ruby-build.git ~/.rbenv/plugins/ruby-build
$ export PATH=~/.rbenv/bin:$PATH
$ eval "$(rbenv init -)"
$ /opt/puppetlabs/puppet/bin/ruby --version
ruby 2.1.8p440 (2015-12-16 revision 53160) [x86_64-linux]
$ rbenv install 2.1.8
...
$ rbenv shell 2.1.8
$ gem install bundler
Fetching: bundler-1.11.2.gem (100%)
Successfully installed bundler-1.11.2
1 gem installed
```

In order for Bundler and Beaker to build correctly, you'll need to install some development packages. On CentOS or RHEL systems, the following command is necessary:

```
[vagrant@client ~]$ sudo yum install -y gcc-c++ libxml2-devel libxslt-devel
```

The Bundler gem is used for local install of all necessary dependencies:

```
$ sudo gem install bundler --no-ri --no-rdoc
Fetching: bundler-1.11.2.gem (100%)
Successfully installed bundler-1.11.2
1 gem installed
```

Index

N

naive autosigning, 353
name parameter, 196
name-based autosigning, 348
namevar attribute, 81, 232
Nano text editor, 23
NetDev standard library
  creating NetDev device objects, 484
  finding NetDev vendor extensions, 483
  reducing duplication with device_hiera, 484
  using, 483
netdev_interface resource, 493
network devices
  best practices for, 499
  managing Cisco Nexus switches, 485-488
  managing infrastructure with Puppet, 473
  managing Juniper devices, 488
  managing with NetDev standard library, 483
  managing with puppet device, 474-483
  overview of, 499
newvalues() method, 232
nginx web server, 306, 379
no operation (noop) attribute, 82
node inheritance, 107, 332
nodejs package, 377
nodes
  assigning environments to, 433
  assigning modules to, 153-158
  authentication process, 347
  avoiding module assignments, 155
  backing up files changed on, 337
  certnames of, 295
  connecting to servers, 323-327
  conventional types of, 291
  defined, 291
  duplicating, 116
  executing commands on subsets, xxxiii
  external node classifiers (ENCs), 360, 383, 394-400
  geographically dispersed, 367
  node scope, 199
  recertification, 294
  report processing, 338-345
  running acceptance tests on, 275
  testing, 333
  unconventional types of, 292
  using a node terminus, 359-364, 433
  viewing inventory of, 460

viewing status on Puppet Dashboard, 389-394
not (!) operator, 67
Notepad editor, 24
Notepad++ editor, 24
notice() function, 59
notify metaparameter, 96
notify resource, 37, 40
numbers, defining, 51
Numeric data types, 51, 110

O

object identifiers (OIDs), 350
octal number, 111
OmniGraffle, 101
Open Source Puppet Downloads, 526
operating system compatibility, 255
operators
  adding values to Arrays and hashes, 65
  bit-shifting, 64
  comparison, 66
  list of, 67
  order of operations, 66
  removing values from Arrays and hashes, 65
or operator, 67
Oracle virtualization drivers, 14
ordering configuration option, 99
OSS License website, 254

P

package repositories, adding, 27
Package {} default, 201
PanoPuppet, 408
parameter keys, 190
params, 231
params.pp class, 512
params.pp, lookup, 214
parent scope, 199
Passenger, 305, 379
PATH environment, adjusting, 10, 29, 33, 126
period attribute, 86
periodmatch attribute, 87
permissions, declarative, 113
Phusion Passenger, 298, 306, 379
ping command, 456
pipe operator (| |), 71
policy-based autosigning, 349
port channels, 495
PostgreSQL, 375

About the Author

Jo Rhett is a DevOps architect with more than 20 years experience conceptualizing and delivering large-scale Internet services. He focuses on creating automation and infrastructure to accelerate deployment and minimize outages.

Jo has been using, promoting, and enhancing configuration management systems for over 20 years. He builds improvements and plugins for Puppet, MCollective, and many other DevOps tools.

In addition to *Learning Puppet 4*, Jo is the author of *Learning MCollective* (O'Reilly) and *Instant Puppet 3 Starter* (Packt Publishing).

Colophon

The animal on the cover of *Learning Puppet 4* is an European polecat (*Mustela putorius*), a member of the weasel family found all throughout Europe. The name "polecat" is thought to derive either from the French *poule* (chicken) because of the species' liking for poultry or the Old English *ful* (foul) for its disagreeable odor.

The European polecat is the ancestor of the ferret, which was domesticated 2,000 years ago to hunt rabbits and vermin. Indeed, apart from having a larger skull, wild polecats are nearly identical in appearance to ferrets. Both have thick, silky brown-black fur with a lighter undercoat and a white mask across the face. The size of European polecats varies widely (11–18 inches long and weighing 1–3 pounds), though males are generally larger than females.

Polecats are polygamous, and before mating, the male drags the female around by the scruff of the neck to stimulate ovulation. Litters of 5–10 kits are born in May or June. The newborn polecats are blind and deaf for a month after birth (and are not independent until 2-3 months of age). In addition to nursing her kits, their mother brings them small pieces of meat. The diet of the European polecat consists of rodents, amphibians, and birds.

Both sexes mark their territories with an oily strong-smelling musk, which is also used as a defense if it feels threatened. While polecats are still hunted for their fur in some European countries, this unpleasant smell lingers on their pelts and is difficult to remove.

Many of the animals on O'Reilly covers are endangered; all of them are important to the world. To learn more about how you can help, go to *animals.oreilly.com*.

The cover image is from an unknown source. The cover fonts are URW Typewriter and Guardian Sans. The text font is Adobe Minion Pro; the heading font is Adobe Myriad Condensed; and the code font is Dalton Maag's Ubuntu Mono.

Have it your way.

Get even more for your money.

Join the O'Reilly Community, and register the O'Reilly books you own. It's free, and you'll get:

- $4.99 ebook upgrade offer
- 40% upgrade offer on O'Reilly print books
- Membership discounts on books and events
- Free lifetime updates to ebooks and videos
- Multiple ebook formats, DRM FREE
- Participation in the O'Reilly community
- Newsletters
- Account management
- 100% Satisfaction Guarantee

Signing up is easy:

1. Go to: oreilly.com/go/register
2. Create an O'Reilly login.
3. Provide your address.
4. Register your books.

Note: English-language books only

To order books online:
oreilly.com/store

For questions about products or an order:
orders@oreilly.com

To sign up to get topic-specific email announcements and/or news about upcoming books, conferences, special offers, and new technologies:
elists@oreilly.com

For technical questions about book content:
booktech@oreilly.com

To submit new book proposals to our editors:
proposals@oreilly.com

O'Reilly books are available in multiple DRM-free ebook formats. For more information:
oreilly.com/ebooks